OFFICIAL REPORT

OF THE

EIGHTEENTH INTERNATIONAL

CHRISTIAN ENDEAVOR CONVENTION

HELD IN

TENTS ENDEAVOR AND WILLISTON, THE LIGHT GUARD ARMORY,

AND MANY CHURCHES.

DETROIT, MICH., JULY 5 – 10, 1899.

First Fruits Press
Wilmore, Kentucky
c2015

THE COMMITTEE OF '99.

First Fruits Press
The Academic Open Press of Asbury Theological Seminary
204 N. Lexington Ave., Wilmore, KY 40390
859-858-2236
first.fruits@asburyseminary.edu
asbury.to/firstfruits

OFFICIAL REPORT

OF THE

EIGHTEENTH INTERNATIONAL

CHRISTIAN ENDEAVOR CONVENTION,

HELD IN

TENTS ENDEAVOR AND WILLISTON, THE LIGHT GUARD ARMORY,
AND MANY CHURCHES.

DETROIT, MICH., JULY 5-10, 1899.

UNITED SOCIETY OF CHRISTIAN ENDEAVOR,
TREMONT TEMPLE, BOSTON, MASS., U. S. A.
1899

Committee of '99.

Mr. W. H. STRONG, *Chairman.*

Rev. W. B. JENNINGS, D.D., *Vice-Chairman,*

Mr. C. R. COOK, *Secretary,*

Mr. GEO. R. ANGELL, *Treasurer.*

Members Ex-Officio.

Rev. NEHEMIAH BOYNTON, D.D.,

Mr. ARTHUR A. HIGGINSON,

Mr. G. J. VINTON.

Dr. J. E. DAVIS.

Chairmen of Sub-Committees.

Entertainment, Mr. D. T. SMITH,

Reception, Mr. HARRY H. BURR,

Music, Rev. W. H. CLARK, D.D.,

Decorations, Mr. FRED J. MASON,

Press, Mr. FRED H. COZZENS,

Ushers, Mr. A. G. STUDER,

Printing, Mr. FRANK KENNEDY,

Places of Meeting, Mr. F. M. THOMPSON.

Local Excursions, Dr. J. E. DAVIS.

Pulpit Supply, Rev. A. H. BARR.

Convention Musical Directors and Singers.

Mr. E. O. EXCELL, Chicago, Ill.

Mr. P. S. FOSTER, Washington. D. C.

Mr. H. G. SMYTH. New York, N. Y.

HAMPTON INSTITUTE QUARTETTE.

2

DETROIT ABLAZE

With Christian Endeavor Enthusiasm and Zeal. — The Best of the Best. — The Opening of Our International Gathering.—A Diary of Doings and Sayings.

ETROIT, Mich., in the very heart of our Christian Endeavor population in America, during July 5 to 10, was very near to the heart of thousands of Endeavorers. Endeavorers came by thousands from the far West and the fervid South, from Christian Endeavor's Eastern home, and from our neighbors, the Canadians, across the northern border. Some came literally from the ends of the earth to attend this Convention, from the antipodes and all the way between.

The committee registered in all 21,000, and, counting the thousands who failed to register, the estimated attendance of young people was at least 28,000. In all, the programme provided for over one hundred and fifty different sessions, which were attended by over *threehundred thousand people*. Never before in the splendid history of Christian Endeavor Conventions has the attendance upon the *meetings* been so constant or so large.

The courteous "white caps" of Detroit's Reception Committee met all trains long before they reached the city, and with maps, registration-blanks, and kindly given information made the delegates feel at home before they arrived. Many of these young Christians had cheerfully waited all night for belated trains, while in the city, in at least one instance, the young women of a church, who had given up hope and gone to bed, arose and dressed themselves again to meet with recompensing smiles the visitors weary of the railroad.

The Delegates Swarm In.

Detroit was found in gala attire ; wharves and stations were manned and womaned with the efficient Reception Committee ; street-corners were guarded by the vigilant Patrol Committee, alert for the often-popped question. Committee headquarters in the great Majestic

Building were humming.   Looking down the handsome streets, the store-fronts were ablaze with glory.

The Convention flag was certainly the most beautiful we have had, with its scarlet and white monogram and its radiant sunburst.   In front of the magnificent City Hall an electric " Welcome C. E." flashed its welcome at night.   In the grass below, the very flowers spelled the city's greeting.   An admirable system prevailed at the registration headquarters.   To one place all lonely men were directed, to another all unattended women, and to a third all married couples.   Everybody was delighted with the pretty badge, with its .neat pictures of Detroit scenes.

Out on the Convention grounds a veritable white city had sprung up.   The committee outdid all others in providing refreshment-booths.   Certainly fifty of them were pitched in appetizing array before the mammoth tents, Endeavor and Williston.

The local arrangements had never been so admirably made.   The decorations of the tents were brilliant and original.   The press tent was a marvel of completeness and convenience.   The Joint Ticket Agency, under the management of Mr. Frank E. Snow, was almost ideal in its arrangement.   We hope that in future convenfions railroad managers will avail themselves of his experience.   The bicycle was recognized for the first time, and the bicycle tent has certainly come to stay.   Two thousand or more bicycles were checked at a time, and the silent steed was whirling gracefully everywhere.   This may well be called, by way of truth as well as simile, " the bicycle Convention."

It was also " the umbrella Convention," and one of the great surprises of the meetings was the good-nature and persistent attention of the audiences under the most trying circumstances.   No one could accuse this of being a dry Convention.   Its temperance principles were unimpeachable, and yet it " went wet."   But if it had n't been rainy it would have been hot, and all of us were delighted to purchase the admirable coolness and freshness at the cost of two or three " umbrella sessions."   It was the most comfortable Convention we have ever enjoyed.

A Part of the Christian Endeavor Museum.

The programme had many features that were novel, and nobly did these prove their right to a permanent place in our conventions.   One of these was the Purpose Meetings, taking the place of the closing consecration meetings, these being transferred to the churches and to Sunday evening.   Another was the Memorial Meeting.   Another was the Yale Band's interesting missionary room, and their practical missionary conference.   Mr. Holley's capital Christian Endeavor Museum well deserves an encore.   So does the arbitration meeting; so do the daily Junior rallies and the daily studies in evangelistic methods.   There were more pastors' conferences this year than ever before, and they treated a greater variety of topics. The "schools of methods" took the place this year of the committee conferences, and every one thought it an improvement. Ten minutes in the heart of each session were spent in quiet meditation and prayer, led by master minds. This was a wonderful uplift to the meetings.

Besides these new features, there were many improvements on old ones. The music was of a much higher order than usual, and the Endeavorers will never be satisfied to go back to poorer music. A greater interest than usual was given to the missionary addresses by the introduction of the more than one hundred home and foreign missionaries, by the appearance of some of them in native garb, and their use of foreign tongues occasionally to render the theme more vivid.

The great question of temperance has never before been presented with so magnificent force, mighty conviction, and splendid effectiveness.

The daily Bible-studies have never before been so well attended as this year, or so valuable. Professors Moorehead, Willett, and Moulton are a rare trio of teachers.

The conference of the local-union officers held this year the most important of all similar gatherings. Plans were proposed which will add new force to the movement in hundreds and thousands of localities.

The evangelistic campaign waged by the Endeavorers was better planned and more elaborately organized than ever before.

If these features were better than usual, yet the other portions of the programme were every whit as good as usual,— the men's meeting, the women's meeting, the State and denominational rallies, the Junior rally, the meetings for pushing the Tenth Legion, prison work, the Floating Society, the Travellers' Union, the observance of the Sabbath.

A very popular novelty was the reception given by the officers of the United Society, the trustees, State presidents, and Convention speakers. Thousands availed themselves of this opportunity to shake hands with the Christian Endeavor leaders. The Junior workers' reception was also new and delightful.

But it, in sober reality, was "the Convention of the presence of God," "the Convention of conversions." Dr. Chapman's Quiet Hours lay at the heart of all the days. The wonderful Sabbath session was the Convention's true climax. Hundreds, yea, thousands, will know July 9, 1899, as their spiritual birthday.

In Pursuit of Information.

"Going and Growing" was given us as our year's motto by the president of the United Society. The secret of growth and of progress is the Quiet Hour, the consciousness of God's presence, the surrender to his blessed will.

The opening meeting of Wednesday evening brought together far more than ten thousand, the monster Tent Endeavor being crammed and overflowing. Praise once, praise twice, praise thrice, ascended in swelling numbers,—praise in popular gospel songs, praise voiced in prayer by Rev. J. G. Butler, D.D., of Washington, D.C., and praise in the grand anthem, " Send out thy light," by the magnificent chorus of which Detroit had a right to be proud, led in a masterly way by Chairman Clark of the Music Committee.

The crowds that had been surging about the blocked entrances strained harder than ever to catch some of the good things enjoyed within, and Dr. Clark requested the ushers to roll up the sides of the tent. It was an auspicious augury for the registration. Never in the history of Christian Endeavor has it been necessary to have an overflow meeting on the first night.

The patriotic temper of the meeting was tested, and responded with overwhelming demonstrations of appreciation, when the following telegram of greeting from President McKinley was read : —

Rev. Francis E. Clark, D.D., President of the United Society of Christian Endeavor : —

On the occasion of the Eighteenth International Convention of your Society, I desire to express to you my cordial interest in its work, my best wishes to those assembled with you in convention, and my earnest hope for the continuance and increase of the great results which the efforts of the Christian Endeavor Society have achieved. WILLIAM McKINLEY.

The genius of Detroit's sons was in evidence more times than one. Chairman W. H. Strong seemed inspired with words of welcome when he said, referring to Detroit's confusing streets, " Don't try to find the points of the compass here. There are none in our geography or in our welcome. We know no north, no south, no east, no west." He proved himself such a master of bubbling humor and happy expression that again and again the tent fairly quaked under the hearty applause.

Address of Welcome, by W. H. Strong,
Chairman Committee '99, Detroit, Mich.

We are glad to see you for the very pleasure of your presence. This is the great convention city, and I suppose the Programme Committee in Boston felt they must do the conventional thing and ask the Programme Committee of '99 to express to you a welcome, which, if not already spoken individually, will come with scant value here.

The rule for chairmen, like children, is that they should be seen and not heard. However, it is an exceedingly great privilege to speak the opening words in this Convention in the name of the allied young people of Detroit. I am unduly honored with the right to speak for those who have planned while I have presided, and toiled while I have talked.

I recognize at this time with special gratitude the cordial co-operation of those societies, not Christian Endeavor, who have joined on our committees, and I welcome you to-night, I am sure, as heartily for Epworth League and B. Y. P. U. and other organizations as in the name of our own Christian Endeavor. Succeeding speakers will give you, far more fittingly and gracefully, an earnest welcome to our city and our city's best.

Possibly it is the duty of our committee to give you a few suggestions as to your walk and conversation while among us. We would not seem too sensitive, but —

Please don't call our city flat; call it level — there is a vast difference between level-headed and flat-headed.

Don't try and learn Detroit points of compass; we haven't any in our city or our welcome. We know no north, no south, no east, no west.

Don't regulate our days here by standard time. Other cities may give you a good time, but we give three good times,— eastern time, central time, and the true time of the sun. Most of you will think that we are thirty minutes either slow or fast, but we are not, we are just right.

Don't race with our bicycle policemen. You may beat and feel fine, but you will feel the Police Court fine still more.

Don't be too superior, even if you are from Massachusetts. At Boston, a thoughtful girl, seeing our Michigan badges, said, "How nice it must be for those people from away out West to ride on our street-cars and see the electric lights!" We, too, are proud — proud of our history, proud of our homes, and proud of the beautiful river which unites instead of dividing those who greet you to-night. Detroit and Windsor are one, both in welcome to

Chairman Strong Captivated Them.

our hearts and homes, and in the lofty aspiration of our motto, "We hope for better things." The words express the fainter faith of our city yesterday, the far-reaching faith of to-day. We are on the summit of a century facing the sunset, a mighty, matchless, magnificent century — man wielding powers undreamed of a hundred years ago; acceleration the key-note of all things; yet ever more increasingly manifest, looking back through history's drama, is history's invisible, yet ever-revealing Creator; and so we welcome you with the courage of our motto, "Hope." We welcome you with the bugle call of our convention hymn,

> "The Son of God goes forth to war,
>   A kingly crown to gain.
> His blood-red banner streams afar;
>   Who follows in his train?"

We welcome in you youth and strength and sunlit days; we welcome new purposes and larger plans. We welcome you to the city whose name comes from other years and a foreign tongue with a ringing meaning, which, alas, has too often been forgotten,— "Detroit," right, straight, direct, onward.

It was destined to be an evening of steppings heavenward ; each part was better than the last. When Rev. Charles B. Newnan, pastor of the Central Christian Church, stepped forward to give expression to the welcome of the churches, he had to rise above in order not to fall below his predecessor. His address was warm in temperature and in tint. It was poetry, oratory, visions of prophecy, everything that appealed to intellect and heart, sense and sound.

Address of Welcome in Behalf of Detroit Pastors, by Rev. Charles B. Newnan.

Honored Chairman and Fellow Endeavorers:— In the name of our Common Master, and as you come to do his work, and to receive the uplift which he will give, we extend you hearty, cordial welcome. When you said you would come we were glad, and the year that has intervened has been to us one of mingled poetry and prose,— the prose of patient preparation, the poetry of delightful anticipation ; prose high and holy, poetry musical and sweet. Happy were we in your promise, happier still in its fulfilment. As the glad earth wel-

comes, with leaf and blossom, the returning spring; as bird and flower, with song and beauty, welcome the rising sun; as the weary captive of Northern night welcomes with exultant joy the Arctic morning; so with song and gladness Detroit welcomes you.

Pleasant to our eyes is the sight of your waving banners and mighty multitude. Welcome is your fellowship as rest at close of busy day. In the name of more than an hundred churches and pastors united in invitation and preparation, and now united in greeting; in the name also of more than fifty thousand Christian men and women who rejoice in this hour, we welcome you. Our streets are wide, our homes are spacious, but our hearts are wider still; and, sure of your sympathy and reverence, we open wide their sacred places and bid you enter and abide. You said you would come, but just how many and from where we hardly knew; but we have sought to make fully ready for you all. Without friction or failure, our committees and our people have wrought together in anticipation of your presence, and from the first hour when we sought your coming until this moment, when we rejoice in the fulfilment of our hopes and the answer to our petitions, we have ceased not to bear this Convention, you and ourselves, before the good Master in earnest prayer, beseeching God that through this gathering his will might be wrought out.

We welcome you because of the lands from which you have come, counting it no small honor that through you Detroit, in this hour, is hostess to the world. One does not soon forget the feeling of universal brotherhood, and the tremendous stimulus to more earnest, faithful work, that come to him when in a single hour in an Endeavor audience he is brought into contact with every portion of the civilized world. He is reminded afresh of Joseph Cook's famous saying, "There are no longer any antipodes; the earth must be healed or poisoned very much as a whole." Such brotherhood-and stimulus are ours as we entertain you. In this Convention we are jostling elbows and striking hands with Endeavorers from every part of the world. From northern snow and southern slope; from where Alaskan glaciers seek the sea; from the great West, where every breeze bears balm; from California's Gate of Gold, fit entrance to that land of fruit and flower; from the Southland, where through forest and canebrake the white sands shine; from the East, where northern pine and southern palm unite in waving loving welcome to the old world, day by day; from Manitoba's mighty plains, where billowy fields of golden grain lie smiling in the summer sun; from Quebec, twin-sister to Detroit in name and early history; from Ontario's broad prairies and richly laden fields, so like our own; from far-off islands of the sea; from under the glowing Southern Cross, where rests, in quiet and quite perennial beauty, Australia, newest of the continents; from Africa, dark continent it is true, but beginning now to glow with light as Christian service and sacrifice are hastening her redemption; from England, island mother of our goodly land, whose gracious, kindly sympathy, so lately and so strongly shown, has been to our people and to the world a new interpretation and emphasis of kinship and brotherhood; from Scotland, the land of the thistle, where seas of steel and skies of grey unite with heather and mist and mountain in weaving for her people character sombre, and yet true and joyous, in all the earnestness of Christian service; from the land of the shamrock, that shall yet, please God, see sunnier days and a happier people; from the land of the Norsemen, and the home of the Vikings; from India, strange land of silence and mystery; from China, just awaking from her sleep of more than two thousand years; from Japan, alert, progressive, eager to learn, and whose tireless patience and artistic insight will build and endow for the indwelling of our God temples most beautiful, and characters that glow with all the graces of Christian life; and from that far-off Mesopotamian border where the cradle of the race still rocks a godly seed; — are you come, following the blood-red banner of the Cross, to this gathering of Endeavor clans.

We welcome you because of the inspiration and uplift which you bring. It will be to us the memory of a lifetime that you met in our city, thronged our streets, and were entertained in our homes. To simply look into your faces and take you by the hand would be glory enough for once; but when we remember that you are to abide, and that we may share your fellowship for days, our happiness is indeed complete.

We welcome you because of the work wherefore you are come. Your pledge reads, "Whatever He would like to have me do." You could have no grander motto. Our own committee motto reads, "Let us hope for better things." Change but one word and it will voice the aspiration of this great Convention: "Let us plan for better things." Yes, better things: better understanding of the Book of God, your one weapon of aggressive warfare. Prominent among the characteristics of Christian Endeavor is its loyalty to the old Book, and well may it be so. We know what it has wrought, the lands it has brightened, the lives it has lifted, the millions it has energized for service.

"What do you put upon your faces to make them shine?" said the Hindoo to the native Christian in the mart.

"Nothing," was the answer.

"But," persisted the Hindoo, "I have seen the faces of you Christians everywhere, and they shine unlike our own; what do you use to make them shine?"

Then the other, comprehending, made answer, "It is the grace of God."

So we trust the old Book that our fathers loved and trusted, that made their faces to shine, and upon whose promises of good they pillowed their heads and fell on sleep in the long ago. You are come that you may catch yet clearer vision of the great world's need. Standing upon the threshold of the new century, across whose borders we can almost look, you will, I am sure, agree that,

> "We are living, we are dwelling
> In a grand and awful time,
> In an age on ages telling:
> To be living is sublime."

In the face of such responsibilities you seek to know how best to bear the burdens and do the work which the new age brings; and that you may better understand the Book and do the work, you covet, I am sure, larger indwelling of the spirit of the living God, who shall enable you for toil, and crown your labor with blessings and success. May this Convention realize, nay, go beyond, your fondest hopes in these regards. May it be to you the mountain-top of spiritual vision. May it be to you the time of infilling with power for service. May the fires of love to God, and sacrifice for your fellows, burn yet more brightly upon the altar of your hearts, and keep you ever in mind that "civilization and Christianity have not come from the survival of the fittest, but by the sacrifice of the best." May those things which divide the forces of the Christ and hinder his work disappear, and may the common basis for faith and love, given by our common Master, be yet more clearly seen, and may it command instant assent and obedience. Have you been lonely or discouraged? May there be brought to you a new conviction of the fact that you are not alone; that in your place you are but keeping step with a mighty army, and that the very mountains around about you are filled with the chariots of Jehovah's protecting hosts. Once more, let me repeat it, not because you need to hear the words, but because our hearts are full, and must utter their message, You are welcome, thrice welcome, to our city. May we prove as worthy hosts as you are worthy guests; and when you have closed your Convention and are ready to depart, may you have it as truly to say that you were well come as we say it now at the beginning.

Then came most inspiring singing by a quartette of men from Hampton Institute.

The patriotic element in Christian Endeavor received impetus in the address of Mayor Maybury. With his opening sentence he swung himself into sympathetic touch with the hosts whom he addressed. An Episcopalian in his church communion, no lifelong Endeavorer could have crowded more genuine Christian Endeavor sentiment into more eloquent rhetorical periods. An Endeavorer's ideal mayor is the official who can speak such words and live up to them in the city hall.

Welcome of the City, by Mayor Wm. C. Maybury.

Mr. President, Ladies and Gentlemen :— On the 24th day of July, in the year of our Lord 1701, the city of Detroit was founded. On this, the 5th day of July, 1899, is founded within the older city a new city. The first city was consecrated by its founders to the service of Nazarene. This latter city, the city of endeavor, is called by his name, "Christian," and consecrated to his work of redemption for the children of man. The foundation of these two cities is separated by two hundred years, yet each is consecrated to the same purpose; viz., the service of God. Does not this confirm our faith that when God and his purposes are the inspiration of the founding of cities, both here and in the world invisible, their foundations are sure and abiding?

You have raised the white walls of this dream city in our midst. We are not jealous of your splendid work. Your architects are no strangers to us, neither were your purposes. The inspiring deeds and helpful influence of this great pentecostal gathering elsewhere is well known to us. We have in the body of our citizenship very many in active alliance with you. It is for these reasons that men and women of every creed and of every kindred join in bidding you a hearty welcome, as we hope to bid you Godspeed and to invoke his blessing upon you when you must go. In the mere statement of revealed truth many of us may differ, but in experience we all agree. The human heart interprets for all and to all alike. It is the seat of the mother language of the world, and breathes the same spirit, whether swelling in the harmony of a great chorus or crooned by the peasant mother as she rocks the cradle. It is the universal language by which the world is united in sympathy, and by which it is at last to be converted to the Saviour of man.

"Endeavor"—I like that word. It means so much. It points out the way, the only way, to those who would win in life's battle. It encourages all to try, and it comforts and consoles those who falter. The secret of all progress in human society belongs to those who aspire; to those who make endeavor. It adds to the sum of human achievement in its every movement. No life can be pure in its endeavors and strong in its strife without at the same time making all life purer and stronger thereby.

What a wonderful growth has been this great upward movement! Founded a comparatively few years ago, and ever since led by one happily present to-night, in whose features there dwells not even the premonition of increasing years; his eyes undimmed, his natural strength unabating, he journeys at the head of his numerous and triumphant family toward the promised land. How heartily do we all join in the wish that the years before him may be many and prosperous; that he may live in the enjoyment of all earthly blessings, health and troops of friends, while late, very late, comes the day when his helpful presence must be exchanged for a sad but delightful memory. It is noted of some lives that they only linger, while others live. The centuries of life of Methuselah were but lingered. Thirty-three years of the life of Christ were years of living. As men live or linger, so is it with institutions like this. Some of them seem to linger. This Christian Endeavor lives. The secret of its living is that it is ordained to uplift and consecrate. It therefore becomes a factor in life, and, like righteousness, exalts a nation.

You come amongst us with no present purpose to subserve, and you have no material interest to consult. The harvest of your sowing and the fruition lie far beyond all earthly desires. From every clime you come, of every kindred you are, and every nation you represent. In every tongue you give expression to the message which you bring—truly catholic and characteristic of the modern spirit that is summoning society everywhere into one vast family, one universal brotherhood. You have overcome the barriers of brotherhood in all the past by annihilating space and distance. Maine and California, Michigan and Florida, Japan and China, the Hebrides and the islands of the outermost sea,—all, all are here, summoned to one duty, consecrated to one purpose, telling the gospel story, blessed of all the ages.   Nations as well as men in the past ages of the world have passed each other as ships pass in the night.   A mere flash of recognition, and they pass beyond the horizon of vision, with no knowledge of the cargoes which they bear, nor the port from whence they come, nor the haven to which they would go.   To-day the nations of the earth and the men of all climes are passing each other in the journey more as ships pass by day,—their names unfurled upon the topmast, their cargoes known, their port of departure and the haven at the end of their journey known.   They exchange salutes as they pass.   They watch for signs of distress.   They go to the aid of the shipwreck on the rocks.   Such is the spirit of the nations as they pass and repass each other to-day.

The conditions under which you meet in this favored city are peculiarly encouraging.   Your mission of peace is the echo of the grand anthem which all nations seem to be singing in chorus to-day.   War's battle-flags are furled. Nations the most warlike have declared for peace, and in The Hague, in peace-loving Holland, are gathered to-day the representatives of all nations, to declare the terms upon which war shall be impossible and peace universal.

There was an ancient prophecy which had its fulfilment twenty centuries ago.   It declared that with the coming of one who should be called the Prince of Peace, the doors of the temple of Janus, the great god of war, should be closed for the first time in its history.   On a bright morning in December, when angels came to proclaim peace on earth and good will to man, by some mysterious agency the doors of that temple were closed, and the reign of peace began.   Another prophecy was then pronounced, for whose fulfilment the nations have been looking.   It declared that the time would come when swords should be beaten into plowshares and spears into pruning-hooks; when nation should not lift up the sword against nation, neither should they learn the art of war, but the reign of the Prince of Peace should be universal and eternal.   In my judgment the nations of the earth

Inside the Information Tent.

stand upon the threshold of the fulfilment of this prophecy to-night, and well may this great gathering be turned into a season of rejoicing, with the sound of anthem and Te Deum, that the ancient prophecy is about to be fulfilled.   You have come to a city that has been loyal to three flags, each in its turn.   For half a century the French flag of the fleur-de-lis floated over this primitive city. It was succeeded by the cross of King George.   One hundred and three years ago the Stars and Stripes were flung to the breeze, and under its sheltering protection this city lives and prospers.   We express the hope and confidence that that flag will continue to wave above the beautiful city of the living, as well as the quiet city of the dead in our midst, until God's purposes among the children of men have been accomplished and the heavens are rolled up as a scroll.

We rejoice in the most beautiful river in the world, and still more in the most magnificent inland commerce that ever was seen in this world.   Twenty-two thousand vessels pass our door heavily laden, in the short season of seven months in each passing year.   They bear only the peaceful products of the husbandman and the rich deposits of the mine.

You are in a city, as I said, consecrated to the cause of religion; and to-day its temples of worship cast their consecrating influences over every neighborhood, while a spirit of delightful tolerance pervades every shade of religious belief and of religious endeavor.   Twenty-eight volunteer societies of devoted men and women minister to every form of disease and distress known to the human family, and homes of shelter for the unfortunate and the afflicted are ample and everywhere. In the long-ago centuries the Almighty dropped an emerald upon the bosom of the river, creating an island, dividing the rushing current of the stream. There this island stood in primitive beauty until a resting-place for tired men and women and a playground for the children called for its use as a public park. Belle Isle holds a place in the imagination or experience of all who travel about, while to us it is the Mecca to which we go for relief from care and the worry of incessant toil. You are in a city of homes, where the land is owned in greater proportion by the dwellers thereon than in any other city in the world. As you go about you will see the evidence of this fact in the garden, cultivated with vegetables for the table, and the front of the cottage home made beautiful with trailing vine and rose-bush. These speak of no temporary abode for the indwellers, but of the continued and substantial home. To all that a helpful and hospitable hand can bestow, to all that hearts warm with a fervent welcome can give, we again bid you a most cordial welcome.

The inimitable Rev. William Patterson, of Canada and Ireland, was first summoned to respond to this cumulative tide of welcome. It was a happy inspiration that prompted some one in the audience to start "God save the Queen" as Mr. Patterson arose. It brought every one to his feet like a flash. And Mr. Patterson stood on the crest of that wave of brotherly feeling, and told in his musical brogue how Canadians love America so much that they had to dig a tunnel under the St. Clair River, that, when they could not cross over the river, they might go under it to their brethren.

Rev. H. J. Tresidder, of London, who as convener of the Hospitalities Committee of the London, 1900, Convention, came to invite us across the sea, felt so warmed in the cockles of his heart by hearing ten thousand American voices sing a prayer for the preservation of a woman loved in two great lands for the eighty years of womanly grace that crown her, that he invited us all to come and enjoy her gracious hospitality ; and we all want to go.

Great Britain's Response to Address of Welcome, by Rev. H. J. Tresidder,
London, England.

However personally unworthy the ambassador may be, he is usually received for the sake of the sovereignty he represents, whether it be that of the people or the throne; and if I speak for the mother country and accept your cordial welcome, I am sure I may claim such consideration. It falls in with nature's order that the maternal party should be somewhat old, slow, and afflicted with infirmity; but where is the son who would not bear with his mother? And I have understood that there is one old lady on the other side, eighty years old, whose praises even Americans can sing,—Victoria, by the grace of God Queen, and by the same grace woman and mother.

Last year your Convention at Nashville was held amid the echoes of war. This year it is happily attended with the looking for a universal peace. I am not sure that a treaty of arbitration will be the best outcome for us. Mothers and daughters are better off without treaties, and if long ago England forgot herself, you may forget the deed as really as last year you forgot the words "North" and "South." For why? We are one — one people with two empires ; we have one language, one literature, one faith, and one Lord and Master, Christ.

Perish the thought that ever conflict and war could prevail between us! Such a day could not dawn; it would be night with a darkness felt. Christian Endeavor is writing the word "impossible" over such a hideous dream.

Standing here in Detroit I realize a life dream. I have longed to visit your land and to look into your faces for many a year. George Washington I love, and not because of that hatchet business. Honest old Abe I revered, and sorrowed for his death; and Henry Ward Beecher's sermons I read as they reached me week by week. I promised myself this visit before I passed to the other side, and now I might almost join in the prayer of old Simeon.

But if I am here in '99, you know we are expecting you in our small village in 1900. We have some five million atoms of humanity there, but a few thousands from America will not make any appreciable difference. Anyhow, my instructions are to say, " Let them all come. " We cannot offer you an American welcome, but you shall have an English welcome.

With respect to the Endeavor in the old land, I speak as an individual observer alone when I say our need is not great speakers or personalities, but to realize the power of the individual society for good. We have had Dr. Clark, and are looking for him again; and we have in old Ireland had Mr. Baer. whom, to quote his own words, we did not find " very bare ; " but we need what the drill-master is to the recruit and soldier,— that our members may live up to their pledge and their consecration, so that, endued with the spirit of God, they may practise everywhere the presence of God. We are younger than you in this way. Your Endeavor is of the age of EIGHTEEN, ours only THIRTEEN years. Have a little patience with our youth.

A Smith was to have responded for the guests in this international feast-day,— Dr. Wilton Merle Smith, of New York, — and though he had been detained, there is, was Dr. Clark said, another Smith always ready for an emergency, and Rev. A. J. Smith, of Savannah, stepped into the breach and filled it in a way fitting an occasion so grand in every other particular.

United States Response to Address of Welcome, by Rev. Arthur J. Smith,
Savannah, Ga.

I am glad I 'm a Smith. I 'm glad I am an American —although I was born on the wrong side of the river. That was an accident, however. We feel very much at home here after the greetings which we received a hundred miles and more away from Detroit by the members of your Reception Committee. And here in the city we see such numbers of white-capped young people ! We see you have thought of us. These tents would not have been erected without it. We see you 've worked very hard, and we want to say we are truly thankful.

I remember of a man who was arrested and taken before the police justice. " What is your name ? " asked the justice. " Sp — Sp — Sp — " the fellow stammered. He could not answer, and finally the justice turned to the officer. " Officer, what 's this man charged with ? " he asked. " Well, your honor, I think it 's soda-water," was the reply.

Christian Endeavorers, listen ! Are we charged with soda-water or with the spirit of God ? Is there too much sweetened wind in our consecration meetings ? If it is soda-water we are charged with, we want to make it the spirit of God. Let us work to that end.

The man who travelled half-way around the world to this Convention, Rev. Joseph Walker, of Australia, drew the next knot in the tide of fellowship that is binding all the world in kindred love. Australia is thanking her stars for Christian Endeavor, and Australia's fervent response elicited from Dr. Clark the suggestion that the audience rise and sing, —

> " Four empires by the sea ;
> Four nations great and free."

Australia's Response to Address of Welcome, by Rev. Jos. Walker,
Australia.

I come here to-night, as the representative of 50,000 Christian Endeavorers in the land of the Southern Cross, to respond for them. It has been a long journey to this magnificent city. As I came to your beautiful Pacific slope, which I had longed to see all my life, I could not help but think that we have many things in common. We have some things from you and you have had some things from us. Your greatest gift to us has been the Christian Endeavor movement. The Christian Endeavor movement has been the greatest boon to our young people. It has solved the social question for them to a great extent. Our country is thinly populated; we have large areas entirely bare, and through the Christian Endeavor these young people have been brought together. It has strengthened the Juniors in character, and their societies are flourishing.

When the news of the alliance between England and America, during your struggle of a year ago, was flashed under the waters, hundreds of our people wept for joy. If we Britains and you Americans stand shoulder to shoulder no peace conference is necessary. Peace is assured and the peace of God is assured.

Picturesque? Yes; not only international songs, sometimes newly adopted, and striking incidents, utterances, and climaxes, but the pageantry of brilliant international costumes. It was for an hour a veritable bazaar of the nations. China, with her flowing silken robes, stood forth in the person of Rev. E. G. Tewksbury, of Pekin. Turkey's warm-hued attire was draped around the form of Rev. L. S. Crawford. Japan, the Yankeedom of the Occident, was represented by Rev. Otis Cary, whose reference to Commodore Perry's Sabbath-keeping example in Yokohama harbor called for the singing of the hymn sung on his ships. Our sister republic of the south, Mexico, sent one of her vigorous Endeavorers, Rev. C. Scott Williams, to breathe upon us the spicy breath of the Occidental tropics.

Mr. Tewksbury Presents
China's Compliments.

China's Response to Address of Welcome, by Rev. Elwood C. Tewksbury,
China.

Detroit is a great city, and your hearts are large to take us all in and give us such a hearty welcome. It is a pleasure to see so many working for the Master. Now, I want to tell you that a Chinaman is not a man who eats rats and does all those things which make Americans shudder. He can endeavor, and when he once gets started on the right road he usually succeeds. When he gets an equal chance with other men the Chinaman usually gets in ahead. In my home in Pekin there are many strong, noble, resolute young men who are endeavoring to serve Christ. As I heard that song, "Send Out Thy Light," by Gounod, to-night, my heart turned back to China, where a number of years ago a group of young men sang one of his songs in their own language. They carried the four parts in perfect accord, and their hearts were in the song, and I assure you they can sing that class of music with telling effect.

The welcome you have extended to us demands a duty from you,—a duty of prayer and your means and yourselves. God grant that your prayers and your means and your best efforts may be extended to help the millions of Chinamen who are in need of the inspiring word of God. I thank you for your welcome.

Turkey's Response to Address of Welcome, by Rev. Lyndon S. Crawford, Turkey.

Turkey is a nation of servitude, and I bring to you the prayers of thousands of Armenians. I bring to you the salaams of the Turks. Lay it up in the hearts of ye who love the Lord Jesus Christ, for these Turks are yet to be the servants of Christ. For political reasons the Turkish Christians have not yet had societies of Christian Endeavor. You little realize how great has been the persecution over in that benighted country.

The robe I wear was that worn by Priest John, one of the many pious Christian souls who have given their lives for their religion. This noble man worked among his little flock until it became known to the Turks. "Give up your Christ or you die," they said. John could not. They cut off his right hand. "Give up your Christ or you die!" Again he refused. Then they tortured him; and as he clung to Christ to the last, they finally put him to death by slow torture. The settlement of the Eastern question, of which this Armenian question is but a small part, is in the hands of the American people. It is in your hands, and to you Christians it has been given. May Christ aid our Armenian brethren as he has those of other lands.

Mr. Crawford, of Turkey.

Japan's Response to Address of Welcome, by Rev. Otis Carey, Japan.

This is an anniversary week with us in Japan. It was just forty-six years ago this week that Commodore Perry sailed into one of our harbors and opened it to the world and to Christianity. When that Christian gentleman went into the harbor it was on a Sabbath morning. A deputation of Japanese officers at once put off from shore on business. He told them that it was a day of rest and worship among the Christian peoples of the world, and that they must go away and return the next day. They did so, wondering at his temerity in thus entering a closed port of a country from which all foreigners were excluded and ordering about the Imperial officers. But to-day they understand and thousands of them are adopting the Sabbath Day as we have it.

Mexico's Response to Address of Welcome, by Rev. C. Scott Williams, Mexico City.

We bring to you the greetings from the land of the cactus and the lotus-flower. We come for many hundred Endeavorers in sunny Mexico. I want to say that the heart of the dark-skinned neighbor of yours across the Rio Grande is with you. Naturally a Republican, he has watched your struggle for humanity in Cuba with a friendly eye. There is a great American question that is arising that will obscure the great Eastern question in time. The Mexican is looking to you for the solving of the great problem. We want your Bible. We have the distillery and the machete. With the Bible we may assist you in solving the American question.

The meeting, that had been going up, up, up, closed on the high plane of a hearty hand-shake among trustees, speakers, officers, and committee-men, and the thousands who had enjoyed the results of their careful planning and splendid efforts. For over an hour a continuous procession passed over the platform, greeting the receiving line.

What happier finish than this to so auspicious a beginning of so full a spiritual feast!

THURSDAY MORNING.

Tent Endeavor.

Delightful and invigorating were the breezes which lakes and river contributed, and elastic were the footsteps by which the streams of eager Convention-goers poured toward every entrance of Tent Endeavor to be sure of seats for the Thursday morning session. And what a promise of rich things looked down at them from the platform! Percy S. Foster, of Washington, D. C., was there, baton in hand; Bishop Ninde, as the leader of the devotional exercises, and President Clark and Secretary Baer, with the annual budgets of interesting facts and stimulating plans. Everybody was expectant, everybody sung, everybody smiled, everybody was happy.

Secretary Baer's glowing report added to their happiness. Over two thousand societies organized since Nashville, — six a day! Mr. Faintheart's criticism that Conventions cost too much was sent staggering off under the broadside of facts concerning what Christian Endeavor is doing for missions. "Christian Endeavor *lives!*" was Mr. Baer's oft-repeated declaration; and the facts he quoted about church debts paid off, Sunday baseball stopped, ballot-fights at the primaries, Sunday-newspaper readers made uncomfortable, and the like, were most eloquent proofs.

Secretary John Willis Baer's Annual Statistical Report.

THE GROWTH OF CHRISTIAN ENDEAVOR.

Each year some self-appointed seer has predicted that the numerical growth of Christian Endeavor could not keep pace with the wonderful development of the earlier years. Notwithstanding it is eighteen years since Christian Endeavor first blossomed, and notwithstanding the further fact that many of the States have few churches at present without Christian Endeavor societies, its increase this year has been remarkable. After taking from the lists the societies that have ceased to exist for any and all reasons, the *net gain in number of societies during the last year is nearly two thousand societies, with over one hundred thousand new members.*

Pennsylvania, including the Junior societies, now has over five thousand societies within its borders; New York, over four thousand; Ohio and Illinois have over three thousand; Indiana and Ontario, two thousand; Iowa, Michigan, Kansas, Massachusetts, have over fifteen hundred; California, Missouri, and New Jersey, not far behind, with over one thousand each.

Does that sound as if Christian Endeavor was decadent, a fad, or had seen its best days? No, Mr. Sceptic, if you are here this morning, listen when I say that Christian Endeavor *lives.*

Since last we met, Russia, at that time the only country in the world without its Christian Endeavor society, has welcomed our principles and methods, and to-day our international fellowship is complete and world-wide. Great Britain has over six thousand societies, and a royal welcome awaits us next July in London. Australia has over two thousand societies, and is represented in this Convention by two delegates that have travelled over six thousand miles to bring greetings from our brothers and sisters under the Southern Cross. India has 454, China 148, Africa 136, Mexico 108, West Indies 103, Germany

101, Madagascar 93, Japan 73, and on through a long list, which I must omit at this time, but cannot pass by Spain, the country with whom we were at war last year. Spain, rent with war and turmoil, has more than held its own, for she has thirty-six societies.

I verily believe we have not begun to appreciate what a great international peace and arbitration society ours is. This development is not man-made: it is of God.

There are now 979 Intermediate societies, — there ought to be more, — 14,680 Junior societies, 85 Mothers' societies, and 49 Senior societies. Over a hundred societies are to be found upon ships, merchantmen, and men-of-war: many societies in the soldiers' camps: and in unexpected places, such as prisons, schools of reform, workhouses, almshouses, asylums, institutions for the blind and for the deaf, schools and colleges; among car-drivers and motormen, policemen, travelling men, life-savers on the coast, lighthouse employees, in large factories, etc., to the number of over two hundred.

I have a right to the exultant ring in my voice when I say that we have crossed the fifty-five thousand line. The official enrolment is 55,813 *societies, with a total membership of* 3,350,000.

If any Christian has lost his enthusiasm, these figures should be a source of inspiration.

In England the Baptists lead in Christian Endeavor; in Australia, the Wesleyan Methodists: in Canada, the Methodists: and in the United States, the Presbyterians.

Always interesting, it is a pleasure to give you the latest detailed information of the denominational representation of Christian Endeavor in the United States. The Presbyterians are in the van, with over eight thousand societies. These figures include the Junior and Intermediate societies. The Congregationalists have over six thousand: the Disciples of Christ, over four thousand; the Baptists, over three thousand: then the Methodist ·Protestant, Cumberland Presbyterians, Lutherans. Reformed Dutch, and Methodist Episcopal, in order named, each with over one thousand societies. Then follow many evangelical denominations, in all, including those already named, nearly forty.

With a commendable spirit of friendly rivalry, our denominational banners are carried in the front ranks, and never lowered. High over all, however, do we raise the blood-stained banner of the Cross, and are amenable to no other authority than that of our Commander-in-chief, the King of kings and Lord of lords, Jesus Christ, the Saviour of the world.

Why should any true denominationalist remain outside of Christian Endeavor? Ours is a happy family. Come join our ranks ; we will do you good. Christian Endeavor *lives.*

The Christian Endeavor "Tenth Legion" now numbers 14,700 members, who are giving not less than one-tenth of their incomes to God. This is an increase of over four thousand members since we met in Nashville. But you are no more satisfied with that growth than I am. Let's work for ten thousand new members this year. When the proper proportion of our rank and file is marching under the banner "Render unto God the things that are God's" such a dilemma as a missionary board in debt, or a young Student Volunteer equipped for service, but prevented from reaching the front because of lack of funds, will never be known. Sit down in my office and read the thousand upon thousand of reports that have reached my desk in the last month, and if you knew nothing of the year's campaign for missions made in our societies by the Yale Band, about the missionary biographies read by the thousand, about the missionary prayer cycles, about the great increase in the membership of the Comrades of the Quiet Hour, now numbering over fifteen thousand, you would have the same hope for coming years that fairly throbs in my heart when I say, God is going to do great things for missions with Christian Endeavor. Here are some of the sentences in the reports that indicate the progress of this mighty missionary and evangelistic force: "Classes formed for systematic study of missions." "Missionary libraries have been purchased." Many a society is supporting its *own* missionary through their *own* board. "We support a missionary, his wife, and three children." "We are educating three orphans in India." "We have our own native preacher." "We support an orphan in Turkey." "We are pledged for six years to educate a child in India." "We pay entire expense of a missionary in Peru." "We are educating three girls in India." "We are responsible for an orphan girl in Armenia." "Our society supports a native preacher in Africa." "We have our own missionary in Japan." "With two other societies we guarantee the salary of a home and foreign missionary." "We are supporting two of our own members in the field." "We are soon to send one of our members to the foreign field." "We now have a live Missionary Committee, and our monthly missionary meetings are the very best." "We have subscribed for our missionary magazines, and keep them going from house to house."

Does that sound as if Christian Endeavorers spent all their energy and money upon conventions? Forget Mr. Faintheart's criticisms. Christian Endeavor is one of the mighty evangels of the gospel. Christian Endeavor *lives*.

Christian Endeavor has done much for missions in the past, and each year the tide has risen higher. This year has been our very best. Never before in the nine years that I have been privileged to serve you as General Secretary have I been able to tell so glad a story. Nearly nine thousand societies in making their annual reports have mentioned the amount of money contributed to their own missionary boards. This amount, augmented by what these same societies have given to other benevolences, and to their own church, is nearly five hundred thousand dollars. The society that leads the list is the one in St. Peter's German Lutheran Church, Allegheny City, Pa.; the total amount given to their mission boards, to their home church, and for other benevolences is $1,583.74. The next society deserving mention is the one in the First Congregational Church of Washington, D. C.; the total amount is $1,371.70. Next is the $1,337.67 contributed by the society in the First Presbyterian Church of Aledo, Ill. Then comes the society in the Second Baptist Church of St. Louis, Mo.; the figure is $1,152. Let me also quote three sentences from the interesting report of this same society: "Held public Sunday night gospel service from June to September; educated two young men for the ministry; had special care of our poor and sick families." The society in the Oxford Presbyterian Church, Philadelphia, Pa., reports $1,283.50 contributed to missions and benevolences, of which amount $842.50 was contributed directly to their missionary boards. So far as I know, the best report made by a Junior society is that of the Juniors of the Brighton, Mass., Congregational Church. This society has for two years led all the Massachusetts Juniors. This year the amount is $247 for missions.

I must close this section of my report with the interesting fact that the Chinese Society of Christian Endeavor of San Francisco, Rev. Jee Gam, pastor, has contributed $689 to their own missionary board, $415.05 to their own home church expenses, and for other benevolences, $108.82; in all, $1,212.87.

Let me share with you some nuggets gathered from my mail-mine.

I have selected them from the thousands of postal-card reports sent in to me by our obliging corresponding secretaries. This is only a small proportion of the wealth that reached my desk. Indeed, I was embarrassed with my riches. Let 's glance at them in the rough. We have n't the time to give them the merited polish and proper setting. These are a few samples of the things the societies have been actually doing : —

"Our Good-Literature Committee has sent books and Bibles to the sailors and soldiers, to hospitals and prisons." "Kept three children in school in Oregon who could not otherwise have gone." "Held gospel meetings in prisons, almshouses, hospitals, old people's homes, car-stations, engine-houses, and wharves." "Furnished dinners to the deserving poor at Christmas and Thanksgiving." "Sent a poor family to the country for one week for fresh air." "Distributed invitations to church in hotels and boarding-houses." "Purchased hymn-books, libraries, church organs, and all kinds of furniture for the church." "Assisted in conducting the Sunday evening service, in many cases taking entire charge." "We give one night every two weeks for work in a mission in the slum district of our city, and go four miles every Sunday afternoon to assist in the evangelistic service in the jail." "Our Fresh-Air Committee arranged eleven picnics, sending 779 persons into the country, our society contributing $152 to carry on the work, in addition to supplying all the refreshments." "Taken an active part in the local fight against the saloon." "Co-operated in a practical way with the W. C. T. U." "Organized, conduct, and support mission Sunday schools in neglected districts in city and country." "Clothed twenty-eight children, thus securing them as regular members for our Sunday school." "Conduct meetings at the Seaman's Bethel three nights in the month." "Furnish a choir for the midweek prayer meeting." "Are responsible for a chorus choir for the Sunday evening service." "Our Junior society gave a concert at the Old Ladies' Home." "Publish a church calendar and conduct our church paper." "Our entire Junior society has organized itself into a committee for the prevention of cruelty to animals." "Conduct a weekly prayer meeting for shut-ins."

Please pass this part of the report along to Mr. Sure-the-society-is going-to-seed. It 's the best of it. I am dealing with plain facts, no fancies. Christian Endeavor *lives.*

"Sent comfort-bags to sailors and soldiers." "Conduct evangelistic meetings among the soldiers in camp." "Support a pupil in a mission school." "For ten years have had charge of a special service at the Old Ladies' Home." "Bought a new carpet for our church." "Secured volunteer nurses for our Relief-Committee work." "Paid off our church debt." "The members of our country Junior society opened their homes for two weeks to eleven poor boys and girls from the city." "We have put our whole strength into promoting Sabbath observance." "Are circulating pledges for total abstinence." "Paid part of our pastor's salary." "Held cottage prayer meetings." "Formation of classes for Bible-study." "Fought Sunday baseball." "Making people uncomfortable who read Sunday newspapers." "Several ballot-box fights at the primaries." "Opened a reading-room in our church." "Secured many names for our Peace Memorial." "Increased the amount given to missions from $2 to $155." "Closed a Sunday barber-shop."

But time would fail me to make the exhibit complete. Ours is an inexhaustible mine.

Now for the last of this annual report. Christian Endeavor has in more ways than those already referred to borne fruit, and is to-day *one* of many other agencies for increasing the membership of the churches of Christ. During the last ten years over one million and one half of our members have joined the church. *Over one million and one half church-members from the ranks of Christian Endeavor in the ten years!* Behold what God hath wrought. *Christian Endeavor lives!*

Rev. Nehemiah Boynton, D.D., a prince among presiding officers, introduced President Clark as "the man whose name is engraved on the hearts of millions of young people." Dr. Clark was most heartily received and soon had all their ears as well as their hearts when he made his annual address; and while it was ringing in the ears of the ten thousand or more present, it was being echoed by the types in every reading land. "Going and Growing" proved one of the most popular themes Dr. Clark has ever presented. Among the important suggestions of the hour was that of a Family Worship Fraternity. "What do you think of that?" asked Dr. Clark. Quick came the hand-clapped approval of the audience. "Then I shall expect you all to go home and do it." Dr. Clark clinched the nail he had driven home.

"Sacrifice and service, living and loving, praying and practising,

going and growing," is a watchword that will ring through thousands
of hearts, as it rang so grandly into thousands of ears that morning.

Annual Address by President Francis E. Clark.

GOING AND GROWING.

The biographer of the youth of King David tells us, in second Samuel, that
" he went on and grew great, and the Lord of Hosts was with him."

I like the marginal reading of this passage : " David went going and growing." Going and growing are inseparable. The boy who does not go does not
grow. The boy who *grows* is very sure to *go*. It is not otherwise with a society, a church, a movement. The movement that has ceased to grow will soon
cease to go; and, conversely, when it ceases to go — to be energetic, aggressive,
outreaching — it will soon not only cease to grow, but will dwindle and fade.
The last part of the verse belongs with the first. Let us never separate the two
ideas. " Because the Lord God of Hosts was with him " — he kept going and
growing. This part, too, we may turn about and in the reverse find a great deal
of force. Because he kept going and growing the Lord God was with him.

Apply this to our youthful David among the movements of the day. To
merit the presence and guidance of the Lord God of Hosts, the Christian
Endeavor movement must *go* and *grow*. " Going " stands for aggressive, outreaching enterprise; " growing " for increase in grace, in power, and numerical
strength.

Going and growing have ever been characteristic of Christian Endeavor.
It was born creeping; it soon began to run.
If ever the promise has been fulfilled:
" They shall run and not be weary; they
shall walk and not faint," it has been to this
organization. Every year of the eighteen
of our history has been marked by some advance : —

1881 by the formation of the first society.

1882 by the first convention.

1883 by growth beyond the Mississippi.

1884 by the formation of the first Junior
society.

1885 by the formation of the United Society.

1886 by the first Local Union and first
State Union.

1887 by the formation and rapid growth
of the State and Local Unions.

1888 by the beginning of work in Great
Britain.

1889-91 by marvellous numerical growth,
every evangelical denomination coming into
the fellowship.

1892 by the extension of the movement
the world around.

Dr. Clark's Message This Year Was
"Grow and Go."

1893 by the adoption of Christian citizenship as a legitimate part of Christian Endeavor work.

1894 by a great revival of missionary zeal.

1895 by the formation of the World's Christian Endeavor Union and a new
sense of our international brotherhood.

1896 by the adoption of the Tenth Legion.

1897 by the beginnings of the Quiet Hour movement.

1898, the last and best of all, by the very rapid and substantial expansion of
the Tenth Legion, the Quiet Hour, of Bible reading, and the sentiment for
peace and international arbitration, as expressed in the Peace Memorial.

Going and growing, growing and going, have been characteristic of every year of our history. All these advance steps have been gained not by ignoring or neglecting the gains of the past, but by conserving them while new advances were made. Thus every advance step for citizenship, missions, international and interdenominational fellowship, church loyalty, and greater efficiency within the Society has been maintained and strengthened, while the next year has seen some higher plane reached, some new duty undertaken, some new responsibility assumed.

In many respects this last year has been the best in our history; there have been more going and growing, more advance and increase, than in any other year. The conventions have been larger and more stimulating; the denominational drift has been more decidedly than ever toward our interdenominational movement; the growth in foreign lands has never been so encouraging; the thought of the Quiet Hour of personal communion with God has taken hold of the Society with a blessed grasp that will never be relaxed; our horizon has been expanded to take in our responsibility for peace on earth and good will to man as never before. There is still room, however, on our Peace Memorial, let me remind you, for hundreds of thousands of signatures.

During the past year more has been done for the prisoner and the sailor than ever before. All honor to the noble Endeavorers who have devoted their lives so unselfishly to this Christ-like service! May their zeal inspire us all to the same heroic endeavor. O Endeavorers, hear the Lord say, " I was in prison and ye visited me. I was on the sea, and ye did not forget me. I was in the camp or the hospital, and ye remembered me; inasmuch as ye did it unto one of the least of these, my brethren—"

I trust that neither you nor I will ever confound motion with progress. There is an activity without action. Our adoption of new plans and new methods of work does not mean that we adopt every new fad that some enthusiast would force upon us. I have been implored, during the past year, to urge Endeavorers to form societies of descendants of slave-holders to ameliorate the condition of the negro; to father many political schemes for the ushering-in of the millennium by which sometimes, incidentally, my correspondents will be elected to a fat office. I have been asked to endorse the wildest of wildcat schemes to evangelize the world, or to revolutionize society. We will beware of the visionary and of the political trickster, whatever moral reform he blazons on his banners, as well as of the selfish schemer who still brings his hatchet to our grindstone.

I do not forget, either, that no amount of progress, of strenuous activity, of earnest zeal, can satisfy some carping critics. I do not forget that, in spite of our best efforts, every thin evening service, every depleted Sunday school, every empty missionary treasury, is by some laid at the door of the Christian Endeavor Society. Some people are still utterly oblivious of the facts, which exhaustive statistics have proved, that the active members of the Christian Endeavor Society attend the Sunday evening service and the mid-week prayer meeting in the proportion of two to one of the older members of the church; that the gifts to denominational missions, home and foreign, from all young people have largely increased within the last ten years; and, better than all, that in three of the great denominations that have most heartily welcomed Christian Endeavor the accessions to the church on confession of faith have more than doubled within the same decade. Let these statistics, until they are disproved, forever silence the fault-finders who lay every temporary or local decadence in religious life at the door of the Christian Endeavor Society and are forever calling upon it to remedy evils for which the whole Church is responsible.

But we will not let visionary fanatics or carping critics keep us from true progress, from real going and growing. We have not yet attained. We are not yet full grown. There are new steps to be taken, new advances to be made. You will, in each society and local union, decide what advance steps are most important for you to take ; how you can best go and grow ; but let me suggest some methods which I think are of very wide application; some steps which I think that God and the times demand.

First. Almost every state, province, and territory affords the opportunity of *larger numerical growth.* There remains yet much land to be possessed. There are school-house districts, isolated communities, even single families, remote from others, where the simple principles of Christian Endeavor could be applied with vast advantage to the spiritual life and growth of all concerned.

There are many denominational societies that would come into our fellowship if only they understood that we seek no control and demand no money or allegiance, but only ask their brotherhood, that we "all may be one." The trend is distinctly and decidedly toward our interdenominational fellowship in all denominations but one, and information wisely distributed among pastors and churches of the real purpose and method of Christian Endeavor would still more largely increase this tendency. Let them know that without withdrawing from their own denominational organization they can be Christian Endeavorers and enjoy our fellowship.

I recommend most earnestly that all State and local union officers give this matter their careful attention. The United Society furnishes literature that will help them. Let secretaries of unions give more effort to this matter than to the gathering of voluminous statistics. It is more important to use our steam in driving the wheels than in blowing the whistle.

Second. *See that the younger Endeavorers go and grow.* This is a matter of vast importance. Ours must never cease to be a *young people's* society, however many older people are connected with it. There ought to be twice as many Junior societies, and ten times as many Intermediate societies as there are. It should be the business of us older Endeavorers to see that every boy and girl between seven and twenty in our church is reached by Endeavor methods. Some of us (shall I speak bluntly?) are growing too long-winded in the weekly prayer meeting. We are doing too much of the work on the committees, because we can do it better than the younger ones. We are not training our successors in the only way they can be trained, — by setting them at work. I would recommend in every society a Junior Committee, whose business it shall be, in co-operation with the pastor, not only to keep alive and foster the Junior society, and the Intermediate, where it is needed, but to promote the participation in service and confession of all the younger people in the older society whose inexperience and bashfulness prevent them from receiving the full training which can only come from practice.

Third. *To Local Unions comes a clearer and more imperative call than ever before to "go and grow."* Plans for some uniformity of topics and methods of work, which have met the unanimous and enthusiastic response of local union officers, are being perfected, which I believe will unify and establish these unions in an unusual degree during the twelve months to come. The local and district unions are immense factors for good when wisely led. Let me urge upon my brethren and sisters who hold positions of influence and office in them to remember that these trusts committed to them are of special sacredness. To advance vastly the fellowship of Christians, the activity of youth, the devotion and loyalty of the young people to their own churches, the unification of righteous sentiment against rampant wrongs, may these unions be used!

Fourth. Two years ago, at San Francisco, I suggested that, since the Lord was more and more setting solitary Endeavorers together in families, *religion in the family should become more and more our serious concern.* How far that thought took root I have no means of judging, but that there is need of endeavor along this line I am more than ever convinced. I am told that among Christians family worship is being more and more neglected, and that many professed disciples never bow the knee in family prayer. My own observation and experience convinces me that this is the fact. Here, then, is a rewarding and most important field of Christian Endeavor. This may well become a theme of prayer and address and earnest consideration, in these days when family life is at the mercy of a Dakota divorce court or a Connecticut marriage statute. Why may not the hour of family worship do as much to purify and sweeten and irradiate family life as the Quiet Hour or the Morning Watch has done to purify and sweeten and irradiate the individual life? Why should we not form among Christian Endeavorers a Family Worship Fraternity, with suggested readings, and help to make of the simple service a blessing and delight?

Fifth. *In evangelistic missionary zeal let us "go and grow."* If the day of the old evangelism is gone by, as many think, — though I am unwilling to believe this myself, — if this be true, however, how much more important that the new evangelism of the young for the young should be urged and pressed! If from conquest from without the church is not making such gains as heretofore, how much more important than ever is it that growth from within, from the children of the church, should keep whole and strong the ranks of the people of God! The task is ours, then, to keep alive the evangelistic spirit of soul-winning.

And with this is inseparably linked the missionary spirit, that conquering, aggressive, indomitable spirit that cannot rest until all the kingdoms of the world are also the kingdoms of Christ.

I would earnestly recommend as an outcome of the Tenth Legion that we all take up the "Forward Movement" of our respective denominations, and that as individuals and societies we either adopt and support some missionary or native worker of our own, or group ourselves with other societies for this purpose.

Nay, why can we not do more than this, and, as individuals, have it for our ambition to support a missionary or worker through our own denomination at home or abroad? The Student Volunteer movement needs this supplementary movement to complete it, and to render it effective.

Young men, make money for God. Pledge yourselves to turn your best ability to the making of money, not for a selfish and sordid purpose, but that through your money the world may be evangelized.

Glorify this meanest of passions with the Godlike light of an unselfish purpose. Transmute this clay into pure gold. Make your purpose very specific and definite. Bring to bear the force of our pledge upon your business. Rout avariciousness with a godly purpose, and say : —

> "Trusting in the Lord Jesus Christ for strength, I will make money for him. I will at the first possible moment support, through my own denominational board, one or more workers for Christ on the home or foreign field."

What a glorious day for world-wide missions will that be when 100,000 young American Christians make that covenant with God!

My brethren and sisters, all these things of which I have been speaking come not forth of the will of man, but of God. I would, if God gives me power, pitch high the key-note of our consecration to-day. I would always appeal to the heroic within you. This is all the natural, legitimate outcome of the blessed Quiet Hour, which, during the past year, has so profoundly affected Christian Endeavor. This is not the ascetic's rapt vision of God, that leads to folded hands and a contemplative Nirvana. It is the vision of God that arms for conflict and victory; the vision that ennobles and inspires the most prosaic business; the vision that sends us about doing good; the vision that carries us to sick chambers, to prison doors, to the haunts of poverty and squalor and vice and wretchedness. It is the vision that nerves to sacrifice and heroism.

A few weeks ago a poor man by a distressing accident had the skin stripped from his arm. That arm would soon be forever useless unless prompt and heroic measures were taken to cure it. Thereupon twenty-seven members of a benevolent fraternity to which this man belonged bared their arms, and allowed a square inch of their healthy flesh to be grafted on his arm. In this way, and in this way alone, could his arm be healed, and his family saved from absolute want.

Ah, brothers and sisters, by sacrificing ourselves alone can the world be saved. Flesh of our flesh, bone of our bone, life of our life, must be given. Our religion, our endeavor, is useless unless it teaches us this. We can neither go nor grow until we learn this lesson, that he that saveth his life must lose it.

This is the spirit of our Quiet Hour. This, please God, shall be the spirit of this Convention. This shall be the watchword of the nineteenth year of Christian Endeavor. Sacrifice and service, living and loving, praying and practising, going and growing, shall bring the time of victory.

Then came forward the rector of Holy Trinity Episcopal Church of Philadelphia, Pa., the Rev. Floyd W. Tomkins, D.D., who conducted a season of quiet meditation and prayer.

"God has no message for a dishonest heart, and we need a period of self-examination preparatory to the message we are about to receive in the sermon of the morning," was Dr. Tomkins's preface to the Quiet Hour. And for ten minutes every eye was closed and every voice hushed except in subdued song, whose soft strains were prayers in melody, meditations in whispered song. Thus the vast audience was led up to a lofty level of heart preparation for the Convention sermon by Rev. F. W. Gunsaulus, D.D., of Chicago, Ill. It was a sermon worthy the man whose pulpit and personal power made millions of Armour's dollars flow into generous philanthropy as the result of a single sermon. The inscription on Christ's cross was the text, and the central thought was that it is the time for Christian Endeavor to take the language of the intellect, and the language of the heart, and the language of the will, and with them write over the cross, "The whole man for Christ."

Convention Sermon, by Rev. W. F. Gunsaulus, D.D.,
Chicago, Ill.

THE INSCRIPTION ON THE CROSS OF JESUS.

And Pilate wrote a title and put it on the cross. And the writing was, Jesus of Nazareth, the King of the Jews . . . and it was written in Hebrew, and Greek, and Latin.—JOHN XIX. 19, 20.

Emerson says, "Language is fossil poetry." In this brilliant sentence the American seer states but one of the features which thoughtful minds behold in that marvellous product of human life called language. For, elsewhere, he himself intimates that language is the unconsciously written history of man; and therefore it is the chronicle of the more prosaic events and movements in the long experience of humanity. It would be interesting to illustrate this proposition by looking into those words — and they constitute a multitude — which have been called into being by some crisis in the life of man, a crisis of which they are the description, words which are sparks struck from steel and rock as they sharply collided in the experience of the race. Every great and many an insignificant hour has furnished to the vocabulary of our humanity its word — a word all instinct with the forces which gave it birth; a word which forever records the fact that at its birth-hour the lips of man moved with an experience which might lie unexpressed in the soul no longer. It would also be interesting to go more accurately and profoundly into the modifications which each great word suffers, and into the transformation through which many an old word has gone, into variations of mood and tense, voice and termination, and to note how the whole manifold life and spirit of humanity has, with matchless honesty and absolute accuracy, told its story. With truth we are told that every word is like a ripple of sand left upon the vast beach of the soul's life, telling how high the tide had risen, how furious or how calm was the mounting wave, what strength manifested itself urging this impulse on from the heart of the ocean, what celestial forces attached themselves to those quivering drops, and dragged them noisily along, in a mass, to tell the tale of the whole sea in that wavelet of sand

which was left when the tide ran out. Such is the truth of these observations
that even the separate peoples of the earth are studied with most satisfactory
results in their language. The smallest difference in construction, the slightest
contrast in method of expression, the most subtle variation in relationship of
parts of speech, mark the very character of one nation from that of another.
A language may be as dead as the people who spoke it, or as living as the man
at your side. The disposition of its words with reference to one another, the
way in which the mind chooses names for its facts within and its facts without,
and above all, the way in which it puts into these words its experience, are the
tell-tale of the mind's own nature, the mirror which reflects its own features, the
sensitive plate which registers the operation of all its powers and shows what
energies are uppermost and what motives ply their supreme influence.

Crisis in History.

Each great crisis is sure to develop such a moment in the history of language
as may mark the advent of a new word. It is also true that every great crisis
in human affairs so commands the human soul, which lies behind all language,
whose partial expression all language is, that a study of the languages of men,
in any such critical hour, will reveal the strong lines which give special character to every feature of human nature. Only a really great event commands the
soul so authoritatively and fully as to bring out all its powers, until they stand
like soldiers in line, none more prominently than the other, one phalanx for
duty. Therefore it is that the study of any time like the period of the Crusades,
or that of the Renaissance, or that of the revolution in France, reveals the fact
that, at times, the whole kingdom of the human spirit is roused to a degree
quite wonderful; that then the intellect of man, the sensibilities of all humanity
and the will of the race are alive and awake, and that all humanity then seems
to have one great soul, in which thought and feeling and will are one. A really
great event seems to gather together the dissevered and scattered lights of the
spirit, each in proper order, and thus to prepare the soul to fling its total energy of
illumination upon the problems which confront it. At such a time some great
capacious human being usually comes to a stand where all humanity may pour
into him the intellect and the feeling and the will of a race, so that he becomes
the spokesman of his kind; and his very vocabulary testifies of the completeness with which his spiritual horizon takes in human nature. So, in one of
these hours, Martin Luther united the thought, the feeling, the will, of an
imprisoned humanity, stood and spoke with something like the marvellous
breath of our human nature, and re-created the German language, so that
Goethe's intellect and Herder's emotion and Bismarck's will might use it with
a sense of freedom and of power. It is, let it be remembered, an exceedingly
significant fact that the language of a people should always in these ways attest
the greatness of its experience and triumphs.

In the event which our text records we have the loftiest example of the
power of great events, or crises, to command the whole kingdom of man's spirit
— the entire soul. Here, and only here, do we behold in history an illustration
of the absolutely complete homage which the greatest of crises and the most
supreme events obtained from the soul of man. Crusades to holy sepulchers,
a matchless morning-tide for the Europe which could not easily get away from
the old Cæsarism, a world-wide rebellion against self-constituted authority and
tyrannical privileges, — each and all of these had their impulse in the cross of
Jesus. If either of these, like a fancied lens, had the power not only to gather
the scattered beams of the soul's power, but also to dissolve them again, so that
the glory of man's tri-personal nature — a being of thought, of feeling, and of
will — should appear, how much more surely might this imperial crisis, marked
forever by Calvary and the cross, so command the soul that it should stand
before it in that awful grandeur of celestial light, with every feature distinct,
every energy manifest, and every fragmentary province of its mighty kingdom
so profoundly and vitally connected with the others that at least once in the
long career of the human spirit this godlike tri-personality of intellect, sensibilities, and will should reveal its supreme unity and glory!

What a crisis that was on Calvary! The age-long battle between evil and good had reached Waterloo. The hour had struck for the decisive conflict. Every contest which the soul of man had felt from the beginning, every silent advance of right upon retreating wrong, every sharp defence of truth against error, every dreadful fight against sin, every bloody march upon selfishness, every terrible charge upon the beast, every defeat, every triumph, was but a prelude to this awfully tragic moment when the Son of God, nailed to the cross, was first to hurl the arrogant power of sin from that solemn height and, next, to make the cross his undisputed throne. Is it wonderful that such an hour should bring the human soul out into such a definiteness of outline that its deepest nature and loftiest possibility should be seen?

Jesus came to be the Saviour of the human spirit — the whole man. He could never be content to merely redeem the intellectual life, or the life of the sensibilities, or that of the purposes and choices of mankind. At his cross, as a trinity in unity, stood a Godlike soul. Thought came in the language of Greece, the land of the intellect; sentiment and feeling came in the language of Hebrewdom, the land of the sensibilities ; the home of the human heart will come in the Latin tongue, the language of imperial Rome, when human purpose had made its arches of triumph. In all these, and by all these, came human nature, dissevered but now united before the cross of Jesus of Nazareth.

" Metlat the Cross."

I do not forget customary explanations, which are true so far as they go. I am aware that this inscription was presented to the eye of the foreigner in Greek that he might understand it ; that it was given to the Jew in Hebrew because Jerusalem and Calvary were located in the province of Judea, a Jewish country ; that it was put into the Latin language because this same Judea was a Roman province, and this was the official tongue. I do not forget that the assertion it contained was probably made in bitterest irony. But behind these facts lies a greater fact. There these three particular languages were.

The mighty powers which make history had so moved in the past, and were so moving in the present, that these three great streams of human life and experience met at the foot of that crucifix, as they had taken their rise long ago in the deep springs of the human soul. The truth is this, — that there was a wondrous drawing-power in that cross. Human nature had been dissevered by evil. Human life was everywhere fragmentary. The soul of man was to be re-constituted. The powers of human nature were to be re-baptized. To save man at all he must be delivered from a fragmentary life. All the

Dr. Gunsaulus Preaching
His Magnificent
Sermon.

energies of history were in sympathy with the work of Christ. Every force carried the soul — carries it still — to the spot of its redemption. As we seek to find in Golgotha a centre for human history, the circle around Calvary seems very large at times : but smaller and smaller does it grow, until at last it has massed humanity — its intellect, its feeling, its will — under Roman eagles, and holds the central position at the cross ; until, in the three languages which most truly stand for the life of this tri-personality,—man,— it announces the death of Jesus and the new life of mankind.

I. *Let us notice how truly these languages express the tri-personal life of man.*

(a) Greece was the land where the flowers of human intellect grew most abundantly ; the Greek language is the language of human thought. In the life of a Greek word lie chapters in the history of philosophy. In the career of a single Greek syllable are oftentimes to be found the results of discussion after discussion in the realms of metaphysics. Dialectical skill, the subtleties of logic-brilliant insight, keen critical power, penetrating analysis, metaphysical genius, the energies of mind which beheld the features of every shadowy abstraction, — all these are revealed in that supple, manifold, and incisive tongue.

The countless transformations of one of the names which the Greek applied to some fact or idea simply indicate the litheness of his thought, as he moved from one to many points of views. The richness of this vocabulary in words, which are names for facts of which the brain is most conscious, attests the power of his intellectual life. A Greek verb can never be so poor as not to show how large a volume of pure thought may circulate from soul to soul.

Supremacy of Greece.

Behind this facile, rich, ductile, strong language was the human intellect supreme. I do not mean to deny to Greece the glory of warm sentiment. I certainly may not with success assume that her history and language, art and life, furnished no great chapters which show how mighty was the will of Greece. But surely her supremacy was not that of will or feeling. It was that of the intellect: her triumphs were those of the brain. Plato was greater than Pericles, though Pericles was, above all things else, a statesman of intellectual power. Aristotle was a mightier conqueror than Alexander. Socrates is a name before which all the triumphs of heart and will in Greece grow pale. Athens was the paradise of the intellect. Of course Sappho's song and the art of Phidias are full of sentiment; the comedies of Aristophanes, the epic of Homer, the verses of Hesiod, are redolent with the heart's perfume; but these are not pages from the literature of the heart, save as the brain leads and commands. The Œdipus of Sophocles, the Prometheus of Æschylus, stand at the head of a literature unsurpassed by their modern representatives, Faust and Hamlet. Herodotus and Xenophon write in the atmosphere of clear thought. The art of Greece had its triumph, not in painting, but in sculpture; and colorless intellect sharpened the chisel-edge, which was held by hands believing Athene to have been born full-armed, not from the heart, but from the head of Zeus. To-day the problems of human thought seem a revival of the questions which stood before Paul as he entered Athens and beheld porch and academy; and the intellect of the present in the midst of her victories feels that her golden age lies afar behind where the archæologist digs in the city of Athene.

(*b*) Palestine was the land where the finest flowers of human sentiment have blossomed most abundantly; and the Hebrew language is the language of the human heart. In the life of a Hebrew word lie chapters in the history of man's best emotions. The whole ocean of human feeling has registered its tides, in stormy grandeur and in solemn calm, in words of Hebrew. The religious sentiment has made its peculiar construction and richness a testimony of its fruitfulness. As the heart knows God in and through the religious feelings, it is not strange that any slightest study of the Hebrew language will reveal a vocabulary at once sensitively open to the approaches of God to man and powerfully expressive of man's approach to God. A beautiful story is told by Mr. Arnold in his "Robertson of Brighton." "A curious conversation," he says, "is related, which once passed between Grimm and Diderot. The two men were walking one day in the fields. Diderot had plucked an ear of wheat and a blue corn-flower, and was attentively regarding them, when Grimm asked him what he was doing. 'I am listening,' was the reply. 'But who is speaking to you?' 'God.' 'Indeed!' 'It is in Hebrew; the heart understands, but the intellect is not raised high enough.'" Other nations have performed other services, but Hebrewdom has uttered the heart of man, and the result is that every characteristic of the emotional nature is impressed upon its language. The spirit of Palestine might fitly look out upon the Pyramids of Egypt and the Stadia of Athens, and say with Tennyson: —

"If e'er when faith had fallen asleep

The heart stood up and answered: I have felt."

The Great Hebrew Heart.

I certainly could not deny that the Book of Job furnishes to the intellect of mankind an impulse and an instruction unmatched by the Prometheus of Æschylus. The laws of Moses and the statesmanship of this great leader, the brilliant thoughts of Isaiah and the Proverbs of Solomon, are witnesses to the strength and depth of thought which ran through Hebrewdom; but the movement of that whole current came from the fountain of feeling, the unsounded depths of the heart. There seems to be no lack of purpose in the personality of Noah, or Abraham, or Moses, or Saul, or David. Surely Hebrew history reveals a people surrounded with enemies, and contesting every inch of soil with courageous will; but the supreme energy behind all these exploits and feats of valor was the Hebrew heart, filled with the sense of omnipotence and resistless with a passionate religiousness. The story of their religion is the story of the heart. Myth and legend may have come into its sweet chronicle; but when you pluck them out with the cold finger of the intellect, the heart bleeds. David's songs are tremulous with emotion. There are tears in the tones of Isaiah, and Jeremiah is the lyrist of the heart. All the sorrow of the soul of man, the disaster of a lost paradise, the perpetual cry of the heart for a sinless life, and the weary weeping for sin,—these made a great portion of Hebrew song. All the desire and yearning of the soul of man, the feverish unrest, the heart-breaking sobs of deathless hope, the noble feeling after the Christ of God,—these not only made unequalled poetry, but these builded temples which were heart-throbs in stone; and these strung together all the events of their personal and national life upon Jewish heart-strings. Athens was the city of the brain; Jerusalem was the city of the heart.

Rome was the social centre of a land where grew most luxuriously the flowers of human purpose and achievement, and the Latin language is the language of the human will. Countless Latin words mark the advent of a new energy in the life of humanity contributed by the all-conquering will of the Roman people. Wherever in our own English and American life some superb purpose leaps to the front with the word of command, it is almost sure to choose a term whose roots run back into the imperial soil of the Cæsars by which to express itself. Seward hesitated long, but at last came to the word "irrepressible," which described the conflict before the nation. Though we are told that "the inhabitants of the Hellenic and Italic peninsulas were ethnically connected and constituted in reality but a single race," the language soon told by the very construction of each sentence how thought dominated in Greece and will in Rome. Wherever the Latin tongue met the Greek, in any of Rome's conquests, the Greek proved that Athenian life flowing along over its way so long had made it a matchless conduit for the advancing life of man. So truly was the Latin tongue the tongue of action and achievement only, that Cicero, who essayed to be a philosopher, occupied himself for days in finding a proper phrase or word for his idea and its belongings. But wherever the supremacy of human will asserted itself, wherever the energy of some mighty purpose was to be named, wherever the sovereignty of conquering volitions felt itself glowing and eager for statement, in military or civil life, in the subjugation of peoples, and in the building of huge works of art and of defence, this stately, concise, and sinewy language, echoing yet, as it does, with the tramp of armies and the sounds of victory, proved itself to be incomparable.

Rome's Noble Life.

Behind this great language was a people which gave it these great characteristics. Rome, in all her grandeur, was incarnate will. Every triumphal arch, every splendid temple, every sumptuous palace, every mighty Appian way, every vast contribution of territory wrested from a subdued people to make up the gigantic empire of Rome, was a witness to the power of the human will. I do not, of course, I could not, deny that a noble intellectual life had its seat at Rome. Another array of great names — Plutus and Terence, Ovid, and Horace, and Virgil, Lucretius and Martial, Cato and Manlius, Cicero, Tacitus, Livy, and Cæsar—would rebuke me if I should. But behind this literature was Greece, and along with it were conquests of will in Rome which far outshine any conquests of the Roman intellect. Certainly no one would think of comparing the emotional life of Rome, its record of the yearnings and struggles of the heart, with that volitional life, that grand record of the will, which made her empress of the world. Rome's characteristic citizen was Julius Cæsar. When we say to Rome, "Show us your man!" Cæsar appears, "the foremost man of all this world." All the intellectual qualities of Rome met in him,—sagacity, learning, a noble imagination, an industrious power of thinking, and a reverence for truth without a love of it for truth's sake. He had Rome's lack of moral feeling. His heart was never passionately warm toward righteousness. But he had also something positive,—Rome's fearless energy of will, her indomitable purpose, her terrible movement, her resistless diligence. Rome was personified in Cæsar, and in Cæsar's hand the will of man attained its greatest power.

II. *Because man is a being of intellect, sensibilities, and will, every social organism or national life which is the embodiment of one of these to the exclusion of others of these powers of the soul has failed.*

Each of these languages which came to that cross was the language of a civilization which had failed to include the whole life and possibility of humanity.

(*a*) Greek civilization failed. It failed to produce a full-orbed humanity. It produced no great symmetrical type of men. Pluto had intellect enough to see the golden rule; he lacked the power of heart, love, and the force of will, the feeling and the purpose, to make it walk the streets of Athens. The statesmanship of Pericles is unmatched in all the forecast and comprehensiveness of the intellect; but it lacked the beating of a human heart and sovereignty of the human will. When up to that cross on Calvary this plastic, flexible, and powerful language came, it bore upon its every feature not only the triumph of thought, but also testimony to the fact that the most splendid thinking the world has ever seen could not lay the permanent foundation for the civilization of humanity. Just as Greek society, Alexander's empire, went to pieces before Roman purpose and power, so a merely intellectual life has never been able to produce and support a full-orbed and victorious manhood. Even the history of learning furnishes the saddest illustration of the fact that the Greek spirit alone is not sufficient for the widest and deepest culture. Intellect is analytic. Life is synthetic. The dominance of thought over feeling and will makes the critic, not the builder, of institutions. A soul in which the intellect is supreme is rationalistic, sceptical, and hesitates in the presence of its own great ideas.

Hebrew Civilization Failed.

What testimony the fragmentary life and the partial results of many a soul give to these truths! Just as the Hamlet of Shakespeare stands for the brilliant incompetency of soul which comes to any man whose power of thinking outruns the purposes of sentiments of his nature and life, so the Paracelsus of Robert Browning stands for the failure of that high but lonely intellectualism in which the enthusiasm of emotion and the strength of courageous will are left out of character and action. In less lasting portraiture, many a sad and wrecked life tells the same story. It is impossible to get manhood so long as the heart is exiled and the will is powerless.

(*b*) And Hebrew civilization failed. That which preserved it for so long was its feeling for the Incarnate God, the Saviour. It did not so picture him as the Saviour of the whole soul as to have waked up within itself a life of intellect and a life of will equal to and co-existent with its life of feeling. The whole manhood of man did not grow at Jerusalem. Their expectation of Messiah lived at last in the sentiment of patriotism, just as the Greek dream of the coming man-deliverer lived in the imagination and made him only a great philosopher.

Each was fragmentary and each failed. No depth of sentiment or strength of emotion can guarantee completeness of character. The man of mere sentiment becomes a sentimentalist and his life has no power of production, more than a boiler bursting with unworked steam. The whole realm of thought and the whole kingdom of the will, in all true hours of every life, that this tri-personality, man,— intellect, sensibilities, and will,— may be complete and true. Feeling needs thought to solidify and mould its warm possibilities; and then will must send the idea to the mark. A single character of Hebrew history will illustrate these truths. David's was a soul of imperial proportions; but David's intellectual and volitional life were, neither of them, equal to his emotional life. Every man, probably, is tempted on the side of his powers. David's power was in his heart; and David's weakness was, also, on the side of sentiment. He shed tears enough — tears of joy, tears of sorrow, tears of repentance, tears of love, perhaps also tears of anger — to have emptied any other heart. But he lacked thoughtfulness, deliberateness, judgment, the intelligent Greek spirit. He also lacked purpose, courage to equal his sentiment of love, will-power to control his passion. He lived all his life in his heart, as his poems and life attest; and when it was broken he died. Man, to be as he ought to be, to be saved in all his possibility under God, must be a trinity in unity. His life of intellect, and sensibility, and will must be one life. The trinity in God must be reflected in his tri-personality if he is to be Godlike.

(c) And Rome failed. Goth and Hun and Vandal waited her hour of weakness and made her an easy captive. Never so strong in sentiment or in thought as in purpose, when luxurious iniquity had broken down that purpose all was gone. The intellect and heart had never been honored in her career; and they refused to defend her gates against the barbarian. No nation is safe without moral sentiment, aflame from the altars of the heart's love, which welds national purpose and national thoughts into one invincible energy. Rome had not sound and healthful heart-life. No nation is safe whose movement from the centre is out of proportion to her intellectual life within. Rome never made her brain equal to her strong right arm. As with nations, so with men; that is a fragmentary and weak character in which will is absolutely tyrant, by the exclusion of intellect and emotions. Such a man is sure to become both reckless and stubborn. His very achievements make him their victim. He cannot hold and rule his own conquests, and at last, as in Rome, he has no sentiments to warm his soul, nor has he intelligence sure enough to itself to keep his victories; and Goth and Vandal conquer him.

The Nazarene their King.

III. *At the cross of Jesus each of these kingdoms of the soul — thought, feeling, and will — had found its sovereign.*

(a) The presence of the Greek language upon that bloody crucifix was a silent testimony to the kingship of Jesus. The very tongue which registered the finest achievements of the intellect of man, and at the same time made memorial of the fact that they alone did not, could not, satisfy man's dream of himself, then made itself witness of the truth that the powers of reason and thought in the human soul had their king in the Nazarene. What a moment of trial was that! Greek philosophy, which brought its sages about that cross, when, in the language of the foreigner, this bitter irony was placed upon its summit, seemed to wake all the old problems, and offer again in vain all the old solutions. The wisdom of Athens was to be judged by, as it judged, the wisdom of Christ. The peerless grandeur of that contribution which Jesus made to the intellectual life of man is never so surely seen as when we stand with the problems of the world and the soul, which called the cross of Calvary into existence, and behold how philosophy fails and Christ succeeds in their solution. His gift to the brain of man of great ideas and a fundamental conception of God, of the universe, and of the soul was so mighty that Homer and Æschylus, Euripides and Aristotle, Thucydides and Plato, all classic life, simply serve by their intellectual work to develop a language in which his thoughts and the musings of Paul might reach the minds of men. Jesus on his cross confronts the hitherto bewildered reasonings of the race as to the meaning of the groaning creation, with himself, — the reason of God, by whom the worlds were made at the first. He is the explanation of the universe. All the abstractions of pure thought bow before this matchless fact, this glorious personality. All the roadways which have been travelled by human feet in the weary search for truth seem to have a common meeting-point as he says, "I am the truth." He has met the intellect with its passionate thirst for truth, and furnished it with a more quenching desire. He has come to the imagination of man and wooed it out into the region of infinity, as he has familiarized it with the fine sense of God. He has met the judgment of the race and taught it from the heart of the eternal justice. The Greek spirit has felt in him its very king and leader. Plato's highest speculation is as authoritative as a law of God from his divine lips; and, as he dies, the language of Socrates, which is used to perpetuate and publish the sneer of Christ's foes, has, then and there, with this same Nazarene, an assurance of immortality such as was never given to it in the songs of Homer or the orations of Demosthenes. At last the intellect had a Saviour and a Lord in Jesus of Nazareth.

All Prophecies Realized.

(*b*) The presence of the Hebrew tongue upon that cross bespattered with blood was another silent testimony to the kingship of Jesus. All the prophecies with which the heart of man has been stirred since the loss of Eden were at last realized in him. All the far-reaching yearnings which in storm and sunshine had gone forth from the human heart at last touched a reality which was to satisfy them in him. Every sentiment of human nature which bound man to God received a divine impulse at that cross. He made the pitiless pitiful at that death-scene by revealing the everlasting pity of God. Humanity's heart was breaking with his when he cried, "My God, my God, why hast thou forsaken me?" He made the vicious, hard life of a thief responsive to his compassion as he manifested in his own blood the quenchless compassion of Jehovah. The heart of mankind learned a new and more powerful movement when he cried, "Father, forgive them, for they know not what they do." All the way through his life he had been toiling at the heart of man, seeking to attach it to the throne of God. "Blessed are the pure in heart," he said, "for they shall see God." He made the moral motive power of his kingdom from his own sacrificial and bleeding heart. Love—that master emotion—became the fulfilling of the law. He gave himself in love to be forever the object of love. "Lovest thou me?"—this was the new question, the deepest man ever heard. Into the heart of man he carried his cross, to move it with the holy enthusiasm and passion of self-sacrifice, and to found there his throne; and to-day our world moves heavenward by the hearts which are ruled by his love.

(*c*) The presence of the Latin language upon that cross suggests the fact that the will of man had found its rightful sovereign in the Christ of God.

Gave the World New Life.

He came into a world whose moral motive power was worn out.

He gave to the will a new moral motive power. It had all the charm of personality. He presented himself. It touched every force within the will and roused it to action. He made man see both God and man in himself; and beholding these, man has found out the way to a Godlike humanity in the willing surrender of his will to that of his Saviour. The human will has never felt itself so strong for great deeds as since giving itself up to the outworking of the will of God under Christ's leadership. It has been able to realize that God's will in Christ for each man is the best will he could have, or adopt, concerning himself. To adopt God's will is to put one's self in the line of omnipotence and to ally one's life with the infinite energies. With this perfect will of God, as it is manifested in Jesus of Nazareth, the loftiest dream of the pagan is in harmony; and the noblest Christian attains his truest manhood when he has learned to sing:

" My Jesus, as thou wilt;
Oh, let my will be thine."

IV. *In the character of Christ, as our Redeemer and King, we behold humanity, and it is to this Godlike manhood that he comes to save us.*

Powers of thought, powers of feeling, powers of will, are equally manifest in his character and career. His ideas are the flashings of the truth of God; his feelings are the throbbings of the love of God; his volitions are the echoes of the will of God. God had perfectly filled him, and he was God's revelation of himself, and God's revelation of ideal humanity—humanity filled to symmetricalness with God. In Jesus of Nazareth you do not see a fragmentary life. He is the monarch of the intellect, the heart, and the will. His thoughts outrun the philosophies, while he weeps at the bier of a Lazarus-like race and pushes his divine will over the altars of Calvary. There was no discord in him, because of the dominance of one set of powers over another. Every tone of thought, and feeling, and will sent its richness into the full melody of that peerless soul. By the side of this peasant, with his commanding powers all contributing to his career, the soul of Plato, the soul of David, the soul of Cæsar, seem but magnificent fragments. In the one Jesus Christ stands a complete humanity. His cross is the spot where he is surest to save each of us from fragmentariness to wholeness; from the sins which come of partialness of character and life unto the holiness (which is wholeness) which comes of completeness of soul. God must fill us up with himself, that every faculty may be brought out. The cross of Jesus alone has been able to attract and develop the thought, the feeling, and the will of mankind and of men. Let us each stand before it until our manhood is complete.

V. *Fellow Endeavorers, let us bring our whole civilization within the influence of the only fact in all the universe which has been able to reconstitute the soul, to mass the forces of human nature and to unify them, to command and develop, along with all others, every power of our common humanity.*

Society is man at large, and has his qualities, powers, and problems. Each faculty, perhaps, has its institution.

(a) Into the school goes the intellect, searching for knowledge, formulating experience, comparing judgments, penetrating mysteries, answering and proposing questions. Thought incarnates herself in these institutions of learning; and just as thought alone is fragmentary, the school is likely to do the work for the intellect alone, and fail. Our education needs the cross.

(b) Into the church go the feelings, trembling under the consciousness of sin, broken with remorse, or yearning for sympathy and comfort, loving God and man, in joy and grief. This institution is the temple of the emotions. There the heart is priestess forever; and just as the feelings are but a part of man's self and life, the church is likely to do only a sentimental work, and fail. Our religion needs the cross to make it intelligent and active.

(c) Into the state goes the will. Its laws are the will's mandates; its government is the will's expression. The state embodies its purposes, choices, and power. The nation is the will's temple. There the will has her holy of holies ; and just as the will is but a part of human nature, the state is likely to become simply an incarnate will, without culture and without heart, unintelligent and irreligious. Our statesmanship needs the cross of Christ.

Let us bring all these institutions up to his cross, that each may behold a rounded, complete manhood in him, that each may get his manhood as an ideal, that each may be so full of God that their ministry shall, under Christ bring forth the ideal of humanity.

Just before adjournment Dr. Clark announced that he had appointed a Business Committee for the Convention, to whom all matters of business, resolutions, etc., should be referred. The committee was composed of Secretary Baer, Mr. Charles B. Holdrege, of Illinois, and Rev. J. A. R. Dickson, of Ontario.

This, the second session of the great Convention, eclipsed the session the night before by at least 3,000 people.

"CROWDED OUT."

BOUND TO HEAR.

IN BELLE ISLE.

AN EARLY-MORNING VIEW.

CITY HALL.

AN EVANGELISTIC SERVICE.

SOME "SNAP-SHOTS."

It was estimated by the Detroit papers that there were 11,000 people seated inside the tent, as every seat was closely filled, and, besides these, there were people four and five rows deep around the entire tent. These "standees" were estimated to number 4,000, so that it is entirely probable that there were 15,000 in attendance and within earshot. There were two or three thousand more people about the grounds.

THURSDAY AFTERNOON.

Denominational Camp-Fires.

"My own church" was the rallying-cry in a peculiar sense on Thursday afternoon. Everybody hurried to his own denominational meeting.

Never before had so much care been given to the programmes of the denominational rallies and conferences, and every hard-working chairman was amply repaid, for the attendance exceeded all expectations.

The Reformed Episcopal Rally.
Bishop Samuel Fallows, D.D., LL.D., Chicago, Ill., Chairman.

The Church of the Redeemer was very tastefully decorated with the Christian Endeavor and national colors, and a fair number of delegates were in attendance. Rev. M. McCormick, of Detroit, opened the proceedings by announcing the old, familiar hymn, "Blest be the tie that binds our hearts in Christian love," after the singing of which the bishop led in the General Confession of the Prayer-Book. At the conclusion of the prayer the Rev. Thomas Mann, of Chicago, read the passage, Philippians ii. 1–11. This was followed by the singing of another hymn from the Reformed Episcopal Hymnal. This concluded the opening devotional exercises, and Mr. C. H. Wilson, of Detroit, delivered a brief but most hearty address of welcome to the visitors from other cities. This welcome was responded to in the same cordial manner by Rev. Thos. Mason, of Chicago.

After some announcements had been given the bishop called upon Rev. M. T. McCormick, of Detroit, to lead the remarks on a discussion of the resolution, "Resolved that the chief mission of the Reformed Episcopal Church is to members of the Protestant Episcopal Church and Church of England." This gentleman declared that the first mission of every church and every individual was to testify of Jesus, the one all-sufficient and most precious and glorious Saviour; but also argued that the distinctive mission of the Reformed Episcopal Church was to testify against a special priestly power of the ministry, baptismal regeneration, the actual presence of Christ in the elements of the Lord's Supper, and the absolute necessity of Episcopal ordination.

These remarks were followed by those of Rev. Thomas Mason, who deprecated unnecessary antagonism, but suggested that much evangelical faith might be inculcated by the systematic distribution of our own church literature, and expressed surprise that the Protestant Episcopal bishop and clergy of Chicago should have practically accepted or permitted the distinctly Roman Catholic Prayer-Book of "Father" Larrabee without any protest or opposition. He also declared that we had not forsaken the Episcopal Church of our forefathers, but that it had forsaken us.

The bishop then called for remarks from all visitors, when responses were made from Chicago, Cleveland, Wilmington, Del., Scranton, Pa.. Moncton, N. B., etc. Rev. Mr. Mason presented the cordial greetings to the rally of Bishop Cheney, of Chicago. Mr. George Oakes, of Chicago, made a brief address. Bishop Fallows, in closing, emphasized the fact that our Reformed Episcopal Church offered the ideal home for every true evangelical Episcopalian. He also spoke with great admiration of the two great principles of the Christian Endeavor movement ; viz., denominational loyalty and interdenominational fellowship. The bishop also described the most cordial and even enthusiastic reception which, as the representative of the Reformed Episcopal Church, he had recently met with at the Presbyterian General Assembly held in June, at Minneapolis, Minn. This interesting rally was closed with the Doxology ; benediction by Bishop Fallows.

African M. E. and African M. E. Zion Joint Conference.

Bishop Alexander Walters, D.D., Jersey City, N. J., Chairman.

The Denominational Conference of the A. M. E. and A. M. E. Zion Churches was held in a joint rally at the A. M. E. Church, corner Napoleon and Hastings Streets.

Bishop A. Walters, D.D., of Jersey City. N. J., was chairman, and Dr. B. F. Watson, of Quincy, Ill., conducted the music.

Rev. J. B. Colbert, president of the Varick C. E. Union of the A. M. E. Zion Church, was on the programme to report "from the field." He was absent, and Bishop G. W. Clinton, D.D., of the Seventh Episcopal District of that church, made the report. Bishop Clinton showed that since 1896, the year the Varick C. E. was organized in his church. over four hundred societies have been established, with a membership of 12,000.

Rev. D. A. Graham, superintendent of the Allen C. E. Society of the Fourth Episcopal District of the A. M. E. Church, was on the programme to report for that work. The illness of Mr. Graham's daughter prevented his being present, but his report was made through Rev. E. A. Clark, of Wilberforce, O. The report showed the organization during the past year of over eighty societies, with a membership of 1,900.

The programme announced an address by Dr. A. J. Cary, of Chicago. but his absence made the substitution of Rev. R. C. Ransom of that city necessary. Dr. Ransom was followed by Rev. E. D. W. Jones, pastor of the Avery Chapel, Allegheny City, Pa.

One of the most earnest addresses on "Junior C. E. Work" was next made by Dr. L. J. Coppin, of Philadelphia.

" Minute-Guns " by every delegate present was the next thing in order. During these reports spirited talks were made by Drs. C. S. Smith and H. T. Johnson. At the conclusion of the delegates' reports Bishop B. W. Arnett made the closing remarks.

A great deal of enthusiasm was created by the excellent singing of Rev. J. W. Becket, of Baltimore, Md., who contributed to the delight of the occasion by special request.

There were sixty delegates present, representing thirty States. besides many visitors from various sections of the country.

United Presbyterian Rally.

Rev. W. H. McMillan, D.D., Allegheny City, Pa., Chairman.

The meeting was opened with a praise service led by Professor McClelland and the choir of the church.

Dr. McMillan, before introducing the speakers, said, " We are always glad to get home. It is pleasant to meet with friends and have a social time and a blessed fellowship, but there is no place like home."

He then introduced Rev. T. H. McMichael, of Cleveland, O., who spoke at length on the theme, " Young Christians in Modern Church Life." He used as his illustration a pod of peas. First pea in the pod, purity. Modern young Christians must be separated from the world ; must live pure, clean lives, be pure in thought, word. and in deed ; be strong in Christ in temptation. Second pea, piety — not long-faced, but joyful, full of gladness, happy. Third pea, presence. Be present at church, mid-week prayer meetings, at the sick-bed, at your Young People's meetings ; show by your presence that you are interested in God's work. Fourth pea, prayer. Observe the Quiet Hour. Spend much time alone with God. Pray with the lost. Pray at your meetings. Spend much time in silent prayer. Fifth pea, paying. Join the Tenth Legion. Introduce it into your society. Study missions. Don't give less than did the Jew. Do without some of the unnecessary things. Give cheerfully. Pay what thou owest. Sixth pea, personal effort. Don't have others to do your work. God has some for you to save. Let every young Endeavorer bring some one to Christ this year. Be not weary in well-doing. Improve all your opportunities.

After the singing of a solo by Professor McClelland, Rev. J. E. Wishart, of Ingram, Pa., spoke on " Young Christians and the State." He divided his talk into three divisions : independence, high ideas, and hopefulness. He urged the young to be independent. Don't follow in the old paths if there are better ones. Don't vote with the old parties unless they are for righteousness. Be independent of the "bosses." Be true to only one King. You are responsible only to Jesus Christ. The hope of *our* country rests with those who think and act for themselves. Have high ideas ; let nothing drag you down. Be hopeful ; Christians should never be sad. In God trust. Be not afraid of the right ; the King is with you. Trust and obey him. Hope for better things and work for that end.

Miss Mary Campbell, a missionary from the U. P. Missions in India, then gave a very impressive talk on missionaries and missions where she has been located for a number of years. She asked that no call for retrenchment would be made, and told a very pathetic but true story of where thirteen girls had to be sent out from their missions to be again among their heathen friends because some one had not paid his tenth to God; how the children had sobbed out their broken hearts when they found out they could stay no longer; and how they wished they had something to send to the poor Americans who had "hard times" and could not let them stay in school and hear about Jesus. Her words, "Who was to blame?" will go ringing down the ages; and who will answer this when the white light of God will be turned on the pocket-book that was closed by the hand of some one?

The meeting closed with prayer by Rev. Dr. Moorhead, of Xenia, O. The benediction was pronounced by the pastor of the church.

A reception was held and a general hand-shaking was in order.

The Moravian Rally.

Rev. C. E. Eberman, Lancaster, Pa., Chairman.

The special features of the rally were : a talk by Miss Minnie L. Cooley, the delegate from Staten Island, on " Practical Methods for Missionary Meetings." The speaker is an enthusiastic missionary. Having been providentially debarred from foreign mission work, her zeal finds outlet in the home activities. She emphasized the need of getting each individual Endeavorer personally interested in missions. " Have a standing Missionary Committee; use books, maps, slides; and have some system of collecting missionary money. Especially, begin mission work with the Juniors. Read them missionary stories." " Missionary Methods for Missionary Meetings;" " Fuel for Missionary Fires;" " Prayer and Missions;" "The Opportunity of the Hour;" and all that line of pamphlets published by the United Society were recommended. Lastly, *pray* daily and systematically for missions.

Mrs. C. E. Eberman not being able to be present, her paper on "The Place of the Child in the Church" was read by a delegate. This paper touched the centre of the subject by referring to the fact that parents do not attend the church and its activities, and thus the children do not learn the habit early enough. A remedy is to raise the standard of church education. Teach the little one to do a few simple things for Christ and the church. Familiarize them with the Bible by constant drill. Have a uniform system in all the societies.

Rev. Mr. Eberman, after giving greetings from Pennsylvania, and referring to the *vitality* of Christian Endeavor. — that it shall not trust in numbers, but in quality and *prayer* for the uninterested, — spoke also on " The Intermediate Society." He said, " I am president of my intermediates, and *live with them* as much as possible, and get them rid of the fear of the minister."

On the question of Junior work in the country were suggested, as helpful methods, the dividing of the society into sections, each meeting in a central or convenient point in the different portions of the neighborhood; also, five-minute sermons for the children, and hymns sung by them in Sunday morning meetings.

The rally ended with a social season in which old acquaintance was renewed and new established.

Methodist Episcopal, M. E. Church South, and Methodists of Canada—Joint Rally.
Rev. A. C. Crews, Toronto, Ont., Chairman.

The Joint Rally for the Methodist Episcopal Church and the Methodist Church, Canada, was held in the Central Methodist Episcopal Church, Woodward Avenue, which was about filled. Rev. Dr. G. C. Kelly, who has attended every Methodist rally at Endeavor Conventions for several years past, said that this was the best attended and most interesting meeting of the kind that he remembered. The chair was occupied by Rev. A. C. Crews, general secretary of young people's work in the Methodist Church, Canada. In his opening remarks he said that he was in cordial sympathy with the Christian Endeavor movement, and rejoiced in the opportunity of meeting with the other branches of the Church of Christ upon a common platform. While he was doing all he could to strengthen his own church, he believed thoroughly in inter-denominational fellowship, and was consequently glad to be present in Detroit.

The first address was by Rev. G. H. Cobbledick, Bothwell, Ont., who spoke of the evangelistic work of the church, making special reference to "The Forward Movement in Bible-Study and Evangelistic Work," which has become a feature of the work in Canada. Miss S. M. Whitworth, of St. Mary's, emphasized the importance of the Junior work, and Mr. Thomas Morris, Jr., spoke some strong words about the claims of the Sunday school upon the church. Rev. Dr. Daniel, Sarnia, Ont., made a vigorous speech upon literary work and the value of the reading-circle.

Rev. W. F. Wilson, Hamilton, Ont., made a stirring address on "Missionary Work," urging the young people to be interested in home missions as well as foreign.

The sunny South was represented by Rev. G. C. Kelly, D.D., of Birmingham, Ala., who complimented the Canadian Methodist Church upon the happy arrangement by which its Epworth Leagues were affiliated with the Christian Endeavor movement.

Rev. W. F. Sheriden, of Pontia, spoke on behalf of the Methodist Episcopal Church. In an eloquent address he referred to the elements which must enter into all permanent work for Christ.

German Rally.
Rev. G. Berner, Buffalo, N. Y., Chairman.

Rev. J. Neumann, of Ann Arbor, gave the opening address:—

Let us discuss real, active Endeavorers, and not fossils. In the plant kingdom there are many specimens that blossom beautifully, but never amount to more than that. They give neither fruit nor seed. This is often true with nominal Christians, and often with the same kind of Endeavorers. Our badges do not count for much unless we are true Endeavorers at heart.

I love Christian enthusiasm and the display of talents. I rejoice we have so much of this in the Christian Endeavor ranks. But the real Endeavorer is the one who, day by day, has silent fellowship with Him, and makes his every little act in humble life count. John xv. says, " Without me ye can do nothing."

One secret of the real Endeavorer is the blessed fellowship with Christ. Another secret is becoming grafted in the Vine. We are to bring fruitage to the glory of our Heavenly Father. The Endeavorer is to be a messenger of cheer and comfort to his fellowman who may be weak. Before we can impart these to others, we must have come in contact with the great power ourselves. We must often find our fruitage ripened by the trying heat of affliction and sorrow. " To him who gives shall be given " should be remembered by the real Endeavorer. Let us go forth, then, and bring the world into direct contact with the Author of all Christian Endeavor.

Rev. G. Berner, who had arrived in the meantime, then took the chair, and briefly outlined the progress of the Christian Endeavor movement among the Germans : —

The German Christian Endeavor has now been in progress for seven years. Since its inception among the Germans in Detroit, in September, 1892, it has met with a wonderful growth, although its development has been through some severe experiences. God has not failed, however, in his blessing.

There are at present 224 German Christian Endeavor societies in America, but the growth has not been confined here. It has spread to Germany, which has 101 societies, making a total of 325. The work in Germany has been propagated under the lead of a most consecrated man, Mr. Blecher.

Since our organization we have had annual conventions in Chicago ; Tiffin, O. ; Sandusky, O. ; Buffalo, N. Y. ; St. Louis, Mo., and will hold our next at Quincy, Ill., next week. Our numbers are naturally not as large in proportion to those of our American brethren, but the quality of the work is sterling. We have a banner in our German union, awarded to the society making the best missionary showing for the year. The Zion Society, of Cincinnati, receives the award, each member averaging a contribution of $4.04 for the year. One German Endeavorer, but a young man, gave, last year, $400 toward the current expenses of his church. We have five district conferences which meet annually : the Atlantic, New York ; Erie, Illinois, Kentucky and Ohio, and Michigan.

We have a task which grows larger from year to year,—to fight the drifting tendency. We need more devoted and earnest Christian living on the part of Endeavorers. We need strength for this, and can get it by a better vision of our Lord and Master.

Rev. L. Wolferz, of Brooklyn, N. Y., then gave a few words of greeting from the Brooklyn society, and Miss Eckhart, secretary of the Buffalo society, followed with a similar message.

Pastor J. G. Hildner, of the Messiah Church, then spoke, very highly commending the excellent work of his local society, and incidentally said that the members alone have been instrumental in raising $1,040 for the church since last January.

United Brethren.

Rev. H. F. Shupe, Dayton, O., Chairman.

United Brethren Endeavorers from ten States and Canada assembled in a typical rally. Rev. H. F. Shupe, editor of *The Watchword*, presided. Rev. Homer K. Pitman, Dayton, O., read the Scripture and led in prayer. Prof. A. F. Myers, Toledo, O., led the inspiring service of song during the rally. The chairman referred to the history of the young people's movement in the church, and to the importance of the contributions of Christian Endeavor to the church's life and interests. One of these contributions is the Quiet Hour, and Miss Mina Gutekunst spoke impressively of " The Quiet Hour for United Brethren Young People." Mrs. G. W. Kitzmiller, of Toledo, O., spoke on " The Joy of Junior Work," giving a number of incidents of the conversion and subsequent development of boys and girls which gave great joy. Junior workers from other States gave testimony to the joy of the work.

The forward movement in the young people's work of the United Brethren Church is tithing, and Rev. W. O. Fries, of Van Buren, O., conducted a " Tithers' Testimony Meeting," in which a number testified to the pleasure and profit of giving the tenth. A pastor said that he sent the church steward to the converts as soon as they were converted to secure their consent to pay the tenth. The Allentown, Pa., society reported over twenty tithers. A pastor had twenty tithers in his church. At a recent Young People's Convention in Indiana fifty declared themselves tithers.

Following this there was a period of introductions and social fellowship greatly enjoyed by the sixty United Brethren present. Rev. W. L. Childress, of Virginia, closed the exercises with prayer.

Cumberland Presbyterian Rally.

Rev. A. H. Stephens, Chicago, Ill., Chairman.

The Cumberland Presbyterians held their conference in the Jefferson Avenue Presbyterian Church. The denomination was well represented. The addresses were enthusiastic. The Rev. A. H. Stephens, of Chicago, presided. The Rev. W. T. Rodgers, of Nashville, Tenn., spoke on " The Centennial Fund of 1900-1910." This discussion was in reference to the one million endowment fund the denomination proposes to raise for the endowment of our educational institutions, thus celebrating the one hundredth anniversary of the denomination. The speaker was enthusiastic in the belief that the amount would be raised. The Rev. A. H. Stephens spoke on " The Church's Home Mission Field and Opportunities to Enter It." The need for aggressive work and the opening for the accomplishing of great things for the Lord were points forcibly emphasized. Pres. A. E. Turner, of Lincoln University, addressed the conference on " Our Educational Policy and Plans." As is characteristic of President Turner's addresses, this one was full of pith and point. The Rev. W. J. Darby, D.D., secretary of the Educational Society, spoke on " Our Ministry — Past, Present, and Future." He discussed the past and the present of our ministry, and called upon the ministers present to express their ideas about our future ministry. Brief responses were made by Revs. J. L. Hudgins, Callin W. Yates, Elonzo Yates. T. Asburn, Shelton, Diskey, McCoy, Curry, and Mr. Noel. These brief talks set forth the future minister as a man of thorough preparation, a man of affairs, and of complete consecration to his specific work as preacher and pastor. Rev. Gam Sing Qua, a young Chinaman, just graduated from Cumberland University and consecrated to mission work in his native land, made an interesting talk, expressing his joy at the thought of going back as a Christian to tell people of Christ and his power to save. Miss Leila Hollingsworth, secretary of the Woman's Board, spoke of women's work, and especially of what they were doing through the Junior Endeavorers. The last topic on the programme was "Our Church a Plant for any Clime," which was briefly discussed by Rev. Callin W. Yates, who emphasized the thought that because of the genius and doctrine of the Cumberland Presbyterian Church, she is especially adapted to carry the gospel to the people of the earth in every clime and condition. This rally was a splendid success. The outlook, as set forth at this conference, is bright for our denomination. The conviction of those present seemed to be that the Cumberland Presbyterian Church is standing right at the front in the great movements of this closing year of the nineteenth century for taking the world for Christ.

The Welsh Rally.
Rev. John E. Jones, Milwaukee, Wis., Chairman.

The Welsh Rally at the Forest Avenue Presbyterian Church was well attended by delegates from some twelve States and Canada. Rev. John E. Jones acted as chairman. The devotional exercises were conducted by Revs. John D. Jones, Ripon, Wis., and C. Morgans, Venedocia, O. Rev. John Hamond, Columbus, O., spoke on "The Welsh Pulpit," in which he referred to a few of the great orators that God in his good providence gave to the Welsh people. Rev. Wm. F. Jones, of Tecumseh, Mich., spoke upon the Welsh Sunday school and its influence in fashioning the character of the Welsh people. Rev. J. C. Jones, Chicago, Ill., spoke upon "What the Welsh Are To Expect from the Christian Endeavor Movement." And following, Rev. Ed. Roberts, Venedocia, O., delivered a very inspiring sermon upon the text Ps. cxix. 42. He remarked that man is a subject of God's moral government. God has revealed his will to him in commandments, and man's highest happiness is to be had in keeping these commandments. But in order to make the keeping of these commandments easy man must be born again. Sin contracts man's heart, but grace has the power to enlarge it. The singing was exceptionally good, especially when the following hymn was sung : —

> Cawn esgyn o'r dyrys anialwch
>   I'r beraidd Baradwys i fyw;
> Ein henaid lluddedig gaiff orphwys
>   Yn dawel ar fynwes ein Duw:
> Dihangfa dragwyddol geir yno
>   Ar bechod, cystuddiau, a phoen;
> A gwledda, i oesoedd diderfyn,
>   Ar gariad anhraethol yr Oen.
>
> O fryniau Caersalem ceir gweled
>   Holl daith yr anialwch i gyd;

Pryd hyn y daw troion yr yrfa
Yn felus i lanw ein bryd:
Cawn edrych ar stormydd ac ofnau,
Ac angau dychrynllyd, a'r bedd,
A ninau'n ddiangol o'u cyraedd,
Yn nofio mewn cariad a hedd.

Presbyterian.

Rev. Teunis S. Hamlin, D.D., Washington, D. C., Chairman.

The large Fort Street Church was crowded to its utmost extent, and an overflow meeting entirely filled the spacious basement. The singing was very spirited. Dr. Hamlin, of Washington, presided. All the speakers announced were present except Dr. Wilton Merle Smith, of New York, who was detained by a death in his parish, and whose place was taken by Dr. J. Wilbur Chapman. The topics were designed to be broad and inspirational, and were so treated by all the speakers. Dr. Jennings, of the First Church of Detroit, spoke of the Presbyterian as an Open Church; Mr. Baer, as a Young People's Church; Dr. Walker, of Los Angeles, as a Teaching Church; Dr. Chapman, as an Aggressive Church; and Dr. Stewart, of Harrisburg, about to take the presidency of the Auburn Theological Seminary, as a World-wide Church. There was an honest pride in the denomination frankly expressed by all, but mingled with the most affectionate tone toward all other branches of the Church of Christ. The enthusiasm of the great audience was very inspiring, and all good points were cheered to the echo. Every one went away, as Dr. Stewart said of himself, more glad than ever before to be a Presbyterian.

Disciples of Christ.

Rev. Allan B. Philputt, D.D., Chairman.

The lower floor of the Light Guard Armory was filled with enthusiastic Endeavorers to the number of about fifteen hundred for the denominational rally of the Disciples. The first speaker was Rev. John E. Pounds, of Indianapolis, recently elected National Superintendent of Christian Endeavor societies, instead of Rev. J. Z. Tyler, resigned. He emphasized the salient features of Christian Endeavor and urged that the young people appropriate them, such as Bible-study, the Quiet Hour, and the Tenth Legion.

The next speaker was Prof. H. L. Willett, of the University of Chicago. His speech was full of the warm spirit of denominational loyalty and yet of zeal for the accomplishment of the larger purposes for which all denominations are striving. He said in part: " We are talking these days about expansion. It is a watchword of the times. We as a people have our mottoes for this jubilee year looking to that end: ' One hundred thousand souls for Christ in '99,' ' $150,000 for foreign missions.' Yet there must go hand in hand with this external improvement an endeavor for real expansion, a filling-out of the lines on the side of true Christian culture, on the side of deeper, purer characteristics, if we would fulfil our high privilege."

The Rev. J. Z. Tyler, D.D., general editor and manager of "The Bethany Christian Endeavor Reading Courses," was then introduced, and gave an outline of the plans for the reading-courses. These little books, on such topics as " Bible-Study," " History of Missions," " History of the Disciples," etc., offer, in a short compass of from one hundred and fifty to two hundred pages, information usually given in much larger volumes. He urged the organization of reading-circles in every society, and spoke of the need of training the young people in the principles and history of the denomination. Mr. Tyler spoke of the similarity between the principles of the Christian Endeavor movement and those of the Disciples.

Following the speeches was a parliament on the question, "The Status and Possibilities of Christian Endeavor Among Us," conducted by the Rev. F. D. Power, of Washington, D. C. This was participated in by State superintendents and leading workers.

After a very enthusiastic invitation from Rev. Mr. Harvnot and F. M. Cooper, of Cincinnati, for the Endeavorers to attend the Jubilee Convention of the Disciples to be held in that city next October, the meeting adjourned. Hundreds remained awhile for social greetings, however.

Episcopal.

Rev. J. B. Richardson, London, Ont., Chairman.

The rally in connection with the Church of England and Protestant Episcopal Church was held in St. Peter's Church, Trumbull Avenue. It was by far the largest rally of Episcopalians held at any convention.

There were present Revs. Canon Richardson, London, Ont.; F. W. Tomkins, Philadelphia; W. Johnson, Huntingford, Ont.; Dr. Clark, Detroit; C. C. Purton, Windsor, Ont.; A. Beverly, Forest, Ont.; J. W. Ten Eyck, Exeter, Ont.; several other clergy, and a large representation of Canadian and American delegates.

A short liturgical service was conducted by Rev. C. L. Arnold, rector, in which all present joined heartily. At the close of this Rev. Canon Richardson presided. He reviewed briefly the onward progress of Christian Endeavor, and noticed its growing adoption by the church in the United States, England, and Canada. He predicted a decided impetus for it in the national church from the convention to be held next year in London. The canon urged the organization of societies in all our parishes as best adapted to successful work among the young men and women of the church.

Rev. Wm. Johnson, Rector of Huntingford, South Lorra, Ont., spoke on "The Church's Problem — Her Young People." He pointed out the obligations which the church is bound to discharge toward the children whom she receives into her fold in holy baptism. These at confirmation need a peculiar fostering care, and Christian Endeavor comes in as a most helpful agent to the church to keep the confirmed members together and build them up in their most holy faith.

Rev. F. W. Tomkins, D.D., Rector of Holy Trinity Church, Philadelphia, followed with an intensely spiritual and earnest address. He said, "Our duty at a convention is to give rather than to get only." This was implied by the word "Endeavor." The idea was that every member should be active for the good of others. The society bound them together to add to their power for Christ and the church. He dwelt upon several features in the Christian Endeavor Society which proved most helpful to our young church-members. It encouraged them to speak and pray alone, and in our church this is needed. He closed with a solemn appeal for more love to Christ and as a consequence more love one toward another.

Mayor Maybury, who is a member of St. Peter's Church, warmly advocated Christian Endeavor as a living and vitalizing force in the churches, and looked for its introduction into the Episcopal churches of Detroit.

At the close of the exercises a reception was tendered to the delegates and others present by the members of St. Peter's Church.

Congregational.

William Shaw, Boston, Mass., Chairman.

To say that it was an overflowing rally does not do justice to the occasion. It was a flood of numbers, enthusiasm, and eloquence. The beautiful and spacious First Congregational Church was a solid mass of humanity. Every inch of space was occupied, and multitudes were turned away. The splendid programme was prepared by Rev. C. A. Dickinson, D.D., of Boston, but at the last moment he was prevented from attending the Convention, and Mr. William Shaw presided in his place.

A telegram of greeting, expressing the interest of the rally in the great work Dr. Dickinson is doing in Berkeley Temple, was ordered sent. Rev. Mr. Pettee, of Japan, led in prayer, and the service of song was led by the splendid First Church choir. The programme was broad and suggestive, and every speaker had a good half-hour's speech boiled down into the ten minutes allotted to each.

Limited space and lack of a sufficient number of expressive adjectives prevents a complete report of each address. They were all the best; or, as Lincoln once said to rival hatters, who each presented him with a hat and asked for a word of commendation, "They mutually surpass each other."

The meeting was full of hope and cheer, and would have convinced any doubter that the head and heart and will of young Congregationalism are all right. The only disappointment, aside from the absence of the leader, was the unavoidable absence of Dr. Jefferson and Dr. Barrows, but there was compensation in the ringing words of President Clark.

The meeting closed with the benediction by Rev. Joseph Walker, of Queensland, Australia. The following was the complete programme : —

WHAT CONGREGATIONALISM IS DOING FOR AMERICA.

"What Is Congregationalism Doing in the Home Missionary Field ?"
Rev. F. S. Hatch, Monson, Mass.

"What Is Congregationalism Doing in the Foreign Mission Field?"
       Rev. Asher Anderson, Meriden, Conn.
" What Is Congregationalism Doing for the Young People?"
       Rev. James L. Hill, D.D., Salem, Mass.
" What Is Congregationalism Doing To Solve the Sociological Problems of the
       Day?"   Charles M. Sheldon, Topeka, Kan.
" Congregationalism and the Municipal Centre."
       Prof. Graham Taylor, Chicago, Ill.
" Congregationalism in Its Relations to Distinctive American Principles and
       Institutions."
       Rev. Nehemiah Boynton, D.D., Detroit, Mich.
" What Congregationalism Is Doing for the New West To-day."
       Rev. F. A. Noble, D.D., Chicago, Ill.
"Congregationalism in Its Relations to the Moral Reforms of the Day."
       Rev. C. E. Jefferson, D.D., New York City.
" What Is Congregationalism Doing in Educational Lines To-day?"
       Pres. John H. Barrows, D.D., LL.D., Oberlin, O.
Closing words by President Clark.

United Evangelical.

Rev. W. H. Fouke, Chicago, Ill., Chairman.

The rally of the United Evangelical Church, held in Grand River
Avenue Baptist Church, in point of numbers exceeded the expectation
of the promoters, and in point of enthusiasm was fully up to the high
pitch of rallies held at former conventions.   Pennsylvania, Illinois,
Michigan, Indiana, Iowa, Ohio, and Nebraska had delegates present.
The president of the Keystone League of Christian Endeavor, the
Young People's Society of Christian Endeavor of the church, Rev. W. H.
Fouke, who is also editor of the *K. L. C. E. Journal,* presided.   Rev.
W. S. Harpster, of Ohio, led in prayer.
   The president said, in opening the meeting, " There is no note of
pessimism in our song.   We are,optimistic to the last letter with refer-
ence to Christian Endeavor.   It stands for many things for which we
as a church have long stood.   The Quiet Hour, family prayer, the
extension of Christ's kingdom, the consecration of *all* to his service,
are familiar doctrines of our faith and practice."
   Bishop R. Dubs, D.D., LL.D., of Chicago, on being introduced, was
received with the Chautauqua salute, and spoke upon " The United
Evangelical Church ; Its Place, Power, and Promise."   Rev. B. F. Judy
sang " I'll be what you want me to be."   Rev. U. F. Swengel, of
York, member of the Board of Trustees of the United Society of Christian Endeavor, and secretary of the Keystone League of Christian
Endeavor, spoke of " Denominational and Interdenominational Endeavor."   Frank J. Boyer, of Reading, Pa., treasurer of the Keystone
League of Christian Endeavor, spoke on " Keystone League of Christian Endeavor Finances," giving methods of raising money in the local
and for the general society.   Rev. J. Q. A. Curry, of Johnstown, Pa.,
vice-president of the Keystone League of Christian Endeavor, spoke on
" The Devotional Spirit," emphasizing the need of realizing the presence
of Jesus himself in every service.   Rev. Frederick Busse, of Chicago,
spoke on " Our German Young People," and paid a tribute to their devo-

tion and steadiness in the work of our beloved church. J. S. Bartley, of Marshalltown, Io., spoke of "The Way to Win Young Men." Rev. H. Schneider, of El Paso, Ill., spoke of the "Inconspicuous Workers;" Rev. M. C. Morlock, of Bay City, Mich., of "Incentives to Personal Work;" Rev. B. R. Schultze, of Freeport. Ill., on "The Value of Co-operation;" Rev. H. C. Stephan, of Terre Haute, Ind., "How Can We Be Helpful to Our Church?" Rev. B. L. Lady, of Cedarville, Ill., on "Persevering in Every Good Work."

After a moment of silent prayer, the president led in a consecration prayer, after which the Mizpah was said, and Bishop Dubs pronounced the apostolic benediction. A social time followed, which was greatly enjoyed by all.

Southern Presbyterian.

The Southern Presbyterian Rally was held in the Church of the Covenant. Prof. J. D. Blanton, who was appointed to preside, was absent from sickness. Rev. A. L. Phillips, D.D., of Nashville, Tenn., presided. The attendance was small, but full of enthusiasm and determination. A conference was held on the condition and progress of the Endeavor work in the denomination. Reports from all the societies present showed them to be in a prosperous condition, with bright hopes for enlarged numbers and greater usefulness. Rev. A. J. Smith of Savannah, Ga., Dr. James Lewis Howe, of Lexington, Va., and Rev. A. L. Phillips spoke earnestly on "The Difficulties in Our Field and How To Remove Them." The rally was stimulative and helpful to all present.

Church of God.
Rev. C. H. Grove, Roaring Spring, Pa., Chairman.

The Church of God Rally was held in the Lincoln Avenue M. E. Church. Pennsylvania sent the largest delegation, over one-half of those present coming from that State. The church has a strong following in Ohio and a few scattered congregations in other States. The rally was presided over by Rev. C. H. Grove, of Roaring Spring, Pa., who made an address on "The Hopefulness of Christian Endeavor," and among other things said the spirit of Christian Endeavor is optimistic.

E. A. Feight, of Roaring Spring, Pa., spoke on "The Church and Its Young People!" The church and Christian Endeavor harmonize. The young people of to-day are the church of to-morrow. How necessary, then, that we take proper care of the young people! What a wonderful power for good is found in the young people of the church of to-day!

Rev. W. N. Yates, A.M., of Philadelphia, addressed the audience from the subject, "The Church and Its Mission." A clean, clear-cut conviction of its duty is necessary. Personal conviction of right and duty makes any one strong and aggressive. A person who can be one thing as well as another is fit for nothing. Be some one thing distinctively, or nothing. To work for God and his glory is our mission. Do not lose sight of the great commission. Reveal Christ to the world in a consecrated, godly life. Be faithful to your mission and leave the results with God.

Rev. C. I. Brown, A.M., of Mt. Joy, Pa., a trustee of the United Society, then spoke on "Loyalty to the Church." The church is a place for us to work out our convictions of duty. Loyalty is doing intelligently the very best we can under all circumstances. To be loyal we need to know what the church is doing, and to do this we must read its literature, attend its meetings and conventions, catch its spirit of growth and development, and be willing to make sacrifices for its welfare. Loyalty is something more than noise. It is conscientious performance of duty and self-sacrificing devotion to its interest.

Prof. Charles T. Fox, of Findlay College, O., gave an excellent address on "Young People and Education." He made a strong plea for more thorough Christian culture and education as an essential factor of usefulness on the part of the young people of the church. The highest type of culture is found in taking for our model Jesus Christ.

The closing address was made by Rev. C. Manchester, D.D., president of Findlay College, O., who spoke in his very happy style on "What Has the Christian Endeavor Movement Done for Our Church?" He said, "It has taught the young people their personal responsibility. It has made them closer and more thorough students of the Bible. It has furnished them a place in which to invest their powers for God. It has solved the society question. It has brought them in closer touch with their blessed Master."

The music was in charge of Rev. T. N. McAfee, of Columbia, Pa.

Reformed Presbyterian.

Rev. Samuel McNaugher, Boston, Mass., Chairman.

The Reformed Presbyterian Rally was held according to appointment in the Second Avenue Presbyterian Church. There were one hundred and fifty delegates in all. The programme as printed in the "Official Christian Endeavor Programme" was carried out, with some additions. The first half-hour was given up to the singing of the Psalms of the Bible. To those of us who are so familiar with these Psalms nothing could take their place. The chairman spoke a few words of welcome. Those present were urged to go back to their several congregations determined to do all that is possible to stimulate all the young people to be steadfast in upholding the banner for "Christ's Crown and Covenant." Rev. W. M. Glasgow, of Beaver Falls, Pa., gave a most helpful address on "The Present Call to Our Young People." There is a present call, and the young people should respond with great enthusiasm.

Rev. David McAllister, D.D., LL.D., spoke to us on "The Relation of Our Church to the Christian Endeavor Movement." This address was indeed most instructive to all present. It was shown most clearly that our church should heartily co-operate with this great movement. Following this we had a very able and helpful address from Rev. T. C. Sproul, on "The Relation of Our Young People to the State."

Rev. Renwick Martin, of College Hill, Beaver Falls, Pa., spoke to us with great force on the subject of "Tithe-Giving." Rev. Joseph Mc-Cracken, of Southfield, Mich., added a few words of an impromptu character. Mr. Wylie, of Toledo, O., also spoke a few words. After singing the Seventy-second Psalm, Rev. Mr. Benn, of Philadelphia, Pa., closed the meeting with prayer. In all our exercises the one great truth of the kingship of the Lord Jesus Christ was made prominent. Christ is our King in the individual life, and also in the Church and in the State. It is our earnest prayer that in our own beloved land and in all the world he may soon be crowned "King of kings and Lord of lords."

Friends.

Rev. Morton L. Pearson, Sabina, O., Chairman.

Trumbull Avenue Presbyterian Church was comfortably filled at the Friends' denominational conference. The Friends have a well-organized denominational Christian Endeavor Union, and the greater part of the time was devoted to a business session. Rev. Charles W. Sweet, of Des Moines, Io., is president. He was re-elected, as also was the efficient secretary, Miss Myrtle Lightner, of Sabina, O. The other officers elected were as follows: treasurer, Lucian J. Thomas, Toronto, Canada; missionary superintendent, Rev. Gilbert Bowles, Oscaloosa, Io.; trustees, Rufus Jones, editor of *The American Friend*, Philadelphia, and Elwood O. Ellis, Richmond, Ind.

Most gratifying reports were made by the secretary and treasurer, showing the society to be in a flourishing condition and accomplishing good results. Next year's meeting will be held at London at the same time the International Convention is held.

Rev. Morton L. Pearson, of Sabina, O., was chairman of the conference, and gave a short talk. Owing to the absence of Rev. Mr. Bowles and Rev. Mr. Stranahan, their places were acceptably filled by Rev. Mr. Mills, of Wilmington, O., and Rev. E. R. Purdy, of Portland, Me., who spoke on "Christian Endeavor and Foreign Missions," and Rev. Mr. Hayworth, of Marion, Ind., who took as his topic, "Christian Endeavor a Spiritual Force."

Brief talks were made by delegates on Junior Christian Endeavor work, proportionate giving, tithing, the Quiet Hour, and Bible-study. Deep interest was manifested in the meeting, and at its close a general hand-shaking was participated in by those present.

Canadian Presbyterian.

Rev. A. L. Geggie, Truro, Nova Scotia, Chairman.

Four Presbyterian ministers of the gospel pleaded with the Canadian Presbyterian Christian Endeavorers at the Central Presbyterian Church to pay more attention to the Bible and less to the works of Shakespeare and other great authors when Christian matters are being considered.

Rev. A. L. Geggie, of Truro, Nova Scotia, was chairman of the meeting. He presented statistics showing that the income for foreign missionary work from the Canadian Presbyterian churches in 1875 was $17,833, and in 1898 the income had increased to $167,662.

"We 're not as big as the Americans," said Mr. Geggie, "but for the size of us, I want to say that we 've done better than the church to the south of us. In 1875 the Canadian Presbyterian Church had sent out fifteen missionaries; in 1898 the number was three hundred. Put that in your pipe and smoke it, you Americans. God grant that this Convention may be an inspiration to the Canadian Presbyterian Church."

Rev. S. J. Duncan Clark, of Toronto, said that there had been a falling-off in the membership of the Christian Endeavor Society among the Canadian Presbyterian churches during the past year.

"What we want," said he, "are the concentrated efforts of all. I think that the falling-off is due to the fact that those who some time ago became Endeavorers have grown up and are occupied with home duties. We should grow Endeavorers from babyhood, and what we must do is to pay more attention to our Junior societies."

Rev. A. H. Scott, of Perth, Ont., thanked God, first, that he is a Canadian, and was cheered by the Canadian delegation. He dwelt upon the substitution of Shakespeare's works for the Bible, and said that it was having a telling effect upon the Christian Endeavor societies. Rev. Mr. Scott brought tears to the eyes of his congregation when he told how his two sisters became missionaries and ended their work in death in foreign lands.

The last speaker was Rev. William Patterson, of Cooke's Church, Toronto.

"Let us be just before we are generous," he said; "let us begin our missionary work at home."

Christian.

Rev. D. B. Atkinson, Merom, Ind., Chairman.

The meeting opened with a hymn, "Onward, Christian Soldiers," sung by the whole congregation. Addresses were delivered by Rev. D. B. Atkinson and Rev. L. J. Aldrich, D.D., Merom, Ind.; Rev. J. G. Bishop, Dayton, O.; Prof. J. N. Dales, Kingston, Ont.; Rev. P. W. McReynolds, Marshall, Mich.; and Rev. Horace Mann, Piqua, O.

The sentiment of all present seemed to be expressed by Professor Dales, when he rose to offer thanks to God that so many of the Christian denomination had been "permitted to come from the East, the West, the North, and the South, to meet here in the body of Christ."

There were between three hundred and four hundred present, of whom the delegates from outside of Detroit numbered over two hundred and fifty.

Reformed Church in America.

Mr. H. A. Kinports, New York City, Chairman.

The conference of the Reformed Church in America took place with the First Holland Church. Three of the most prominent persons attending the Christian Endeavor Convention addressed the young Endeavorers. The church had been neatly decorated with Christian

Endeavor banners, and the pulpit was tastily set off with palms and vases of cut flowers. The singing was led by an excellent chorus of young people. H. A. Kinports, of New York, presided. Rev. Cornelius Brett, D.D., of Jersey City, N. J., clearly outlined the progress of the Holland Church; Rev. W. I. Chamberlain gave an interesting account of his experiences in India; Rev. John H. Elliott, of New York, delivered a brief address on Endeavor work. After the services, refreshments were served in the Sunday-school room.

The Lutheran Rally.
Rev. M. F. Troxell, D.D., Springfield, Ill., Chairman.

Along with many other features of the Detroit Convention which touched high-water mark, we are glad to name the rally of the Lutherans. In both attendance and interest it was declared by those who have at-

In the Men's Hospital and Ladies' Retiring-Tent.

tended previous rallies to have been among the very best. There being no General Synod Lutheran Church in Detroit, the Committee of '99 assigned the rally to the handsome Westminster Presbyterian Church; and the fine choir of the church aided the musical features of the programme very songfully, among other selections, helping to give the battle-hymn of the Reformation, " Ein Feste Burg," and also a special hymn written for the Lutheran Rally at Detroit by an ardent Endeavorer of Washington, D. C.

A very timely and providential character given to the rally was the presence of a young Lutheran minister and missionary who had just located in Detroit for the purpose of founding a Lutheran Church of the General Synod. His reports were received with enthusiasm, and the next convention season in this beautiful city will not find Lutheran Endeavorers without their own church home. Those present at the rally counted it a good time to give an offering for the good cause, which they did liberally and cheerfully.

The programme was in charge of Rev. M. F. Troxell, D.D., of Springfield, Ill., who was re-elected as the president of the National Lutheran Endeavor Union. Rev. E. Lee Fleck, of Dayton, O., was made secretary and treasurer, and Rev. John Weidley, of Pittsburg, Pa., was elected vice-president.

Rev. M. Rhodes, D.D., trustee of the United Society for the Lutherans, gave the cordial greetings of the Endeavor officials, and spoke on the subject of "Our Larger Fellowship." Rev. J. W. Kapp, D.D., of Richmond, Ind., dealt happily with the theme, "Our Family Fellowship," and Rev. G. W. Eichelberger, of Illinois, made an inspiring and spiritual address on "Our Highest Calling." Another most helpful family feature of the rich feast was a triplet of brief addresses on "The Lutheran and History," "The Lutheran and Citizenship," and "The Lutheran and the Bible," by Revs. J. M. Cromer, of Missouri, J. G. Butler, D.D., of Washington, D. C., and W. H Blancke, of Iowa, respectively. The interest was such that the order of exercises ran an hour over the allotted time. When the question was asked by the president at the close if the Lutherans should endeavor to hold a rally in London, in 1900, there was a unanimous shout in the affirmative from those present. Endeavor enthusiasm is on the increase among the Lutherans, who have now over one thousand enrolled societies in the National Endeavor Union.

Baptist.

Rev. C. A. Barbour, Rochester, N. Y., Chairman.

The Baptist Rally thronged the beautiful and spacious auditorium of the Woodward Avenue Baptist Church. Rev. Clarence A. Barbour, of Rochester, N. Y., presided. The singing was led by Mr. Percy S. Foster. The meeting was clean-cut, spirited, and enthusiastic — a splendid example of denominational loyalty with interdenominational fellowship. The speakers were men widely honored, and worthy of their eminence.

Devotional services were led by Rev. A. C. Kempton, of Janesville. Wis. Rev. Howard B. Grose, of Boston, from the beginning a trustee of Christian Endeavor and influential in its councils, brought hearty and wise greeting from the "Hub" of Christian Endeavor. He emphasized the "Hub" principles of loyalty to the pledge and fidelity to the local church. He who is false to his own church is false to Christian Endeavor. Next to the Christ is the church, and about them the wheel turns.

Rev. H. J. Tresidder, of London, England, the honored secretary of the London Endeavor Council, spoke on "Baptist Gains through Christian Endeavor." These he conceived to be: (1) The Bible recovered in the daily reading and study of the weekly prayer-meeting topic; (2) the Baptist principle of loyalty to Christ enthroned, especially instancing this in the presence of children in the church membership; (3) Baptist practice endorsed, obedience to the Lord in all things increasingly the watchword; (4) the righteousness of denominationalism assured; (5) a recoil from sacerdotalism in close obedience to the Word.

Rev. Wayland Hoyt, D.D. of Philadelphia, was brilliant and forceful as ever, speaking on "Baptist Endeavor and the Fellowship of Believers :" —

Our Christ is the Christ of amplitude. He is the one significant exception to the law of rigorous heredity. He is the one universal man. As all birds flock to the summer, so all men of all times, of all climes, flock to and find resting-place in him. One who accepts this Christ of amplitude as his personal Saviour and Lord passes into similar experience with all believers.

A fundamental doctrine of the Baptists has always been the doctrine of the great, one, indivisible, spiritual church. I value and rejoice in Christian Endeavor because, without in the least demanding that I lessen my denominational loyalty, it allows me to say forth and to set forth this structural truth of the spiritual unity of all believers in the one great Christ.

Rev. W. W. Boyd, D.D., of St. Louis, was warmly welcomed and spoke on "Baptist Endeavor and Its Sources of Power :"—

Baptist Endeavor, in its ideal, expresses Christian life and fellowship. To realize this ideal, teach the young people to recognize three sources of power: the physical, or the body, the essential vehicle of power, and therefore not to be sinned against, but thoroughly developed; the intellectual, the invariable law of mental health being the self-direction of mental power; and the spiritual, the immanence of God in nature and in the soul of man.

Next came the honored pastor of the church in whose house the rally was held, Rev. D. D. MacLaurin, D.D., in a ringing address on "Baptist Endeavor and the Conquest of the World for Christ :"—

That the church on earth is a militant host no one acquainted with the New Testament will venture to deny. Her very existence foretokens conquests for her Lord. The duty of the church is to carry the word of life to a perishing world. *The plan of campaign* must be definite. A new and definite plan is known as " *The Forward Movement*." Its purpose is to secure as many churches as possible to assume the support of one or more missionaries. The fields of these missionaries will become parts of the churches' parishes. *The plan has been successfully begun.* In one denomination in the past five months thirteen churches show a guaranteed increase of nearly three hundred per cent in contributions; an increase in *per capita* contributions from \$ .45 to \$1.71. In our own denomination the plan has recently been adopted in nine churches, with an aggregate membership of 2,707. By the old haphazard method they gave last year \$1,647.35; by this definite method they have pledged this year \$6,935.05,—a gain of \$5,287.65!

There is but one Dr. Henson. He lives in Chicago, but his friends live everywhere. He spoke as he can on "Christian Endeavor and Baptist Expansion : "—

There's a kind of expansion greatly to be deprecated,— a gaseous expansion that goes ballooning with André, to share a like fate. But there's a solid expansion of head and heart and aggressive energy that is greatly to be desired.

As Baptists we should seek intellectually to take in the uttermost truth; sympathetically, the uttermost man; aggressively, to conquer the whole world for Christ.

If there were better denominational rallies than this they must have been superlatively good.

Free Baptists.

Rev. J. M. Lowden, Olneyville, R. I., Chairman.

Sixty Free Baptists assembled in the Woodward Avenue Congregational Church at the meeting of that denomination. Rev. J. M.
Lowden, of Olneyville, R. I., was chairman, and a number of eloquent
addresses were made. The first was by Rev. W. A. Myers, of Cleveland, and following him was H. S. Myers, of Hillsdale, Mich. Miss
Nelsine O. Aagleson also talked interestingly of the work among the
younger Endeavorers.

THURSDAY EVENING.

Tent Endeavor.

" Let those who are so given to the study of philosophy and the evolv-
ing of esoteric problems to suit their individual temperaments study
such pictures as were presented at the Endeavor Convention grounds
last evening," said the *Detroit Free Press.*

" Let them analyze the cause of the perfect contentment, self-poise,
rational sociability, and invariable courtesy of the men and women who
are on the grounds ; dig into the sincere atmosphere which fills Tent
Endeavor when, in the twilight, before the electric illuminators are put
on duty, the audience of over 10,000 persons from all over the United
States and Canada begins the singing of a convention song. What is
it that makes the musical 'attack' so genuinely musical ? How does
it happen that the magnificent volume of tone is so well balanced as to
part-singing ? Whence comes the unity of articulation and the spirit of
enthusiastic devotion ? It was not that there was a leading chorus and
a director, any more than the presence of policemen and firemen was
the cause of good order and uniform gentility.

" What was it, a little later, when a man, a total stranger to nine thousand nine hundred of those before him, led the vast assemblage in
prayer, that caused even those who stood around the outside circumference of the vast auditorium to bare and bow their heads in reverential silence and sympathy of thought and action, while over all and
through all was a supreme condition or sense of thankfulness for and
glorification of facts as they existed for those present ?

" It was a series of pictures which no man or woman of intelligence,
without regard to creeds, theories, or condition in life, can afford to miss.
The very sight of so many thousands of people seated on a level plane
is of itself worth studying, and to the seeker after striking factors the
appearance of the uncovered heads of ten thousand people, all practically of the same height and all on the same level is, to say the least,
very interesting. Viewed as a whole, it had the appearance of a wide
area of hair, with bald heads and gray heads — in this instance — so
few that they were utterly invisible, the dominant color being brown.
The dodging about of white-capped ushers only emphasized the general

effect, so that under the brilliancy of the illumination and with the colors of the decoration, the composition was as impressive as it was singular."

Rev. A. C. Crews, of Toronto, Ont., presided in Tent Endeavor and Mr. E. O. Excell, of Chicago, Ill., marshalled the singers. After the devotional exercises, which were conducted by Rev. W. F. Richardson, D.D., Kansas City, Mo., the Endeavorers came in contact with the living, burning question of Mormonism.

Address by Rev. W. M. Paden, D. D.,
Salt Lake City, Utah.

THE REJUVENESCENCE OF POLYGAMY.

With us in Utah polygamy is again a living issue. The majority of our people still believe in the righteousness of this form of marriage, and scores of our leading men and hundreds, if not thousands, of their followers are now living in polygamous relations. In spite of the manifesto of 1890, as interpreted under oath by Presidents Woodruff and Snow, old relations consummated in defiance of the Polland Bill and the Edmunds-Tucker law have been resumed; and it is not seriously doubted by those who know but that new plural marriages have been consummated. At least two, probably four, of the apostles have within the last few years taken new plurals. It is acknowledged by those most interested that President Woodruff was lax in the enforcement of his own manifesto; and it is understood by all that the church has done nothing to encourage the enforcement of laws interfering with polygamy. So conceding, as we may, that under the pressure of the present agitation something of a check has recently been given to new plural marriage, it is still certain, beyond the peradventure of a reasonable doubt, that at no period since the Edmunds-Tucker raid have polygamous relations been so openly acknowledged as during the last two years.

But for the election of B. H. Roberts to Congress, this question might have remained, for awhile at least, a State or local issue. But the demand that this man, who is living with at least three wives, be permitted to sit in our National Councils makes polygamy a living issue for every American citizen. Will you, through your representatives, permit what we by majority vote have made possible? Will you permit a man who lives in and defends polygamy to assist in making laws for this nation? Will you permit this man who is breaking the covenants made by his people and living in open violation of the laws of his State, and the marriage code of Christendom, will you permit him to sit in honor with those who are shaping the destiny of America?

You need have no doubt as to the validity of the charge that Mr. Roberts is living and associating in the habit and repute of marriage with at least three women. His friends do not deny it. He himself does not deny it. If he did, we have evidence which if held and used by you against one of your public men would doom him politically, disgrace him socially, and probably either drive him into exile or land him in the penitentiary. Mr. Roberts is as surely a trigamist as Dr. Clark is a monogamist.

Ten years ago he was serving out his sentence in our State penitentiary. The people of the United States had, through their courts, indicted him for polygamous cohabitation. He left the country for some months to avoid arrest, but finally returned, went into court, plead guilty. and was dealt with mercifully. Since then he has manifested his penitence and gratitude by continuing the offence for which he was fined and imprisoned; and as if to make his penitence more evident. he has added Dr. Maggie C. Shipp to the list of his plurals. His penitence reminds one of the gamin's account of the penitence of Peter. When asked by his teacher how Peter manifested his penitence he promptly answered, " The rooster went out and crowed three times. " The gamin's conception of penitence was hardly fair to St. Peter, but it exactly fits Mr. Roberts. Sent to the penitentiary for living with two wives, he manifests his penitence when released by living with three. When the rooster got out he crowed three times. And now, as if in further defiance of the courts and monogamic code which condemned him, though at least one more of a polygamist than he was when he was sentenced to wear the stripes of a criminal, he demands a place in the House which is responsible for the laws under which he was indicted, disfranchised, and condemned to prison.

What are you going to do about it? *Ten* years ago you gave him four months in the penitentiary. Will you now give him two years in Congress? *Nine* years ago you forced the church to which he belongs to suspend the practice of polygamy. Will you now by your inaction wink at the resumption of this violation of the seventh commandment? Hardly more than *three* years ago you gave Utah statehood on the express condition that polygamy should be forever prohibited. Will you now accept as Utah's representative a man whose life is qualitatively, if not quantitatively, quite as polygamous as was that of " the prophet Brigham." Not quite one year ago those who sympathized with Mr. Roberts in his candidacy virtually said, " We will send him to Congress; if he is not unseated we may take it for granted that the people of the United States have no desire to interfere with our peculiar domestic relations, and that hereafter we may settle such matters to suit ourselves." Are you going to permit Mr. Roberts and his co-polygamists to fasten their marriage code on the State of Utah and thus on our nation? Do you mean to encourage the re-establishment of polygamy in the heart of our commonwealth? If not, what are you going to do?

I hold in my hand a certified copy of the court process in the case of the United States *versus* B. H. Roberts. This process culminated in his pleading guilty of unlawful or polygamous cohabitation and his sentence to the Utah penitentiary for a shortened term. That was in the spring or early summer of 1889. Now you have his case on your hands again. Again it is " The United States *versus* B. H. Roberts." But this time, while tacitly acknowledging that he continues the old offence in an aggravated form, he comes with the credentials of a congressman elect, and demands as a right one of the highest honors within the gift of the American people. What are you going to do?

Do not suppose that the final overthrow of Utah polygamy will be an easy task. The history of such endeavors in our State is against the supposition. The polygamous beliefs of our people are against it. The fact that men who live in or believe in polygamy are dominant in the political and ecclesiastical affairs of our State is against it. And do not suppose that to rid our State of polygamy you have only to push over a few old stumps with decaying roots. Men like Roberts. Whitney, Grant, and Thatcher are no row of old stumps with decaying roots. They are vigorous, masterful men in the prime of life ; men who are as influential and popular with the young people of Utah as any of your young leaders are with you. Mr. Roberts, a man of about forty, is easily the most popular and eloquent leader in the Young People's Association of the Mormon Church; and his popularity has increased rather than diminished since his election to Congress. Do not mistake. The Young People's Associations of the Latter Day Saints are as unanimous in their desire to see Mr. Roberts retain his seat as you are to see him lose it.

On the other hand, do not say that you are helpless ; you are not.

> " So near to glory is our dust,
> So near to God is man,
> When duty says to him, You must,
> The youth replies, I can."

As the people of the United States, through their representatives, thrust Mr. Roberts into the penitentiary in '89, you, through your representatives, can thrust him out of your national councils in '99, Only let the three million members of your 40,000 societies go to work and the thing will be done : your congressmen can do as you please in this matter, and they probably will if you let them know your pleasure.

That is the practical thing to do. Write to your congressmen ; get your fathers, brothers, and neighbors to write to them. Send them petitions; enlist the ten thousand communities in which you live in signing and sending such petitions — not petitions to Congress, but petitions to the President and your own congressman. Add petitions for such an amendment to the National Constitution as will make polygamy a crime against the United States. So you may deliver the young people of another generation from the humiliating necessity of asking the question, "Shall a man who is living in polygamy be permitted to sit in the American Congress?"

The Utah delegation is prepared to furnish you copies of the needed petition. Every name appended to such petition is a vote against polygamy. We cannot vote for you; we can only offer to furnish the ballots.

In the name of God and the marriage code of Christendom we ask of you to vote them and to see that your votes are counted.

For obvious reasons, the State Prison Endeavorers sent no delegates to the Convention, but Mr. Frederick A. Wallis, of Kentucky, spoke for these brothers in bonds, one of whom, a bloody-handed desperado who had repeatedly attempted to lead a mob against the meetings in the prison, is now pleading with his fellows. "You would not follow me against Christ when I asked you to; now follow me for him."

Neither could "Jack" come to Detroit, but our Jack tars had a tongue to speak for them. Treasurer William Shaw told how a master-at-arms on one of our war-ships expressed himself emphatically for Christian Endeavor, "praying at one end of the ship as against the drinking going on at the other end." "Bill the Soak," on one of the ships, has, by the help of Christian Endeavor, become "Bill the Salvationist;" and this is a sample of the work Christian Endeavor is doing on shipboard and in the Nagasaki Christian Endeavor Seamen s Home.

If it is true that trade follows the flag, Mr. Shaw felt sure that his second topic, "The Travellers' Union," very properly followed the first. He described the up-to-date commercial traveller, who knows more about the prayer meetings on his route than about the bar-rooms.

Address by Treasurer William Shaw.
FLOATING CHRISTIAN ENDEAVOR WORK.

The heroic dead in Havana Harbor and the living heroes of Manila Bay and Santiago have called the attention of the world to the splendid material of which our sailor-boys are made; but years before these events happened Christian Endeavor appreciated the worth of these men, as well as their need, and under the consecrated leadership, first of Miss Antoinette P. Jones, of Falmouth, Mass., who is known and loved by perhaps more sailor-boys than any other woman in the world, who organized the Floating Christian Endeavor work, and later of the wide-awake committees on Floating Christian Endeavor work in all of our lake and seaport towns, we were enlisting them in the Lord's Navy, and sending them out upon the seas to fight his battles and win victories for the cross.

Nobly have they responded to the call, and if time permitted me to rehearse the moral and spiritual victories "Jack" has won, even Manila and Santiago would be cast into the shade. It takes courage to stand by the guns or in the fiery heat of the stoker's hole in the excitement of battle, but it requires no less courage to stand before one's mates in the forecastle and during the deadly routine of a sailor's life in times of peace, and acknowledge Jesus Christ as King, and live a pure and manly life for him. No one who is unacquainted with the details of a sailor's life can have any conception of the temptations that assail him on sea and land. All honor to our sailor brothers who often amid the jeers of their mates hold their Christian Endeavor service of prayer and testimony on board ship, and stand by their colors when on land!

Floating Christian Endeavor work stands for the direct spiritual training of the individual, and to unite individuals in Christian fellowship; and also to interest the Christian Endeavorers on shore in their brothers on the sea.

On one ship the master-at-arms looked in on an enthusiastic Floating Christian Endeavor prayer meeting, which had been unwittingly prolonged over time. He closed the door with no word of rebuke, and next day said, " Praying one end of the ship, drinking at the other." On another ship, " Bill the Soak " has become to his mates " Salvation Bill." Another Floating Christian Endeavor member has become a Baptist missionary, and is stationed in Japan. Another is studying for the ministry.

Nine years of loyal service for the sailors has only deepened our sense of the importance of this work, and our conviction that there is no agency so effective as the Christian Endeavor Society. Through the home societies the sailors when on land are brought into direct touch with the churches, and with noble Christian women, who have such a refining influence upon the sailor. The work is world-wide, organizations existing in Canada, England, Japan, New Zealand, Australia, Sweden, as well as in the United States.

The Christian Endeavor Home for Sailors in Nagasaki, Japan, is a light in a dark place. It is the only place of refuge for sailors in that city, which is visited by thousands of sailors every year, where liquor is not sold. It is doing a splendid work. It is incorporated under the laws of Massachusetts and under the provisions of our new Japanese treaty, so that it will stand forever as a beacon-light to the storm-tossed sailor in that sea of sin.

I hope that you will all take a personal interest in this work for the sailors, than whom no better missionaries can be found, and that many of you will attend the Floating Christian Endeavor Conference, Tuesday afternoon, at half-past two, in the Forest Avenue Presbyterian Church.

We hear a good deal in these days about the trade following the flag, so that it is appropriate that my second topic should be

THE TRAVELLERS' CHRISTIAN ENDEAVOR UNION.

Christian Endeavor has been travelling ever since that first society was born, eighteen years ago, in Portland, Me., until to-day, when its banner flies in every country under the sun.

But I am not to speak to you about the travels of Christian Endeavor, but about Christian Endeavor travellers, or drummers, as they are sometimes called. The time was when a travelling-man, to be successful, must drink and smoke, and be ready at all times to stand treat for the buyers. The bar-room was the place where contracts were usually closed. To-day this is all changed, and the most successful travelling-men on the road are earnest Christians who are strangers to the saloon, but can tell you about the condition of the churches on their route, and know when the prayer meetings are held. Hundreds of these men are, or have been, active members of Christian Endeavor societies, and many of them are doing the very best kind of missionary work in organizing new societies and helping those who are weak or discouraged. I have in mind a travelling-man who, instead of loafing around the hotel after the business of the day is done, looks up the pastors of the churches, and if they have Endeavor societies, makes them a friendly visit, and brings them inspiration and help. If they do not have Endeavor societies. he takes samples of organizing literature, a package of which he always carries in his grip, and calls upon the pastor and tries to interest him in the movement. Arrangements are usually made for a meeting of the young people to be held on his next visit, which results in the organization of a society.

The Travellers' Christian Endeavor Union was organized in Philadelphia, in 1892. Mr. F. D. Wing was the first president, and Mr. J. Howard Breed, secretary. A pledge, adapted to the peculiar conditions of a travelling-man's life, with a simple constitution, was adopted, and for several years much interest was manifested. More recently the work has been allowed to lag; and some of us, who are specially interested in travelling-men, feel that the time has come to re-organize the Union and put new life and vigor into it. We believe that in this movement there are possibilities of great blessing to the men, and of great usefulness in the extension of the Master's kingdom.

Before the closing address, given by Rev. F. A. Noble, D.D., of Chicago, Ill., a profitable quiet season of prayer and meditation was had, with Rev. Edward M. Noyes, of Newton, Mass., as leader.

Christian Endeavor has a war upon its hands, but it is a "war against war," and Christian Endeavorers believe in that kind of war, as their Peace Memorial will prove to the world. If any others came not believing in peaceful settlement of international difficulties, after hearing the strong presentation of the cause by Dr. Noble they went away convinced that war is hellish, if not hell, and Endeavor's face is set against it.

Address by Rev. F. A. Noble, D. D.,
Chicago, Ill.
ARBITRATION.

The recent assembling at The Hague of the Peace Conference called by the Czar of Russia to consider certain specific topics relating to the general subject of war, and the fresh impulse which the deliberations of this conference have given to the hope that methods less sanguinary than the battle-field and the naval conflict may soon be devised and accepted for settling international disputes, would seem to make both the hour and the occasion eminently suitable for pressing home upon the hearts and consciences of all lovers of humanity the high claims of arbitration.

It is little, perhaps, that any one man, or any hundred men, or even any generation of men, can expect to accomplish in bringing about a change so vast as the substitution of an appeal to reason for an appeal to arms in the adjustment of such differences as may arise from time to time between sovereign peoples: yet every tiniest brooklet of opinion and testimony helps to swell the common stream, which by and by will become mighty enough to carry all before it.

Just now the skies are aflame with the promise of a new and better state of things. Echoes of the bloody encounter between Spain and the United States still linger in the air; the boom of guns from across the sea continues to vex the ear; nations mutually jealous and watchful, aggressive in temper, and armed with every conceivable appliance of defence and destruction, stand ready to fall on each other at the slightest word of command; nevertheless, more voices than ever before, in more quarters of the globe, and in more places of power and influence, are pitched to the key-note of universal peace. The special encouragement is that so many of the rising generation are committed to this sacred cause.

The question of arbitration naturally divides itself into two subordinate questions.

I. *Is arbitration desirable?*

To this question there can be but one answer. If justice, or anything like an approximation to justice, can be secured by submitting the cases in controversy to the honest judgment of disinterested parties; if aggression can be warded off and the rights of the people to themselves or their institutions or their territory can be maintained; if freedom and the precious opportunities of freedom can be either held or won by this process; then the method of arbitration must be conceded by all well-disposed persons to be preferable to the method of war. As it is better for individuals to settle their difficulties in this quiet way than to resort to blows or rush into court, so it must be better for communities of individuals to fall back on this same simple, natural plan.

In a brief discussion of the subject, such as that to which we are now limited, it is not possible even to mention, much less to pass in review, all the objections which may be lodged against war; but there are some facts which, even though they are already familiar to many minds, must not be allowed to escape mention.

In the first place, war is an immensely expensive method of harmonizing differences and reaching agreements between nations.

It is expensive in money outlay. The thirteen years of war in which Napoleon was engaged cost France alone $1,000,000,000. Add to this what these wars cost England, Italy, Austria, the German States, Russia, and other nationalities which were more or less involved in these terrific struggles, and the grand total is a sum well-nigh incomprehensible. The suppression of the Southern Rebellion called for an expenditure of not less than $4,000,000,000 by the United States Government; while the Confederacy put at least $3,000,000,-000 more, or everything within reach, into the wicked venture to disrupt the Union and establish a new system of civil order on the explosive corner-stone of human slavery.

A distinguished German writer, in a pamphlet recently published, shows that the Crimean War cost $1,700,000,000; that the war of Italy involved an expense of $300,000,000; the Franco-German War, if the $1,000,000,000 of indemnity be included, absorbed $3,500,000,000; the war of Turkey with Russia, $1,250,000,000; and that of Prussia with Austria, $330,000,000. Adding to these other sums expended in other wars within the last half-century, such as the enormous amount required to carry on our own Civil War, the author reaches the astounding total of $13,175,000,000. The imagination is baffled, as the heart is sickened, by these figures.

Nobody knows yet what our late war in behalf of Cuba will have cost this nation before all the bills are settled; but if what it will have cost the enemy as well be put into the reckoning, the sum will run easily up into the hundreds of millions.

There is no such maelstrom to suck in wealth as war. It is as greedy as all the misers rolled into one. It is as reckless as a whole congress of prodigals. If a nation has an embarrassing surplus, let it go to war, and very soon its surplus will change into a deficit, and its agents will be hawking government bonds on the street.

It is expensive in human life. The Crimean War cost 600,000 lives. The Franco-German War was at an expense of 215,000 lives. Our Civil War called for a sacrifice of 800,000 men. Within the fifty years now rounding out to a close, more than 2,500,000 soldiers have surrendered their lives to the stern necessities of war. If this number be increased by those who have fallen victims to the diseases and accidents which are incidental to war, the list would be something appalling to contemplate. It would be like taking the State of Michigan and adding to it the State of Maine and then instantly wiping out every human being, man, woman, and child, within their borders.

In the second place, war, not alone in its prosecution, but in its preparation, imposes enormous burdens on the state, and in this way seriously hinders the material progress and comfort of the people.

First of all, immense annual appropriations are required to keep up standing armies. Consider for a moment what the leading nations of the Old World are paying out year by year for the support of their military establishments. According to the latest available statistics, these are about the average figures for each succeeding twelvemonth: Russia, $175,000,000; France, $200,000,000; Germany, $125,000,000; Austria, $100,000,000; Great Britain, $200,000,000. In the estimation of their rulers nothing less than these vast sums — something like a total annual expenditure of $800,000,000 — will keep the armies and navies of Russia and France and Germany and Austria and Great Britain up to the proper standard of efficiency.

Turning to Italy, Spain, Belgium, The Netherlands, Norway and Sweden, to poor Portugal, and to proud but smitten Greece, the same ugly facts confront us. Sums immense in themselves, and out of all proportion to the amounts voted to education and moral improvement, are deliberately devoted to the ends of preparation for war.

Then, in addition to the oppressive weight of taxation under which the people groan in order that the rulers may keep their several states on a proper war-footing, these preparations for war necessitate the withdrawal of large numbers of able-bodied citizens from remunerative industrial pursuits.

In the five nations just named, Russia, France, Germany, Great Britain, and Austria, — named for the purpose of getting some trustworthy measurement of the extent to which the leading nations of Europe judge it necessary to go to meet the contingencies of possible bloody conflicts between themselves, — there are hardly less than 3,000,000 men under arms in one and another branch of the service.

It is true that war furnishes employment for considerable bodies of men in foundries and shipyards, in providing and concentrating supplies, and in other incidental ways. Wars are gold-mints to not a few manufacturers. Here, however, are 3,000,000 men, taken from their farms and shops and ships and stores and mills and mines, and forced to spend their time and energy in forms of activity which bring only small personal return and add nothing to the wealth of the community.

These figures, astonishing as they are, do not, after all, cover the case. Soldiers in actual service, especially in times of peace, are only a small contingent of the male population who have been trained to the life and duties of a soldier. Europe is practically a huge military camp. Everything points to possible war. Great Britain is in part an exception; but it is an exception only in part. What seems to be the military necessity of the situation dominates the Powers. No policy, no measure, no discipline, which promises to add to the aggressive energy of any one of these nations, or to increase its defensive resources, is overlooked or neglected. This is a fact which must be allowed its due weight when we are trying to make an estimate of the resources of mind and body which war diverts from the channels of rewarding industry.

The German Empire has carried what is known as the Prussian system of enrolment for military service to the highest point of completeness yet reached; but the other nations have been quick to catch the idea and follow on in the same path. The plan is not without plausible support. For, as another has defined it, "This system is based upon the theory that military service is not a trade or craft, to be adopted by a portion of the population, but a duty owed by every male citizen to his country." Acting on this theory, Germany requires that every man between the ages of twenty and thirty-two, who is in proper physical condition to render service, shall form a part of the army. For three of these twelve years the man has to be out in the field and under severe military discipline. No man is allowed to put in a substitute, or to secure exemption from duty by payment of money. In addition to those between twenty and thirty-two, if emergencies arise, all between the ages of seventeen and twenty, and also all between the ages of thirty-two and forty-five, have to fall into line and serve the state in the ranks of the army.

This is a superb military scheme. Inside of two weeks the Emperor William could set not far from 2,000,000 men in battle array, with more than half of them in fine trim and splendidly trained in the art of war, and with all of them ready to move with the awful momentum of an avalanche against the foe. These vast forces, perfectly organized, are on call at any moment. What it means to have an army of this size and with this discipline, ready to move like a railroad train, France could tell.

But in converting a nation into a tremendous fighting-machine like this, think how men are robbed of the opportunities and rewards of productive labor. When the numbers who are in the armies, not of Germany alone, but of the various nations of Europe, are contemplated, and when account is taken of the amount of time and talent and toil which go into army service, one cannot help thinking of it as a sad and criminal diversion of energy to ends which are not constructive but destructive. Were all these brains and all these hands busy with peaceful pursuits,—with improving fields, growing stock, cultivating gardens and orchards and vineyards, developing mines, erecting and managing mills, sailing ships, conducting financial enterprises, building houses, training minds, adorning homes,—how much better it would be for all concerned, and with how much more certainty society would advance!

This is one of the persuasive points made by the Czar in his now historic peace proposal. Speaking in reference to the unprecedented increase in these recent years of military forces and military armament, he says, "The financial charges following the upward march strike at the very root of public prosperity. The intellectual and physical strength of the nation's labor and capital are mostly diverted from their natural applications and are unproductively consumed. Hundreds of millions are devoted to acquiring terrible engines of destruction, which, though to-day regarded as the last work of science, are destined to-morrow to lose all their value in consequence of some fresh discovery in the same field. National culture, economic progress, and the production of wealth are either paralyzed or checked in development." He calls the "armed peace" now existing "a crushing burden" on the people, and one from which they ought to be relieved.

In the third place, war means to large numbers of the soldiers of the countries engaged in war hardship and sickness and wounds and lifelong disabilities and death; and to the friends of the soldiers, consuming anxieties and heartaches and blinding tears and the bitter sorrows which are associated with broken plans and baffled hopes.

There is no call here for attempts at realistic pictures of battle-fields at the close of hot engagements; nor for descriptions of hospitals crowded with fevered patients and the maimed victims of fierce carnage. All this may be left to sentimental poets and painters and dramatic historians and the correspondents of newspapers and magazines. Our illustrated weeklies are sure to teem with the reproductions of these horrors.

But dwelt upon or passed over in silence, the horrors of war are painfully real. There can be but few lands in the earth where there are not fathers and mothers weeping for sons slain in battle; where there are not widows who have been made widows by the exposure of their husbands to the casualties of army life; where there are not orphans who have come into the pitiable inheritance of orphanage because the fathers whose names they bear have had to yield to the slow onset of disease or the fierce charge of the bayonet; where there are not smitten homes and desolate lives and blasted futures in consequence of the havoc wrought by cruel war.

Men with any sense of patriotism in their souls, and with any appreciation of the high courage and magnificent loyalty to duty which leads a man, if he does it voluntarily, to put his life in peril, or to sacrifice his life, for a cause, will never cease to bow reverently at the grave of a soldier. But each grave, no matter how humble, stands for a death which pierced some heart with agony, and wet some face with tears, and changed the entire outlook of some life, perhaps of many lives, on things here and things beyond.

When wars are in progress — now on the far frontier of China, now in some mountain pass of India, now in the heart of the Soudan, now in Cuba, or Porto Rico, or the Philippines — the daily bulletins assure us that only a few were slain on one side, while scores and hundreds were killed on the other side, and the statements make only a slight impression on our minds. Each one of the men who fell, however, whether on the side which has our sympathy or on the opposite side, had a life that was dear to him; a life which, when once surrendered, could not be recalled; a life which was gladdened by the sunshine of stars and the opening of flowers and the greetings and intercourse of friends; a life which was full of plans, and that throbbed with hope; and each one of these men, too, rude as he might have been, had hearts that were bound up in him.

Thus, whether thought of from the view-point of property or of human life, war is waste and cruelty. War does not cultivate fair fields; it turns fair fields into deserts. War builds ships; but it does not build ships for the purposes of commerce and trade, but to blow other ships to atoms. War forges guns; but it forges them that shot and shell may be dropped destructively down upon armies and towns. War takes the labor which should have gone into the creation of something to meet the needs or to add to the comfort of men and fashions it into death-dealing bombs and bullets. War takes the money which foresight and thrift have accumulated and explodes it in powder. War takes life and smites it with death War accomplishes its purposes and wins its victories by filling graves.

Here falls in the second question which a study of the subject in hand forces upon us,

11. *Is arbitration practicable?*

Unquestionably arbitration is desirable. The considerations just brought forward in support of this view, and the many more which might be advanced, would seem to settle this point beyond all controversy. Few things, indeed, in the sphere of international relations, can be imagined which are so desirable as finding out and applying some method other than a resort to deadly encounters on battle-field and high seas by which the privileges of liberty and the ends of righteousness and the objects in general which make for the welfare of humanity can be secured. Is arbitration this method? Can the scheme of settling differences between nations by referring the matters in controversy to disinterested parties for decision be worked?

There are two answers to this question.

First, it is fair to presume that in the course of time and the progress of events, some method similar in its spirit and aim to this method of arbitration would be hit upon to reconcile differences between nations and hold peoples in the bonds of mutual good-will. Considering what the horrors of war always have been, and what they still are and must be so long as war continues ; and considering that man is a creature of intelligence and conscience, and under the guidance of the Divine Spirit might well be expected to find out some more rational and humane way of reaching satisfactory conclusion on disputed points than fighting to the death, there could be no other thought than that the rude and brutal savagery of war would sooner or later give way to a better plan of composing alienations and adjusting conflicting claims.

This has been the hope of the world and one of the sustaining assurances in the long conflict which good men have waged with evil. Prophets foresaw the good time coming when swords should be beaten into plowshares and spears into pruning-hooks. Angels put it into their songs. Jesus by his life and death made the realization of the hope a glad certainty.

It was the fascinating dream of a better way than the marshalling of mighty armies for straightening out misunderstandings and reconciling variances between nations which led the Italian Parliament more than a quarter of a century ago to take the initiative among legislative bodies and by a unanimous vote go on record in favor of the principles of arbitration. Nor did the members of this Parliament stop there; but they emphasized their sincerity and earnestness by incorporating in their vote a recommendation to their own king and his advisers to do their best in the foreign relations department of the government "to render arbitration an accepted and frequent means of settling, according to justice, international controversies in matters susceptible of arbitration." It may be said that it was the war-burdens under which Italy was then groaning which made her statesmen so ready to take this humane action. Be it so. Precisely this is the lesson which war-burdens ought to teach and the attitude which war-burdens ought to lead the nations to assume. It is one of the glorious missions of sorrow and distress, and of the straits into which men are brought by their folly and wickedness, to teach higher lessons of life. But be this as it may, here was the distinct feeling of a better policy to be pursued, and the foreshadowing of a time when the representatives of the nations would consent to have their differences reasoned out and settled on the basis of the calm and deliberate judgment of what sober, second-thoughtful men might deem right. It has been both a conviction and a yearning of humanity-loving men that a time would come when "war drums" would throb no longer, and " battle-flags " would be furled, and there would be a "parliament of man " and a "federation of the world."

Men have not felt that they could believe in the uplifting and renewing power of the truth of God, nor cherish any encouraging hope for the future of the race, without anticipating an hour when reason shall bear full sway in the conduct of great affairs, and when the interests of the world at large shall have become so interwoven that the common conscience and the common sense of the many will make war unpopular, and make it unpopular by making it unnecessary.

But there is an answer much more effective than that which is afforded by the mere presumptions of the case. It is the answer which is found in the fact that arbitration has already been adopted, and its principles successfully applied, in numerous instances of controversy. In some of these instances there was not much at stake; though in the past, wars bitter and fierce have often been waged under provocations less sharp than these differences would have supplied; but in others of them the issues involved were of sufficient importance to attract and hold the attention of the whole civilized world.

Fortunately for us in this discussion, arbitration is not an experiment of yesterday. While it is a fruit of our modern civilization, yet the plan of it has been in operation for a hundred years, or more.

The famous Jay Treaty, which was concluded between Jay and Grenville in 1794, and which for many reasons was unpopular in this country, had nevertheless the distinguished merit of providing for the settlement of three disputed questions by reference to mixed commissions. In 1814, or twenty years after the Jay Treaty, the Treaty of Ghent, which was conducted on the side of the United States by Clay, Adams, Gallatin, Bayard, and Russell, remanded three other questions which were in dispute to mixed commissions. This shows at once the origin of arbitration, as we have come to know it, and how long the system has been before the minds of statesmen of the highest order. Arbitration is not a mere whim of the hour. It is not a fad. It is a growth; and the principle of it has had more than a century of application.

In speaking on this point of the length of time during which arbitration has been on trial, and of the success which has attended it, Trueblood, in his "Federation of the World," says: "The merits and practicability of arbitration need no longer be pleaded. It has already won its case at the bar of international public opinion. Beginning in a tentative way with the United States and Great Britain a hundred years ago, it has been applied with increasing frequency, in recent years particularly, to disputes of nearly every conceivable kind. The cases which it has disposed of have ranged all the way from those involving damage claims of a few thousand dollars to those more serious controversies touching territorial limits and transgressions against national rights which have cut deeply the national pride and sense of honor, and given rise to hot and long-continued diplomatic debate. Wherever it has been employed it has succeeded. There is not a real exception to be noted."

Our author then goes on to affirm that the cases which have been settled by arbitration have stayed settled. It has been tried by thirty-one nations, great and small, in the Old World and the New. In these cases, as was fit, and as might have been expected, the United States and Great Britain have led; the former with about one-half the whole number, and the latter with nearly one-third. Recall one or two of these cases.

It would be difficult to conceive of a more delicate and complicated question arising between two governments than that which was forced upon the United States and Great Britain by the outrages of the Confederate cruisers which sailed out of English ports in the time of the Southern Rebellion to prey on the commerce of the Republic then struggling for its life. Both nations were sore and sensitive. The United States was stung with a sense of the cruel wrong which had been inflicted on the authorities at Washington and the people alike ; and Great Britain was sustained by a sense of national pride which made her rulers and her people also shrink from the possibility of humiliation in a matter so grave. But the question, after years of annoying debate and fencing diplomacy, was submitted to arbitration. The result is familiar to everybody and the story of it need not detain us. It is enough to say that the settlement of the Alabama Claims by arbitration was not only a distinct triumph of modern civilization, but a marked event in the progress of mankind, and a shining prophecy of better things yet to be. For this was a typical instance, and in it the fact was made clear that there is a more reasonable and fraternal way than a resort to mutual butchery to settle differences; and that this more reasonable and fraternal way, so far from being an idle dream, or a mere fancy of the visionary brain, can be put into practice and utilized on the plane of the gravest questions and the highest statesmanship.

The settlement of the Behring Sea controversy by this method of an appeal to reason belongs to the same class of delicate and difficult problems of diplomacy. The time is not long gone when a difference of this nature between nations of the commanding importance of the United States and Great Britain would have precipitated a war of sufficient bitterness and magnitude to jar the world. But here there was no marshalling of forces and no clash of arms; but when each side had submitted its claims and made its arguments, the seven eminent gentlemen to whom the controversy was referred took up the case, carefully considered the facts, and rendered their decision, and the controversy in the main issue of it was settled forever. How much wiser, how much more humane, how much more creditable to two great Christian nations to have adjusted their difficulties in this fashion than to have summoned the hardy yeomanry of their lands to put on the garb of soldiers and go at each other with sword and gun!

> " Were half the power that fills the world with terror,
>   Were half the wealth bestowed on camps and courts,
>   Given to redeem the human mind from error,
>   There were no need of arsenals or forts."

Another of these cases which might have led to war, so embarrassing and irritating was it, from the way in which it was handled, to both sides in the controversy, is the Venezuela Boundary dispute. But this case is to have amicable and final settlement by a Board of Arbitration which is now in session on the other side of the water. One cannot help thinking what a splendid object-lesson this commission will be, sitting there at Paris or at some other convenient point in France, to the Peace Conference at The Hague, when the members are deliberating on the question of adjusting international contentions by referring all matters in dispute to a carefully selected body of intelligent and impartial men. Providence would seem to have timed these two remarkable events with a view to the best results for humanity.

These instances of a resort to the method of arbitration to settle international controversies might be multiplied to the extent of a hundred or more; but enough are here cited to show that the plan is practicable, and that even when the case is of gravest importance and has reached an acute stage arbitration may be employed with assurances of success.

It is no part of my thought that arbitration will be immediately and universally substituted for war as a way of getting on among the nations. Arbitration implies the idea that both nations which are involved in a controversy are willing to do right and want only justice. This level of moral advance the world has not yet reached. Men are climbing toward them, but not yet do their feet press these heights. There are cases in which strength is used, not to uplift, but to grind and crush; and there will continue to be these cases. There are cases in which the weak can get rid of their yokes of bondage, not by patient waiting, and groans and tears, and pathetic supplications addressed to the dull ears of heartless sovereigns, but by rising up in such strength as they have, and in the name of Him with whom right is might, and sternly breaking away from the tyranny which binds and oppresses them. It is not only useless, it is a perversion of all ethics, to say that there have been or that there can be no just wars. There are circumstances in which men owe it to

themselves, and to their posterity, and to their country, to fight. Who will ever
venture to charge it upon Lincoln and Grant that they were wrong in resorting
to arms to save this Republic?

While the Peace Conference which was called by the Czar of Russia has
been in session at The Hague, and all good men and women the world over
have been praying that the deliberations of that body may mark an era in
the advance of mankind, the Czar himself has stood with his heavy crushing
foot on poor Finland. Deaf alike to appeals and protests, indifferent to the
claims of righteousness, in violation of express pledges, and in criminal disregard of the oath which was taken on his accession to the throne, he has
refused to lift his foot, or even to condescend to the courtesy of receiving the
officials of that smitten people and listening to their cry, when they have
sought audience with him that there in his presence, there, face to face with
him, they might make known their wrongs and secure redress.

When Finland was dissevered from Sweden, and made a part of Russia, it
was expressly stipulated that no law relating to life, liberty, property, education, religion, taxes, military service, or any form of local government could
be enacted without the sanction of all the four Chambers of the Diet. But all
this was flung to the winds by the Czar. This brave people has been reduced
to practical slavery.

Such wrongs plead trumpet-tongued to heaven for redress. Such wrongs
justify war. Such wrongs call for war, if there is any reasonable assurance of
succeeding. For so long as there are rulers who will not listen to reason and
justice, and so long as there are nations which will insist on employing their
resources for ends of injustice and oppression, force may be called into requisition to resist them. There are objects more sacred than property, or even
than life.

As there are cases which arbitration cannot reach, as in instances where
the wrongs inflicted or the oppressions practised lie within the boundaries of a
sovereign people, and the way must be left open to remedy by force evils
which have ceased to be endurable, so it is not wise to put too much strain on
arbitration or to expect too much from it by attempting all at once to operate
the principle of it through a great World-Congress.

There are those who think this scheme feasible, and who have at hand
ready answers to the objections which may be raised against it. Both the
United States and the British delegates have submitted plans — differing
from each other only in the matter of details — to the Peace Conference looking toward the establishment of a permanent tribunal of arbitration in which
all the nations shall be represented.

It is not strange that the imaginations of men are kindled and set aglow
by this idea. It is a magnificent conception, and one that has in it not a little
of the radiance and beauty of the millennium dawn. But a great international
tribunal of arbitration implies and also requires too much to be immediately
successful. Professor Woolsey of Yale College has shown that this kind of
court, to be effective, needs three things: first, a code of law recognized by the
powers; second, a body of arbitrators to apply this law; third, military power
to enforce the decisions of the court. Granted that arbitrators might be easily
secured, granted that a code satisfactory to the powers might be constructed,
it would still remain that there would be no way, any more than there is now
outside of military power, to enforce the conclusions to which the tribunal
might arrive. In other words, an effective international tribunal will be possible only when there has ceased to be much call for such a tribunal. It is a
scheme that will not be workable on that scale and in that manner until the
good time coming when there will be little for it to do.

It is wiser, therefore, to attempt to fly with a more modest wing. Arbitration has been splendidly vindicated in the sphere and after the manner in
which it has been operated. The prospect is that it is to win new conquests
in the same fields and along the same lines. This is to get individual nations
to enter into solemn league and covenant with other individual nations to
settle, not alone some particular difficulty, but all their difficulties, by a ref-

SOME OF THE OFFICERS TRUSTEES, AND MEMBERS OF THE UNITED SOCIETY OF CHRISTIAN ENDEAVOR.
HOTEL CADILLAC, DETROIT, MICH.

erence of the matters in debate to a board of well-informed and conscientious men.

A superb example of what may be done in this direction has been set by Italy and the Argentine Republic. As has been seen, the Parliament of Italy was the first legislative body in the world to take action with reference to the acceptance of the principles of arbitration. So it is Italy, acting conjointly with the Argentine Republic, which adopted the first general treaty of arbitration which was ever established.

The first article of this treaty runs as follows: "The high contracting parties hereby bind themselves to submit to the decision of arbitration all the disputes, whatever may be their nature or cause, which may arise between the said parties, when such cannot be adjusted in a friendly way by the ordinary courses of diplomacy." This provision was made to extend over disputes which might have arisen prior to the treaty. Other articles of the instrument are to the effect that "judgments rendered shall decide definitely every point of the dispute;" and that "there shall be no appeal from the judgment," and that "its execution shall be confided to the honor of the nations signing the treaty." This eminently Christian agreement has been in force for a year; and it is to continue for nine years more. If it is not denounced six months before the date of its expiration, it is understood to be renewed for ten years more, and so on ever after.

Here is a model action for all peoples. Here is a challenge to the civilization of the hour. Why may not all the leading nations of the earth enter into the same kind of agreement? Great Britain and the United States have tried to do it once, and failed; but let them try it again. What a splendid

In the Well-Appointed Press Tent.

direction it would be for diplomacy to take, and what a splendid achievement it would be for statesmanship,— this of mutually binding Great Britain and the United States in bonds, like those into which Italy and the Argentine Republic have entered; and of inducing France and Germany, Austria and Russia, Spain and the Netherlands, and all the rest of the nations, to come into an understanding, one with another, and each with all, not to settle their difference by fighting, but by arbitration!

This is the glorious victory which now awaits to be won in the international relationships of the world. This is the glorious victory which will be won when the intelligence and virtue of mankind have reached a degree of development which will enable our leaders to see that mind is diviner than muscle, and that justice is infinitely safer than injustice.

It all comes round, therefore, to a question of the moral education of the people, and the creation of a public opinion which will hold the rulers of nations to high standards of duty, and to the faithful recognition of the rights of men to liberty and justice, and the best opportunity possible for the cultivation and use of the faculties which God has given them.

One of the most impressive of all the Beatitudes, as well as a beatitude most suitable to a world of strife, is that in which our Lord emphasizes the blessing pronounced on peacemakers, by declaring that they should be called sons of God. Whether there was any attempt at logical arrangement in these immortal sayings with which the Great Teacher began his discourse on the Mount may be an open question; but it is not without significance that the blessing which is associated with peacemaking follows immediately upon the blessing which is to wait upon purity of heart. Men will not be peacemakers, sincere and earnest,

until they are pure. Men will not be in the moral and spiritual condition to
entitle them to be called sons of God until they have had a transforming vision
of God, and through this transforming vision have come into fellowship with
him in his thought and feeling and purpose. They will be selfish and aggressive and headstrong, bent on having their own way,—and all the more so if
they have authority and power,—if a better mind has not been wrought in them
by the Spirit.

Is not this what James says? "Whence come wars and whence come
fightings among you? Come they not hence, even of your pleasures that war
in your members?"

Things will go right when the people are right and public opinion is informed with the principle of justice. Cabinets will reach fair and humane conclusions when the members of cabinets are broadly intelligent and lovers of
their kind as well as of their country. Rulers will rule in equity when their
hearts are set on righteous ends and there is a sentiment abroad which will
tolerate neither duplicity nor oppression.

Micah, along with Isaiah, anticipated a time, as has been intimated already,
when nations should beat their swords into plowshares and their spears into
pruning-hooks, and the learning of the art of war should come to an end, and
toilers should be permitted to sit under their own vines and fig-trees, and without molestation enjoy the fruit of their labors. His anticipation, however, of
a coming time of peace and good-will was based on his further foreglimpse of an
hour when the people would be walking with God. He did not venture to reverse the order and say that if men would stop fighting they would walk with
God; but he said that when they reached the point where they were willing to
walk with God then wars would cease in the earth.

This is the underlying truth of it all. · Whoever, anywhere, is bringing men
into the faith and fellowship of God, or is aiding in the development within the
soul of a suitable sense of the dignity of our human nature, and of the responsibilities of life, and of the sacredness of the common brotherhood that is ours in
virtue of the common Fatherhood of Him. in whose image we are all made, is
·working toward the direct realization of universal peace.

Practically our duty settles down to the twofold, but distinct end. It is on the
one hand to hold aloft the high ideal of nations dwelling side by side in amity,
or locking hands across wide spaces and keeping step to each other's forward
movements; and it is on the other hand to understand that it is only as the individual is set right and filled with thoughts of justice and good-will toward all his
fellows that any real progress can be made in persuading men and states to
dwell together in the spirit of love and unity. When the kingdom of our Lord,
which is a kingdom of righteousness, shall have been brought in there will be
no more wars; and the same agencies and influences which operate to bring in
the kingdom of our Lord will operate to bring in the universal reign of good-
will to men.

> " And like a bell, with solemn, sweet vibrations,
> I hear once more the voice of Christ say, ' Peace.' "

Tent Williston.

It was no question by Thursday evening whether both of the vast
tents would be crowded. Indeed, when no more could find place in
Williston or Endeavor, or in the packed churches down-town, there
were still thousands unprovided for. Doubtless as many as thirty
thousand were on hand. President Clark presided, and Mr. Foster
kept up the musical end of the programme. The great audience was
led in Scripture reading and prayer by Rev. W. E. Strong, of Jackson,
Mich.

The first speaker had a suitable topic, when one remembers the English monetary system, for it was Mr. Pounds, and he spoke on " Dollars and Duty." Every sentence was an epigram. Every epigram rang true.

Address by Rev. John E. Pounds,

Indianapolis, Ind.

DOLLARS AND DUTIES.

The interest in this subject is significant. It denotes that the Endeavor Society is growing, as it has always done. It has grown from the smallest of seeds to be the largest of trees. Indeed, it was so little at first that the wise-acres said it was too small to grow and too weak to get stronger! Now the same dismal prophets say that it is too strong to lift loads and too healthy to live long! And still it grows and will grow. He who doubts it has not read the signs aright. The red on the clouds is the blush of the rising, not the setting, day, and betokens the coming, not the passing, of the grateful shower. Endeavor may be changing somewhat; but change is not always to be regretted, for sometimes it means being unclothed of the things that perish and clothed upon with the things that abide. Christian Endeavor is ceasing to be an ex periment, and is becoming more and more an experience — a real part of religious life. The glorying may have passed somewhat, but the glory remains. The boasting of the future will not be so much of the increase of size as of the decrease of sin. True. Endeavor *is* changing.—changing from boasting to business, from fire-crackers to Mauser rifles, from kite-string to the life-line, from doll-nursing to motherhood. As children we built fires in the back yard for the smoke that could be produced; but becoming men, we use smokeless powder, judging success by the execution done.

And such a change, such a growth, is but the unfolding of the real life and purpose of the society. Christian Endeavor was not intended to be an institution, but an inspiration. It has served an end when it has caused service to begin. It does not aim at triumph, but at training. It prefers service in the slums to a seat in the synagogue. The greatest word among its members to-day is "service," and this is well. The spirit of the pledge —" to do what He would like to have me do "—is active, as it should be. Unless there is action in Christian Endeavor there will be reaction. The co-operation of God is conditioned on the operation of men. The Spirit comes to those that go. The Master has help for him who stumbles in the path of duty, but none for him who does not start. Inactivity is infidelity. Perhaps the activity most of all needed to-day is activity in giving. The treasury of the Lord is empty, while the treasuries of the Lord's people are full to overflowing. Spirituality cannot be high when liberality is low. When the church lacks funds the members lack faith. We have the truth which the heathen need so sadly. There is lacking but the golden wire over which to telegraph the message of God's love. We have the gold, too, but not the heart to give it.

There are three nerve-centres in the spiritual man.— the head, the heart, and the pocket-book. The reason congregations start when money is mentioned is because the last is the most sensitive of the three! And yet, did they but understand it, the philanthropists are the happiest of men. True joy is in giving, not in getting. The child who runs after the rainbow. expecting to find the end of it resting on a pot of gold, is not more sadly disappointed than the man who runs after a pot of gold, expecting to find resting on it the rainbow of joy and peace.

And the giver is as useful as happy. While the missionaries are making the future geography of heathen lands the philanthropists are writing the future history of all lands. How sad that we are so slow of heart to learn this!

The fault is not wholly with the pew, either. When darkness covers the preacher gross darkness will cover the people. Self-seeking should have no place at all in the pulpit. When every man is for himself the devil will take the foremost as well as the hindmost. Were the Master on earth again, the man who views his preaching on Sunday as a necessary preliminary to drawing his salary on Monday would be driven out of the pulpit with a whip of small cords. If your congregation can get a certain preacher by offering him an increase of salary don't get him; for he who mistakes the jingle of the guinea for a call to preach will mistake the tread of the wolf for the rustle of the dove's wing, and the flock will be destroyed. After all, the worst that can be said of Judas is that he was mercenary; for the love of money was the root of all the evil he did. The Judas kiss of to-day betrays the love of women as well as the Lover of men.

Not that I am pessimistic regarding the pulpit. The world's deepest consecration and highest devotion is there. Men have chosen it preferring to give themselves empty-handed to the Lord, rather than to give the fulness of their hands to him. The true preacher chose the ministry on the principle, not that the world owed him a living, but that he owed the world a life. The noblest gift is to put one's self beyond the power of making a gift. The greatest benefactors are those who can say with Peter, "Silver and gold have I none, but such as I have give I thee." The most princely givers the world has ever seen are the Judsons and the Livingstones, who sometimes begged to be fed with the crumbs that fell from the heathen's tables. Yet Livingstone said he had never made a sacrifice! The Lord owned the man and he had no money. The same spirit should always characterize the pulpit. The ministry must live before it can lead. The walk is more heeded than the words. People are guided by footprints rather than by sign-boards. The sheep will follow the shepherd whether he leads them to the green pastures or not. The heroic spirit of giving must be begotten of the ministry.

Concerning the actual giving there are three important considerations: the *method*, the *measure*, and the *motive*.

The *method* is important. The impulse of the first Christians to lay all at the Apostle's feet was as beautiful as it was simple. But our duty is more complex. The channels of benevolence are multiplied a hundred-fold and there are no apostles to distribute our gifts with special wisdom. God requires of us the same liberality as of the early church, and in addition asks us to use our best wisdom as to the best way to give our treasure.

There are four methods in common use: the go-as-you-please,— the collection method; the please-as-you-go,— the respectable method; the giving a part of what is laid by,— the emotional method; and the laying by a part to give,— the devotional method.

The go-as-you-please method — taking a collection — is really the lack of a method. A collection is what people would rather give than be bothered, and leads to the time when people would rather be bothered than give at all. When a collection is taken up for missions enthusiasm for missions is taken down. The missionary offering should be the culmination of the year's work. When the hat is passed the opportunity for a large gift passes with it. The preacher who merely passes the hat deserves to lose it, for he has no head to wear it on.

The please-as-you-go method —giving enough to be respectable — is the most common one. Most business men give enough to maintain good standing with their fellow members. But thus measuring themselves by themselves, and comparing themselves among themselves, they are neither wise nor liberal. And as the standing with men becomes more assured the giving becomes less so. The liberality naturally diminishes as the social recognition increases. The trumpet-blowing method sounds well, but is generally lacking in cents and always in dollars.

The giving a part of what is laid by — the method of cheap emotional appeal — is uncertain in its present effect for good, and certain in its future effect for evil. The people who have given because of your passionate appeal will afterward feel that they were trapped, and will harden themselves against you in the future. If you depend on impulse to-day you may depend on repulse to-morrow. And then the appeal to emotion is not sure for even once. The people may give as they feel, and yet not give until they feel. And they will think they are giving of their own, taking a part of what they have laid by for themselves, and this is trying. It is so much harder to give a part of one's principal than to give a part by principle. And doing so, they will feel heroic while they are only hysterical.

The laying by a part to give — the deep, devotional method — is commended by practical wisdom as by Scripture precedent. If there were no authority for any method, the obligation to have the best one would be sufficient. That is not deficient in theory which is efficient in practice. It is hard to prove heresy against that which really gives bread to the hungry. It is well to work what works well.

The Tenth Legion is making a valiant and successful fight for larger liberality. Some object to giving a tenth because it is Jewish; but the Jews can teach us a great many things about money yet. Besides, tithing antedates the Jewish law by at least some centuries. And then, God always commended the Jews for their way of giving, except when they made it a substitute for the giving of heart and life.

Others object to the Tenth Legion because of its pledge, feeling that it may be difficult to keep it. But if the Endeavor pledge is good, then this one is. The pledge principle is good. Make a pledge to do better every time you get a chance! You may say that pledges are made at a time of religious fervor. True, and that is their value. Do not wait until your heart is cold and the hold of the world is strong upon you to fasten your life. But when you are on the heights claim yourself there if you can. Tie your life to the highest point it ever reaches. Fasten yourself up by a pledge of faith, not down by a fear of failure. That is the purpose of any resolution. The pledge was made for man, not man for the pledge. It is helpful to take any pledge that is helpful. This feature is a recommendation, not an objection.

Laying by a part is a pleasant way to give. Having made a decision once for all, one is not always torn between his desire to help and his desire to keep ; between his conscience and his courage. And God loves a cheerful giver.

And then, giving by a regular method tends to giving through regular channels — a most important consideration ; for it does not pay to starve the missionaries who have been sent out in the regular way in order to send others out in an irregular way. Special and foolish appeals have less chance of winning with those who give regularly for the more important things. It seems to me that the Endeavor Society is the special prey of wild schemes and schemers. Two views are taken of the Society : that it is a chance *for* the young people, and that it is a chance *at* them. It is surprising how many hold to the latter view. A chance to ride a hobby before them, a chance to teach peculiar doctrines to them, a chance to preach old sermons at them, a chance to have them adopt some new scheme, a chance at their pocket-books! The safeguard is to do regular work, and to give to it in a systematic way.

And giving a tenth leads to larger things. It is not ideal, may be, but it is educational. It teaches us how little we have given.— a lesson we sadly need to learn; for we overestimate our gifts. I do not know why, unless it is because what we give to the Lord's work goes so much harder with us than what we give to anything else that we remember it better and longer. Ask a man for money and he will say, "Why, I gave a dollar to something last year." Yes, and he bought a hat last year, too, but he does not remember what he paid for it! Thus, without the stern accuracy of a mathematical calculation we overestimate our gifts.

And then it is educational in that it tends to larger things. Systematic giving becomes constitutional — a habit of life. The tenth idea is only the beginning. It is not intended as a limit above which we are never to act in giving, but a limit below which our giving is never to react. Liberality should be a growth — must be, in fact. To ask a man who has never given largely for ten thousand dollars for some large benevolence is to startle him beyond measure. It is with him very much as it was with Goliath when David threw a stone and hit him, — such a thing had never entered his head before! It quite overcame him!

Large gifts are the crown of many small ones. This leads to the second consideration, — *the measure.*

How far *beyond* the tenth should giving go — that is the hard question? How much for education of self or of children, how much for adornment of home, to make it beautiful and attractive, how much for a competence in old age, and how much for the immediate and pressing needs of the work, — each must decide these things for himself. But there should be some cases in which the scale would dip toward sacrifice. There might be a few choice ones who would deal more generously with the Lord than with even themselves.

The need and the chance to supply it should enter into the solution of the problem. Liberality should be in proportion to opportunity. The Endeavor Society has furnished the trained workmen, and the time is ripe. The dawn of the new century is also the sign of the world's largest opportunity. It was thought worthy to be recorded in the Divine Record that in Paul's time there was one man in one nation saying, "Come over and help us." And when Paul got there he found it was not a real man, but only a vision of some who would hear when he had labored patiently. But in our time there are a thousand men in every province of every nation standing with outstretched hands and begging for the bread of life. He who falters at the moment of such supreme opportunity is twice craven. Some are awake to the opportunity. The world is not worthy of such, although the Master is.

Not long ago a member of a large city church came to the Missionary Committee and gave them a hundred dollars, asking that they use it at their discretion for missionary work. The name of the giver was to be kept secret. But I said to the chairman of the committee, whom I knew, " Is that member so much more able to give than others ? " He hesitated, and then answered, " The member who brought that money is a servant-girl, working in one of the homes here on Central Avenue." He hesitated again, and then added, in a husky voice, " I am sure there are a hundred members in this church who could give a thousand dollars each more easily than this girl gave the hundred." That would be a hundred thousand dollars, and only one-tenth of our church giving anything ! And yet we are talking to-night about proportionate giving !

What do you think of her, Endeavorers? Is she a fanatic? Do you fear she will lack daily bread? "Consider the birds of the air, they sow not, neither do they reap nor gather into barns, and yet your Heavenly Father feedeth them." Think you she is of no more value in his sight than many sparrows? Oh, ye of little faith! Or do you think she has less joy in his service, or that her crown will be less bright than that of others? Rather, the Master will say, " Let her alone ; she hath done what she could." Would that all had the same spirit, that all might have the same commendation!

A word in conclusion about *the motive.*

The motive is of first importance. The old saying, " Aim high and you will shoot high " is not necessarily true. Aim high and you will shoot high — if you have some power behind the ball. The only true motive is love. Giving should be religious — indeed, nearly all giving is so. People give not in proportion to their riches, but in proportion to their religion. The love of Christ is the true constraining power. The Lord opens the hand when he seals the heart. The Quiet Hour and the Tenth Legion have the closest connection. He who prays in the closet with closed door will pay in the congregation with open hand. Worldly motive must be shut out of our living before worldly measure will be shut out of our giving. He who does not keep the Quiet Hour when others are praying will keep quiet the hour when others are paving.

The best way to show our love for the Christ, and to increase it, is by ministering to the needs of men. When we say to Jesus that we love him, he will answer, " Feed my sheep." He who does not love men does not love the Saviour of men. The measure of a man is the number of people he loves, and his value is what he is willing to do for them. When the story of the cross is driven home it drives the hearer away from home — to tell others. He who would feel the electric current of the Christ's life pass through him must join hands with his neighbors that the circuit from heaven to earth and back again to heaven may be complete. The knee is most reverently bent in devotion and praise to God when one stoops to pour oil and wine into the wounds of a stricken neighbor.

Painters have drawn a halo around the face that is upturned to heaven, and rightly so. But there is a diviner attitude even than that — it is the look toward men. Moses spent forty days in the mountains, looking up toward God, while listening to the revelation of his law; and when he came down those who saw him said, " Let us step back from before the glory of his shining face "— and no wonder! Stephen was permitted to see beyond the mists and behold the Son of Man standing at the right hand of God. And those who saw him while he gazed said that his face looked like the face of an angel. But Jesus was raised upon the cross-tree, and from there he looked down to fallen men. And those who saw his face said, "Surely this is the Son of God!" Faith, like Moses, climbs to the mount of vision and looks up while listening to God's word. Hope, like Stephen, looks beyond the vail and sees the glory of the risen Lord, and the beauty of the loved ones gathered round his throne. But Love, like Jesus, climbs upon a cross and looks down upon the perils and possibilities of men. And the greatest of these is Love. He loves Christ most who gives most heed to the commandment, "Go and do likewise." True Christianity inspires philanthropy as true philanthropy expresses Christianity.

The spaces of quiet communion in each session were among the chief delights of the Convention. The one in Tent Williston was conducted by Rev. Clarence E. Eberman, president of the Pennsylvania Christian Endeavor Union.

Then Dr. Henson, Henson the witty, Henson the eloquent, Henson the wise and kindly friend of all. His theme, " Satan and Cities," gave him a chance for his best work, and he took it. He argued for the existence of a personal devil, in the face of that thing called Advanced Thought.

President Clark, in introducing Dr. Henson, said : —

You will see that the next subject concerning which we are to hear this evening is " Satan and Cities." I was wondering whether Dr. Henson had seen one of the enterprising Detroit papers before he picked out his subject, or whether the paper saw his subject before they printed their cartoon ; but some of you remember the picture. His Satanic Majesty was going along at a rapid gait, with his gripsack or bag. He was going away from Detroit, and he was saying, " The climate suits me all right, but I don't like the company " We are glad if Christian Endeavor has had anything to do with turning his face away from Detroit, and we will join our Detroit friends in the prayer that he may never return.

Address by Rev. P. S. Henson, D.D.,

Chicago, Ill.

SATAN IN THE CITY.

" Satan in the City" is the theme assigned me — a theme not pleasant nor popular. No matter for that, if it needs to be treated ; for the things that men most need to hear are often the things that men least like to hear. In discoursing on my uncanny text, I propose to consider who Satan is, where Satan is, and how we should proceed in order to dislodge him. First, as to the reality of his personality. And touching this there is undoubtedly the widest incredulity. One of the shrewdest devices of the devil is to persuade the world that there is n't any. And in this regard, in recent years, his success has been extraordinary. Many causes have contributed. The caricaturists have done their share, and all of us, from earliest childhood, have been familiar with the ridiculous representations of the Evil One, with horns and hoofs and a forked tail. Milton pictures him as "squat like a toad" at the ear of Mother Eve, and whispering softly infernal suggestions — and one may imagine him in like attitude by the side of the comic artists, who have made the whole world laugh at their grotesque portraits of him, for he knows right well that in matters of religion what is made ridiculous very shortly becomes contemptible and is then dismissed as incredible. And well-meaning, but ignorant evangelists have been influential in the same direction by the very extravagance of their language in denouncing the devil, as if he were the author of all the evil in the universe, and as truly omnipresent as the Lord of Hosts, and so we should have two gods in the universe, one supernal and the other infernal,—a doctrine so repugnant alike to reason and to revelation that men in revolt against it are tempted to swing away to the other extreme, and deny the existence of any other devil in the universe than the evil disposition in human nature.

Another thing has powerfully tended to the exorcising of the devil from this mundane sphere, and that is the victorious march of the scientific method. Men have been penetrating into the very penetralia of nature, and uncovering secrets that have been hidden from the foundation of the world. Many things that were accounted supernatural have been found to be only the outcome of natural causes. And the philosophers, elated and inflated and intoxicated with their marvellous successes, have been tempted to believe that if they were only given time enough they would pluck the heart out of every mystery in the universe. They have not yet grown bold enough to deny outright the existence of a Great First Cause; but instead of frankly acknowledging his personality, they vaguely discourse of "a power that makes for righteousness" and a "universal principle," not distinguishable in thought from the universe itself — and so God is going, and as for ghosts and spooks, angels and spirits, they are gone already, the devil heading the procession.

We are constantly assured by our modern philosophers that from a scientific view-point such things are utterly incredible.

But why incredible? Has not science itself, with its far-reaching telescope, shown us myriads of mighty worlds undreamed of awhile ago? And has it not with its microscope disclosed innumerable living creatures, including the horrid microbe, of whose existence we had heretofore no conception?

Why should it seem so absurd a thing to suggest that there may be other beings in the universe mightier than any we know of now, for the recognition of whose presence we have no adequate faculties? To deny such possibility is not to exhibit breadth of knowledge, but the narrowness of ignorance and the intolerance of bigotry. And why among these spiritual existences may not some be benignant and some malignant? There are such distinctions in the creatures that we know. And why among the malignant may there not be some one masterful spirit that towers pre-eminent? And what objection is there to calling him the devil?

Philosophy itself in this foremost age can urge no valid argument against his personality. But after all, philosophy is not the tribunal of highest appeal. The Scriptures alone can lift the veil that hides the secrets of the spirit world, and in the light of the Scriptures the devil looms colossal.

In the book of Job, perhaps the oldest in the Bible, he comes conspicuously to the front.

In the book of Genesis, the first book in the Bible, we hear his infernal whisper, and have a taste of his satanic subtlety. And all along through the pages of the Old Testament we can see the slimy trail of the old serpent, and hear his hiss.

And if it be said, as it is said, by the modern higher critics, that the Old Testament represented a dispensation of types and shadows, and of myths and allegories, we reply that the New Testament throws upon the devil a still more lurid light, and more vividly reveals the reality of his personality. John represents him as "a sinner from the beginning." Paul speaks of him as "the god of this world," who "blinds the minds" of men to the light of the gospel, and who does it most successfully by disguising himself as an angel of light. He warns his brethren not to "give place" to him for an instant, and urges them to put on the whole armor of God that they might be able to stand up against him. And Peter represents him as "a roaring lion, going about seeking whom he may devour." If it be said that these are the picturings of men whose minds were tinctured with the coloring of their times, then we join with them in crying "Back to Christ;" and going back to him we find that his very first experience after his baptism was in a conflict with the devil in the wilderness, and it was after that experience he taught his disciples in their daily prayers to repeat the petition, "Deliver us from the Evil One."

The fact of the matter simply is that the personality of God is not more clearly taught in the Bible than is the reality of the personality of Satan, and if we reject the one we may as well reject the other, and bundle the books of the Bible off to be buried or burned, that thus a priest-ridden world may be rid of the absurd superstitions that so long have served to keep it in awe. But the Bible will not down, nor will the devil.

No sound exegesis can banish him from the Book, and no true philosophy of history can ignore his presence in the world.

But if so, where? And this, for all of us, is a question of no mean importance. As he is only a finite being, he can only be in one place at one time. He has doubtless myriads of subordinates, — "demons," the Scriptures call them, — and these can carry on his work in his absence; and for aught we know he can reach them by some sort of wireless telegraphy in which he may have anticipated our own electrical magicians; but he himself must be, at any particular time, somewhere and not everywhere. And that somewhere, if a place of supreme strategic importance, he may for a protracted period make his headquarters. Where his headquarters were in the time of Christ's incarnation here on earth we can hardly have a doubt.

The devil, in Eden, had had the first intimation of the coming of One that was to bruise his head. He had heard a repetition of it in God's promise to Abraham. He had seen a singular simulacrum of himself uplifted by Moses in the wilderness. He had heard Isaiah ask, "Who is this that cometh from Edom?" and he wondered who it was. He had heard it said that "he should tread upon the lion and the adder; the young lion and the dragon he should trample under foot," and the reference seemed to be to him. He was a student of the prophecies and so he was looking for his coming, and probably knew better than the scribes that the advent was to be at Bethlehem. He doubtless knew that star, and he may have heard that angelic choir. He came with the shepherds, and later with the Magi, and he it was that instigated Herod to the slaughter of the innocents. And how he must have gnashed his teeth as he saw the babe spirited away beyond the reach of Herod's wrath, and guarded, it may be, by angelic legions! And on the return to Nazareth we may well imagine that the devil, like a beast of prey, perpetually prowled about the carpenter's home and the carpenter's shop.

And when Jesus laid aside his carpenter's tools, as if he never meant to return again, the devil dogged his steps to the scene of his baptism, and followed him up into the wilderness where was to occur the most mysterious and momentous conflict that earth or heaven ever saw. But though the adversary was utterly discomfited, he was not utterly discouraged. He betook himself to desperate methods: he marshalled all his forces. Europe, Asia, and Africa might temporarily be left to devilish men, but that little strip called the Holy Land was to be the great decisive battle-field — for that time, aye, and for all time. And hence that whole land swarmed with demons. God was there manifest in the flesh, and so was the devil, as never either before or since. He dogged our Master's steps through every stage of his life-journey, and closed in upon him with all his cohorts toward his journey's end. He inspired the chief priests and scribes and Pharisees; he entered into the heart of the unprincipled Judas; he nerved the arm of the cowardly Pilate; he egged on the mob; he gloated over the cross; he planted his minions around the tomb; and these were the principalities and powers that were spoiled when Jesus rose triumphant from the dead.

Dazed was the devil and bruised by that victorious heel, but he still lingered in Jerusalem, and after the Lord's ascension sought to strangle the infant church that he left behind — but with what ill success the record shows.

He shook the tree of life with the blasts of persecution, but he only scattered the winged seed to spring up in every land.

He tried to stamp out the fire, but the sparks flew through the whole wide world and kindled a conflagration whose flames licked the heavens. And yet, with an infernal persistence worthy of a better cause, he has continued down through all the ages to carry on the fight, and never was the fight so thick and hot as now. And never was there greater need for the soldiers of the cross to gird themselves and bestir themselves, and with highest courage and supremest strategy to compass and beat down the strongholds of the enemy.

To meet the enemy and to beat the enemy we must seek as best we can to locate him, and this we believe it will not be difficult to do.

We may be sure of this: that he has lost none of his ancient subtlety, but has whetted its edge the rather against the hard experiences of the centuries.

Some things he has learned undoubtedly. One is that persecution is not adapted to accomplish Christianity's extinction, for the blood of the martyrs has ever been the seed of the Church.

He has discovered that sugar-coated pellets charged with poison do deadlier work than lion's claws, and that to counterfeit Christianity is a better way to beat Christianity than to come out into the open and fight it; and that such infernal delusions as spiritualism and theosophy and Christian Science will more effectually accomplish his purpose than blatant infidelity and blasphemous atheism.

But some things he practised in the beginning that all his experience and cunning have never been able to improve upon.

One is the suggestion of a question as to the truth of the Word of God. "Hath God said?" That was the first satanic whisper, and that is also the last; and strangely enough, it is sounded forth from our loftiest seats of theological learning, and from the lips of men who have been put there as the trusted guardians of the faith once for all delivered to the saints. Another stroke of strategy he early made, and so successfully that he still persistently employs it. He suborned a woman, and it is not without significance that in the matter of the three most dangerous delusions of the present century he has had recourse to the same most potent agency, — spiritualism by the Fox Sisters, theosophy by Madam Blavatsky, and Christian Science by Mrs. Eddy.

The other device was a master-play. He would found a city, and he employed the first murderer to go forth and build it. I mean no disrespect to the beautiful city that gives us hospitable entertainment, and I would not cast reproach upon the magnificent metropolis where I am proud to have my home; but there cannot be a question that of all things below the stars the city is the best adapted to the devil's uses.

For saints and angels a city would be an ideal place, and so their eternal dwelling-place is represented as a city with gates of pearl and streets of gold. But for creatures fallen and depraved such proximity as the city brings is perilous. Contiguity means contagion, and congestion issues in putrefaction. It may not be good for men to be alone, but it surely is far from healthy to be too much together. And the devil delights to pack them. And yet I would not make a packhorse of the devil, and charge the growth of cities altogether to his account. A thousand natural causes contribute. Men, and women too, are instinctively gregarious. There was a great deal of human nature in that old woman who was found nearly starving in the slums, and was sent by some good woman away off to a comfortable home in a newly settled part of the country, but who was presently discovered back in her old haunts, and who, when reproached for returning, gave as an excuse that she "would rather see people than stumps." There is a great deal to see in the city and a great deal to enjoy, whether you be young or old, vicious or virtuous, pious or profane. Provision is made abundantly for religious privileges, for æsthetic tastes, and especially for the lust of the flesh, the lust of the eye, and the pride of life.

Provision is made for "old fools," as is shown by the number who from time to time make a spectacle of themselves struggling like silly flies in the webs in which they have been caught. But especially all the arts of satanic seduction are brought into requisition for the destruction of the young. Money they must have, for life is costly in the city and appearances must be maintained, and it is early discovered that money rather than mind is too commonly the measure of the man. " Put money in thy purse " is supposedly the first and great commandment. But to earn it means "to labor and to wait," and young Hotspur is not much disposed to either. And here the devil comes in with all manner of infernal suggestions of getting money without the stern and hard necessity of honest toil and frugal saving. Hence all the shameful category of wild-cat speculations and peculations, the frauds and forgeries, the pool-rooms and the gambling-hells, and finally, the burglaries and murders that make our American cities so perilous to live in. And *amusement* they must have, and ought to. The Lord never meant us to bend forever beneath the yoke, and forever to pull the plow. There is need of relaxation and diversion after the stern, exacting toil of life. But the mischief is that the devil, for the most part, is allowed to provide it.

Take the theatre as an illustration. The theatre ought to be an ideal school of morals, where the loftiest sentiment should be exhibited in heroic action. Unfortunately, the real theatre, like Sir John Falstaff, has "a proclivity for sinking," and in order to give piquancy to its plays, must needs abound in double *entendres*, and salacious suggestions, and indelicate situations such as ought to bring a blush of shame to the cheek of modesty ; and yet, side by side, young men and women sit to listen and to look, until the blush has faded out, and by and by comes no more.

The appetite for the sensational and the sensual grows by what it feeds on until ultimately it seeks gratification in the vaudeville, and the concert saloon, and the infamous dive, where blear-eyed brandy-blossomed men and painted and bedizzened harlots congregate. Sitting side by side with these are girls just brushing off the bloom of maidenly modesty and boys just putting on the airs of precocious depravity. It is enough to make one's heart bleed to see the crowds of roystering young people surging in and out of these devil's dens even on God's holy day. But worst of all these schools of debauchery is the accursed saloon, the omnipresent saloon, which like an infernal octopus is reaching out evermore, and grappling on with its remorseless tentacula to men and women and children, and dragging them down to death and hell.

Talk of the cost of blood and treasure in the Spanish War, and that now waging in the Island of Luzon ! This is but a bagatelle, and yet our yellow journals howl not over the wreck and ruin wrought beneath our very eyes. They tell us of "imperialism," and we are vociferously warned against its creeping shadow, but here is imperialism of a type so insolent that the wonder and the shame is that American freemen have borne it so long. It is the imperialism of the saloon, which, while debauching youth, and blighting homes, and breaking hearts, and wasting substance, dominates our politics, rules our cities, controls legislatures, and dictates the manifestoes of attorney-generals.

Did I say that the worst of all the devil's devices for debauchery is the saloon ? Perhaps in this there is a measure of exaggeration, for I am not sure but that after all a venal and licentious press has even a wider reach of malignant power. I say not that every press is venal or licentious : far from it, for I gladly and gratefully recognize the fact that in the press liberty, philanthropy, and piety have ever found their mightiest helper. All honor to the editors and publishers whose high ideals of the mission of the press have made them the most potent of our public benefactors. But the fact remains that in a lamentable measure the press has been subsidized by the devil, is run for revenue only, is a panderer to the basest elements of human nature, and is daily deluging us with sewage that threatens to breed a moral pestilence. This is the pabulum on which we feed — this the stream of which we drink. Not everybody frequents the dramshop, but everybody reads ; and thus through an agency supposed to be educational and uplifting the devil finds easy access not only to the so-called "submerged tenth," but to the so-called "upper ten." For, know all men by these presents, not all the devilishness is done in the slums. The devil is no respecter of persons or places, and gets in his work in the avenues as well as in the alleys, in the aristocratic clubs as well as in the dives, in the "salons" as well as the saloons — only in the former the danger is the greater, because of the softer seductions of vice that is gilded and refined.

But time would fail me to tell of all the innumerable agencies through which the devil operates to debauch the city, and through the city to destroy the land ; for the city is like a mighty heart, pulsating ever with tremendous throb, and sending forth a mighty stream of influence to poison or to purify every part of the body politic. "Out of the heart are the issues of life," and if the devil control "the issues" then presently the whole body will be putrefied and will perish.

How to dislodge the devil from the city, how to capture it and hold it for God and humanity, — this is a question of supreme importance.

I am not unmindful of the country — nor lacking in love to it. I was brought up in it, as was everybody else who is good for anything — unless exception be made in the case of Detroit. I sympathize profoundly with the pitiful plaint of that New England governor over the decline of the churches in the rural districts. But what 's the matter with the churches? Why, the people have moved away and left nothing behind but the silent graveyards and the deserted barn-yards. What then? Shall the minister stand and wail in the graveyard or the barn-yard over the loneliness and desolation that prevail around him? I trow not. Let him go to the city where the people have gone and seek to save them and the city too. The apostles were masterful strategists, and they sought to capture first of all the world's great capitals. Joshua struck straight at Jericho before he went skirmishing at large in the land of Canaan.

First capture the city and from that high vantage-ground you shall command the whole land. And to capture the city you must marshal the youth. I am not disposed to disparage age, for some of us here are not so young as once we were, but every man has his own proper gift and sphere. They say, "Old men for counsel and young men for war." This saw must be taken with a grain of salt, for "fighting Joe Wheeler" is no longer a youth, and Dewey — God bless him! — was not born yesterday — but let us be thankful that he was born at all. There are graybeards that are mighty fighters; but the great body of our nation's warriors are still so young that we may call them "our boys." The city is all alive with such youth — in the streets, in the shops, in the marts of trade. They are literally "the rising generation." The future is all before them. They are to be its arbiters. The devil is after them. We must beat the devil. We must capture them for Christ and then mobilize them for his service. The proportion of them in our churches may be only inconsiderable, but "one shall chase a thousand, and two shall put ten thousand to flight." What we need is the gathering of bands like Gideon's, courageous, heroic. self-sacrificing, who will not abase themselves by bowing down and abandoning themselves to even innocent enjoyment, but who, with girded loins, and eyes that look right on, shall stride ahead with lamps and pitchers and trumpets well in hand, ready to flash their lights and sound their trumpets, and so stampede the enemy in disastrous rout.

We need to utilize our young people ; aye. and to utilize our churches, — I mean our houses of worship, — and make each one a power-house whose mighty throb and thrill shall far and wide be felt and known.

The Germans call the burying-place of their dead "God's Acre." There is poetic beauty in the name, and yet it would seem as if God's acre should be rather the very seat and fountain of light and life. Sadly enough, however, it is true that God's house for the most of the time is the darkest. dampest, deadest place in all the town. Shame on us that we should allow it ! Day and night it ought to hum like a hive, and be ablaze with light and aglow with warmth. The children of this world are wiser than we, and they get their inspiration from their father the devil. And it seems to be in order to ask why the theatres and saloons, and every place of worldly pleasure and of riotous debauchery should be open day and night and utilized to the utmost of their possibilities, while the house of the Lord is hermetically sealed. as if there were danger that religion would spoil if exposed to the air. A religion that must be kept on ice in a cold-storage warehouse is more worthless than any embalmed beef that ever nauseated the stomachs of our modern war critics.

We must have larger conceptions of Christian life, and must crowd out the baser by the inflow of the better. We must make a business of religion and a religion of business. We must write "Holiness to the Lord" not only on the bells in the steeples, but the bells on the horses. And above all else, we must pour into all the devil's dens broadsides of sunbeams.

The powers arrayed against us are the powers of darkness, and the one thing that they cannot stand is the incoming of the light. "They that sleep sleep in the night, and they that be drunken are drunken in the night." The devil is a footpad that does his hold-ups in the dark. Arc-lights in all the streets and alleys furnish better protection than an army of patrolmen. One reason why the devil *cannot* break into heaven, and why he *would not* if he could, is because there is "no night there." John saw the new Jerusalem coming down from God out of heaven. Let it come — the devil cannot live in it, because it shall be filled with the light of the glory of God.

Two theories have obtained as to the regeneration of the city; one is that it must be accomplished by evolution from forces below, and the other by the revelation of power from above. According to John's vision it was accomplished by power from above. Zechariah also had a vision, and it was a vision of a glorious, golden chandelier, all radiant with celestial lamps. He saw mountainous masses of difficulty in the path of God's purposes, and he might have been disposed to be discouraged; but he heard a voice crying, "Who art thou, great mountain? Before Zerubbabel, thou shalt become a plain." Not by pick-axe and shovel, not by tunnelling or discharge of dynamite, was that mountain to be levelled, but rather was it to be "melted" away by the silent shining of the golden lamps that God had lit. "Not by might, nor by power, but by my Spirit, saith the Lord."

And thus shall Satan's strongholds be brought low and thus shall the city be redeemed. And then shall be heard the exultant shout which rings out in the Apocalypse: "Now is come salvation and strength, and the kingdom of our God and the power of his Christ; for the dragon is cast out, that old serpent called the devil and Satan, which deceiveth the whole world."

And if it be asked how it was they won the victory, the answer echoes like a clarion:

"They overcame him by the blood of the Lamb, and by the word of their testimony, and because they loved not their lives unto the death."

Woodward Avenue Baptist Church.

Notwithstanding both large tents were filled and a great throng in another church listening to Rev. Charles M. Sheldon, a large audience in the Woodward Avenue Baptist had an opportunity to see what a Chinese Christian Endeavor society looks like. A stereopticon lecture of more than ordinary merit was delivered by a missionary from Pekin, Rev. Elwood G. Tewksbury. His topic was "The Hope of China."

In turn, the lecturer took up in interesting style the political, intellectual, and religious future of the Celestial Empire. From his intimate and analytical knowledge of the Chinese, Mr. Tewksbury was able to present clearly to his hearers, in an hour's talk, a graphic picture of the situation.

Mr. Tewksbury, among other things, said that the hope of China lies in the educating and Christianizing of the boys and girls, and in marrying the male native helpers to Christian native wives. By this means he said that the influence of Christianity is certain to spread.

The intrigues of the Dowager Empress to control the Emperor were related in part, and the attempts of the Emperor to institute valuable reforms against the wishes of the power behind the throne were spoken of. It was shown that the advancement of China would be more rapid if the Emperor were aided in his attempts by some civilized nation.

The religious beliefs and the language and literature of the Chinese were presented briefly. The lecture was intensely interesting to all persons that have followed, to any extent, the changes that have been going on in China for the last dozen years or so.

An entertaining praise service preceded the lecture, and the singing of "Showers of Blessing" concluded the programme.

First Presbyterian Church.

A novelty in Christian Endeavor programmes was introduced at the special meeting held at the First Presbyterian Church. A famous author and minister of the gospel read a story, written especially for the occasion, whose salient features were an interview between the devil and a pastor of a church, a sermon by the preacher on the interview, the resulting revolutionizing of the church-members' attitude toward the church, the breaking-up of the more than friendly relations between the soprano and tenor of the choir, and the triumph of the president of the Christian Endeavor society in establishing exceedingly friendly relations with the aforesaid soprano.

The church was crowded to the doors. Hundreds stood up in the aisles and near the doors and along the side walls.

Rev. Charles M. Sheldon, of Topeka, Kan., author of " In His Steps; or, What Would Jesus Do? " and " The Crucifixion of Philip Strong," and other tales, read his new Christian Endeavor story, entitled, " For Christ and the Church." He was introduced by Rev. J. Wilbur Chapman, D.D., of New York City.

The story consists of a prologue and four chapters, and the reading of it occupied just an hour.

SYNOPSIS OF THE STORY.

In the prologue the author told of Rev. Mark Spencer's interview with the devil, who had suddenly appeared in his study while he was preparing a sermon. The minister of the story, on glancing at the half-finished sermon, hopelessly said aloud, " I can never finish it. I have not the heart to go on with it."

" Of course not," calmly said the devil, who had taken a seat on the edge of a table where the religious papers were kept, with a triumphant sneer on his face. " Of course not," repeated the devil: " when you know that more than one-third of your entire membership are liars."

The devil then went on to explain that more than half the church-members, among whom were many Christian Endeavorers, were neglecting the solemn pledges to attend church services and prayer meetings, and spent their evenings in going to parties, receptions, or entertainments. The devil was sarcastic, but the minister finally acknowledged that he was telling the truth. While the minister was on his knees in prayer His Satanic Majesty quietly withdrew.

The first chapter of the story opens as follows : —

" Oh, dear! " said Miss Brooks, the soprano, " I 'm so tired this morning that I had half a mind not to come to church at all."

" You don't look tired," remarked the tenor, as he distributed copies of the anthem to the chorus.

Miss Gertrude Brooks did not answer the tenor. Her face had a little more color in it as she took the music and hummed over her part. The tenor's slight remark conveyed more than the spoken words. He said very plainly that the face of the soprano was so beautiful to him that it never looked tired. He did not say all this out loud, but Miss Brooks understood what he meant.

Rev. Mark Spencer, the pastor, looked unusually grave and preoccupied. To the surprise of every one, he abruptly proceeded to graphically relate his personal interview with the devil. The sermon had an immediate and lasting effect. The members of the congregation went home profoundly stirred by the pastor's sensational remarks.

Some of the business men privately took exception to their pastor's frank statement that they were liars. Judge Morton afterward met Bruce Carter, a business man, and laughingly said, " I say, Carter, that was a great sermon, was n't it? Hit you pretty hard, did n't it ? "

" Hit some other people, I guess," Bruce Carter replied, rather stiffly.

The author described the effect upon others as follows :—

" Scores of men and women in the Morgan Street Church had similar conversations as they walked home from service that day. A good many men, like Bruce Carter, were angry. The sermon had been too personal for them. A good many others acknowledged the truth of the minister's position, as Judge Morton did, but the result of the sermon was not a determination to do anything more than they had been doing. When a business man in a church has not been in the habit of attending a prayer meeting for years, when he considers it a bore, and a stupid, dull place without any entertainment for him, it takes something more than a sermon, even so unusual a sermon as that one, to change his habits and bring him into a cheerful, loyal attendance on a service he has neglected so long."

The president of the Christian Endeavor society decided to do the right thing. He called a meeting of the officers and committee chairmen that night, and looked attentively at the soprano, who was an officer, as he made the announcement. At the meeting it was decided that those present should observe their pledge and attend the next mid-week prayer meeting of the church. Later the tenor met the soprano and asked her to accompany him to a grand concert the next Thursday night, but was surprised to have her decline, saying she had promised to attend the prayer meeting that night. He sneeringly referred to her " sudden conversion," and she bade him a simple " good-night," and went away.

The story then ran :—

" She might have learned to love him — was that all gone now? She said to herself something had taken place which made such a possibility out of the question now." " For Christ and the Church, " she kept her promise and attended the prayer meeting. So did many others — in fact, more than half of the two hundred members.

In the concluding chapter another interview between the minister and the devil is related, and many new evidences of the reconsecration of the members of his church ; and the devil finally disappointedly and sheepishly withdrew.

The chapter concludes as follows :—

That same evening the soprano went up to her room singing lightly. " I was glad when they said unto me, Let us go into the house of the Lord. I was glad when they said unto me — "

She bowed her heart in thanksgiving and knew that the crisis of her temptation was passed and the pledge of her Christian life would henceforth be kept for the Master.

When the president of the society came in that same evening, the mother was still awake. He went into her room to kiss her good-night and told her a little about the meeting.

" The Lord bless thee, laddie," she said simply.

" He has blessed me, mother; I feel a new strength and joy. The church means more than ever to a good many of us. Please God, we shall be true to our motto."

And as he went out after kissing the dear face, he whispered to himself, "For Christ and the Church, Amen."

NOTE.—Mr. Sheldon's complete story " For Christ and the Church " can be had of the United Society of Christian Endeavor, Tremont Temple, Boston. Price, 25 cts., post-paid.

FRIDAY MORNING.

Tent Endeavor.

Well, it did rain in Detroit. None of your effete Eastern drizzles, but a majestic downpour,— swift as a charge of cavalry, comprehensive as the sweep of the sky. In a trice the great streets were rivers and every gutter a Niagara rapid. There's nothing half-way about Michigan.

Friday — unlucky day indeed, so far as ribbons were concerned — will long be remembered as furnishing the Umbrella Session. The throngs at the Armory at the first Quiet Hour made it necessary to transfer those meetings to Tent Endeavor. Arrived at the tent, it was found to be a double tent,— dripping canvas for the top story, black umbrellas for the second, and underneath all, seven or eight thousand laughing faces. Endeavorers never get "*under* the weather." If they could n't sit on the seats, they could perch themselves on the backs thereof. If they could n't do either, they could stand.

The force of vigorous cornets led the singing in loud defiance of the heavenly artillery. "There shall be showers of blessing," — that was sung with a will. Then, "Lord, I hear of showers of blessing." "There's sunshine in my soul," — of course there was. "Let a little sunshine in," — the best kind of sunshine was there already.

"The programme of the morning will be carried out," said Mr. Baer; "the speakers can't be kept from speaking."

It was well, for the "Practical School of Methods" was indeed practical, brisk, enjoyable. There would be a short talk to set all brains humming with ideas, and then an open parliament to relieve the tension.

Secretary Baer presided, Mr. Excell had charge of the singing, and Bishop Clinton, of North Carolina, led the devotional exercises.

The first speaker was Mr. W. E. Sweet, of Denver, Col. His topic was "New Ideas for the Prayer-Meeting Committee."

Address by Mr. William E. Sweet,

Denver, Col.

NEW IDEAS FOR THE PRAYER-MEETING COMMITTEE.

I am persuaded that to make the work of the Prayer-Meeting Committee more effective, new or novel ideas are not so much needed as a downright earnestness of purpose, — a definite aim, with a deeper realization of the fact that the committee's pledged duty is to raise the standard of the prayer meetings, not always by new methods, but by conscientiously working and putting into practice those we already have. I believe in this little book, " Prayer-Meeting

Methods," by Amos R. Wells, published by the United Society of Christian Endeavor. There is material enough to keep the Prayer-Meeting Committee busy the entire year. There is no lack of methods — whoever will take the trouble may be fully informed.

In general I believe it is the particular business of the Prayer-Meeting Committee to direct and advance in every way the spiritual life of the society. Never since the society was started has such great emphasis been given to this side of Christian Endeavor. The columns of *The Endeavor World* are full of helpful articles, while "The Quiet Hour" and kindred topics have been the burden of Dr. Clark's letters and addresses. The chief inquiry of the Prayer-Meeting Committee should be that of how it may best advance the spiritual life of the members. Hence it shall be my aim to put before you a few best methods for the advancement of this spiritual life; some may be new to many of you, and they will at least be worth trying by all.

First. It is the duty of the Prayer-Meeting Committee to see that all Christian Endeavor "forward movements" are made known to the society; to see that the Quiet Hour and the Tenth Legion are frequently mentioned in the meetings. Speakers from outside the society always lend interest and freshness to our meetings. They can be especially useful in meetings of this kind. Request the pastor's aid, and in every way bring these questions before the society members.

Second. Is it not practicable, under the leadership of your pastor or competent laymen, to organize in your society or church a Bible training-class? The Sunday school does not attempt this work. Such a class would work wonders in a society of Christian Endeavor. Let the motto be, "Every young Christian trained."

Third. Timid members need help. The Prayer-Meeting Committee or its chairman should meet for half an hour each week with the younger members for the advance study of the topic, and prayer. I knew of the character of the participation of six young girls to be completely changed by this plan, the result of which was also the development of beautiful Christian lives. There is nothing so inspiring, so helpful, in all our Christian Endeavor work as to witness the development, the gradual unfolding of the spiritual life, in our boys and girls. Let us pray and plan for this end.

Fourth. Earnestly persuade the members to attend the mid-week prayer meeting of the church. Most Endeavor meetings are held on Sunday evenings; have the pastor at this time announce his prayer-meeting subjects. If he outlines them in advance, print them on the topic-card right with the Christian Endeavor topics. Cause the members to be mindful of this clause of the pledge. Keep at it until the young people outnumber the older ones at this service, so that there may not be the distinction too often made between the Endeavor meeting and the church prayer meeting. Splendid advances are being made in the way of increasing the attendance of Endeavorers at the mid-week prayer meeting, but there is room for greater improvement still. I am sure.

Fifth. A serious difficulty with most of our prayer meetings is the lack of plan and purpose. Many committees stop when the leaders have been selected. See that, so far as the Prayer-Meeting Committee can effect it, every meeting has a purpose. When the meetings get off the track, as they sometimes will, switch them back. Be on the alert, when an inexperienced leader is in the chair, to help out, to direct and to keep the meeting pointed right. This cannot be done without frequent meetings of the committee, — if possible with the leaders, — not alone to pray, but to plan and give ideas.

Sixth. Anything which will promote thought on the part of the members is valuable. Some people are mortally afraid of a pause, but a pause can be made as effective as a testimony, and often more so. Therefore plan for pauses by requesting the members to think for a few minutes on the subject or a phase of it announced on the blackboard. Let there be no word spoken; close this period of silence with a few moments of silent prayer.

Seventh. Lend variety to the Scripture reading by the leader not always reading the passage, but verse about. This will compel the Endeavorers to bring their Bibles. Occasionally call on some one person to read; then alternate between the young men and the young women; then altogether, etc. Use the revised version, and then have the same passage read in the authorized version. In every way lend variety and freshness to this part of the meeting.

Eighth. Appoint a member of the Prayer-Meeting Committee to assist the younger leaders in planning for an attractive meeting. Some inexperienced leaders have *gone back*, discouraged over the outcome of their first attempt at leading. Let this not happen through any failure of the Prayer-Meeting Committee to assist and aid the leader with suggestions.

Ninth. Encourage younger members to take part briefly. Too many of them have the idea that they must have all the fluency, ease, and originality of the older members. To encourage the timid have them learn sentence prayers from the Bible. In this way they make the prayer their own much more really than when thinking what to say that they may please their friends, themselves, and the Lord. This will be found a splendid way to discourage verse-reading.

Tenth. Push all plans to the point where results are obtained. Don't try too many things, but pin your efforts to definite things, and put life and snap and go into things. This requires earnestness of purpose, without which we can accomplish very little. Therefore, I emphasize, in closing, this same quality which I mentioned in the beginning: —

> "Pray in earnest, ye that pray,
> Work in earnest while ye may.
> Very few shall wear the crown
> Who would lay their armor down;
> Very few shall enter in
> Who have not *in earnest* been."

There was loud applause and cries of "Hear! Hear!" when Mr. Sweet said, "If you can't attend but one meeting during the week, let it be the mid-week prayer meeting." His remarks about the necessity of brevity in prayers were appreciated.

Secretary Baer than presented Mr. W. H. Ball, of Philadelphia, whose topic was "New Views for the Lookout Committee."

Address by Mr. W. H. Ball,

Philadelphia, Pa.

New Views for the Lookout Committee.

"He that sat upon the throne, said : Behold, I make all things new."

As it will be in that great day, let us make our lives, our work, and our ideas or views each day; and now, the beginning, and not the ending, of another year of service for our Master, let us make it verily a new year, with newer purposes than ever.

So if we in any way should reconsider some of the plans that worked well last year, may it be coupled with the new inspiration and enthusiasm we have, or will gather from this greatest of great Conventions. Therefore, "let the dead bury their dead," and bygones be bygones. If our work has been a failure or not as it ought to have been, begin with now and put the new zeal in it. Don't consider them as old things, but new things to be accomplished this coming year.

There must be a preface to our new views, — a preparation, or getting right. We must first be right with God before we can do his work successfully.

Let us, then, first consider what is success in his work. It is not necessarily what the world would adjudge successful; nor even that which man himself might pass judgment upon favorably. A large society may or may not be just as God would have it. A Lookout Committee which has been able to secure a large number of new members, irrespective of the right kind, is far, far away from the right principle. All that glitters is not gold. Sad to say, some of *our* success may have been failure; and happy to say, some of *our* failure God's greatest success. Some of you will recall the story of Lyman Jewett when the American Baptist Missionary Union considered to abandon the Telugu Mission, because apparently there were no results. He said, "*I* will bear no part in the fearful responsibility. If encouragement and aid are refused me by the Union then I will return *alone* and spend my remaining strength and days among the Telugus."

" Well, brother, if you are *resolved* to return, we must send somebody with you to bury you; you certainly ought to have a Christian burial in that heathen land," said the secretary.

They returned him to "The Lone Star Mission," and with him Mr. Clough. The results finally came.

Have we not been discouraged on account of no results according to our standard? I do wish I could emphasize the importance of being right with God, which, after all, is our only requisite and the panacea of all spiritual ills.

It will not be from the lack of good things said at Detroit that next year will not surpass all others in our local society, but from a lack of taking home what we get. We might generalize in our remarks, but I believe in being definite. Although I think it difficult, especially so with Lookout-Committee work, to give many views, as most of our work is personal, and no one can tell us just how to do that. Earnestness and sincerity must be our motto to be able to win souls and members.

Fellow Endeavorers, take Christ into your Lookout Committee more than ever before. Consult him, and, as I have already said our work is mostly personal, he will direct you. We do too much planning ourselves and measure our own results. We want more of Mary's religion in our lives, — to sit at the feet of Jesus and learn of him, instead of being cumbered about much serving, as Martha was. *More* prayer for the Lookout Committee is the old, old story, and still it is to be our new view. I say *more* prayer, so that it will apply to all; for we cannot have too much. We are young and consequently ambitious, but don't let it run away with us.

Last year, at the Lookout Committee Conference in Nashville, I reported that our society had decided for one year to look in and not look out. I feel encouraged to again make this statement, as it was thought well enough to be quoted in the official report. By the looking in we were unquestionably blessed, for we saw improvement in our members; and not only that, but we were rewarded for so doing, as there was not a month that year without accessions to our membership, which practically came unsolicited. Try this, friends. Many, however, labor all their lives, as Dr. Jewett did, without a harvest.

Are you careful about getting new members in your society? Some are not. We never should make it too easy to an applicant. Don't frighten them off, but fully explain the pledge and your society's requirements of its members. I have known of Lookout Committees, in speaking to those who were doubtful about being able to take some part in the prayer meeting, to say, "Can't you read a verse of Scripture?" as though that was all that was necessary. The new view of our pledge is that we expect of every member *all* that Christ would have us do. Not only read the verse of Scripture, if he wants us to, but speak and pray, if he prompts us. These have been spoken of as "the next step," I believe.

Still further, I have had applicants come to me and say they would join if they did not have to lead a meeting. While, of course, I could not answer for another as to whether they should or should not lead, I did say that I thought they ought to, as, in the first place, just simply as one of an organization, they should take their turn and be willing to do what is expected of others; and, in the second place, as they promise to strive to do whatever He would like to have them do, that they would have to put themselves in the position of Christ not wanting them to lead, which to me is very unlikely. Christ's command to his disciples was, " Teaching them to observe *all* things whatsoever I have commanded you. "

Do I believe in striking from the list of members those who are absent and unexcused from three consecutive consecration meetings? Yes; most emphatically so. But, Lookout Committee members, be careful you are not the cause of such a one ceasing to be a member. Have you gone, at the first and second defaults, in a definite way, and one that could not be mistaken, to learn the reason of their absence, or have you helped them make their excuses? The first unexcused absence seems to me to be almost the most important, for if this is met in the right way the chances are against a second and a third. Nevertheless, if it should come to three times, I would strongly advise carrying out our Constitution on this subject. Be sure and make no distinction among your members.

These have really not been new views, and will not be of any service to you unless you yourselves put the newness into them in applying them with new energy that God will give you if you will ask him.

Then came the first open parliament of the session. It was a free-for-all discussion of the ideas advanced by the two speakers. Mr. W. C. Perkins, of Baltimore, Md., was the leader of the parliament. He started out briskly by saying, " Now is your time to talk back. Give us the kernels of success that you have achieved along these lines. We don't want a sprinkling of remarks. We 've had enough ' sprinkling ' through the tent. What we want is a downpour."

He got it. He had hardly ceased speaking when the first person stood in the audience to begin the general talk. And the time was profitably taken by many making pointed and practical suggestions.

" Some Novel Socials " was the next address.

Address by Rev. E. Lee Fleck,
Dayton, O.
SOME NOVEL SOCIALS.

The Christian Endeavorer is a socialist. He believes and she believes in socialism. They revel in socialistic principles — but they are of a kind that are right and pleasing in the sight of God. In speaking of that which is new and novel in the social, let me have just a word to remove anything that may have put an erroneous idea into your minds.

I believe the idea of any social must be that which is advancement, which is stimulating to the great work,— and that which is light and frivolous only cannot be considered by such a magnificent body of socialists as this is this morning. In order, therefore, that we may speak of those things only that shall be full of helpfulness to us, it is not necessary that we should have excluded from it that which is of a mirthful or a cheerful or a happy nature. I guess that is enough of an introduction, and we will now go on with methods.

The first social that I would call your attention to is that which would come from the Music Committee. I believe you may have any number of these and each one different, if a little time is taken to prepare for this social. I would suggest that possibly from the number of members in the society three-minute accounts — and they had better be written than otherwise — be offered of the biographies of authors of music. This would give your society, for that evening, very many things of a helpful nature.

Again, a short series of talks or papers descriptive of the hymns and songs you are singing every day and every week. How many of those things we notice here and there in the public press that are never associated with our worship and our singing in worship! I think a similar plan with this could be followed in the Good-Citizenship Committee. You know just what is to be accomplished; plan well for it. Have short presentations of the question, and for the remainder of that evening I am sure your society will not lack for some stimulating topic over which to converse. Nay, more than that; you will have an opportunity for uniting your effort with that of every other member, and that society with every other society of the union of your city, of your country, of your state, or of the world, for Christ. Probably this appears to you too much like work to be of a social nature. I understand that we are here for work; and if we can make that work the most pleasant thing of our life, then indeed is it that which God would have us be and do.

Another social would be a hunting party. Use as the object for distribution a nickel, a dime, or a penny. Let it be understood by the one who prepares this that there will be a list of objects that are to be found on this coin that is to be distributed. Now, then, the committee that has prepared this list will number them. There may be fifteen objects found on this coin. Any one who will find more objects on the coin than this committee have found will ·be honored for the evening. I am sure there will be a conference by nearly every member with some other member in that social gathering.

Another social I would suggest is a portrait gallery with the advertising question. I am sorry that the advertising mediums do not have a great many of these pictures; but with the magazines you have access to, you will find a good many pictures of authors and of prominent men and women. Cut these out and paste them on a piece of cardboard. Have those named and numbered, and pass them to one another, and let them, according to the number of the card, attempt to name the men and women thus presented, and see how many of them will go immediately to their right hand or left-hand neighbor. It is for the purpose of breaking up formality, and it is also for the purpose of making you acquainted with some of our best and noblest men and women.

A friend of mine sent me another, a railroad social. You arrange the seats in the manner in which seats are arranged in coaches, with an aisle through the centre. Tickets are distributed, and these tickets are numbered and represent the objects which you are to converse about. There is a conductor who calls the time according to these numbers, and the gentlemen must change seats at the stations, beginning conversation with some other one. There is introduced a newsboy, who may have any objects for sale at a nominal price.

One minute more. I am going to suggest a Mary's Little Lamb social. There are in our recitation-books any number of paraphrases which can be gathered together: there are a number of different songs that can be set to them; and you will find they will introduce, as far as that is concerned, much sociability.

And lastly, don't forget there is another very important social. It is to play mouse — mouse. Don't allow socials to run to the midnight hour. Each one ought to know when to go to his own house.

The open parliament following this was conducted by Mr. John H. Carey, of Baltimore, Md. Numerous suggestions were made from the audience, and experiences along this line of work were related. An interesting one was a "bicycle party," in which the young men in attendance were reported to have raised one-half of the pastor's salary.

Mr. H. N. Lathrop, of the Clarendon Street Baptist Church, Boston, delivered an address on "Fresh Missionary Meetings."

Address by Mr. H. N. Lathrop,
Boston, Mass.
FRESH MISSIONARY MEETINGS.

Among the "new things worth doing," I will try to suggest in the few minutes allotted to me how to have interesting missionary meetings, for if they are interesting they must be fresh. It is possible to have "fresh missionary meetings." Some societies are having them right along, every month or oftener.

Perhaps your Social Committee gives you superb socials; perhaps your Music Committee furnishes the society with masterly music; perhaps your Temperance Committee keeps your thought on temperance tenaciously; perhaps you have most precious prayer meetings; but if you have miserable missionary meetings, or, worse yet, are minus missionary meetings altogether, your society is falling far short of its highest Christian Endeavor duty and privilege. Not only that, but its very life is in danger. Dr. Gordon used to say, "A church that is not a missionary church will soon be a missing church." It is equally true that a Christian Endeavor society that is not a missionary society will soon become a missing society.

The one great aim of all Christian effort is the extension of God's kingdom on earth. It is the business of the Missionary Committees to inspire the society to undertake definite work along this line. You notice I say "committees." I use the plural form because I believe in separate Home and Foreign Missionary Committees just as much as I believe in separate Prayer-Meeting and Lookout Committees. In a society in a large city I would even carry it a point farther, and have a separate committee to look especially after the interests of city missions. At any rate, I should certainly advise the two committees for home and foreign work, and it will naturally follow that you will have separate home and foreign missionary meetings. If you can create a generous rivalry between your two committees to see which can have the best meetings and raise the most money, so much the better for your society and for the cause of missions.

To be successful in this age you must be a specialist. Specialize your missionary meetings. Don't go "from Greenland's icy mountains to India's coral strand" in one night. Have an Alaska meeting, a Congo meeting, a night among the Indians, a night in Japan, and another night for a visit to the Philippines or among the West Indies. Don't take up the evening with the spiritless narration of a lot of dry statistics that nobody cares anything about. That is a sure recipe for a dull and stupid meeting. To make it fresh and interesting, get fresh missionaries, real live ones — they won't hurt you. If there are none near you, spend some money to get them from a distance. Is n't it a gilt-edged investment for the Lord's money, if you spend ten dollars getting a missionary and the missionary gets fifty dollars out of you for missions? This takes no account of the unexpected dividends which may accrue from the interest thus awakened.

You may wonder why some society near you, no larger or richer than yours, gives five or ten times as much for missions as you do. It is because they are on fire with missionary zeal, kindled by missionary meetings at least once a month, and fanned by the latest news from mission fields concerning missionary heroes. Your live Missionary Committee will watch the daily press as well as the religious press for missionary news. History is made very fast nowadays, and no kind of history faster than missionary history. Not a month passes but some notable achievement is recorded. Have some member whose heart and soul is in missions give these current events to your society, in that way making every missionary meeting fresh and up-to-date. Incidentally, much instruction in ethnology, biography, geography, and history will be gained.

Put your brightest and best members on your Missionary Committees. Don't make up your Prayer-Meeting Committee, your Lookout Committee, and your Social Committee, and then fill up your Missionary Committee with any old fossils that are left.

Your fresh missionary meeting will be a prayer meeting as well as a missionary meeting. Missionaries use the Bible a great deal. You will, if you want missionary inspiration fresh from the Throne of Grace. Sing often the grand old missionary hymns. Above all, make every meeting cost the members something. Touch people's pocket-books and you touch their very souls. Christian Endeavorers are no exception to this rule. Every member who makes a definite pledge for missions will be eager to know how and where his money is spent.

That brings me to my last thought. Have your own missionary, one that your society supports wholly and entirely. You will then have a definite work and a definite worker to pray for and to work for. Perhaps you say you cannot support a whole missionary; but I say you can. Not every society can support a trained missionary in Africa, Asia, the Islands of the Sea, or benighted portions of our own land, whose salary is from $300 to $600 per year. Some are doing it, however, and every meeting with them is a fresh missionary meeting. But there are few societies that cannot support native workers in China, India, Burma, Africa, and other Oriental countries. Such missionaries can be kept at work for a whole year for from twenty to fifty dollars. Your own denominational boards will be glad to find for you as many of these earnest, consecrated workers as you will support, and will keep you thoroughly interested in them by frequent reports of their work.

Widen your missionary vision to an encircling of the entire globe. Keep posted on the missionary activities of other denominations besides your own. The biography of every missionary will be a new " Acts of the Apostles " to you and a well-spring of inspiration for " fresh missionary meetings. " And finally, believe in the greatness and enduring character of your work.

During the meeting, just after Mr. Lathrop's address, Secretary Baer scored a point. He said, " I don't know how you feel, but I am having a good time. Every one that is having a good time just say ' Amen.' " There was a loud response from all over the tent, and the grand chorus of " amens " was on record as a new means of voting.

Mr. H. H. Grotthouse, of Dallas, Tex., conducted the next open parliament in a lively manner.

Mr. Baer then introduced Mr. S. J. Duncan-Clark, of Toronto, Ont., and asked the audience to arise and shake hands with the speaker. With one accord the vast audience arose and greeted Mr. Clark with a waving of hands. Mr. Clark's topic was " Some New Committees."

Address by Mr. S. J. Duncan-Clark,
Toronto, Ontario.

SOME NEW COMMITTEES.

First of all, I want to suggest that we should have an Endeavor Training Committee in connection with our society, into which we should take associate members and train them to be active members ; teaching them the spirit and the principals upon which we stand; training them well in our constitution; training them in the pledge; teaching them what the pledge means, so that when they come to sign that pledge and put their names to the constitution and assume their places in our society as active members, they will know what they are doing and be able to take an intelligent part in all our work.

Another committee, something along the same line,—a Denominational Committee,— a committee to keep your young people in touch with the work of their own denomination, to teach them what the denomination is doing, what the denomination stands for, what it hopes to do, and how it is going to do it. In fact, a committee of this nature in our societies would be very helpful in strengthening that denominational loyalty in which we believe as Christian Endeavorers.

Another one. I want to recommend to you a Comfort Committee; I mean a committee that will look out for the comforts of those present, in order to make our meetings helpful and enjoyable. The very best programme carried out in the best room in the world with the windows closed on a hot night will not be interesting. This committee means relief to the members, and should be well looked after. If you had a committee to look after the small points, to see that the windows were open, to see that there was a jug of ice-water, to see that there were fans for the comfort of those present, it would add greatly to the interest of the meeting. A Comfort Committee that would look after these small things that are so important, after all, would be found very helpful.

Now, another committee. I want to suggest the advantage of having a Committee of Encouragers—I would not let it be known just who they were, perhaps, but two or three of the brightest and most sympathetic people in the society, who will go to the weak members and say to them, "I was glad to hear your voice to-night, let us hear it again;" who will go to the pastor after he preaches a good sermon and say, "Your sermon was exceedingly good and very helpful;" who will go to any one who seems to be in the blues and let the sunshine in and give them a vision of Jesus Christ, the one who settles all our difficulties and problems for us.

Now, then, one other committee,—a Rest-Givers' Committee; you can change the name if you like, but I want to give you the idea, that is all. A committee that would look after the tired people, the people who have too many home duties; a committee that will assume another's burdens; a committee that will go and look after the baby and let the mother get out to the meetings, because some of the young mothers long for the meetings of the society. Let some motherly, loving young girl go and spend an hour and a half at the home in the evening, and let the mothers get out and get the helpfulness and pleasure out of these meetings that should come to all of us. A Rest-Givers' Committee, a committee that will take up the burden of some earnest Christian, who can afford to give an outing of two or three days for those who need it to go to the country, and pay their expenses for a breath of refreshing outdoor air, praising God for the sympathy and health that is conferred upon them.

Now, I want to suggest some committees of the whole; and every member of the society should belong to these committees. First of all, an Intercessory Committee. I do not believe you and I have half reached the estimate of value of intercessory prayer, and its value is being emphasized more and more every day. Let your society be resolved into a committee of the whole on intercession. Get hold of the names of several young people who you know are not as much interested in the task as they ought to be, and make them the subjects of pleading, definite, earnest prayer until the Holy Spirit comes. Call your society together for one night and say, "We are going to organize as a committee of the whole for personal work; join us to lay hold of some one individual, and use your best efforts to bring that man or woman, boy or girl, into closer touch with God."

Then a committee of the whole for Bible-study. *The Christian Endeavor World* has started that already, but it is in your hands to carry it out. Each one of this committee will have an interest in the Bible-study; and let your society make this committee of the whole to be composed, not only of Bible students, but of Bible workers.

And now, my closing thought to you. We have been talking about new committees. We are like the Athenians this morning, we are reaching after some new thing. There is an interest in some societies at any rate in renewed committees; committees that have been made over by the new baptism of God's holy spirit, and fitted for better and more faithful, more earnest, more truthful work. As we go back from this Convention, having listened to the words of exhortation that have come to us, let us not forget that this will amount to but little unless we have heard through all the voice of God speaking to our hearts. Let us go back, each one, saying, "By God's grace, I will become a renewed member of that committee," and you will have renewed life, and you will be filled with the renewed spirit of Jesus Christ, and we will have renewed life all along the line.

Three speakers then took up the subject "New Blood for the Society." The Rev. Charles M. Oliphant, Wheeling, West Va., spoke about "New Members;" Mr. J. W. Dalrymple, president of the Philadelphia Christian Endeavor Union, gave an address about "Our Associate Members;" and Prof. James Lewis Howe, Lexington, Va., handled the important topic, "Our Graduate Members."

Address by Rev. Charles M. Oliphant,
Wheeling, W. Va.
NEW MEMBERS.

Blood is life. New blood is new life. To the Christian Endeavor Society is given this new life. These new members are changed. In this change there is not the new beginning of the man, but the beginning of *the best good in the man.* No fresh faculties or sensibilities are conferred, but those already in existence are awakened, restored. The relationship simply is changed, which means new impulses, new motives, new desires, new actions, new conduct, new life. What shall he done for these new members *by others and by themselves* that this new relationship may serve its holy purpose?

I. *What shall be done for them by others?* This has to do with the duties of the Society toward its new members.

First. The Society should make them feel that they are *in a new fraternal atmosphere.* They have a right to feel that when they enlist under the banner of Christian Endeavor they are going into a higher and better atmosphere than that in which they moved before; into a brotherhood, where kindness and sweet charity are carried on to a higher degree than outside. The Society, to them, is to be more than a spiritual boarding-house, where each lodger has his own room, calls for what he himself needs, and does not feel bound to care for any other lodgers; *even a home*, where the members are "members one of another," and where "each for all and all for each" is the principle, so lived that the members are looked after, followed up, comforted, strengthened as well as instructed, *by and through* the fellowship whose large sympathy and broad love, whose unselfish motives and generous desires, whose helping hands and cheerful eyes, whose willing feet and goodly looks, whose warm hearts and Christlike lives, inspire with hope and love, strengthen with confidence and power, elevate with lofty aim and sanctified purpose, these new members to holier thinking, kindlier speaking, more beautiful acting, and more consecrated living.

Second. The Society should direct its new members into larger usefulness. The individual is too often lost sight of in the generalization. He must be reached or lost to the cause. He has a place to fill, however humble it may be. If not filled by him the cause suffers irreparable loss.

> "I cannot paint, nor write, nor sing;
> And yet there seems for me some quiet niche to fill
> Some where in God's great world; I stand and wait,
> Where he may find me ready for his will."

His usefulness depends upon filling his place. In the solid phalanx, the individual soldier keeping his place in the moving mass, is indispensable. His usefulness lies in the compactness of the body of which he forms an essential part. Powerless alone, yet *in his place with others in the Christian Endeavor army* the individual member is eminently successful "for Christ and the Church." It is the work of the committees to help the new member *find his place and direct him to fill it* to the glory of God.

Third. The Society is to present to the new member the highest possible ideal of life. This is one of its aims. This ideal is the test of character. What we are is what we aim to be. No ideal, no success. Small ideal, small success. Great ideal, great success. If the new member has a great ideal, he has something upon which to feed and live. If he does something great, it is because he thought something great. Christ is his ideal. Christ ever before him, standing high, bright, and pure, though by this ideal condemned; Christ, his polar star, though he forsake his aim and be nearest to his ideal, when reason comes again he can resume his journey; Christ above the horizon, bright, always in sight, though the voyage intermit, he has that by which he may begin again, and at whose sacred light he may kindle the quenched torch of his most holy purpose! The society furnishing new fraternal atmosphere, directing to larger usefulness, and presenting Christ as the highest ideal of life will have done its part.

II. *What must the new member do for himself?* He is not to be simply receptive. He has his part in making his new relationship helpful to him.

First. *He is to eat the food furnished by Christ.* Many new members die because they do not eat the bread of life. Food is fuel. We need it as the fire needs coals, for we are burning away. Christ can offer us, *but we must do the eating.* The good shepherd places the food in the rack, *but the sheep must eat it or die.* So the Christian Endeavor member will die if he eat not the bread of heaven. He must digest it, and allow it to become a part of his being, to nourish him, strengthen him, support him. (Jer. xv. 16.) Eating will prepare him for the next step.

Second. He is to serve. He has been saved to serve. Like his Master he is to say, "I am among you as he that serveth."

Service is the condition of greatness.

> " For He before whose sceptre
> The nations rise and fall,
> Who gives no least commandment
> But come to pass it shall,
> Said that he who would be greatest
> Should be servant unto all."

His service is to be continuous to keep him from the influences of sin. A train was moving at the rate of forty miles an hour. The thunder roared, the lightning flashed. A passenger, an old lady, was much alarmed. The conductor asked why she was so fearful. She said she feared the lightning might strike the train and all would be killed. The conductor said that lightning never struck a moving train. So the lightning of sin never strikes a *moving* Christian Endeavorer.

Third. The new member must not allow the insignificant things of life to keep him from this greatness of service.

> " A great temptation waits us all
> Who long for great things and do small
> We toil among the trivial sods
> Within the garden of the gods.
> While dark clusters hang above,
> Rich with the juice of life and love;
> We cannot reach and pluck them down,
> These fair pomegranates of renown,
> Whose juice life's early hope restores,
> For we must work — and do the chores.

> " Above us loom forever
> The mighty mountains of Endeavor,
> And whoso on their summit stands
> Looks on sun-kissed table-lands.
> We grasp our mountain-staff to climb
> Their sky-enshrouded peaks sublime,
> Up where the crystal torrent pours,
> And then — we stop and do the chores."

"He that endureth to the end shall be saved." Receptive to what the Society has done for him, feeding and serving, the new member will be fruitful. He will be quickened by Christ's spirit, will have all the means of divine grace, the dew of divine love, the sunshine of divine righteousness, the showers of divine mercy. *He will not be found wanting.*

Address by Mr. J. W. Dalrymple,

Philadelphia, Pa.

OUR ASSOCIATE MEMBERS.

As I take it, we are here this morning to consider a tie which, in the natural world, binds us closer to some person or persons than to others, that of blood relationship; for cannot this be characterized as a blood relationship which exists between our active and associate members? Are not these our associate members our nearest relatives — our cousins, shall I not say, coming next to our own brothers and sisters in Christ in our affections and in their claims upon us?

In the discussion of this topic let us consider first the important position these associate members occupy in relation to our society, as it presents itself in a threefold manner.

First, the important part it bears in the preservation and continuance of our society. As the blood which courses through our veins is continually changing by throwing off and taking on, and needs ever to be renewed and kept healthy by the continual production of new corpuscles, so the life of our society needs also that the active membership shall be renewed by the addition of new material and new energy. This new material must come from one or two sources of supply,—our associate ranks, or from without the pale of our society altogether. It is obviously apparent that it is easier to win from the associate membership than to draw from those who have perhaps taken no interest or active part in our society's welfare. Therefore, for the future good of our Christian Endeavor societies do we need the new blood of our associate members.

Second, our associate members, by their association with the active members of the society, stimulate them to better service, larger growth, purer living, and holier consecration; for where is the true Endeavorer, recognizing the presence of one who is not yet ready to openly confess Christ, in the midst of our little Christian Endeavor family—yea, a part of it—who will not be constrained by loftier aims and purposes to be found more in the image of his blessed Master? Our second deduction, then, must be that the individual members of our societies need these associate members as a stimulus to a larger growth and development of their own spiritual life.

Our third argument would be that the associate members themselves need other associate members. We must not lose sight of the fact that this class of our members has not openly confessed Christ. While God can and does manifest his saving power in any place and under any circumstance, where is one more likely to be brought to the foot of the cross than in some of our deep spiritual prayer meetings? How many of the many thousands of associate members who joined the church this past year gave themselves to the Master in and through our Christian Endeavor prayer meetings? We cannot tell; but this we do know from the personal testimony of a pastor, — that he has been unable to secure in the regular prayer meetings of the church the deep spiritual tone which characterizes his young people's meeting. In such an atmosphere are we surprised at finding our associate members crying out, "Men and brethren, what must we do to be saved?" And through the influence of one associate member following Christ other associate members also being led to confess him?

But how shall we win those outside of our society and secure them for associate members.

First, by keeping the meetings of the society deeply spiritual in their character and tone. If Christ be lifted up and exalted in our prayer meetings, there will indeed be that power manifested which will draw men unto him. The gospel of Jesus Christ is not a repellant, but an attractive power, which, when presented in sincerity and in truth, must always appeal to the conscience of men. Aim, then, for an exalted spiritual life.

Second, these associate members must be sought out. If we sit idly by and wait for them to come knocking at the door of our society for admission, or if we leave the entire seeking to the hands of the Lookout Committee, be they never so efficient, the very natural probabilities are that another six months or a year will see but few additions to the associate lists of our society. As every Endeavorer is responsible for the larger or smaller influence which they exert on others, let him realize that this responsibility extends to those who might become associate members and thus be brought into the fold of the Master. We should be keenly alive to the fact that while there is a positive responsibility arising from the presence of our associate members, there is also a negative responsibility resting upon us for the absence of associate members in our societies.

Third, strengthen and intensify the relationship existing between the active and associate members. What so quickly chills the interest of an associate as, after becoming a member of the society, to receive no more recognition than a mere shake of the hand at the close of the prayer meeting? Converse with your associates about the work of your society, enlist their sympathies, and above all, forget not to remember them in your prayers. When praying for a blessing to rest upon the members, divide them into two classes, and mention both active and associate. Great care and tact should, however, be used in this, as we believe that sometimes our associate members are brought out so conspicuously and obtrusively in our prayers that, instead of accomplishing the good intended, they, on the contrary, give offence.

While looking after the spiritual side of their nature, also remember that they have a social side which clamors for recognition. They cannot say that "old things have passed away, and all things have become new," and because of this fact our prayer meetings do not appeal to them so strongly as they do to those who have experienced that change ; and if we would hold and interest them we must be ever keenly alert to throw around them those social environments which by their unquestionable character will be morally and intellectually helpful to them.

Fourth, employ them in the work of the society. While in our judgment there are committees in the society which should be composed of only recognized followers of Christ, such as the Lookout and Prayer-Meeting Committees, there are other committees where they can render most excellent service, and by their active participation in these interests of the society will have their own interest not only in the society but in Christian work increased, which may ultimately lead to their conversion. We have known of some committees, like the Ushers Committee, being composed almost entirely of associate members.

In conclusion, the Christian Endeavor Society, as a natural result of its training, is becoming more than ever a recognized evangelistic power. No nearer field of usefulness is to be found than that which lies with the unsaved young people of your own church. No better opportunity for soul-saving is afforded than through the open door of your society.

May it not be said by a single young person of your church, because your society failed in its duty toward its associate members and those who might have become associate members, "No man cared for my soul; " but "go ye up and possess the land."

Address by Prof. James Lewis Howe,
Lexington, Va.
OUR GRADUATE MEMBERS.

The chief aim of Christian Endeavorers from the first has been the training of the young people in the church for Christian service. In all our natural sciences to-day we have laboratory work; in our medical colleges we must have our clinics for the practical training of the students; and I think that the Christian Endeavor Society is thus in some sense the laboratory and clinic of the church. There the young people are learning how to work; and while that work is not their chief aim, they must have opportunities for that work in order to learn how to work; but with this there is also implied, if Christian Endeavor is a school, that graduation must come. We hear that in China the old men of eighty or ninety years old oftentimes go up for their examinations; but Christian Endeavorers are not, in this country at least, Chinamen, and we do not want to stay on and stay on until we are eighty or ninety years old before we are ready to graduate into larger church work.

There is a practical difficulty that has appeared right at this point; we have been getting the new blood into our society, but we older members, so to speak, the old blood, fill up the arteries and the veins, and there is no place there for the new blood to circulate; we older members are doing all the work in the society, and there is nothing for the younger members to do. Well, we say, let us graduate. We used to hear, eight or ten years ago, so much said about the wonderful changes in our churches that there was going to be when this power of trained young people should be available. It is available to-day, but many of our churches are not availing themselves of it. We speak to-day more and more of graduating students, and not of students graduating themselves. I think that is necessary in Christian Endeavor. The truth is that many of our churches are not ready for the trained graduate members of Christian Endeavor societies.

At a State convention not long ago I stopped at the house of a prominent church worker, and the good lady said, "I do not quite like Christian Endeavor. We had an election of officers in our church the other day; we elected an elder, and he was a young man; we elected a deacon, and he was a young man." I happened to know that they were active and prominent Christian Endeavor workers; but she resented it. We find sometimes dead churches with live Christian Endeavor societies, and you let the elder members of those societies go into the church organizations, the prayer-meetings, the ladies' missionary society, and so on, and oftentimes that will really be resented. I know a ladies' missionary society that would absolutely resent anybody waking them up out of their sleep.

Then the appeal must come to the older members of the church, to the pastors, to the officers of the church, to graduate the members who are ready for graduation in the Christian Endeavor societies. Not that the Endeavorers should try to push themselves into the work, the broader work of the church, where possibly their presence may be considered an intrusion, but rather that the elder members — and there are lots of elder members and older church workers here before me this morning — should help to graduate those who have been trained in the Christian Endeavor Society and are ready for that broader and larger phase of church work.

But here comes also a responsibility upon those who are in the society. It is our duty to train, to help to train, the new blood that has come into the society. Get out of the way and make room for that new blood, and then help in training those younger members. We oftentimes feel that our societies could not get along without us; we recognize our great importance in those societies; we recognize that we have built those societies up; and we sometimes feel that these young folks cannot ever take our place; but do not be one bit afraid of it; they will come and fill our places and do a good deal better work than we have been doing, because so much more is known now of Christian Endeavor work. We had to solve a great many problems; and they have been solved now, and the young generations coming have all the advantage of our experience and can well-nigh begin where we left off. Do not be afraid to allow yourselves to be graduated if there is broader work for you; and above all, help to train the new blood that is coming into the society — help them on; do not be afraid to throw the responsibility upon them. They will be able to take care of that responsibility.

It is like that which we find in our schools. In one sense our schools do not progress so much — the individuals do not progress; they go on and up to graduation, and then go out into other work, and the new generation comes on and fills their places. I remember when I went up to my High School a year or two after graduation I thought to myself, What little children they have in that High School now! I failed to remember the fact that I was little myself once. We ought to carry out this same system further down. If we have our Intermediate Society, then we must be graduating those young people of the Intermediate Society into the Young People's Society; and we must see that those who have entered into the society must be trained along in that for their graduation. And in our Junior societies the same principle applies. In some of our Junior societies the children there are getting altogether too old for Junior societies. I do not blame them for loving their Junior society and not wanting to get out of it, but we must not think only of our self-interest, but of our duty; and when they are old enough they must be graduated into the Intermediate, or into the Young People's Society, and the little ones as they are coming on, trained in this same way, must be trained for their work. And so we have possible a system, as it were, of Christian Endeavor education in our churches, where young people, starting from the cradle, I might say, come into the Junior Society, and then on and on, trained in the phases of Christian Endeavor work, applicable to their age and experience, on and on, up through the Young People's Society, until they are fitted for grand, trained, useful work for our Master.

The last address of the morning was intensely spirited and interesting. The subject was "Don't Stick in Ruts." The speaker was the Rev. William N. Yates, of Philadelphia, Pa.

Address by Rev. Willam N. Yates,

Philadelphia, Pa.;

DON'T STICK IN RUTS.

The pathway of Christian Endeavor is enclosed on either side by the fence of righteousness. Within this enclosure, between where we are now and heaven, is the sphere of our methods. Whatever method you may adopt, don't get into a rut, and if you do get into one, don't stick ; for the man who sticks in a rut is a continual jolt-maker.

But how shall I keep from sticking in ruts? By constantly keeping before your mind the purpose of the Christian life. That purpose is not to get something, or to learn a certain number of facts, but "to know Him whom to know aright is life eternal." Never fall in love with a method, for one generally sticks where he loves, and a method used too often becomes a rut, and if you love the method you will stick in the rut. I know no deeper rut than that of method, and he who sticks there is in so deep that he sees nothing but the rut. He is just like a wagon that is in the rut up to the hub,—if you go to turn him out you break his tongue. Many a man can pray when he is on his knees who declares he cannot when he is on his feet. That man is in a rut knee deep. Then there is another man who cannot pray unless he is standing. That man is in a rut over his head. The form, to such an one, becomes more than the substance, and while he toils the practice is his only reward.

Don't get into the rut of imitation. Truth belongs to no one man ; it is as much mine as it is yours. But the manner of expression is an individual possession, and just as part of the wheel disappears while it is running in a rut, so the individuality of a man disappears when he becomes an imitator. Roadways that might otherwise be pleasant and inviting become actually impassable because everybody has driven in the same track until a dangerous rut is formed. A few years ago a prominent worker in Christian Association work, in a telling address, used the expression "getting in touch with Christ." Immediately almost every address by lesser lights had that "touch" in them, until a clause otherwise beautiful and expressive became common and almost repulsive.

Repetition is a twin sister of imitation, and is a great rut-maker. Don't think that a method used in leading last week's prayer meeting, and which proved successful, should be used every week during the coming year. The horse is a noble animal, and when young and spirited excites admiration; but if you ride him for an hour some of the vim will be out of him ; and if you ride him a whole day without stopping he will lose all his attractiveness; and if you keep on riding him you will soon find yourself astride a dead horse. Now the horse is not dead because of old age, but because you used him too constantly. Our methods, like our horses, need to be stabled frequently and well fed.

If you get into a rut, don't stick in it. About the only way to overcome the disadvantages of being in a rut is to increase the speed. If you are going rapidly you are not so apt to stick. If you are determined to do what some one else has done, and in just the same way, then do it with a vim. Get momentum enough to carry you through. Get your personality into your speed.

There is danger of sticking in ruts by our trying to get out of them too suddenly. Never try to twist out at right angles; nine times out of ten something will break and you will stick. I believe there are as many people sticking in

ruts to-day because of the time and way in which they tried to get out of them
as there are of those who are unable to go on in them. Unless you are confident that the horse is strong enough to pull out, you are a poor teamster if you
try to pull out. The result of such drivership would be a balky horse that
never could be depended upon; and there are thousands of Christian workers
to-day who cannot be depended upon because of being forced to do things for
which they at the time did not have the strength.

Love is the greatest rut-destroyer in the universe. Heavenly in its origin, it
is miraculous in its effects. It takes the common things of earth and transforms them into images divine. It may be the same thing that others do, but
if love controls the action, personality destroys imitation, and it becomes a new
creation. Those of you who are married, or soon will be, know this truth by
experience. When you stood, sat, or kneeled by her side, and laid your heart
at her feet, you felt that Gabriel had blown the trumpet and eternity had dawned.
Before you on the one hand were the pearly gates, and she had the keys, while
on the other hand was the bottomless pit, and she had the chains. Was there
anything commonplace in your feelings then? Yet you were doing what all
manly men have done. No wonder the good Book says, " If ye love me, keep
my commandments; " for when we love Him, and his smile means our heaven
and his frown means our hell, there will be no rut there. There are no ruts
near Jesus. His loving power fills them with the throbbing life of consecration. Embarrassment, imitation, and repetition fade away, and the man walks
in the light of divine love, surrounded by an " innumerable company," and at
the same time is "hid with Christ in God. "

Mr. Baer asked, " Can any one of you say you have had a dry time?
Your note-books as well as your umbrellas will prove that you have n't.
Let all members of committees rise. We 've had it reported that but a
few real workers were in attendance at the Convention." Almost all
present arose. "Let the press men take note of this. We are workers,
you see, not shirkers."

Mr. Baer then introduced Rev. John Pollock, of Glasgow, Scotland,
and Rev. James Mursell, of London, England, who had just arrived.
An ovation was given them by the audience. Rev. N. H. Burdick, of
Rochester, Minn., pronounced the benediction, and thus closed the
morning session.

Tent Williston.

Amid a pouring rain delegates flocked to Tent Williston as usual.
True, the canvas house was very wet, the seats were all damp, and
people had to sit on the backs of them and hold umbrellas during
nearly the entire service. Treasurer William Shaw presided, and his
opening words were : —

" The attendance this morning, amid this awful downpour of rain,
and these people sitting here where the rain is almost as bad as outside, demonstrates that Christian Endeavor is the best thing in the
world. You can't drown it; you can't burn it up. It is never too dry
nor too wet for the Christian Endeavor Society to thrive. Let us show
the world what a great Christian Endeavor Convention like this can
do in a rain-storm."

The big audience arranged itself as comfortably as possible, and the singing began. Some people who have attended all of the meetings in the big tents said that the singing was more enthusiastic than any that has been heard at any of the large meetings of the Convention.

Mr. P. S. Foster, of Washington, was in charge.

Rev. D. A. Graham, of Indianapolis, Ind., led the devotional services.

The ten-minute addresses on "Best Things" were all bright and especially interesting to the delegates, as they took copious notes of each speaker's remarks. Rev. Otis A. Smith, Bay City, Mich., spoke on "Best Things that Can Be Done by the Prayer-meeting Committee."

Address by Rev. Otis A. Smith, D.D.,

Bay City, Mich.

THE TEN BEST THINGS WHICH CAN BE DONE BY THE PRAYER-MEETING COMMITTEE.

It is a significant fact that men have almost invariably chosen hill-tops as places of worship. Pagan nations have built their altars and temples on "high places." The ancient Jewish temple was erected on a mountain. We read of Jesus himself going up into a mountain to pray. By his selection of an exalted *place* of worship man seeks to represent the loftiness of the *act* of worship. Our Christian Endeavor prayer meeting is our mountain-top, our highest act as a society. It is the place in which, as a body of believers, we touch God; the time when we become conscious of his holy presence.

To make a good show of success along other lines of work in which we may be engaged and to fail here is to fail utterly. The prayer meeting alone is great enough to justify this great movement in which we are engaged. To afford a place where the young people of our churches can exercise and cultivate the grace of public prayer is no insignificant matter.

When we remember that it was in a students' prayer meeting that the Volunteer Missionary Movement was born; in a prayer meeting that modern missions on this side of the Atlantic came to be; that it was in a prayer meeting that the Church itself was born; — we begin to see something of the place and power of the prayer meeting.

To have this, the highest function of our society, administered with judicious oversight and reverent care is a consummation devoutly to be wished. This part of the work is largely in the hands of the Prayer-Meeting Committee.

Before we can intelligently prescribe *the ten best things which can be done by the Prayer-Meeting Committee* we must ask, "Ten best things for what purpose?" What is the chief purpose of the prayer meeting?

Now I am convinced that most of our young people have very indefinite and obscure ideas upon this point. But we ought to settle this point, i. e., the end to be sought, before we can determine the way to reach it. The answers to this question will invariably run along one of three lines,— *instruction, sociability, worship.*

Now, which of these three possible ends is chief? To my own mind, the highest object of the prayer meeting is to meet with Christ; to honor him in prayer and praise and the reverent use of his Word. This lifts it out of the category of a social club, or a literary society, or even a class for Bible-study. Put Christ in the supreme place and you will have accomplished for your religious life what was accomplished for the world by the Copernican theory of a central sun.

Here you will find the right *centre*, around which all other enterprises, as well as all the other parts of a prayer meeting, will harmoniously adjust themselves. Here you will find a source of life; of deep-seated emotion and out-

QUIET HOUR IN TENT ENDEAVOR.

spoken praise; of words heart deep which soul speaks to soul, never dreamed of before.

The trouble with us all, when we go to a prayer meeting, is that we go to get something or to render something which will sound well in the ears of man, while we make God merely a side issue. If we shall, as Endeavorers, make the supreme object of our prayer meeting to honor Christ by prayer and praise and the study of his Word, we shall find it, like the Urim and Thummim of the ancient High Priest, emblazoned with the glory of the Divine Presence; we shall find the promise of Christ true, "There am I in the midst of them."

What, now, are the ten best things which can be done by the Prayer-Meeting Committee to keep worship first and everything else subordinate?

First. The committee must co-operate with the Holy Spirit. This they may do individually and as a committee before they make any plans. They may do this after their plans are made. They must seek his guidance in all that pertains to every meeting of the committee and every meeting of the society.

Nothing has been found more helpful than sacredly to observe the five or ten minutes of prayer together with the leader before every Christian Endeavor prayer meeting. The meeting really begins in this preliminary prayer meeting. Secretly, reverently, quietly, must this part of the work be done; but it will be found to be a vestibule to the true temple of worship and praise.

Second. The Prayer-Meeting Committee must impress upon the society that the meeting is a *prayer* meeting. A prayer meeting always lacks fire if it lacks prayer. Only at the altar of God can our cold hearts be set aflame. Neither verse-reading, speech-making, quotations, music, nor machinery can take the place of prayer.

Third. In no better way can the committee promote the spiritual welfare of the society than by distributing books upon the nature, the power, and the form of prayer. I recommend Phelps's "Still Hour," and "Guidance in Prayer," for sale by the United Society. I have studied to my own profit Dr. John Hall's "Family Prayers," and the prayers of George Dawson, a famous English preacher.

Fourth. The committee must help the leader. Nothing will encourage a leader more than to know that he has half a dozen persons who stand ready to do anything they are able to do by way of preparation, and anything which the Spirit may prompt them to do,—to pray, testify, or expound a verse of Scripture,—in the progress of the meeting.

Fifth. They must seek to develop the latent talent of the society. Here is one of the best opportunities for judicious work. The best meetings are not those in which some attraction is offered, but those in which each member does something himself to honor Christ.

Sixth. Make much of special occasions. I would name especially Easter, Thanksgiving, Christmas, and the New Year, but above all, the regular monthly missionary meeting. Occasionally have a praise meeting, a memory verse meeting, or a promise meeting.

Seventh. Extend the influence of the society by means of cottage prayer meetings. This form of work has been most helpfully carried on through my own society.

Eighth. Induce members to take part in the regular church prayer meeting. Indeed, this is the natural result which we ought to expect; but there are many who need much encouragement. The Prayer-Meeting Committee can co-operate with the pastor to bring this about.

Ninth. Co-operate with the other committees of the society. We are all parts of the same society, working for the same end; therefore let us always have harmony and a living, active co-operation.

Tenth. Advertise the meetings. Make much of the meetings of the society in the Sunday school and the church. Interest the church, as well as the outside world, in what is taking place in our society.

I am glad my topic emphasizes the *doing* of things. It is often a great evil to make much of the *plan*, and much of *how* to do things, and then leave the things *undone*. Many attempt great things, but few persevere. " Many go out into the wilderness, but few come into the promised land."

Upon the base of Raikes's monument, on the Thames embankment in London, are engraven his own memorable words concerning the time when he began the first Sunday school for the ragged boys of Gloucester : " I said, ' Can anything be done?' A voice said, ' Try!' I did try, and, lo! what hath God wrought ! "

O ye young people who are charged with the oversight of the Christian Endeavor prayer meetings, in the name and by the strength of God, " try!" And I am sure, if you persevere, you too will be able to say, " Lo! what hath God wrought ! "

The next speaker was the Rev. T. H. Hanna, Jr., of Steubenville, O. His subject was " Ten of the Best Things that Can Be Done by the Lookout Committee."

Address by Rev. T. H. Hanna, Jr.,
Steubenville, O.

TEN BEST THINGS FOR THE LOOKOUT COMMITTEE TO DO.

First. The first best thing for the Lookout Committee to do is to *look in*. As I understand it, the Lookout Committee, without any presumptuous meddling, has the spiritual oversight of the entire society; and that there may not be a disastrous leading of the blind by the blind, the members ought to examine themselves.

St. Francis, the pious monk of Assisi, so the story runs, once stepped into the cloisters of his monastery, and, laying his hand upon the shoulder of a young novitiate, said, " Brother, let us go down into the town and preach." And they walked down the hillside, through the principal streets, and around the alleys and byways, until they found themselves back at the monastery. Then said the disciple, " Father, when shall we begin to preach?" And Francis answered thus : " My child, we have been preaching while we were walking. We have been looked at, and our behavior has been remarked, and so we have delivered a morning sermon. Ah, my son, it is of no use that we walk anywhere to preach unless we preach as we walk."

Fellow members of the Lookout Committee, our activities will be of little avail — they will be worse than useless — unless they are backed up by the testimony of our workaday lives.

Second. The second best thing for the Lookout Committee to do is to *look up*. By that I mean they ought to be men and women of prayer — not merely opening their meetings with a brief petition, but men and women who in secret have " the gift of the knees."

It is told of a Christian mission that it built on the borders of its settlement a small prayer house, bare of all furnishings save a Bible and a chair and a table, to which the missionaries might resort for private devotions. A path was soon worn from the village to this mercy-seat, and God richly blessed their efforts. But by and by ill times came to the mission; strife sprung up; the workers lost their power with the heathen; and the anxious church at home wondered why, until a former member of the mission, who had known it only in its forceful days, returned, and pointing to the rank grass and weeds that overgrew the path to the place of prayer, he said, " There, brethren, is the reason for the sad and shameful history you have been making."

Christian friends, it is a lack of prayer that makes our work so fruitless. Now, for the altruism of our efforts.

Third. *Secure new members*. Societies, like armies, need reinforcements. Every Lookout Committee should set up a recruiting-office and enlist more volunteers. One committee I know of does this systematically by appointing among the committeemen all non-members who are eligible and desirable, and then personally soliciting them.

Fourth. *Watch old members.* Many grow careless and indifferent and may slip out of the ranks entirely. Our loss by leakage is enormous. Delinquents are a drag. They are dangerous, like derelicts at sea.

It was said of General Gomez, late Commander-in-chief of the Cuban army, that he was more inclined to take off shoulder-straps than to put them on. Perhaps we are too anxious to swell our list of new members and not careful enough to improve those we already have.

A minister said, "We have had a good revival at our church." When asked how many they took in, he replied, "Oh, we did not take in any; but we put a lot out." That is the saddest part of the Lookout Committee's work, cutting off the dead wood, but it needs to be done.

On the other hand, there are some among the old members who need assistance. A botanist not long ago discovered that a certain plant under proper environments would bloom beautifully. The poor flower had never had a chance to show what it was capable of. Some people need a little care and culture, and they may surprise us by their blossom and fruitage.

Fifth. *Look after associate members.* As Moses said to Hobab, "Come thou with us and we will do thee good . . . and thou mayest be to us instead of eyes." Use this double-barrelled argument in persuading them to become active members, — "We need you; you need us."

Sixth. *Remember the absent ones.* The Young Men's Christian Association can teach us wisdom here. The Roman Catholics can give us pointers that are valuable. Never let a member move away without following him. Let some minister in the town or city to which he goes know about him. Certificates of membership ought to be freely used One society, through its Lookout Committee, sent topic-cards and letters to all members temporarily absent, requesting that some message be sent home at least for each consecration meeting.

Seventh. *Don't have drones.* Wesley's motto, "All at it, always at it, and all together at it," ought aptly to fit our societies. To bring about this happy consummation, one Lookout Committee sends cards to each of the other committees, with names of new members. To illustrate: —

To Chairman of Tithe Committee: —

　The undersigned was recently received into our society.

Please give .... the opportunity of joining our Tenth Legion.

　　　..... ....

To Chairman of Calling Committee: —

　Will you and your helpers as soon as possible call

upon ....

　　..... ... .

Eighth. *Have an eye open for improvements.* A merchant who makes his business pay watches his stock carefully. If certain goods are not selling well he pushes them. If one form of advertising does not work he makes it more attractive. Be as alert to see needs for change in society work. We might paraphrase Pope a bit: —

> "In Christian Endeavor schemes, as fashions, the same rule will hold,
> Alike fantastic, if too new or old ;
> Be not the first by whom the new are tried,
> Nor yet the last to lay the old aside."

Ninth. *Exchange plans with other societies.* Immigration and emigration are not wholly bad, either of men or of ideas. Correspond with other committees; and even though you are not acquainted, Ruth Ashmore's spirit will not be shocked. Thus doing, you will find that some society away out in Oregon is improving the business meetings, both attendance and interest, by holding each committee in turn responsible for the success of the meeting, either by refreshments, or a novel social, or a literary and musical programme afterwards. You will learn that a society down in Florida distributes neat invitation-cards among the hotel-guests on Saturday nights. You will hear how committee reports have been improved both in quality and quantity by the Lookout Committee in a New York society having report-blanks printed, indicating in outline the items naturally expected, *et cetera.*

Tenth. Which is like unto the first and the second, *watch and pray.* No other committee needs more to follow George Herbert's advice:—

> " By all means use some time to be alone ;
> Salute thyself ; see what thy soul doth wear ;
> Dare to look in thy chest, for it is thine own,
> And tumble up and down what thou findest there."

No other committee needs more to follow the Master's advice whom Herbert loved: "Enter into thine inner chamber, and having shut thy door, pray to thy Father which is in secret."

Christian Endeavor is always right on the temperance question, and Rev. E. W. Clippenger believed in sacrificing method to establish principles. A Temperance Committee should be sober, but need not be dry.

Rev. Address by Rev. E. W. Clippenger,
Warrensburg, Mo.

THE TEN BEST THINGS THE TEMPERANCE COMMITTEE CAN DO.

These suggestions are given as the best for the average society. If directed specially to the large city society, or to the village society, they would be somewhat changed.

The weakness of our Temperance Committees is largely due to a lack of definite, specific effort. There has been too much of mere sentiment without concentrated effort for the accomplishing of some definite purpose. Hence I trust these suggestions will commend themselves to you for definite lines of work.

First. My first suggestion among the best things for this committee to do is pray. If I were asked to name the best things that any Christian Endeavor committee could do I should unhesitatingly name, among the first of them, prayer. To pray earnestly for the success of a cause demands earnest work for that cause on the part of the one praying. Hence prayer is a means of enlarging one's personal interest, stimulating his energies, and impelling him to more concentrated and consecrated effort. And further, who shall measure for us the part that God takes in all reform, and in response to the prayers of his people? Surely God's help is not small, nor his co-operation unimportant.

Second. Insist upon temperance meetings in your society from time to time, with programme specially prepared and adapted to your community. If your pastor does not preach occasionally on the subject of temperance, wait upon him as a committee, and make a special request of him, in the name of the young people of his congregation—and few pastors will refuse such a request. By all means see to it that temperance is a subject of public discussion in your church and society.

Third. Work for temperance organization both in and out of your particular church. Temperance work has been too much limited to sentiment and spasmodic effort. Organization means power. In this age every class of people who want power organize. An army fights its best battles and gives its country the most efficient service when thoroughly organized. We would never think of sending an army out to fight the nation's battles except under the most perfect organization possible; and yet our temperance advocates are scattered, disorganized, fighting independent of each other, and yet hoping to defeat man's arch enemy of to-day. I am firmly persuaded in my own mind that whenever the temperance-believing people will get together in the power of a compact organization, on that day the death-knell of the saloon will be sounded — but not till then.

Fourth. And this leads me to the next suggestion. Work for the co-operation and unity of all temperance believers. This is the vital place in our work to-day. Christian people are practically a unit in the belief that the saloon is an accursed institution and must go; but we differ among ourselves as to the method of driving it out of existence. We must learn that method is not principle. A man must never sacrifice his principle, but he can sometimes afford to sacrifice his method for the sake of a forward movement in the cause of moral reform. We must remember that high license, low license, local option, government control, prohibition, and other such are only methods in the cause of temperance reform. I stand for the prohibition method, but if I cannot get the prohibition method I will clasp hands with my community in the best method we can get. My message to temperance believers is, Get together. Get together and the victory will be ours.

Fifth. Work for the affiliation of all temperance organizations. Why should we stand apart from the Anti-Saloon League, when they are striving to bring about the very thing we desire? Why should we leave the Women's Christian Temperance Union to fight their battle single-handed while we fight single-handed in the same community and for the same cause? More brotherhood between temperance organizations. More united and harmonious efforts in our common cause.

Sixth. Seek to enlist the sympathy and effort of influential men and women in the special incidents and opportunities arising in your community. There is no soul without influence, and by tactful, judicious effort one may be able to influence some of the most influential men and women in a city. The politician who wants the support of influential men not only studies his man, but also the best man to approach him. The saloon-keeper seldom asks favors of the community in a personal, direct manner, but rather he works through other parties who represent more than he does. A Christian Endeavorer, working for the accomplishment of a definite, specific object, can often multiply his personal influence a hundred-fold by working through other parties.

Seventh. Make a wise use of temperance literature. Study men and women and study temperance literature in order to meet particular cases. A little temperance tract of the right kind often represents more influence than an hour of argument; indeed, the Temperance Committee can clasp hands here with the Good-Literature Committee by seeking to place particular articles in the hands of special parties. I have seen this tried with good results.

Eighth. Dare to do personal work with some soul already cursed with drink. Through the personal work will come the largest blessing both to you and to the one for whom you are working. Too often we shrink from the men or women who have taken a false step, instead of giving them the love and counsel of a true Christian spirit. There are men in the gutter to-day and women in the brothel who would be known as upright and honorable citizens if some soul had taken a personal interest in them and made them see a Saviour's love in their kind and noble actions.

Ninth. Study the temperance laws of your State and work for their enforcement in your community. The temperance laws of every State in the Union are better than their enforcement. The officers of a community ordinarily follow the general sentiment of the people rather than the technical enforcement of law. By our silence in these matters we often give false impressions of public sentiment. Saloon licenses are constantly being granted which could not be given if even a few citizens knew something about the temperance laws of their State and really demanded their enforcement.

Tenth. Agitate, and keep on agitating. Don't slumber in indifference, nor let anybody else slumber. Agitation is a means of wholesome education; and education is essential to progress. Make people think about temperance. Make people see its accompanying evils. Force them to take sides either for or against. Let the people know where you stand; stand square, and then make it warm for the fellow who does n't stand square with you.

The Social Committee appeals strongly to young people. If the society does not provide one, the young people are likely to form a number, of two members each. Rev. A. C. Miller, D. D., believed that the Social Committee should steer between the rocks of moroseness and the quicksands of silly levity.

Address by Rev. A. C. Miller, D.D.,
Plymouth, Ohio.

, TEN OF THE BEST THINGS THAT CAN BE DONE BY THE SOCIAL COMMITTEE.

Before the best things to be done by any committee can be enumerated, the necessity of having a wisely selected committee should be emphasized. A Prayer-Meeting Committee should be a praying committee. A Music Committee should be a musical committee. A Lookout Committee should be a committee with spiritual eyesight. So the Social Committee should be composed of members who by nature and culture are equipped for their specific work. Adaptability should be thoughtfully considered. Being precedes doing. What the committee is is more important than what a committee does, just as character outranks deeds.

First. The members of the Social Committee should consider the serious character of their work and the responsibility assumed. The one supreme object in the mind of the ideal Social Committee is expressed in the words, "Socials to Save." Any lower standard than this will not fill the requirement. In order that precious souls may be won to Christ the Social Committee has been given birth. Its essential qualifications are those of a soul-winner. Only that Endeavorer who appreciates the value of an immortal soul is equipped for service in this capacity.

Second. Feeling the glad burden of responsibility, the next step is devotement. This implies dedication of the heart to God, and devotion of talents to the work.

Third. Walk with Christ. That means harmony with God, looking upon the great issues of life as God views them. In "The Tempest" Shakespeare makes Ferdinand and Miranda fall in love at first meeting. A glance and they "changed eyes." The true Christian worker changes eyes with God. As a result he becomes Christlike. Then his social touch, like that of his Master, becomes a benediction. All of life is sacred. The heart beats in sympathy with the holy purpose of God. To him every human soul is a valued jewel for heaven's diadem.

Fourth. Prayer and Bible-study. Contact with God precedes contact with souls. When taught by the Holy Ghost in the Quiet Hour the Christian can go forth with a sanctified presence and a heavenly touch. He sits at the feet of Jesus and learns his will and studies his methods.

Fifth. Be cheerful and optimistic, avoiding foolish frivolity. Then there will be no need of borrowing a smile that will not fit the face. A Xantippe at home and a smiling Christian Endeavorer at church or in society is an incongruity. The Social Committee, above all others, should "scatter smiles and sunshine." He is a wise Endeavorer who by cheerful conversation and happy manner, "steers between the dark rocks of moroseness and the quicksands of silly levity."

Sixth. Show special regard and consideration for the older people. While this is the age in which youth is prominent,—the golden age of which the prophet speaks when he says, " Your daughters shall prophesy, and your young men shall see visions,"— this heritage is due to the devotedness and sacrifice of the fathers and mothers. Endeavorers, " Don't forget the old folks." While winning the young, carry cheer and comfort to the hearts of the old soldiers of the cross.

Seventh. Be social as a Christian and not as a committeeman. Avoid official air or bearing. The only badge needed is a heart full of holy love. Be your own Christian self. Do not wear the blue coat and brass buttons of official dignity, which means, " I am a member of the Social Committee of the Christian Endeavor Society, and it is my official duty to greet you and shake hands with you." A great heart is a leading qualification for the social Endeavorer. This will keep him close to souls. Bear in mind that you must stand by the stream to fish.

Eighth. Share responsibility by a division of labor. This should be arranged in the committee meeting. These meetings should be regularly held. The work should be gone over carefully and prayerfully, and the needs considered, even to individual cases : but certain details should not be reported outside of the committee meeting.

Ninth. Have social gatherings with distinct Christian Endeavor earmarks. There ought to be no imitation of the social functions of the world. All should feel a pervading atmosphere of purity and holiness. Christian Endeavor socials should inspire lofty ideals. And as ideals lead mankind, these socials may lead to a higher and nobler life. The sweet, helpful, and inspiring touch of humanity is not enjoyed without the intermingling of people. Hence the need of social gatherings.

Tenth. Be tactful. Use sanctified common sense in approaching friends and strangers. Never make an assault upon any one. Make the stranger in your community feel at home. Be a panacea for homesickness. Above all, keep in mind that the true aim of the Social Committee is to introduce souls to Christ.

And finally, " Whether, therefore, we eat or drink, or whatsoever we do, let us do all to the glory of God," remembering that " they that turn many to righteousness shall shine as stars forever and ever."

Mr. Vickrey, one of the famous Yale Mission Band, believes with all his heart that the monthly meeting can be made the most interesting meeting of the society ; and those who heard him carried away note-books full of such happy suggestions as that a postage-stamp a day for missions is better than a check for a thousand dollars at the end of the year.

Address by Mr. C. V. Vickrey,

Bartley, Neb.

THE TEN BEST THINGS FOR A MISSIONARY COMMITTEE.

First. Make free use of the missionary headquarters of this Convention, located in the High School Building.

Second. Organize the committee, placing definite responsibility on each,— chairman, treasurer, secretary, librarian, missionary meetings, etc.

Third. Read, study, and master books on methods of missionary work; e. g., Park's book on " Methods," Miss Brain's " Fuel for Missionary Fires," etc.

Fourth. Use the " Missionary Prayer Cycle " in the weekly devotional meeting, copy to be had of the United Society.

Fifth. Study and pray to make the monthly missionary meeting the most interesting and helpful of the entire month.

Sixth. Plant missionary literature freely, (a) by securing subscriptions for the denominational missionary papers and magazines: (b) by distributing, selling, and loaning missionary pamphlets and books.

Seventh. Have a monthly committee meeting, much of the time to be spent in prayer for the guidance and the power of the Holy Spirit in the work.

Eighth. Organize a missionary-study class or reading-circle.

Ninth. By tactful, prayerful, persistent, personal canvass, secure systematic giving for missions from every member of the society.

Tenth. Co-operate with the pastor in the diffusing of missionary spirit throughout the entire church, acting as the pastor's assisting committee in the distribution of literature; canvass for systematic giving and collection of subscriptions.

It fairly thrills one to think of the latent power of our Young People's Societies. Has it ever occurred to you that if your society, by a personal canvass, was to secure an average of a postage-stamp per day from each of your six hundred church-members, it would mean the support of six American missionaries who otherwise could never be sent to the fields? It would mean eternal life to scores and perhaps thousands who could never have heard the story of love had it not been for the power of God working through you.

We missionary committeemen may not be able to go to the fields ourselves, but in answer to prayer God will use us and make us instrumental in securing the support of perhaps half a dozen missionaries, which may be a great deal better than if we went to the field in person.

We admire such men as Judson, Carey, Livingstone, and Paton. Our blood warms at the very mention of their names, and yet it may be that God has opened the way for your Missionary Committee, through prayer, to send not one, but two or three or four such servants to the field. When God invites to large service let us not insist upon our present two-penny methods of playing at this work.

> " Attempt great things for God.
> Expect great things of God."

When the Hampton Quartette sang " De ol' ark 's a-rollin' " " the audience burst forth into tumultuous applause over the prophetic announcement, " De rain, it subsided."

" The great danger of the consecration meeting," said Rev. A. C. Kempton, "is that each meeting shall be so like the one before it and the one after it that a rut will be worn as deep as a grave."

Address by Rev. Arthur C. Kempton,
Janesville, Wis.

THE BEST CONSECRATION MEETING.

The consecration meeting has been called "Our Crowning Meeting." It should be our crowning meeting in that it is *the best meeting* of the month. It should be our crowning meeting in that it places the crown of consecration upon the brow of every member. It should be our crowning meeting in that it crowns Christ the King of every life. Hundson Taylor says, "Crown him, crown him Lord of all. If you do not crown him Lord of *all*, you do not crown him Lord at all."

Three things are essential in the best consecration meeting : —

First. *The best consecration meeting must have a leader who understands what consecration means.* We sometimes think that any one can lead the consecration meeting, for all that he must do is to preside while the secretary reads the roll. A greater blunder could not be made. The "crowning meeting" has a right to claim as leaders the spiritual kings and queens of the society. Upon the leader depends almost entirely the success of the meeting. He should come fresh from "the secret place of the Most High," where he has been face to face with the great King; he should come with the dew of the Gethsemane of prayer sparkling upon his garments; he should come with the crown of consecration in his own hand, that he may place it upon the brow of others; he should come with a deep spirituality manifesting itself, not in many words, but in such a spirit of reverence that every word will be transfigured, every act become a prayer.

With such a leader the flippant response at roll-call, "Want to be re-consecrated"—uttered, as has been said, with no more serious feeling than if one should remark, "Want a glass of soda-water," and indeed a fit type of such religion, all froth and bubbly with emptiness—will seldom be heard. In place of it, testimony and prayer will be uttered as in the very presence of Christ himself, and even the most careless will somehow feel that the Master is most surely present.

Again, the best consecration meeting must be different from the one preceding it and different from the one that follows. Variety is essential to success. The danger is that all consecration meetings will be alike, until the ruts become as deep as graves, and all spirituality is buried in them. Instead of the crowning meeting, it thus becomes the crownless meeting. Let me hint at some ways in which variety may be gained.

Have an Alphabet Meeting. Ask all whose names begin with "A" to rise, calling on each one for some response. Then, those whose names begin with "B," and so on through the alphabet, interspersing the testimonies with singing.

Have a Birthday Meeting, referring not to the time when first they were born, but to the time when they were "born again." Ask all who have been born again within one year to rise; then those within five years, ten, twenty; perhaps at last some old patriarch of fifty years will inspire all with a testimony of God's faithfulness through a lifetime.

Have an All-Prayer Meeting. Let the whole time be taken up in prayer, the secretary calling the names of three or four at once, the prayers to be followed by hymns of prayer. A meeting of this kind will frequently open the doorway of the "holy of holies."

Have a Definite Consecration Meeting, asking each one in his testimony to pledge himself to consecrated service in some special work during the coming month.

Have a Consecration Meeting of Confession, at which members will be encouraged to frankly confess where they have broken the letter or the spirit of the pledge, asking forgiveness of the society and of God.

Above all, have variety in every meeting. Never allow anything to drag. Always have some surprise in reserve. At unexpected moments introduce concert features, such as the Lord's prayer, twenty-third Psalm, repeating a hymn instead of singing it, or silent prayer. Occasionally have a "Silent Moment," when with bowed heads all will silently consecrate themselves to God. To give such variety in consecration meetings will require both planning and praying.

Thirdly, and most important of all, *the best consecration meeting is the meeting that brings all present face to face with Christ.* It matters not how it is done. A meeting may have all else, but without this it will be a failure; a meeting may lack all else, but with this it will be the "best." To accomplish this purpose all should unite. Leaders, singers, officers, secretaries, committees, ALL, should be ready to drop out of sight themselves that they may reveal Christ.

One afternoon in the National Art Gallery, London, I had searched in vain for the famous painting of Christ by Murillo, until at last I went to one of the ushers, who took me to a locked room, and lifting a heavy veil that hung over a picture he stepped back, without a word, and left me face to face with the Christ. The best consecration meeting is the meeting that takes us into the "secret place of the Most High," and leaves the soul face to face with its Master.

The open parliament to discuss "The Best Thing Your Society Ever Did" was conducted by Mr. A. G. Leffingwell, Appleton, Wis., who said, "The Convention has had the ideal presented by speakers; now we want to know what the best things are that have been accomplished in your society."

A Chicago Christian Endeavor society had brought over fifty into their church last year. A Pennsylvania society, with one hundred members, had subscribed $200 for missions the last year. West Virginia had founded three Junior societies in the State Reform School. An Ohio society is supporting a Bible woman in Japan. Bridgeport, Conn., had sent two missionaries to India and is supporting one of them. Bay City had established a mission Sunday school, which is a great success. Mt. Vernon, N. Y., is holding services among the Chinese. Warren Avenue Congregational Christian Endeavor Society is supporting two native field missionaries in India. Kansas, Illinois, Indiana, Tennessee, and other States reported also, many of them receiving hearty applause for the good stories they told.

Then came the " snap-shots," by prominent delegates. The first, " The Best Secretary," by Miss Jennie T. Masson, State secretary of the Indiana society.

Address by Miss Jennie T. Masson,

Indianapolis, Ind.

THE BEST SECRETARY.

The corresponding secretary is the connecting link between the society and its denominational headquarters, the United Society, the state, district, and county unions.

The best secretary is like the shirt-waist,— he fills a long-felt want; he has come to stay, if not forever, at least for a long time; he adds much to the comfort of his society and the aforementioned headquarters and unions.

The best secretary writes a hand you can read without calling in the assistance of your family. He understands that prompt replies are indicative of good breeding and kindness of heart. When called upon for information that it takes time to secure, he at once sends the inquirer a postal-card expressing his determination to furnish the information as soon as obtained.

He is a blank-receiver, blank-filler, and blank-returner. Blank is here used in a legitimate way. Secretaries will understand. On this subject, I once had a letter from a " best secretary." It read:—

Dear State Secretary: — I always try to fill all the blanks sent me, but I have a vague idea I have omitted one sent by you for some purpose. I have filled about a peck. I love to do it. If you have one you want me to fill, I will be glad to do it.
                                   Yours sincerely,

The best secretary, you see, is cheerful even if it pours when it rains. Right here is the place to observe that the best secretary is doing his best to teach the various Christian Endeavor Unions not to waste their substance in riotous sending-out of blanks for statistics. He knows that a blank filled once a year by a society can be made to do for county, district, state, and international convention reports.

Saint Paul appointed Phœbe corresponding secretary to the church at Rome, and gave a recipe for making the best secretary. To that society he said, " I commend unto you Phœbe, our sister (the best secretary comes well recommended), which is a servant of the church at Cenchrea (the best secretary is an active church-member). She hath been a succorer of many, and of myself " (the best secretary is one who likes to help people, especially the pastor).

General Secretary Paul says further regarding the corresponding secretary, " Receive her in the Lord as becometh saints." The best secretary is made so largely by the treatment of the society. To " blow up " the secretary, as some phrase it, and as many seem to delight to do, is not going to make him better. Besides, "blowing up" the secretary is not receiving him as becometh saints. Saintly conduct toward him is to know his name, to remember him in prayer, to recognize him in business meeting by calling for his report, to introduce him in social meetings by his official title.

Paul finishes this recipe for a best secretary by adding, " Assist her in whatsoever business she hath need of you." The best secretary has much business. He needs the expressed interest of the pastor. She needs the judgment of the president to help decide what communications and how much of same shall take up the time of the society in presentation. She needs always to have her name published in list of officers on the topic-cards. She needs to be supported in her resolution never to permit the list of members to be used by advertising schemers. He needs to be invited to the meetings of the various committees, so as to be well enough informed regarding their work to tell to those who ask by letter for helpful suggestions from his society, and to keep the society in touch with the various departments of Christian Endeavor. In order to give dignity and authority to her correspondence. she needs postage and the society's official stationery.

He needs the expressed interest of individual members in such queries as, " Will you be able to announce the mass-meeting of the Local Union to-night?" or, " Have we received information this week regarding the District Convention?" or, " What is the latest news from Boston?" or, " Will you please send an account of our last unique and interesting missionary meeting to *The Christian Endeavor World?*" or, " Can I help you on your report to the State secretary?" etc.

I notice that in this talk I have used the pronouns " he " and " she " indiscriminately. That is all right. The best secretary may be just " a little lower than the angels; " that is, he may be a man; or she may be the next thing to an angel; that is, a woman.

Rev. J. F. Cowan, D.D., of Boston, one of the associate editors of *The Christian Endeavor World*, spoke for a few minutes upon " The Best Information Committee." In opening he said that there are some Information Committees that should be informed, others that should be reformed, and others that should be deformed.

" Good Information Committees are scarce. The duty of a good Information Committee is to inform and demonstrate to the societies what is going on in Christian Endeavor. It is not the duty of an Information Committee to get up in meetings and read pretty poems, nor to read a two-column newspaper-article to the society; but the true duty of such a committee is to select the most interesting bits of news and dish them up so that they will please the palates of the members of the society and make them wish for more. It is my advice that the members of the society read good religious papers and keep in touch with the other parts of the Christian Endeavor world. If every member of the society would do this there would be no need for Information Committees. Now, some Information Committees take any old thing in the shape of news and dish it up to the society. This sort of thing is not right, for, in time, it will debilitate the society."

The chairman announced, with deep regret, that two of the prominent Endeavorers who were to have spoken, Mr. George McDonald, of Altoona, Pa., and Mr. A. E. MacDonald, of Chicago, were unable to attend the meeting. Mr. A. E. MacDonald sent his paper upon " The Best Executive Committee," and it is herewith printed.

Address by A. E. MacDonald,

Chicago, Ill.

THE BEST EXECUTIVE COMMITTEE.

The best Executive Committee is one that executes. The nature of its work and its make-up, being composed of the officers and chairmen of all the other committees,—the picked people of the society,— make it a very important committee.

Its business is to plan and map out the work for the society to do and *see that it is done*, not *do it*, mark you.

An ideal Executive Committee should have as its motto " We will do nothing ourselves which we can get others to do, but all we plan as necessary to be done for the best good of the society must be done." It requires a much higher type of mind, a greater ability, to set ten people to work and keep them at it than to do the work alone that these ten would do, and it is much better for the ten or eleven to have all share in the work.

The best Executive Committee has a regular time for meeting. It ought to be as often as once a month. In large societies I believe it ought to meet once a week for a few minutes (besides its monthly meeting) at the close of or just before the weekly Christian Endeavor prayer meeting.

The president of the society is of course, *ex-officio*, the presiding officer, and he should be the *de facto* presiding officer. He should have and hold the committee well in hand, conduct the meeting in a business-like manner, have matters taken up and discussed orderly and expeditiously, and hold the members to the discussion of the question. I believe in having a regular order of business,—in having each person address the chair, and not speak till recognized thereby. It is best to require each officer and chairman of a committee to have his report in writing at the monthly meeting of the Executive Committee. He will then have matters arranged in shape and be ready to present and discuss his report intelligently, and the others will be able to understand what is wanted or needed.

While I believe in conducting the business matters of the Executive Committee in a business-like way, I would give place for informal discussion and conversation bearing upon the question under consideration, and would *always* have a time in *every* meeting of the Executive Committee for a season of prayer, either at the opening or the close — not one formal opening and closing prayer, but a season of prayer, usually for some specific purpose suggested by some point that has come up during the session, or for a spiritual awakening among the members, a greater devotional spirit, more power in prayer, a consciousness of the Holy Spirit's presence, or along some such line. Such a service, participated in by every member of the committee, all kneeling throughout, cannot but result in profit and spiritual growth on the part of each person present; and its influence will be felt throughout all the committees, as it will be carried away by the chairmen, and so will permeate the whole membership of the society; for when the leaders are deeply spiritual it will have a wholesome effect upon the society as a whole.

One other point: I have a conviction that is wise to take up, after the reports have been discussed and disposed of, some topic at each meeting of the Executive Committee for discussion, such as " Our Prayer Meetings; How Can We Improve Them?" "The Quiet Hour in Our Society," "How To Develop More of a Missionary Spirit Among Our Members." Such topics are profitable for consideration because they are of practical application and will bear fruit in the greater fidelity and earnestness of the individual Endeavorers of your society.

Another thought that I wish to emphasize is that the president, while he is the head of, is not the whole Executive Committee, and should not *run* the committee, but should be the leader and direct the work and see that the others do their part.

My last point is that it is the duty of this committee to discharge from office any officer or member of a committee who is unfaithful in the performance of his duty, or who neglects his work to the extent that he practically does nothing and makes no effort to. A committee is recreant to its trust that allows such a person to continue in office.

"Seconds," in trade parlance, do not go with Christian Endeavor. "Don't Be Satisfied with Second Best," interpreted by Rev. J. H. O. Smith, meant what the color-bearer did when he said to his colonel, "I'll bring back the colors or report to God."

Address by Rev. J. H. O. Smith,
Chicago, Ill.
DON'T BE SATISFIED WITH SECOND BEST.
In the name of our God we will set up our banners.—Ps. xx. 5.

A sarcastic woman once remarked, "Man's first desire is to *eat*; his second and last desire is to *beat*." "Me first" is not shouted alone upon the playground, but its ominous echo is heard in church and state, often relegating honest men to obscurity and condemning real excellence to the stake.

Every well-poised soul possesses an inherent ambition to excel, which, wrongly used, "grows to an envious fever of pale and bloodless emulation."

Whether ambition is a blessing or a curse depends upon the ideal. There is a battle of the standards — God's banners arrayed against human standards. "Don't be satisfied with second best" is not, I take it, an exhortation to emulate or excel the victories of others. Spiritual egotism is more insufferable in the church than flagrant worldliness.

The Lord Jesus Christ has a programme for every life, every Endeavor society, every church, every nation, and every world. When brought to judgment, the burning question will be, Have we followed the programme — have we builded according to the plans and specifications in the mind of the Master? In that great day God may show us the life we might have lived — the work our society might have done: and because his hungry heart was unfed, his thirsty soul cried unheard to us for drink, and behind prison-bars he begged in vain for a friendly visit; because he turned his weary eyes for sympathy in sickness, and, through humanity's need, pleaded in vain, like angel strumpet-tongued; — because we neglected these easy opportunities behind which Christ was waiting for our coming, we neglected the only opportunity we will have throughout eternity to know Him whom to know aright is life eternal.

> "Of all sad words of tongue or pen,
> The saddest are these: It might have been."

God so loved the world that he gave you, his child, to serve it, and you fail, or fall below the divine intention for your life!

Dissatisfaction with second best in an Endeavor society does not mean a contest for supremacy above the societies of your town or city; not a struggle for members and social influence; not a contest for the greatest number of testimonies in a given time, or a banner in a Christian Endeavor rally, or even the greatest enthusiasm in committee work, as the sole object of our endeavor. No; God so loved the world that he organized your Endeavor society and put it into a community where human need extends its withered hand for help, and you pass on singing,

> "Onward, Christian soldier,
> Marching as to war!"

and heed not the skeleton fingers clutching at your saintly robes begging for the bread of life.

What was the indictment against the strangers to the king? They had prophesied in his name, had cast out devils, and in his name had done many wonderful works. They had not done the Father's will. His will for ourselves and for our society is best. To substitute something else, even second best—is it not idolatry? The struggle is not between individual workers or societies, but between God's ideal and our actual character and conduct. In recognition of this sublime truth our pledge reads, "Trusting in the Lord Jesus Christ for strength, I promise him I will strive to do whatever he would like to have me do." That is the measure of responsibility and duty; but the battle of the standards goes on between the programme as he would like it and the programme as we would like it.

In the Civil War a boy eighteen years old was made color-bearer of his regiment. The colonel, in presenting the flag, said, "Take this flag, fight for, it, die for it, but never surrender it to the enemy." The intelligent, heroic face of the boy lighted up with a great resolve as he replied, "Colonel, I'll bring back this flag with honor or report to God the reason why." In an awful battle he went down with a bullet through his heart, and the colors fell across his breast. He did not bring back the flag, but his comrades and God Almighty knew the reason why. It was one which he could conscientiously give to his Lord and Master. In the name of God hold up his standard in your society, or report in the hour of death from your post of duty the reason.

John said, "I saw the dead, small and great, standing before God." Can we not see to-day the dear young people and Endeavor societies facing—the twentieth century? No! facing God and eternity. God stands within the shadows, waiting for his legions. The question when we stand at the grave, the gateway of time, will not be, Have we accumulated a fortune or won a name which the world applauds? but, Have we disappointed God? To be satisfied with second best is to disappoint the Master. He will make due allowance for imperfection. He does not expect impossible, but reasonable, service. First in the sight of God does not always mean first in the opinion of men. The one-talented Endeavorer striving for the Master's ideal may lift the world nearer God than the splendid five-talented man conspicuous only by his commanding ability.

In the country community where I was reared the dear old church nestled by the roadside in the edge of a forest. For many years the light of love burned brightly on its altar; but adversity came, followed by indifference and neglect. One snowy Sunday morning a motherless girl, who worked in a farmer's kitchen, completed her morning task, and with her Bible under her arm started down the unbroken road toward the church. A man, once an active member of the church, looking across the fields, saw her try one of the doors only to find it locked. She waded to the other door—in vain. All was silence and desolation. Then the patient, uncrowned daughter of a King dropped upon her knees in the snow, turned her wistful face toward heaven, and in silent prayer poured out her heart to Him whose hand was not shortened that it could not save nor his ear heavy that it could not hear. Then she returned home. No one heard a word of complaint. She had done the best she could and God did the rest. The solitary witness of this church service in the snow noised the matter throughout the neighborhood; strong men wept; a meeting was called and a pledge recorded that the doors of that church should never again be closed upon the Lord's Day. The whispered prayer of the humble girl was answered in a revival. More depends upon obscure workers than upon many who are more prominent. In our national cemeteries thousands of graves are marked with the simple word "Unknown," yet these unknown heroes have made American valor illustrious around the world. Your humble life of duty God will weave into the splendors of his plan.

"First best" with men means some lonely, lofty position toward which we struggle and climb and finally attain only when we have pulled down and crushed the last proud victor in the race. Men look down upon the masses. God dwells with them, suffers with them, leads them one by one to victory. We are too willing to worship in a temple made with hands, its gleaming marble cold with our philosophies, its fretted gold ablaze with our vain theories.

When the veil of this temple is rent in twain we stand face to face with God's ideal, and then we realize our individual responsibility. Once innocent blood was upon the hands of a king, and a deeper crimson stained the robes of

Israel's royalty. The princely hero of an hundred battles had gone down before the marshalled passions of his own guilty soul, and now uncrowned, unsceptred, in the sight of God had fallen face downward in the dust. Was it the sudden crash of a sycamore, rent by the forked lightning, or was it the sullen fall of the forest oak, hollow with slow decay? Was it a swift yielding to awful temptation, or one more concession to the besetting sin, creeping upon him like a panther, velvet-shod? It matters not; somewhere in his lofty career his heart had departed from God's programme for the king, and that heart of gold, once purified in the flames of persecution, once steadfast in the hour of tempting ambition, now carried a fearful secret whose dread unrest would haunt him forevermore. The prophet of God, anticipating the judgment-day, sketched David's real character, and the king said, "The man that hath done this thing shall surely die." "Thou art the man" swept away spin-thin-ian philosophy and left the cowering king face to face with God's ideal — the individual alone with his Creator. In the Gethsemane of repentance the rebel died and the broken-hearted king of Israel accepted once more God's programme for his life.

There may be terror in the thought of individual responsibility, but there is also comfort and true inspiration. It makes men brave. "Every one of us must give an account of himself to *God*," said Paul to the subjects of powerful Nero. It makes men loyal to conviction. "We cannot but speak the things we have seen and heard." "We will obey God rather than man," said loyal Peter. Once catch the vision of God's ideal for your individual life, and it is not so difficult to be faithful unto death. No second best is good enough for you,— no second best can atone for one sad, disappointed look upon the Master's face. In angry old Jerusalem a man once stood before a council — a tender, loving man, yet fearless, stern, uncompromising. Quietly he faced his perjured accusers. Angry faces, flinty stones, and flintier hearts surrounded him. Powerful arms were already bared of outer garments, that were laid at the feet of a stern-faced, attentive listener. His life hung by a thread as he began his defence: "Men, *brethren* and *fathers*, hearken!" That is a gentle beginning. O Stephen, thou wilt be careful! Thou wilt be satisfied to conciliate thine enemies until thy life is out of jeopardy! Listen! His gentle voice is rising. Down through the history of Israel he sweeps his puzzled auditors rapidly, vividly, his voice accumulating ominous thunder and his eyes flashing the lightning of a great purpose. Beware, Stephen! The wrath of Judah's mob means death. There stands *one* man in that fierce audience in whom are centred the daring, the perseverance, the fierce loyalty to conviction, of all thy chosen race of kings and prophets. He is listening to you. Your gathering eloquence is burning into his brain, but he is *against* you. Hold back the denunciation already whirling from thy tongue. For once be satisfied with second best, for Saul of Tarsus is thy judge — a glorious friend, a terrible foe! But thy face is the face of an angel, radiant from the bursting vision. What matters death, to thee, for the *truth* has been spoken.—has gone straight from thy lips to the mark,— tearing through and through the bleeding, but still rebellious, heart of Saul of Tarsus? "First best," Stephen, in thy dying coronation. "First best," Saul of Tarsus, when later on thy blinded eyes shall behold thy vision,— God's ideal for *thee*.

As churches, as denominations, let us not be satisfied with second best. Second best means sectarian emulation that has wrung the heart of God from Calvary to the year of our Lord 1899. "*We* have a law," and the man must die. That woful spirit rent the church and held rival diets and conclaves. It lighted the fire-brand of persecution, and hunted God's ideal from the caves of Switzerland along the lovely Rhine, through shrieking France and shuddering Spain, over the plains of England, across the ocean, and even up and down our fair New England hills.

Infidelity laughs to-day, while sanctimonious egotism counts noses and gloats over false church statistics. If the lost ever laugh, hell must echo with ghoulish glee when sectarian emulation lays its grasping clutches upon the fresh young hearts and Christlike resolves of our *young people*, ordering them back from the conquest of the world, bidding them break step with the onward march of endeavor, and commanding them to train their guns upon each other. We have had enough of sectarian emulation.

Don't be satisfied with second best when God's ideal for the church is before you. "On this rock I will build *my* church, and the gates of hell shall not prevail against it," said the Master. There it stands, its stones set with fair colors,—its plans and specifications, its ordinances and observances, its creed, and its rules of faith and practice. He who runs may read the inspired description of God's ideal church.

Look away from your piles of brick and stone! Look away from your proud church history and long church rolls ! Nay, you can afford to look away even from your great missionary records to God's ideal church government, his ideal of self-sacrifice, his ideal of world-wide evangelization.

Study it! Strive for it! Suffer for it! Sacrifice pride and prejudice; consecrate time and talent toward it! Second best means strife and emulation, disappointment and delay. Second best means sorrow in heaven. *First best* means the church for which Christ prayed. *First best* means Christian union and the world for Christ.

We still see through a glass darkly, but the vision grows upon us. The eyes of our young people, the church of the future, are steadfastly fixed upon the great ideal. The nations of the earth are making ready for the Church Universal. The banner of Christ encircles the globe, and powers and potentates recognize our King of kings and Lord of lords.

When the autocrat of all the Russias called the Peace Conference at The Hague, he wrote at the head of the famous document, "Anno Domini,—In the year of our Lord,—1899." The mighty empire who has stretched her shaggy length across all Europe; who, as has been said, "Moves down the map of the world as the glacier moves down the Alps, patient and relentless, startling the jealous rivals that watch its course, and granting contemptuous peace to the allies that shiver in its shadow"—Russia crouched for one moment at the feet of her Lord and her banner went down before the standard of the King of kings. Her old foe Germany received the message—Germany, who bows to no ecclesiastical potentate. Her emperor began his answer of acceptance, "Anno Domini,—in the year of Germany's Lord,—1899," and the banner of the Fatherland went down before the banner of the Prince of Peace.

France received the call of Russia — troubled France, who once refused to write her Anno Domini, who established a date of her own, and thus threw down her gauntlet to the God of time and of eternity. The President of France began his reply to the old Nemesis of Napoleon, "Anno Domini, 1899," and the banner of the Fleur-de-lis went down as she laid her diadem of lilies at the feet of the King of kings and Lord of lords.

The message went across the channel to old England, who for centuries has stood like a lighthouse in the sea for the cause of Protestantism. The Christian queen wrote her reply, "Anno Domini,— the year of England's Lord,— 1899," and the mighty crest of the British Lion, reared aloft, as never before, to watch the troubled principalities of the world, was lowered submissively before the Lamb of God.

The call of the Czar came over across the sea—to America, magnanimous, a city of refuge for the world's oppressed, standing among nations for non-sectarian Christianity; America, beautiful, powerful, conscious of her strength !

Our President took up the pen,—"Anno Domini, eighteen hundred and ninety-nine,"—In the year of America's Lord, 1899. Down goes our starry banner, never lowered in the presence of foreign or domestic foe, at the feet of the King of kings and Lord of lords.

In the name of our God, International Christian Endeavor will set up its banner, the snowy standard of the Prince of Peace.

The Christian world is looking toward the ideal — God's ideal. The vision grows upon us. We see not yet all things put under him, but more and more we see Jesus, with a programme as perfect, as beautiful, as the love of God.

As nations, as churches, as societies, as individuals, we shall be satisfied only when we awake in *his* likeness.

FRIDAY AFTERNOON.

Westminster Church.
Important Conference upon Parish Problems.
Conducted by Rev. Charles M. Sheldon, Topeka, Kan.

It was a marvellous conference; not so much for what was said, though many good things were said, as for the spirit of eager inquiry, of ardent reaching out for the Christlike thing, that evidently possessed the many hundreds of ministers present. The great churchful had evidently come together, not so much for a tribute to Mr. Sheldon, though all showed how much they loved and honored him, as because they were earnestly seeking light on the great problems treated in his books.

The famous author of " In His Steps " first told, in his steady, self-effacing way that seems almost timid, how he had himself made use in his own church of that searching test and pledge, " What would Jesus do ? " first with his Endeavorers and then with their elders. He gave us many examples, from all parts of the country, of the practical carrying-out of that great principle.

Address by Rev. Charles M. Sheldon,
Topeka, Kan.

A great many ministers have written me, and some of them are here to-day I presume, asking if the story " In His Steps " had any foundation in fact, and when it was written. It had no foundation in fact whatever. It came out of the ideal, out of what I dreamed might sometime be, and there were no such places, no such people, anywhere in the wide world. Another question that has come very often which is pertinent to our topic this afternoon is whether in any of the churches we have adopted this motto, and put it into practical working shape. When that question first came to me, a year ago, I had to answer I didn't know. A great many pastors wrote me asking if my own church had adopted such a motto, and I was obliged to say no. When the story was finished, in the summer of 1896 and 1897, my young people in the Christian Endeavor Society, which is composed of a very large part of the members of the church, — my Christian Endeavor Society is composed of a hundred members, — they came to me and wanted to form an organization at once about the pledge of " What would Jesus do? " They were very eager and earnest about it, but I said to them, " Let us wait. If this thing is good it will last; if it is not, it will go back; and we don't want to do anything here hurriedly without the light of the Spirit;" and we waited a whole year. The question asked oftenest by pastors is, Is your church practising this which you preach? and finally it led me up to the point where I saw the time had come for us practically to put this question into practical shape in our own church life, and try and live it out.

One night, after the Endeavor service, I asked all those who wanted to do so to remain and talk over the matter. We have only one service in our church in the evening, and it is along the line of the topic of this afternoon, which has grown out of that pledge; and it is used in this Christian Endeavor service. In the evening we have evening service, and the young people have their own service with their own leader, just as if I was not present. I am there sometimes at the opening, or perhaps at some other time; but at the close I come in, and I talk upon the same topic they have been talking about for fifteen or twenty minutes. So on this particular evening we began this second service a little after eight o'clock. I think it was eleven o'clock before we started to go home. The young people wanted to ask a great many questions, and many of them were puzzled about the two pledges; thought that they might conflict. They said, "We have already taken one pledge, that we would try to do as Jesus would have us do. What do you mean by asking us to take the other pledge?" I tried to explain it in this way: that one pledge simply included the other, and, if I may say so, explained the other, and they see it now more clearly. I do not think there is a member in my society to-day who took the pledge to do what Jesus would do who would not say that it was an explanation of the Endeavor pledge already taken; that is, what Jesus would have them do is what he himself would do if he were in their places; and I don't think they are perplexed about that any more.

Another question they ask a great many times: "If we take this pledge, won't it oblige us to have one standard of conduct? Shall we all have to do the same thing?" Well, they found they didn't. This was illustrated in a beautiful way when the war broke out, — I may say that before the meeting closed every one of my society took the pledge; practically our whole Endeavor Society has taken that pledge.

The illustration of the difference of conduct in two Christian disciples was illustrated this way. Two young men who were among the most earnest and consecrated of my congregation, two strong, vigorous young men who were football players, came to me. One of them said, "Mr. Sheldon, I don't think I can play football any more and keep my pledge; because I cannot imagine Jesus in my place playing football." I said, "That settles it for you. If you can't do it conscientiously, you will have to get out of the team;" and he did. He was one of the best players, and all the influence of the college was brought upon him to make him play football; but he resisted that effort and has not played since. His brother came to me a few days afterwards and said. "Mr. Sheldon, I've been thinking about this matter with all solemnity, and I think I can play football, and Jesus would if he was in my place;" and he has played football, and the result of his example and the way he played football made that football team the best college football team in the State of Kansas. That team had an opportunity in Denver to make $100 if they would do a tricky thing, and they were running behind in their expenses, and there are a great many tricky things in athletics; but they refused through the influence of this young man and other young men like him.

One of the most devoted and consecrated young men I had in the Christian Endeavor Society came to me in my study one day, and he said to me, "Mr. Sheldon, it seems to me that the Lord wants me to enlist in this war: and if Jesus was in my place I believe he would go, and work among the soldier-boys in the camp, at the front on the battle-field, and take the Christian work with him." I said, "Very well. The Lord bless you. Go;" and he went. A few days afterwards another young man came in. He said, "Mr. Sheldon, I would like to go to war; I would like to enlist, but I don't think I could do it and keep my pledge. I don't think Jesus would do it." I said to him, "Why?" "Well," he said, "my motive is not the best of motives." I said, "Why do you want to enlist?" "Well," he said, "to have a good time; to have a picnic with the boys. I am tired of college. I want to get out." I said, "That motive is not strong enough, is it?" He said, "No, I can't do it;" and while he longed to be with the other boys, he stayed at home.

This illustrates the way that the young people are influenced. I notice as time goes on the young people are defining their positions more clearly every week. I may say here also in this connection that two or three weeks after the Endeavor Society had been carrying out this pledge the time seemed ripe to call upon the church to do the same thing, and at the close of the communion service a year ago last February I asked all the members of the church who were willing to take this pledge to stay at the close of the communion service. Not so large a portion of the church-members remained as at the En-

leavor Society, but I think I can say that at least two-thirds of the members
of my church have taken the pledge, and the membership is about 320.

We have this consecration service at the close of every communion service.
At the close of the service, we remained seated without the social greetings we
usually have, and go right on with this service, which centres around the
pledge " What would Jesus do ? " That service is as simple as possible. We
have nothing printed. All we say is, Are you willing to try to do just as Jesus
would do in your place regardless of the results, you college men, you business
men, you housekeepers, you clerks in the Santa Fé Railroad office ? That is
all. We talk together about our difficulties. We ask each other questions.
We give our testimony. Lately there has come to us from all over the land
testimony from disciples who have taken this pledge who send to us the results
of their pledge. For instance, here is one young man at this Convention who
tells me of a young man out West who held a responsible place at a good salary with a Denver newspaper. He was obliged to write a newspaper letter on
Saturday, which was to appear in the Sunday morning edition of the Denver
paper. He had a very large Sunday-school class, and one Sunday a great
many of the boys were late to the class, and he asked them why they were
late. They said they had to deliver the Sunday morning paper, and they
couldn't get there — that was before he had read the story. Finally he read
the story. He got mad ; he threw it on the floor and went away ; and when he
got back home he took it up and read it. Finally he said, " I cannot retain
this position if I take this pledge. " He was urged to take it. He said to himself, " There are only two things before me. I must be false to my pledge,
which I want to take, or I must keep the pledge and resign my place." And
he had a little conference there all by himself, all alone in his desert, and he
conquered ; and he gave up his place and took another at $400 less, and he is
filling that place now, and he is winning his boys "for Christ and the
Church." That is one example out of the thousands that come in. That
answers the question, Is this practical?

I want to say that pastors in a great many churches have sent word that
they are beginning to try the same thing, and I have here in my pocket now a
card given me by a brother at the door which reads, " I this day consecrate
myself to Almighty God and the service of his Son, my Lord and Redeemer,
who died to redeem me ; and with his help, I promise to do this year what
Jesus would do if he were in my place. "

This is only one out of a great many similar illustrations which have come of
the practical working of the pledge itself.

And then Mr. Sheldon opened the floodgate of questions. How they
poured in from that audience of men ! They were thoughtful, piercing
queries, questions of duty and of privilege, questions that touched the
foundations of society ; and Mr. Sheldon answered them all with rare
insight and skill. It grew into a testimony meeting, illustrating possibilities of self-sacrifice. It seemed impossible to stop it, and many
scores pressed up to Mr. Sheldon at the close with fresh questions, before
which he retreated into the vestry, and from that to the sidewalk, where
still when last we saw him, an eager crowd, that seemed as large as ever,
was besieging him.

Q. Has it ever occurred to you that there possibly might be a very large
class in this community who do not care what Jesus did, or they would embrace
him ? How do you answer this apparent indifference ?

A. I should question the truth of that question. I don't think there is a
very large class who believe that. In fact, it seems to me all over the world
men and women in every class of life are interested in Jesus and in what he
did, and in how he did it. The world to-day is more interested in Jesus, in what
he said, and what he did, than in any other topic or subject in the world.

Q. Do you believe that if the people in this city would rule their conduct by the query, What would Jesus do? the results would be a real moral uplift for humanity?

A. Why, it would turn the city bottom side up in twenty-four hours. It would revolutionize the business of this place. It would put it on a new basis. It would revolutionize the political history of this city most decidedly. It would revolutionize the journalism of this city. Can you imagine any greater revolution than would take place in this city if every man in the newspaper world would try to do as Jesus would do? It would involve revolutionizing of the churches, of families, of individual life. The millennium would dawn here to-morrow morning.

Q. Would you call Christianity a failure if after 1.800 years of effort there are still hundreds of thousands of men and women upon whom preaching has made no impression?

A. There was a while that marriage was talked of as a failure. Some marriages are: but marriage is not as an institution. Christianity is not a failure. The failure to apply it is a failure sometimes. Christianity is not itself a failure any more than Jesus is a failure. Jesus himself when he was on earth could not draw all men unto him, and the saddest thing he had to say was, "They will not come unto me, that they may have eternal life." Men are sometimes a failure in their refusal of the gospel; but Christianity, never.

Q. Why is it that nations do not turn one cheek when the other is wounded? Is not the result of such humility annihilation for any nation?

A. Well, I don't know of any nation that has ever tried it. I do believe very largely with Tolstoi in the non-resistance of nations as well as of individuals. I do not know why there should be one law for individuals and another for nations: do you? for nations are nothing more than aggregations of individuals. Do we have two standards of conduct, one for the preacher and one for the business man? one standard for business and another for religious life? The nations are amenable to the same law that individuals are, and I hope to see the time myself when nations will be humble enough to turn the other cheek. In the long run, I know that Christ's teaching of non-resistance will work to the direct good of every nation in the world.

Q. Can every man by the exercise of his own free will follow in the footsteps of Jesus Christ, or does it still remain true that no man calleth Jesus Lord but by the Holy Ghost?

A. We cannot do it by our own strength. That opens up the question of criticism that comes from over the water. People think the atonement is left out, but the book takes it for granted that people have already accepted the Saviour.

Q. I should like to say it was for the sake of those across the water that I asked the question.

A. I have had to write long papers to tell them that I believed in the atonement, and if I ever go to England I will tell my English brethren that.

Q. The newspaper in your book was supported by a fortune and succeeded. Suppose it had not been thus supported; what would have happened?

A. I don't think that a paper of the kind I had in mind can succeed without financial support. I think the Lord intends us to use means to carry on his work, and I do not yet myself see how a man that wanted to found a daily paper could do it without means. I don't know of any such paper. The nearest thing that comes to it is the Montreal *Daily Witness.* I want to say here what I am going to say again to-night, that this paper ideal in the book will be real in a few years, I hope. I have had letters from newspaper men in every part of the country saying they are willing to throw up the positions where they are and go upon the staff of just such a paper as that. I have a newspaper man in my own church, a young man who has had experience in newspaper work, a graduate of your State University, and who worked upon the newspaper at the college. who has since been trying to run a political paper on the basis of this pledge. He says. "I can't do it. I am going to give up the paper; and I want to start a paper of the kind you mention if somebody will come to the front with the money." I have got a man of experience in newspaper work, a man ready to lose his money and everything except his reputation. I have got other men to go into places as reporters and pressmen, a corps sufficient to start this paper in Topeka or Chicago to-morrow, if some man who has substance will raise the money.

Q. How much will it take?

A. A million dollars. Why not? Why not, my friends? The colleges have had their millions; is n't the time ripe for some one to advance a million dollars for a newspaper of this kind?

Q. Was Mr. Bruce doing wrong by preaching for a wealthy church? Do not wealthy churches need a pastor as well as poor ones?

A. Why, of course. The thing was right, of course. It is only this man, the bishop, and the young girl who go into the slums. Maxwell does n't. Each man must bear his own burden. It was the last thing I had in my mind that a man must get out of a rich church and go into the slums. If the bishop felt he had to go, that was the thing for him to do. Dr. Bruce felt he must go, so that was the thing for him to do. It does n't mean that no one must go into the churches and preach for the rich people.

Q. Do you not believe that there are men who would run many things as Jesus would if some one would give them millions of dollars to start it? Do you believe there is not a man to-day who can do it unless he has a million dollars to lose?

A. That is a hard thing to answer, but it is a practical question and a practical thing to do. I made a thorough examination in my town once. I went up and down both sides of the business street, and asked them if they were conducting business on religious principles or not? I could find but one who could say he was. He is a successful business man, and the people of the town say that he conducts his business on Christian principles. I don't think he makes a great amount of money, but he makes a living. I don't think it is necessary for a man to have large sums of money. I heard lately that two women started a store in London, after reading the book, on this basis. They had about three thousand dollars, and the report came afterwards in the press that they had failed, lost their stock, which would seem to go to prove that one single individual could not conduct his business under this plan in the present selfish competitive system; but other men say they can. I understand that Mayor Jones says he did, and he said that he was going to pay his men living wages whether any other man did it or not; and he has the means to get along. What are we to do, brethren? Are we all going to wait until the millennium? I know of a Topeka German who keeps a meat market. It is a little market. He has no horse to deliver his meat. He works by himself; he gives the best meat he can find on the market and delivers it from house to house. He has in his shop texts from the Bible stuck about, and he shuts his shop up for prayer meeting and shuts it on Sunday, and it is the only one in the place that is shut; and while he is doing a little business he is doing a good business and strictly on this basis.

Q. Has any religious reformation the right to succeed that is dependent upon large riches? Must not these begin at the bottom?

A. Well, yes: but when we speak of success, the most success that a man or woman could have sometimes is to lose every cent they put into it, and some more people in the world have got to be crucified besides Jesus Christ.

Q. Would Philip Strong have reached the point he did if instead of making his church in the slums he had left it in the rich neighborhood? Could he not have accomplished all he did without being crucified at once?

A. Yes, he could if he had been another man. A great many pastors have written criticisms of that character. I do not mean to endorse everything he did. I don't think it was the highest wisdom.

Q. Is it not assumed always in conducting business upon a Christian basis that other features must be equal — common sense, and business judgment?

A. Why, certainly. The Lord does not bless foolishness.

Q. May I ask you what your idea was in picturing Philip Strong in the way you did if you do not endorse it?

A. I will tell you. It is simply a caricature, a cartoon drawn in that way to call attention to the things in the church itself. The difference is between real and assumed religion. We must remember that it was not the common people that crucified Jesus. It was the aristocratic element. It was not the people in the slums that killed Philip Strong.

Q. Are not the reports coming over from Russia such as to show that it would be better and a greater help if some one city was made a headquarters for this work?

A. Do you know about the town of Ruskin in Tennessee? Do you know about the commonwealth settlement of Gibson in Georgia? These are living illustrations of what men are trying to do; go off in a little town by themselves and try to organize the primitive Christianity of Jesus.

Q. Do you think if the church would follow Christ that there is any portion of the human family that could not and would not be saved?

A. No, sir, of course not — if they tried to live as Jesus did.

Q. The question is, Is there anything too bad for the church to save?

A. No, sir. I believe, as Phillips Brooks once said to his aristocratic congregation, " If one hundred men in my congregation would actually live," — he used these very words too, — " would actually live the life of Jesus here in Boston, they would revolutionize this whole city ; " and if in a church such as this, in this city, every member took this pledge and lived up to it, it would transform the city.

Q. Ought not Jesus himself to have produced more effect than he did?

A. I think not. He said that greater works than he did we were to do.

Q. Do you not think the time is also coming for ministers to quit inquiring into the sort of salaries paid them before they will accept a church?

A. Yes. One of the saddest letters I ever had came to me some years ago from a man in one of the large churches. He said that during the hard times when the men in the churches, the retail clerks in the stores, and others had their salaries cut down, the ministers went on with their salaries the same ; and he says that the working men found it out and that ended the churches for them. He said that the ministers were not willing to share with their people in the reduction of salary.

Q. How shall we get our people in churches to adopt this plan?

A. This is about the hardest question that has been asked yet. You know your people better than I do. I had to think for a year with my people, and I had been used to this idea for a long time before I ventured to propose to them that they take their pledge. Begin with the young people first. That is your entering wedge. They are freer to act. They are not bound down by custom. They have no great sums of money to lose by taking the pledge; and believing in the pastors, you can trust them.

Westminster Church.

Special Pastors' Conference.

Rev. George B. Stewart, D.D., Harrisburg, Pa., Chairman.

Westminster Church was entirely too small to hold the visiting ministers who assembled there in special conference. One little realized the number of pastors who are attending the Convention until the gathering in the church was seen. When the time came for opening, at 3.30, there was not a vacant seat. The seats intended for the newspaper men had been filled by ministers, and even the steps to the pulpit were filled, while all around the walls and in the rear was a solid mass of humanity, packed so thickly together that it was an impossibility to work one's way out by the rear entrance. It was one of the most important conferences of the Convention, bearing as it did upon the direct relations of the pastors to their Christian Endeavor societies, and among the speakers were some of the most noted Christian Endeavor workers. Rev. George Black Stewart, D.D., of Harrisburg, Pa., presided, and Rev. L. Y. Graham, D.D., Philadelphia, Pa., conducted the opening devotional exercises.

Dr. Stewart, as he looked upon that magnificent body of pastors, was moved to declare his confidence in the stability of Christian Endeavor under the evident leadership of the God-appointed leaders of the churches. The nine eminent ministers who spoke — Rev. Messrs. Barbour, of Rochester; Anderson, of Connecticut; Lowden, of Rhode Island; McMillan, of Pennsylvania; Hatch, of Massachusetts; Spencer, of Michigan; McCauley, of Ohio; Philputt, of Indiana; and Dr. Clark — spoke right out of long and sympathetic connection with practical Endeavor work as members of societies. Theirs were no air-spun theories. Go to the meetings. Plan with the Executive Committee. Form a band of outdoor workers. Get church prayer-meeting topics in which the young people will be interested. Establish pickets throughout the congregation to greet the strangers. Every speaker brought out plans as practical and pointed as these.

One remarkable point was the emphasis laid by many of the speakers on the fact, for which they vouched, that in every case within their knowledge where a society died or lived to little purpose it was because the pastor took little interest in it and failed to direct and inspire its work.

First Congregational Chapel.

Travellers' Union Conference.

Mr. William Shaw, Boston, Mass., Chairman.

A Travellers' Union Conference was held in the chapel of the First Congregational Church, Treasurer William Shaw, of Boston, presiding. As a result of this gathering the Christian Endeavor Travellers' Union was reorganized and placed on a new footing. It is considered a noteworthy achievement, and will rank as one of the important things accomplished at the Detroit Eighteenth Annual Convention.

There were about fifty active travelling-men present, but the chapel was filled with other men and women who were interested in Christian Endeavor work, particularly the department for travelling-men.

There has long been a conviction that the Christian Endeavor Society throughout the world could be of great benefit to the travelling-man at home and particularly on the road. Wearing the Christian Endeavor button, he would meet friends that would look after his welfare, and make him feel at home when he was perhaps thousands of miles away from the point he looks to as his headquarters.

A Travelling Men's Union was formed some time ago at one of the conventions, but it did not exactly fill the bill. As Mr. H. H. Grotthouse, of Dallas, Tex., said to a *Free Press* representative after the meeting: —

There was too much red tape about it, I guess. There was a set of officers, and all that sort of thing. They are really unnecessary. The idea is fully expressed in the pledges that have been accepted by the travelling-men here to-day, and that pledge, with the accompanying application-blank, is entirely sufficient.

The travelling-men do not want much in this case. The idea has been to form a union composed of those who sign the membership pledge, get their application out in proper form, and forward it to the general secretary of the United Society of Christian Endeavor, Tremont Temple, Boston. The pledge is kept by the signer.

The following is the membership pledge : —

Trusting in the Lord Jesus Christ for strength, I promise him that I will strive to do whatever he would like to have me do, and that I will make it the rule of my life to pray and read the Bible every day.

As a member of the Travellers' Union, I promise to take some part in a Christian Endeavor prayer meeting at least once a week, unless hindered by some reason which I can conscientiously give to my Lord and Master, Jesus Christ.

I will also help to organize societies of Christian Endeavor wherever possible, and aid existing societies that I may visit in my travels.

I will endeavor to report any items of interest at least once a quarter to the general secretary of the United Society of Christian Endeavor, Tremont Temple, Boston, Mass.

The application-blank is as follows : —

Having carefully examined the principles of the Christian Endeavor Travellers' Union, I would be pleased to join the same, and do hereby subscribe to the above pledge, and agree, with God's help, to live up to its requirements.

Then there is a place for the name and address, and the following " pastor's voucher " is attached : —

I hereby certify that —————— is in good and regular standing in ————— church of —————.

The pastor must sign this voucher, to be forwarded with the application for enrolment. Therein is no expense whatever.

All of the travelling-men present accepted these cards, which they intend to fill out and send to the Boston Christian Endeavor headquarters.

Forest Avenue Presbyterian Church.

Floating Society Conference.

Miss A. P. Jones, Falmouth, Mass., Leader.

" Floating " Christian Endeavor work was discussed in all its phases at the Forest Avenue Presbyterian Church. Hundreds of delegates and visitors who are interested in that church work attended. Miss Antoinette P. Jones, of Falmouth, Mass., a prominent worker of the " Floating Society " of the world, which devotes its attention strictly to seamen generally and the navy, presided over the meeting.

One of the speakers of the afternoon was James A. Tenney, of Portland, Me., who has devoted nearly twenty years of his life to " sail loft " meetings and work among the sailors. Mr. Tenney dwelt upon the fact that there were hundreds of mission seamen unsaved in the world, and that it was a vast field to work upon. Several Detroit ladies, who are interested in the marine hospital work, also spoke. Donations of comfort-bags were asked for. The devotional services were conducted by Rev. W. F. McCauley, of Dennison, O.

Miss Jones made the following address on the work:—

Address by Miss A. P. Jones,

Falmouth, Mass.

When, last year, naval triumphs filled our thoughts, our brothers on the sea were hailed heroes indeed. None the less were they heroes, previous to the war, in their life of isolation on their ships before the red fire of battle glorified them, nor since, after hardship and depression has succeeded. Their real war is against sin and Satan, and that is on all the time. The true victory was not gained at Manila or Santiago, but in the daily overcoming of sin within and without. "Faith is the victory" on the sea as well as on land.

It appears almost unnecessary to "stir up your pure mind by way of remembrance," when nearly every one in a Floating Christian Endeavor conference has either had long experience in the work among seamen, or has an earnest desire to extend to them the hand of true Christian fellowship, to win and train them for Christ.

It is not easy to imagine the loneliness of a single Christian life, lived out in the love of Christ in the midst of a godless crew. Neither is it easy to imagine the tight band of temptation and sin drawn about the boy or young man when he is isolated from the helps to good and hindrances to evil experienced on land.

You who are in ports realize the necessity for work being carefully planned in order to reach the greatest number most effectively. The whole field should be carefully reviewed, districted, and co-operation arranged for by all the Christian Endeavor societies in the port, or the local union, if there is one. Societies nearest water-front can render personal assistance in services. Those farther away can arrange for regular supplies of good literature, comfort-bags, and help furnish the means for carrying on the work. No previous knowledge of sailors or the sea is necessary, but a thorough consecration, tact, some experience in evangelistic work as a soul-winner, and prayerful judgment are all needed.

In each port the work must be adapted to existing conditions. In some ports the work converges to a comparatively small point, while in another port it is extended along many miles of frontage.

Where work has already been established and has right of way, it should be cordially respected and no plans made which will encroach on their field. Usually such work and workers can be materially benefited by the Christian Endeavorers assisting in the regular services. Almost immediately a necessity is forced upon you for a regular meeting-place, a reading-room, or a "home."

While the men from ships can be cordially invited to regular church services, these do not usually afford the time nor variety nor freedom for personal work that gospel services do, arranged to meet the special need of the sailor.

The permission for ship services should be obtained of the captain of a naval ship, or officers of any ship. The most convenient time for Sunday service on a naval ship, where no regular service is held, is following morning inspection, when it interferes less with duty and recreation. When a week-night is chosen, the hour should be very early, and in any case the service should be prompt, pointed, cheerfully and well sustained, and by no means prolonged. A very few judicious workers should mingle with the sailors for personal conversation, while the others should continue brief song service to cover this effort.

Great carefulness should be observed that earnest impressions resulting should not be dispelled by levity. Remember, moments are precious and decisions for eternity involved. From such services usually can be gleaned enough earnest ones to attend meetings on shore, when, having voluntarily placed themselves in the way of spiritual and moral assistance, they are more likely to accept it.

Hospitals and barracks more easily reached with regular services and visitation afford grand fields for personal work, as some of you have experienced. How much is a home needed by a sailor who comes into a great city alone, without friends, save the saloon-keeper?

I want to tell you what " Bill " says, and he knows: —

" Jack is n't as bad as he is put up to be. Of course there are good and bad in every flock, but a man in a uniform is more noticeable than a man in ordinary dress. If you want to win a sailor to Christ, love is the only way to conquer. Take him by the hand and lead him home. But first you must have a home he feels he is welcome in. Have something different from what he comes in contact with on shipboard. Put him on a level with men who stay ashore and don't go to sea to defend the country's honor. Treat him as a man, and he is as good as the one who stays at home and never sees life in foreign climes.

" The reason he goes to the bar for grog is because he has no other place to go, as a rule, and the saloon-keeper gives him the glad hand; and Jack, being afloat in a strange land, is easily led by the invitation, for he is like a ship without a rudder, adrift in a strange land, with nowhere to lay his head. If there is a home and some one to bid him welcome, he is just as easily led to the good as he is to the bad, if you catch him in time, before the land-sharks grab him.

" So, when you have him in tow, make him comfortable and make him feel welcome. Let him have a good meal, for Jack likes something nice and tasty; then a nice warm room to sit in and read and write a letter, the ink and paper right at hand for him; and then he is landed, provided you have for him a nice, clean, soft bed for the night. If you have n't the bed, clean and soft, no good having the rest, for that will knock him off his course quicker than anything else, and off he will go on another tack, and, of course, no other place than a rum-shop.

" In he goes, gets all in a muddle, and don't know where he lies, and don't care, for he knows he is away from home and friends, with no one to care for him, and he thinks he is making the best of his time. Therefore he is lost, when a good bed and home might have been the means of bringing him to the Saviour and putting him on the road to the ' Home, Sweet Home' where he would meet his friends, never more to part."

Do you know what an average sailor's boarding-house is like? Then investigate. Would it be a suitable " home " for your own brother? Ask the Lord what you can do toward founding a real " home " in your home city.

The Christian Endeavor Home at Nagasaki, Japan, has proved a great blessing, and while great improvements can continue to be made there, it is a light in a very dark place. The home has recently been incorporated under the laws of Massachusetts, to insure its continuance under American and Christian Endeavor control, anticipating the new treaty provisions.

The Young Men's Christian Association Army and Navy Christian Commission has been called into prominence by the late war, and they have done good work; but there is a work for the Floating Christian Endeavor that the Y. M. C. A. cannot do.

Floating Christian Endeavor has in its nine years of existence proven to be a plan of God, and its place cannot be relinquished until it has ceased to be spiritually effective. Co-operation along Christian lines can dispel any shadow of rivalry, which need never exist in the Master's work.

First Presbyterian Church.

Local and District Union Conference.

Secretary John Willis Baer, Boston, Chairman.

Christian Endeavorers sat on the topmost rows of seats in the galleries of the First Presbyterian Church and peered over at the Christian

Endeavorers that sat on the row of seats next the chancel rail. Christian Endeavorers were crowded in between these two extremes of seat locations as tightly as they could be. Every nook and corner of the edifice held some person with a crimson-and-white badge and a happy face.

It was the important conference of the city and district union officers. Nearly every person in the church was an officer of some local or district union in some part of the country. During the meeting almost every State in the Union was heard from, and the benefits derived by the officers through this intermingling of ideas was said by prominent workers to be invaluable.

The meeting was full of interesting features, and important ideas were evolved which promise to bear fruit in no small quantity. One important piece of business transacted was the decision to appoint a committee to co-operate with the executive officers of the United Society in Boston in carrying out a programme for the coming year, presented by Dr. Clark to the meeting.

The relations existing between the Christian Endeavor Society and the Epworth League, that strong Methodist organization, were quite freely discussed, and ways and means of creating a close union between the two great organizations were suggested. There were persons present, belonging to the Methodist Church in different parts of the country, who said that a union of the two associations is not at all impossible. Following is the programme, which shows how profitable was the free discussion of methods of work : —

" Report on President Clark's Letter to the District and City Union Officers."
" An Advance Step for Unions: Uniform Topics, Their Usefulness and Flexibility."
" How Often Should Meetings Be Held ? "
" Prison Work."
" Why Have Local Unions ? "
" What Good Can They Do ? "
" How Shall They Be Supported — Financially ? By Attendance ? "
" Elements of Disintegration in City Unions ? "
" Where Can We Strengthen Our Unions ? "
" How Get the Pastors Interested ? "
" The Necessity for an Advisory Board of Pastors."
" How May the Union Help (*a*) the Local Society ? (*b*) the Local Churches? (*c*) the Union's Missionary Committee ? (*d*) the Denominational Boards ? (*e*) the State Union ? (*f*) the Juniors ? "
" The Possibilities of the Press Committee."
" The Duties and Results of the Union Lookout Committee."
" What Can Be Done by Unions toward Organizing New Societies ? "
" Intervisitation of Societies."

FRIDAY EVENING.

Tent Endeavor.

By Friday evening the tents that had been so drenched in the morning were thoroughly dry and confortable again, and they were filled with vast companies, the people standing around the outskirts in hundreds upon hundreds to catch what words of eloquence they could, or at least hear the singing. In Tent Endeavor Mr. Baer found it necessary to say something about the absurd statements concerning the "small" attendance spread abroad by the newspapers. How these statements originated or what could be their motive is a mystery. As Mr. Baer justly remarked, Christian Endeavor has never before held a convention with all the meetings, the tents, conferences, Quiet Hour services, so crowded. "But are they Endeavorers?" piped up some one; whereupon Mr. Baer asked all that were Endeavorers to rise. The ten thousand in the tent immediately sprang to their feet.

Bishop B. W. Arnett, D.D., Wilberforce, O., presided with a tact and good humor that came well into play later in the evening. Mr. R. R. Patterson, of San Francisco, Cal., conducted the devotional exercises. The quiet season of meditation and prayer was led by the president of the Minnesota Christian Endeavor Union, Rev. George E. Soper, of St. Paul, Minn. After the announcement that Dr. Quayle was kept at home by the serious sickness in his father's family, and after silent prayer for God's blessing upon the absent speaker, after the Hampton Quartette and Mrs. Ellis, of Detroit, had delighted us with sweet song, Dr. Barrows was introduced, and received with a Chautauqua salute because he is president of Oberlin, and another because of the Parliament of Religions, and another because he is a great Christian Endeavorer. Now Dr. Barrows is a weather Jonah. Last year, at the Nashville Convention, he had to speak against a terrific storm, and this year his opening sentences were emphasized by the mutterings of thunder, and soon the rain came down and the umbrellas went up, and "Let a little sunshine in" rose from beneath. Newspapers became temporary protectors for pretty hats. Now it was a chorus, now a solo; always it was cheery. And before long the storm ceased, and the grand oration could be completed.

For it was indeed a grand oration, perfect in form as a Greek statue, large with spacious studies and experience, and all aglow with the warmth of Christian ideals. It swept the whole world in its wide review, carrying us to the college campuses of many foreign lands and of earlier days. Rich in scholarly allusions, fine in poetical phrases, definite in sturdy teaching, we do not believe that our language contains an oration in praise of Christian education worthy to be placed for a moment beside it. Even if the discomfort of the storm had not brought its own recompense, this address would have well repaid us.

Address by Rev. John Henry Barrows, D.D., LL.D.,
Oberlin, O.

THE SUPREME VALUE OF HIGHER EDUCATION.

The Christian college cannot be understood without understanding its purose,—to mould the heart and character, to shape the will and the life, as well s to sharpen the intellectual faculties of the students. "Education," as Ierbert Spencer has said, "is to prepare us for complete living." Man, being he kind of person he is, needs right ideals and something besides. He needs he spirit and the heavenly forces which help him to fasten his affections on ight ideals. The purpose determines the quality of an action, and also, in a reasure, the results of it. If religion is something worth while in education, re ought to be willing to declare it, to announce it in every wise way. Through he life which the student lives there should ever run the olden thread which leads to God. The aim of the Chris-fan college is not reached by turning out students who re merely believers in Christianity, who consent calmly nd indifferently to its creed. It aims to fill its students rith the spirit of St. Paul, to make them alive in the ervice of Christ, and to fire them with the enthusiasm of iumanity. It purposes to send them forth equipped with he knowledge of that Book which more than any other ias kindled the imagination and the moral sentiment of nankind. The president of Clark University believes hat the Bible "is being slowly re-revealed as man's text-iook in psychology; dealing with him as a whole,— his iody, mind, and will." And President Gilman affirms hat "the ethics of the New Testament will be accepted iy the scientific, as well as the religious, faculties of iian."

Dr. Barrows Was Equal to the Test of the Storm.

The president of a State university has affirmed from his own expe-ience the conviction that a State institution cannot exist unless it is founded ipon a religious basis. Agencies to promote religion among students in State :olleges are, however, no part of the education provided by the State. State iniversities which began by requiring church and chapel attendance have given ip this requirement. State institutions cannot discharge a teacher who is hos-ile to Christianity. Christian schools can.

There are special reasons to-day which show that the part taken by the Christian college in our national life is growingly important and strategic. America, already the richest of nations, is to become far richer. The number of the wealthy will be increased, and millions will have most of the comforts and :ven luxuries which the very rich now enjoy. The tendency of opulence is to inervate. Christian character needs to be hardened and fortified against luxury. And a manhood "that can stand money" is what the Christian college aims to produce, and what Oberlin College has produced in the few men of her gradu-ites who have given their lives, successfully to the getting of great fortunes. Education, refinement, culture, wealth, luxury, are among the most powerful forces of misery, restlessness, and vicious discontent that exist in the world to-day, unless they are penetrated and controlled by the religion of Christ, which gives peace, love, courage, faith, hope, and joy. Our civilization rushes to a vast and fatal plunge unless God is enthroned in the educated minds of our people. Education without religion is architecture without foundation and roof.

On every side of us we hear the loud demand for educated men who are fit-ted to the world's present work. Character comes from character; and nothing in the way of culture or machinery or wealth can take the place of Christian-ized personalities. The households need them. Our churches need them, oh, how sadly! And sometimes two or three devoted, well-trained, sensible men and women will do far more for the life of a church, for its growth and pros-perity, than hundreds of inefficient, poorly trained, even if not indifferent, members.

As a character-building institution the Christian college holds an unrivalled place. Some studies, as already intimated, are difficult; but the forming of character is both the most difficult and the most important task given to the Christian teacher. It is the most difficult, for "it is a far harder task to form a single moral virtue than to become a philosopher." Virtue is the habit of doing good; and habits go with us longer and more potentially than the knowledge of the facts of science and history. Germany does not think it safe to educate her children leaving out religion. In France the schools are proving a prodigious ethical failure, because, owing to a not unnatural fear of despotic priestcraft, the highest truths and motives are omitted from the school life. Criminal statistics in France, as well as in America, indicate that there is a horrible failure somewhere in the education of the youth. We are witnessing a strong reaction in favor of ethical training; but it is plain that the code of morality which ignores religion is both incomplete and ineffective. Morality without religion Frederick Harrison pronounced "a rattling of dry bones." Those who have the administration of schools and colleges should give heed not only to character, but to convictions, in those who are called upon to teach; for it has been truly said that "one man can sow more tares in a single day than a dozen men can root up in a month." What men need is not only truth, but an inclination to obey the truth. And a code of morality, however pure and perfect, has no more motive in it to make a man obey it than the knowledge of geography has to make a man travel around the world. A college training that does not mould right character, that leads to dilettanteism and selfish refinement and exclusiveness like those of the later Roman Empire, or of the brilliant era of the Italian Renaissance, does not meet the requirements of true education. Such a culture does not help forward human development. Such a culture among the mandarins of China to-day is a chief obstacle to the regeneration of that thoroughly terrestrial Empire.

The whole educational system of our country, both in the common school and in the University, is the outgrowth of the Protestant Reformation. The spirit and the convictions which resisted the bigotry and tyranny of the English Stuarts, and which colonized New England, have changed the moral life and exalted the moral standards of Saxon peoples in all lands. It may be safely said that no other force has entered the life of our world in the last three centuries which has given so broad an extension to the domain of intelligence as the Puritan force; and this is shown from the fact that John Calvin was the father of the common-school system of Geneva; that the spirit of Calvin created the common-school system of Holland; that, as embodied in John Knox, it created the common-school system of Scotland, and, as embodied in the Puritans, established the common-school system of America.

I find it difficult to account for the tremendous influence of the colleges first established in America without connecting their intellectual life with the profounder life of the spirit fostered by Puritan doctrines. The theology which "makes God big," and makes man know himself as a child of God, directly responsible to the awful power of an infinite holiness, is bound to have a greater influence over life than any superficial training of the human understanding, whose primary concern is with the facts and laws of the material world. Science may be made deeply religious, and I greatly appreciate its value. It is now becoming allied to the highest poetry. But if it is treated only as a knowledge of facts and laws, and the scientific spirit becomes oblivious of the Infinite Spirit whom the Christian poet feels "in the light of setting suns, and the round ocean and the blue sky, and the living air, and the mind of man," then it does not do for the modern student any such service as the Puritan theology rendered to our ancestors.

What a mighty source sprang from the sort of training which Puritanism fostered! If we could enter the Princeton College of a hundred and forty years ago, we should feel that it scarcely deserved the title of a grammar school. Its library was a miscellaneous refuse of cast-off theological works; its astronomical apparatus was an orrery; its museum was a few stuffed alligators; and yet that school, with John Witherspoon at its head, graduated during the presidency of that great divine, of that great teacher, of that great statesman, twenty senators, twenty-five representatives in Congress, thirteen governors, three judges of the Supreme Court, one Vice-President, and one President, all within a period of twenty years, when the institution seldom had more than a hundred students. Of the thirty-two college men who sat in the Constitutional Convention, nine came from Princeton. The better history of the Southern, Atlantic, and Gulf States might be written in the biographies of Princeton graduates. It is not without vast significance that from a college in whose halls once sat the Congress of the Colonies, and on whose platform could once be seen Washington and Witherspoon side by side, nine Princeton men had gone forth to sign the Declaration of our Independence, and that this institution was the mother of Brown University, Union College, Hamilton, Washington-Jefferson College, Washington-Lee University, Hampden-Sidney College, the University of Ohio, the University of North Carolina, the University of Cincinnati, and a score of others. The Lees, Bayards, Debneys, the Pendletons and the Breckenridges, who have come from its halls are but representatives of the greater host who are worthy to be classed with the most famous Americans.

As democracy insists on having its educational life crowned with the State university, so the Christian church must have, in order to realize its ideals, its own institutions of higher learning. I need not argue that Christian education is required to meet the chief dangers by which the twentieth century will be overshadowed. With agnosticism not yet extinct, with materialism penetrating like a poison the minds and hearts, as well as the external life, of modern men, with the immense accumulations of wealth, and the growing appetite for pleasure, secular education alone will be utterly powerless to furnish the moral force and spiritual power demanded by the perilous ages before us. Wendell Phillips once said, in speaking of Wade Hampton, that it was impossible to conciliate him. And then he added this striking figure: "You might as well pour 'lasses on a rattlesnake." There are serpent-like and poisonous forces in our modern civilization which no sweetness of culture will either conciliate or regenerate; and therefore, the Christian college and the ideas which it represents are more necessary to our national well-being at the present hour than even in the early beginnings of American life.

Tent Williston.

"Onward, Christian Soldiers!" The song arose from the chorus in Tent Williston, softly at first, like the anthem of some angelic band far away. Then, as if it was taken up by the great host of Endeavorers before the platform, the song waves seemed to meet and to rend the curtain of separation between them and the souls of the leaders that had left them for another land, and in whose memory they had gathered. The two waves of song met and, in harmonious action, swelled into power that was irresistible to every heart present.

A memorial service to Christian leaders was the occasion that stimulated the happy enthusiasm that is the unit of strength and success at all the meetings. There were present those in the audience that had come to listen, and were not professing Christians; but when one of the grand old hymns that they had heard in past years arose, their lips moved in song, and the remembrance of the words becoming clearer, they sang aloud and the outside world was forgotten in an hour of spiritual enjoyment.

After devotional exercises led by Rev. E. D. W. Jones, of Allegheny City, Pa., and just at the conclusion of the song service, a company of

Michigan's Fighting Seventh, from Fort Wayne, came upon the platform, and their glorious conduct at El Caney during the Spanish war was honores with the Chautauquan salute from all persons present. Then came "America," with the audience standing, and the last verse was sung in honor of the soldier-boys.

President Clark said the welcome given to the Endeavorers last Wednesday was sufficient, but that Mayor Maybury had handed him a poem of welcome, which was so good he wanted it read to the audience. Professor Howe, of Lexington, Va., then read the pretty "Welcome," written by Minnie McArthur Laing, of Detroit, and it was well received.

Welcome.

By Minnie McArthur Laing.

Youth of America, children of liberty,
 Dawn on your faces and faith in your eyes,
Great in intensity, grand in simplicity,
 Mighty in unity — lo, how ye rise!
Out of the country whose craigs are the eagle's perch,
 Bold as her emblem and free as her gale,
Under the banner of Christ and his mighty church,
 Hail to ye, Christian Endeavorers, hail!

Back roll the mists of the centuries, over us
 Loometh the cross and its figure on high;
From it the path is traced where now your feet are placed
 Firm in a faith that was born not to die.
Youth of the risen Lord, children of destiny,
 Born of the death of the Master of men,
Soul of the Fatherland, light of the age ye stand,
 Buds of a branch that shall blossom again.

Lo, how the present reflects from its grandeur
 The shine of the smile through the pain on the cross;
Lo, how the world forgets; lo, how it sneers and frets —
 Feebled in faith and appalled at its loss!
But in the strength of her youth, the sublimity
 Lights the great heights "In His Steps" they shall climb,
Leading the works along, tuned to a morning song,
 Into the truths of the stronghold of Time!

Youth of America, children of liberty,
 Dawn on your faces and faith in your eyes,
Great in intensity, grand in simplicity,
 Mighty in unity — lo, how ye rise!
Out of the country whose craigs are the eagle's perch,
 Bold as her emblem and free as her gale,
Under the banner of Christ and his mighty church,
 Hail to ye, Christian Endeavorers, hail!

It was a thrilling scene when, just after the singing of "America," Dr. Clark led to the platform Mr. Mazarona, a Cuban minister, and Chaplain Shields, of Fort Wayne. Mr. Mazarona spoke a few words of gratitude for the political deliverance of his people, and of hope for their spiritual deliverance, and concluded by throwing his arm around Chaplain Shields, who represented his country's deliverers.

IN THE WELL APPOINTED-PRESS TENT.

Miss Jessie Ackerman, of Chicago, the first speaker of the evening, touched a deep chord when she called Frances Willard the greatest woman who had ever enlisted in Christian Endeavor. She thanked God that Christian Endeavor had established the precedent of this memorial meeting in honor of the year's great dead.

Miss Ackerman set before the Endeavorers as a noble ideal these words of Miss Willard : " My applause shall be not for the great or successful, but for the men and women who try and fail."

Address by Miss Jessie Ackerman,

Chicago, Ill.

FRANCES E. WILLARD.

Early in February, before the year '98 had waned, and while its pages were still unwritten, a record of sorrow was penned,—when the news of the death of Frances E. Willard — that household name — was sent over the world. Upwards of half a million of women paused in their usual occupation, and, with bated breath and bowed heads, echoed the words that rose with the dawn and swept on with the circling light in its course, until they girdled the world: A woman is dead.

Yes, a woman is dead! and the portals of the celestial city never opened wider than to receive the pure, beautiful spirit of Frances Willard when it took its flight. For the first time in Christian effort, one day each year has been set aside as a time when the people of the nation might meet to honor her sacred memory. For the first time in the history of this Republic it has been decreed that the statue of a woman shall find place among the mighty dead of this nation. All honor to the brave men of the great commonwealth of Illinois who have had the courage not to follow old precedents, but have established a new one by daring to honor the memory of a woman who has " made the world wider for women and better for men." The legislators of Illinois have not only " done that State proud," but have paid a fitting tribute to the womanhood of the land. For gallantry, chivalry, and deference to women, the men of America score one point beyond the men of any other nation.

For many years Miss Willard has stood out upon the horizon of our day, a central figure around whom centred every force that makes for righteousness. We are so familiar with the beauty of her classic face and the outlines of her stately form, so familiar with the sweet smile, gracious manner, "imperial intellect," and irresistible personality, that there seems nothing new to say about this marvellous woman.

To-day we do not mourn that she is no more, for she has earned her rest and entered upon her reward ; our sister does well that she sleeps : but we fain would honor her memory and pay tribute to an unexcelled womanhood, that, in all the years, reflected the graces that adorned the life and beautified character of the Nazarene.

Her career is well known to nearly every school child. We recall that she achieved her first success as an instructor in high places in some of the leading institutions of learning in this country, during which time more than two thousand young lives passed through her hands and received the indelible imprint of her influence. The fires of a holy ambition and mighty zeal were kindled in many a heart, and to-day men and women in high callings — ministers, evangelists, teachers, lawyers, professors, and journalists — all gladly acknowledge that their success in life is, in a great measure, due to contact with Miss Willard in their school days.

Miss Willard, however, is best known to the world as a philanthropist and reformer. As a philanthropist Miss Willard lived out her highest ideal. It is a small matter to give gold and silver, houses and lands ; it is a small thing to autograph a slip of paper and send it on its way to carry relief to the oppressed, food to the hungry, and light into dark places ; but there is a philanthropy that is higher than even this. It was taught nineteen hundred years ago, by One who had neither gold nor silver, when the very sun of heaven, as it looked upon the richness of his giving, fairly faded from view, ashamed of its own weak light. When at mid-day this old world was rolled in darkness and from the depths was heard a voice saying, "It is finished," then and then only did the world learn the lesson of true philanthropy in that "He gave himself."

Following his blessed example, our beloved leader always lived out his highest ideals; nothing was too small a service to render. On one occasion she made her way through the streets of a great city, hurrying to the jail to fulfil a promise to a sorrow-stricken mother in search of a wayward daughter. Reaching the place, she followed the keeper down a long row of cells, and finally, halting before one, he said, "She is in here." In the corner of the cell, on a rude bed, lay the form of a woman. Hearing footsteps approach, she covered her head and face with an old blanket and made no response to the entreaty to come to the bars and speak.

Finally, Miss Willard, in tones of tender sympathy, said, "I'm your very own sister; won't you come and speak to me?" Touched by the spell of that matchless voice, she arose and came to the bars. Taking hold of the grating with her shapely hand, she leaned her head against her arm and wept like a child. Seeing she had no handkerchief, Miss Willard passed hers through the grating, and the poor girl buried her face in its soft white folds and between her sobs, said, "I once had clean handkerchiefs of my own."

Passing her hand between the bars, our dear leader placed it upon the weary head, stroked the tangled locks, and then gently putting it over the shoulders, tried to teach her how to be good. Long after, a woman who had devoted her remaining years to a blessed work, because of her own deliverance, told me the touching story. Deeply impressed by it, I inquired, "What did Miss Willard say that so influenced your life?" Her reply was, "It was not what she said, but she put her arm about me, *she touched me.*"

The secret of Miss Willard's success was due to the fact that she never avoided touch with those whom she desired to reach, but, like the Master, she even "sat at meat with publicans and sinners."

Her sympathies were always with those who had gone down in the struggle of life. When I was about to leave this land for others she handed me a printed slip, saying, "Child, here is a great thought for you, as you journey from land to land; learn these lines, and the time will never seem long, for you will never lack an object in life." Continuing, she said, "You know it is the way of the world to applaud the victor. Men and women reach the topmost pinnacle of fame, wealth, or genius, and half the world bows at their feet to do them honor, while the other half would fain climb those dizzy heights to crown them with the laurel wreath: but for the one who has tried and failed the world has no applause. I always feel like cheering those who can record the effort of doing, though it end in failure. Learn the lines! I did, and ofttimes they have been the inspiration of weary and worn days. I pass them on to you:"—

> "I sing the song of the low and the humble,
> The weary and broken in heart,
> Who strove and who failed, bearing nobly
> A silent and desperate part;
> Whose youth bore no fruit on its branches;
> Whose hopes burned in ashes away;
> From whose hands slipped the prize ere they grasped it;
> Who stood at the dying of day,
> With the failures of life all around them,
> Unpitied, unheeded, alone—
> With death sweeping down on their failure,
> And even their faith overthrown."

She loved, pitied, and helped those who stood "with the failures of life all around them," and it has been her loving attitude toward the lowly that made her the ideal philanthropist among women.

My most blessed recollections of her are as a woman in the home. It was my privilege to live with her some months under the hospitable roof of our gracious friend Lady Henry Somerset, at Eastnor Castle. It was our custom those days to set aside work for a time and assemble in Lady Henry's sitting-room for afternoon tea. The room was decorated with plants and flowers, and in the season of them there was always a bunch of heliotrope, Miss Willard's favorite flower. It was not the sweet perfume or delicate tint of this flower that attracted her, but the sentiment for which it stood. The heliotrope — " turning toward the sun; " such an emblem of her own sweet self! With her fearless face turned toward the heavens, she always looked to the Light of lights, the Sun of suns, from whence came all the inspiration of her life.

On these occasions she always came down in some dainty teagown. She frequently wore one of which I was especially fond, for in it she looked like some embodied spirit from another and better world. Its soft, pale-blue folds seemed to cling to her in almost a fond embrace, and the tints were reflected in her mild eyes — those eyes that looked upon all things only to see the good. It was there that I learned to know Miss Willard as a woman, the character in which I wish the whole world might better know her.

Miss Willard's motto was, "*Mea vita vota*" (My life is a vow). In early childhood she made of life and all its powers a sacred vow; and as the days, weeks, and months passed by, each was a partial fulfilment of that early vow. She once gave expression to what was a lifelong conviction with her, in saying. " Man is immortal until his work is done. " When about to leave this country, the mother of Miss Willard expressed a desire to see me before sailing. Accordingly I made a last visit to Rest Cottage. While sitting on a stool at her feet, dear old Saint Courageous put her hand upon my head as if in parting benediction, saying, " Frank always believes that man is immortal until his work is done. You will live to do your work, no matter what it may be. "

Once while Frances was away at school her mother sent her a motto saying, " Though you forget all else in the world, remember this: 'To be carnally minded is death; but to be spiritually minded is life and peace.'" Few indeed among the daughters of women ever attained a deeper spirituality than did our leader, for she always took for her example the One who alone has left us a perfect pattern, and ever dwelt upon his mission to the lowly.

Her faith in God was eternal, and her faith in humanity abiding. Her chief glory in the work to which she gave her life was in the fact that the foundation and four corner-stones were laid in the gospel of Jesus Christ. She rejoiced in a message that brought hope even to the evil-doer. When she went to the saloon-keeper to say, " Woe unto him that putteth the bottle to his neighbor's lips, " she always added, " Come now, let us reason together, saith the Lord; though your sins be as scarlet, they shall be white as snow; though they be red like crimson, they shall be white as wool. " She faithfully warned the drunkard, " No drunkard shall inherit the kingdom of heaven. " From a loving heart warmed by heavenly fires, she gave the promise, " Come unto me, all ye that labor and are heavy-laden, and I will give you rest. "

She was zealous to have our banner, with its motto, " For God, Home, and Humanity, " unfurled in every land; but much more did she desire that the banner of the King Immanuel should float in every valley, and be planted upon every hill-top. She never grew weary of telling what women had achieved in her day, but she affirmed it was because of " the story that transforms the world. " She always declared that Jesus Christ was the first and only emancipator of women, and marvelled much that the world had been so slow to learn the lesson taught by him when he looked upon the sinful woman and, looking her sins away, bade her " go in peace and sin no more. "

Strong as was her faith in Christ, equally so was her faith in that institution, founded by him, called the church. In these days when so many reforms rail at the church, let it be forever placed on record that Frances Willard stood for, and by, the church. She honored the institution that had braved all the storms of infidelity and scepticism, and handed down to us, unsullied, the Word that has been a " light to our feet and a lamp to our path. "

Yes, because of her faith in God and the church she was enabled to go on. When she saw the poor drunkard's wife, with her life ebbing fast away, she would take from her arms the half-fed, half-clad child, and as she pressed it to her own bosom of love, looking into its innocent face, she could sing to it a lullaby of prophecy, as she declared, in the name of the church of the twentieth century, that such a thing as a drunkard's child would be unknown, and a drunkard's wife would be a forgotten language; because back of and over against all she stood for were the eternal, everlasting arms of the Lord God of Hosts, and the Church of his Christ.

This was the foundation of her life and work; and, beloved friends, our sister does well that she sleeps; that she rests from the stupendous labor of her hands and brain.

We sit, not in tears and mourning, as those without hope; but, with hearts baptized with new courage, and new cheer, let us learn the lessons of her beautiful life, and dwell upon her triumphant entry into her eternal home. What rejoicing there must have been in some unseen, unknown sphere! Methinks I hear the glad welcome as the angels echo around the throne, "Rejoice, rejoice, for the Lord has claimed his own!" And the great organs of eternity peal out the notes, and the heavenly host echo and re-echo the sweet refrain, "Rejoice, rejoice, for the Lord has claimed his own."

She is not lost to us! From the highlands of glory and at the beautiful gate she watches, waits, and beckons to us; and methinks if her sainted lips could speak, her message to us would be, "To be carnally minded is death; but to be spiritually minded is life and peace."

May the mantle of her boundless love descend upon us, the spirit of her abiding faith be ours, and the star of her hope guide us to build well, wisely, and faithfully upon her works.

The Convention learned a bit of a lesson which will be serviceable to those who go to London next year. Dr. Clark bespoke for Mr. Pollock, of Scotland, who was to eulogize Gladstone, a hearty English reception. English speakers, he said, are accustomed, as we shall learn next year, to robust hand-clapping and exclamations of "Hear, hear!"

Both the hand-claps and the "Hear, hears" were forthcoming in abundant quantity when Mr. Pollock arose; but billows of laughter rolled over the audience when Dr. Clark hastened to explain that the "Hear, hears" should have been kept until the speaker said something good.

"This makes me feel very much at home," said Mr. Pollock.

"Hear, hear!" promptly shouted the audience. "Hear, hear!" came again when he declared Washington to be the greatest man of the eighteenth century and Gladstone, the loftiest figure of the nineteenth century.

Address by Rev. John Pollock,
Glasgow, Scotland.

WILLIAM E. GLADSTONE.

Permit me, at the outset, to express my sense of the honor of representing, with my beloved friend, Mr. Mursell, the Council of the Christian Endeavor Union of Great Britain and Ireland. It is an additional pleasure to speak on behalf of the General Executive of the Scottish National Union, and to convey to the United Society of America, and to all the delegates present, the cordial greetings of our Scottish Endeavorers. Nowhere on the face of the earth are the principles of Christian Endeavor better understood or more steadfastly adhered to than in the good old country of the Covenant, the illustrious little land of my nativity.

We in Scotland claimed William Ewart Gladstone as our own, and that claim he always lovingly acknowledged; for, though born in Liverpool, he belonged to Leith, in the historic county of Midlothian, which he represented in Parliament during the richest years of his life. And if, in the few precious minutes allotted to me, I speak of my fellow countryman in terms of highest eulogy, my apology must be found in the constitutional tendency of a Scotsman to regard a just and reverent appreciation of a godly man as the most practical expression of divine thanksgiving.

Gladstone belonged to you as well as to us. His patriotism was cosmopolitan. With him "the enthusiasm of humanity" was no empty phrase. In his home policy he was a Republican, a Democrat in the truest sense, thinking and toiling for the people, in whom he had all but unbounded confidence. His foreign policy meant national righteousness, international justice, and the deliverance of the oppressed. If the throne of the British Empire stands to-day more stable than ever, "broad-based upon the people's will," and commanding, as never before, the respect of the civilized world; if the great Anglo-Saxon race, to which you and I equally belong, occupies a position of influence among the nations which has neither precedent nor parallel; and, best of all, if principalities and powers have been led to pay more homage to Christ, and greater heed to the claims of righteousness and peace; — the results are traceable in no insignificant degree to the large-hearted statesmanship of Mr. Gladstone. I join with you most cordially in regarding Washington as the most commanding figure of the eighteenth century; and possibly some of you may agree with me in thinking Gladstone the greatest name on the roll of the nineteenth. But whatever may be your estimate of Gladstone's greatness on this side of the ocean, certainly there was much truth in the generous remark made by a member of the present Tory cabinet when the news of his death reached the House: "That finishes the Victorian era!"

Time would fail me to make adequate mention of his erudition. His mere information was colossal in its magnitude. He came as near as possible to being a universal specialist. He was learned in the law, and an eminent theologian and apologist. It was an enemy who said of him that, had he not been Prime Minister, he might have been Lord Chancellor, or Archbishop of Canterbury. As a linguist and ethnologist he had few equals. He was an intellectual athlete, a master of debate before whom Disraeli and Chamberlain shuddered, a platform orator without a peer, — or with but one, to be eclipsed by whom was no dishonor, his friend and fellow gladiator, John Bright. Endeavorers. what lesson can possibly reach you and me from such a giddy eminence of genius? It comes down to us in no uncertain sound. Let us strive after the fullest development of the powers God has committed to us. Let the mute, inglorious Gladstones among us bear in mind that his great abilities were not seconded by good luck, but by incessant labor.

Two great moral qualities stand out conspicuously in the character of Gladstone: honesty and enthusiasm. Even in the blinding heat of controversy his motives were seldom seriously questioned by his most bitter opponents. He laid himself open to the charge of inconsistency, alienated some of his staunchest friends, rent in twain the great political party of which he was the leader, and which he might almost be said to have made, prepared for himself a great defeat, and caused failure to be written over the closing years of a brilliant career, — all because he could not disregard the command of conscience. And he threw himself whole-hearted into every task he undertook. The motive power of his life was spiritual, — the enthusiasm of conviction and of duty: the religious fervor of a man who lived consciously under the eye of God. Without this consuming zeal, even with his magnificent mental endowment, he could never have been the great man that he was. For he was not a bookworm, but a student, never losing the freshness of enthusiastic interest in the them's that engrossed him: not a politician — most contemptible of men! — but a broad-minded statesman, turning his honest face in every direction, and sweeping with his far-seeing eye the whole circle of his horizon. Like all great enthusiasts. his faults were so patent that the blindest love could not lose sight of them; but they "leant to virtue's side," and sprang, in a sense, from the very nobility of his nature. He could bear with calmness the most virulent personal attacks. The great patience of the old man under the most acute physical suffering was the wonder and admiration of the world. But he could not endure meanness, and had nothing but short shrift for cowardly oppression. It was the great, meek man who sat, Testament in hand, by the bed of the little London crossing-sweeper who counselled the "bag-and-baggage" policy as the only satisfactory solution of the Eastern question. And was not Christ himself an impatient reformer? Was not the whip of small cords the instrument of a divine indignation? And were not some of the angriest words Gladstone ever thundered from the hustings, or hurled across the table of the House of Commons, uttered in the spirit of the Master himself?

The memory of such a man cannot perish. We who have seen and heard him, and the few of us who have met him face to face, and felt the grasp of his hand, can never pass from the influence of his personality. Four long years of seclusion, following upon political defeat, only enhanced men's estimate of his greatness. Among the millions who may be said to have walked on tiptoe around his couch of pain were many whom he counted his foes; but when the end came the nation burst into tears! This world has seldom seen such a mourning. As one who parted from him said of him once in the old days of comradeship, "This generation stands too near such greatness to comprehend it. Far in the coming century it will be seen in truer perspective." Beheld from the plain, the height of the highest mountain is deceptive. It needs to be seen from a distance. And the greater the space of time over which Gladstone is seen, the greater will he appear.

My remaining seconds will not suffice for the pointing of a moral. I cannot more powerfully suggest it than in the well-worn but never hackneyed words of one of the noblest of your own poets,—

> "Lives of great men all remind us
> We may make *our* lives sublime!"

The rain thundered down upon the roof of the tent at the conclusion of Mr. Pollock's address, and continued during the season of meditation and prayer conducted by Rev. F. D. Power, D.D., Washington, D. C.

After the memorial hymn had rung out grandly, with the rumbling thunder and the falling rain as an accompaniment, Rev. James Mursell, of London, England, began his oration on George Müller, looking out upon a sea of black umbrellas instead of bright faces. But he made the beautiful life of that man of faith shine out luminously. Mr. Mursell's reception was most hearty.

Address by Rev. James Mursell,

London, England.

GEORGE MÜLLER.

I need scarcely repeat what my friend Mr. Pollock has said; viz., that I regard it a high honor to be allowed to speak to American Endeavorers as one of the representatives of British Endeavor. We are samples, sent to Detroit, '99, in the hope of inducing all of you to speculate largely in London, 1900. Samples are often better than bulk. That may be so as regards my comrade. It does not apply to me. As you sample me to-night, please remember, the bulk is better.

You have given me a great subject, and little time in which to speak of it. If William Ewart Gladstone was the grand old man of politics, George Müller was the grand old man of prayer. "Prayer and faith," he says, "helped me over all my difficulties."

George Müller was born in Prussia in 1805. His youth was like Augustine's, marred by vice. Theft, falsehood, immorality, stained his early years. He often made resolutions to be different, yet broke them almost as fast as they were made. He was converted at a little meeting in a private house when he was twenty years of age. He came to England in 1829; settled as a minister in Bristol in 1832. There in 1834 he formed the Scriptural Knowledge Institution for Home and Abroad, which was really a missionary society, a Bible society, and a R. T. S. rolled into one. There, in the closing days of 1835, he founded the Orphan Houses with which his name is forever linked. Thence he set forth on those wonderful missionary journeys in which the old man told to believers in every land the wonderful works of God; and thence, also, in March, last year, he passed, as by one step, through the thin veil that hides from mortal eyes the face of God.

The life of George Müller has special lessons for Endeavorers.

First. The first of these relates to prayer, and the study of God's Word. The man who is converted at a prayer meeting is likely to make much of prayer. George Müller did. Prayer was indeed his vital breath. Right from the outset of his Christian life he set apart an hour every day for secret prayer, and soon the one hour was multiplied to three or four. Up to 1839, he tells us, he had risen "only between six and seven, but from that year he came to see that the best part of our time should be especially given to communion with the Lord." The result was that he was able to secure what he calls "long and precious seasons for prayer and meditation before breakfast." Mark this, Endeavorers, especially you who take short and not peculiarly precious seasons for these things after supper.

George Müller prayed about everything. When the drains were stopped up, and the obstruction could not be found, he prayed, and it was found. He prayed money out of chancery. He prayed the north wind into the south. You may smile; but one has said, "Elias was a man of like passions with ourselves, and he prayed earnestly that it might not rain, and it rained not on the earth," etc., and he prayed again, and the heaven gave rain. It is still true: "the spirit-possessed prayer of a righteous man availeth much."

George Müller prayed when he was tired. He was glad on one occasion to be left alone inside a coach, for it permitted him to pray aloud, and having already travelled forty-eight hours uninterruptedly, he says, "My body was too tired to allow me to continue for any length of time in mental prayer."

George Müller prayed without ceasing. Some people pray for a little while and then cease. Not he. In 1841 he began to pray for the conversion of five men of his acquaintance. Says he, "I prayed every day without one single intermission, whether sick or in health, on the land or on the sea, and whatever the pressure of my engagements might be." In eighteen months one of them was converted. "I thanked God, and prayed on for the others." The second was not converted for five years; the third for six. In 1897 two of them were still unsaved. They had been prayed for every day for fifty-two years. "They are not converted yet," George Müller said, "but they will be." He was prepared to offer, as he says elsewhere, thousands and tens of thousands of prayers, to exercise much faith and patience, persuaded that the servant of God who trusted in him would not be put to shame.

Most of these prayers were offered with an open Bible in his hands. Some of us are reading through the Bible in one year. George Müller read his through four times every year, and that not hurriedly, but "with prayer and meditation." "The first thing I did . . . was to begin to meditate on the Word of God, searching . . . into every verse to get the blessing out of it . . . for the good of my own soul. The result I have found to be almost invariably this: that very soon my soul has been led to confession, or to thanksgiving, or to intercession, or to supplication; so that, though I did not give myself to prayer, but to meditation, yet it turned almost immediately into prayer."

That, Christian Endeavorers, was how George Müller prayed. Do you pray anything like that? Do I? The future of Christian Endeavor depends upon our answer. No movement, however big, no Christian, however gifted, can maintain spiritual life and spiritual strength apart from prayer and pondering the Word of God. Think of George Müller's "long and precious seasons for prayer and meditation," and then with new solemnity and earnestness recall the sentence in our pledge which says, " I promise God that I will pray to him and read the Bible every day."

Second. George Müller was also an example to Endeavorers in giving. We think of him as a man to whom a great deal of money was given. So he was; but he was also a man by whom a great deal of money was given. Some of you belong to the Tenth Legion. That may do to begin with. Before long you should enlist in the Fifth. George Müller began in the Third. When his income was £150 per annum he gave £50 of it to the Word of God. When it was £288 he gave £120. When it was £2,600 he gave £2,230 to the Lord's service, and used the balance for his own necessities. That is to say, he gave away six out of every seven dollars that he had. A man who gives in that proportion has the right to pray for money. If you do not give in *that* proportion, see to it that you give in some. Proportionate giving, decided on as in the sight of God, cannot be mean. " Many of the children of God," George Müller says, " lose in a great measure the privilege and also the blessedness of communicating to the Lord's work . . . for want of a regular habit of giving." An old woman, poor, and a cripple, sent sixpence to the orphanage on Ashley Downs, wrapped in a piece of paper, on which she wrote: " Give, give, give; be ever giving. If you are living you will be giving. Those who are not giving are not living."

Third. Finally, George Müller is an example to us all of faith. He practised faith. He did so for his income. Sometimes he was brought so low as not to have a penny left, or to sit down to a meal with the last loaf on the table, and no money to buy another; but God came to his help in the nick of time, so that his servant never lacked daily bread.

He practised faith for the support of the Orphanage. He never asked man for a farthing. He told the Father of the fatherless his needs, and was not put to shame. " Greater and more manifest nearness of the Lord's presence I have never had," he says, " than when, after breakfast, there were no means for dinner, and then the Lord provided the dinner; or when, after dinner, there were no means for tea, and yet the Lord provided the tea; and all this without one human being having been informed about our need."

George Müller practised faith in sorrow. In the deep waters of bereavement he cried out, " God himself has done it. We are satisfied with him." He practised faith for guidance in the smallest things. One evening there was only a farthing in hand, and all the orphans to feed. Next morning, before breakfast, George Müller took his usual walk, but was led by inward promptings out of his usual track. " Perhaps God has a reason for this," he said, as he got over a stile. Less than five minutes afterwards he met a gentleman who gave him £2 for the orphans. " Then I knew the reason I had been led this way." He practised faith in the hour of difficulty, and he had more than most men in his life. But he was not daunted. " Nay," he declares; " I had a secret satisfaction in the greatness of the difficulties which were in the way. So far from being cast down by them, they delighted my soul. I did nothing but pray."

Fellow Endeavorers, one of the greatest needs of the present day is lives that are really lives of faith. So many of us only have the faith which believes when it has seen. Our Lord does not refuse such faith, but he cannot bless it. " Blessed are they who, like George Müller, have not seen, yet believe." " I judged myself," he tells us, " bound to be the servant of the church of Christ in the particular point on which I had obtained mercy; viz., in being able to take God by his word, and to rely on it." Let each of us, inspired by his example, bind on ourselves the same high obligations. We, too, are called to live the life we live *in the flesh* by faith. George Müller was not a greatly gifted man; but he achieved great things. He proved impossibilities possible, and did it all by faith. " Great faith," perhaps you say. I do not know if it was great or small. I do not think it matters. A little faith in a great Saviour always produces wonderful results. Faith as tiny as a grain of mustard-seed removes mountains. The tiny seed opens a door in itself, and nature, which is

God, steps in and makes a great tree. The whole ocean can pour itself through a narrow channel, if you give it time. I have given up asking myself whether my faith is little or great. I have a great God, a mighty Saviour, an omnipotent Paraclete, and if I have any faith, any real faith, in him, and practise it, it is enough; he will come into my life and use me to the full. George Müller is a shining instance of the marvellous use God can make of an ordinary man who really trusts in him.

"What a wonderful man George Müller was!" some of you say. No, he was not. George Müller was not at all a wonderful man; but he had a wonderful Saviour. His name shall be called wonderful; that is the lesson of George Müller's life for us Endeavorers. If he could step out of the glory where he dwells with Christ, I think he would repeat the words he spoke when he was still a pilgrim and a sojourner on earth: "The glory of God — that it might be seen by the whole church of God that yet in these days God listens to prayer, and that he is the same in power and love as he ever was. To illustrate *that* I have devoted my whole life."

One of the best and truest things Dr. Wayland Hoyt, the last speaker, said in his oration on the Endeavorers that died in the Spanish war was that the victory at Manila and the issue of the war did not *happen.* They were the results of a military system almost as perfect as the system of the stars, which held in his place every man behind the guns and in the stokers' holes.

The rain had entirely passed over and the umbrellas were down, and gesticulating hands and echoing voices were raised at every mention of Manila and Dewey.

"The heroism of transfigured duty" was one of Dr. Hoyt's fine phrases. He was speaking of the Harvard graduate and society man who washed dishes for the Rough Riders, and of the coal-heavers who made it possible to overtake Cervera's fleet. It is a phrase that will live and fire many an Endeavorer's heart for lowly, heroic service.

Address by Rev. Wayland Hoyt, D.D.,

Philadelphia, Pa.

Lessons in Heroism—Our Soldiers and Sailors.

So they went sailing forth on the last days of that April but a year ago. War had been declared. Therefore all the neutral ports were closed. There was no refuge anywhere. They were amid mighty hazards — no more coal could be had when that upon the transports should have been consumed; the officers of the fleet had never been in the bay whither their ships pointed; the number of hostile vessels they were seeking was beyond their own; the alternative confronting them was victory or sheer destruction.

But as the United States cruiser *Boston* steamed out of Hong Kong harbor with her sister ships, the captain of Her Majesty's ship *Immortalité* hailed Captain Wildes of the *Boston* to say. "You will surely win; I have seen too much of your target-practice to doubt it."

And they did win, on that May-day morning a year ago — how magnificently, how demolishingly, you all know; never in the world's history such a battle, such shattering defeat to the black and blood-red banner which for centuries had been flaunting for the worst oppression, such limitless and even bloodless victory for the glorious flag of freedom.

But that surprising triumph did not simply happen. It did not fall out, the careless issue of a blind luck. It was the exact result of rigorously working causes. The captain of Her Majesty's ship *Immortalité* exploited the secret when he shouted," You will surely win; I have seen too much of your target-practice to doubt it."

Why, as for long time our brave Jackies *had been* practising, so up to the moment of attack they *kept on* practising. On the voyage to Manila gun-drills, and drills of every other necessary sort, were steadily maintained. Every man, from Dewey to coal-heaver, knew his exact place and was exactly fitted for it. Disciplined intelligence loaded every gun, aimed it, fired it. System, as splendid almost as the system of the stars, clasped every man, stationed him, set his duty at his hand, taught him the precise doing it. Why, when the battle was raging fiercest, and two black torpedo-boats pushing out from Cavité straight for the *Olympia* would have utterly destroyed her could they have reached her, a spectator of that anxious moment says, " Our gunners stood as calm and collected, as sure of themselves, as if they were no more than on their ordinary gun-drill." And the torpedo-boats did not reach the *Olympia*. The straightest shots prevented them. But those balls whizzed so straight, and the guns whence they whizzed were so calmly managed and so intelligently aimed, because there had been beforehand such constant and painstaking, ordinary gun-drills. What could the happy-go-lucky, undrilled, unprepared Spaniards do against men so steadily and sternly prepared for the awful gauge of battle?

The heroism of *unshirking, patient, noble preparation* is the lesson we ought to let our achieving sailors teach us, as we give acclaim to their great victory at Manila.

And this lesson of patient and dutiful preparation is a lesson peculiarly pertinent to Christian Endeavor; for this, if it is anything, is Christian Endeavor — not an end in itself, but always a means to an end. And that end? The best possible service for Christ and his church, and in order to that end of service, preparation for it by means of Christian Endeavor. Drill of prayer meeting, drill of consecration meeting, drill of business meeting, drill of prayer, drill of testimony, drill of committee work, drill of daily loyalty to the pledge — that is to say, unceasing preparation for service, that, as soldiers of Christ and marshalled members of his church, we may do vanquishing warfare in the great conflict our Lord and his church are waging.

Dr. Hoyt's Eloquent Tribute to Our Dead Heroes.

" Onward, Christian soldiers,
Marching as to war;
With the cross of Jesus
Going on before."

Yes; but we do not want to be raw recruits of soldiers and awkward squads of them. We want to be trained veterans for the Holy War. And Christian Endeavor means such training and preparation. The heroism of a sedulous and submissive *preparation* is a sort of heroism our triumphant sailors at Manila should infect us with.

———

It is at San Antonio in Texas. It is the camp of the Rough Riders. He is a graduate of Harvard University. He is a gentleman of wealth. He was on the deck of the *Defender* when she outsailed the *Valkyrie*. He was wont to drive a four-in-hand in Central Park. By position and culture he is as far removed from menial things as a man can well be. But when the war struck he felt it his duty to enlist. Nor would he seek any position of distinction. And Colonel Roosevelt says, " When I went down to the camp at San Antonio he was on kitchen duty, and was cooking and washing dishes for one of the New Mexican troops; and he was doing it so well that I had no further doubt as to how he would get on."

The good ship *Oregon* is making that marvellous sail from San Francisco around the Cape. Much of the voyage is done under tropical sun-heats. What with the sun and furnaces, down below there, where the fires must be kept raging, the temperature often averaged a hundred and fifty degrees. Such, also, was the temperature below during that magnificent chase after and destruction of Cervera's fleet when he sought escape from the harbor of Santiago. And most of the men down there — most of them, save the engineers, not charged with any lofty duty, though with duty irrevocably necessary. They were coal-heavers; amid the grime and awful heat they were but hauling coal for the greedy furnaces. They were, and must be, absolutely ignorant of what was going on above. For them, where the conflict clashed, there were immensities of danger, but there could be little of the excitement of the conflict. For them only the dimly lighted darkness, the dust and grime, the suffocating heat.

I count that heroism of the noblest sort — that washing dishes, that lowly coal-heaving. It was the heroism of lowly duty glorified by lofty motive. Such menial things as washing the dishes and heaving coal must be done for the country's sake. Well, then, for the country's sake they would do it all, uncomplainingly, strenuously, in fashion the best they could. Heroes all of them, because a great motive was behind their doing even the inconspicuous things at which their country set them.

Such lesson as our brave soldiers and sailors can so well teach us of the glorifying and transfiguring of lowly duty by heroic motive, we all of us need the constant learning.

Listen to Thomas Carlyle a moment. In that prose-poem of the French Revolution he has been telling of Louis the Fifteenth, — his resplendent throne, his kingly chance of helping his fellows, and how, both as king and brother-man, he miserably failed. Then Thomas Carlyle goes on to say. and I think his words the truest and the weightiest, "And yet let no man lay flattering unction to his soul. Louis was a ruler; but art not thou also one? His wide France, look at it from the Fixed Stars (themselves not Infinitude) is no wider than thy narrow birdsfield, where thou didst faithfully or didst unfaithfully. Man, ' symbol of eternity imprisoned in time,' it is not thy works, which are all mortal, infinitely little, and the greatest no greater than the least, but only the Spirit thou workest in, that can have worth or continuance."

Be you, too, heroic, then, O Christian Endeavorer, in the least things your Christ and his church would have you be. Make what men call smallest greatest by the motive, " For His sake." Do not daintily pick and choose. Do not say, " Somebody else can do the inconspicuous and distasteful service." Seize you it, rather, for Jesus' sake, and by the great motive with which you work turn drudgery to delight, and show how high and noble it is and possible to be heroic, even though your hands are set at what men call common things.

Says Colonel Roosevelt of his Rough Riders, " They were just as ready to fight when the Spaniards made an attack at three o'clock in the morning, although they were hungry and shivering from lying out at night — where they had been drenched by the tropical rains — as they had been to fight in the daytime on full stomachs, and that is the test. To wake men up at 5 A.M. who have had nothing to eat, nothing to cover them, — wake them up suddenly and have them all run the right way, — that is the test. Such men are a good lot. There was n't a man who went to the rear."

It was on that Sunday morning off Santiago harbor. Yonder, behind the hills encircling this harbor, some smoke was rising. On the forward bridge of the *Brooklyn* Lieutenant Hodgson was intently looking at it. "That smoke is moving, sir, " cried the man at the masthead. " Give me the glass," said the lieutenant. Barely looking through it, he dropped the glass and shouted, " After bridge there," and to the commodore and captains report was made that the enemy's ships were coming out. " Signal the enemy is escaping," commanded Commodore Schley. " We have already done so, sir," replied Lieutenant Sears. " Signal the fleet to clear ship," instantly commanded the commodore. Every gun was ready; fresh fires were started under four boilers;

every water-tight compartment was closed; the ammunition was ready for the reloading of the guns; the decks were wet — *all in but three minutes.*

See our brave soldiers and sailors teach us the heroism of *prompt* duty. Laggardness is always loss. Promptness is at least the beginning of triumph. If you are a true Christian Endeavorer you will be prompt in your service for your Lord and his church. That hesitant pause in your prayer meeting — obedient to your pledge, you will instantly spring to fill it. That service on your committee — you will quickly seize it. That unusual duty the circumstances of your church suggest — you will never be among the halting ones exclaiming, " I pray thee, have me excused; " but like the soldiers in the trenches about Santiago, like the sailors getting the ships ready almost in the flash of an eye, you will rather say, " Here am I; send me," and you will at once be at it. Promptness is heroism.

———

The fight was over. The *Maria Theresa*, the *Viscaya*, the *Colon*, the *Oquendo*, the *Furor*, the *Pluton*, were all sunk or stranded or burned or surrendered. Commodore Schley is on the bridge of the *Brooklyn*. The decks are crowded with the joyful men from the fire-rooms, from the magazines, from behind the guns. Pointing to them, Commodore Schley said, " Those are the fellows who made this day." And what was true of the *Brooklyn* was as utterly true of the sailors, marines, helpers of every sort, aboard the other ships. Those were the fellows who made that glorious day. Every man in his place; every man doing his whole duty; all, from commodore to coal-heaver, in assisting interdependence.

It is the heroism of *united* service which has given such fresh lustre to Old Glory on that great day; every man doing his part, and all doing their parts together.

Why does your society lag? — if it does lag. Why is the onset of your society feeble? — if it is feeble. Is not this the precise trouble? There has been failure of united service. Each has not lent his hand. There is a lot of latent strength lying around unused. While some have wrought others have waited. Perhaps while others wrought *you* have waited. By so much you have weakened your society. By so much you have set limit to the success of your Lord's cause and church. The heroism of united service — from our brave soldiers and sailors let us get that contagion.

———

The splendid charge was almost done. The top of that hill of San Juan had been almost reached. Lieutenant Ord was leading his men magnificently. Just then, a few yards from the summit, a boy private from Ohio, who had kept close to Lieutenant Ord — himself so soon to fall — was stricken with a mortal wound. Lieutenant Ord heard him give a faint cry, and stopped an instant in his rush to kindly say, as he saw the "dying pallor" on the boy's face, " My poor fellow, I can do nothing for you." Then came back gasping answer like this: " I did n't call you back for anything like that, Lieutenant. I 'm done for; but I thought you had better take my steel nippers. There may be still another fence beyond that hill, and I won't be there to cut it for you."

It was after that battle of Las Guasimas. In the hastily contrived field hospital the wounded were lying. The night had shut down. Suddenly a voice started: —

> " My country, 't is of thee,
> Sweet land of liberty,
> Of thee I sing " —

Other voices joined : —

> " Land where my fathers died,
> Land of the pilgrim's pride " —

One voice joined, lagged, yet would keep on. It was a weak voice, and gasping. But it kept on, though the others had finished : —

> " Land — of — the — pilgrim's pride,
> Let — freedom " —

and the voice failed and was stilled forever.

The heroism of *devotion to the death* — surely this is the lesson for us.   O members of Christian Endeavor, let such be our heroism, — devotion to our Christ and his church to the last breath!

Well, they wrought, they endured, they fought, they were wounded, they died, many of them, some on the battle-field, some lingeringly in hospitals.   It is terrible and fateful business — this business of war.   And what have they accomplished?   Was it worth the while?

By blood and wounds and sickness and death they have illustriously set forth the fact that ours is a united country.   The one flag is the flag for all. Bagley, Ord, Fish, Capron — and hundreds like them; the slain on Cuban battle-fields, on battle-fields in the far Philippines, dead heroes all.   They are from the South, the North, the East, the West; but farthest down of all they are Americans.   For the one glorious flag they died.   The one flag enfolds them.   To show forth the mighty fact that blood of South and blood of North, that heart of South and heart of North, are indestructibly one was worth the while.

What else have those heroes of ours accomplished?   And again, was it worth the while?

They have shattered the worst oppression, both civil and religious, the world has ever seen from twelve million people.   They have opened the gates for civil and religious liberty for twelve million people.   They have done it for humanity.   Yes, that was worth the while.

And what responsibility of opportunity have they laid on us!   O Christian Endeavorers, into Cuba, into Porto Rico, soon it shall be true in the far Philippines, you may go with civil liberty, with the free, pure Gospel.   See to it that you go — or certainly that you send.

There in the trenches about Santiago, as each night came, all along the lines, the regimental bands played "The Star-Spangled Banner."   Then all, officers and men alike, wherever they were, stood with heads uncovered to salute the flag.

By the heroism of preparation, of high motive in even little things, of promptness, of united service, of scathless devotion to the right; by passionate patriotism, by thorough good citizenship, by the patient and strong solving of the great new problems which confront us, by trust in God, O members of the great and noble army of Christian Endeavor, do you salute the flag.

First Congregational Church.
Literary Study of the Bible.
By Prof. R. G. Moulton, Chicago, Ill.

It has been especially perplexing during the Convention to know which to choose: the varied and splendid programmes of the tents, or the alluring lectures and conferences often scheduled for the same time. Among the most conspicuous of these "special meetings," as they were called, were the two lectures on the Bible given by Prof. R. G. Moulton, of Chicago, on "The Literary Study of the Bible" and "The Romance of the Bible."   These were attended by large and most interested audiences.   Professor Moulton understands, as few understand, how to make the Bible fascinating.   His "Modern Reader's Bible" proves that. His talks were most dramatic.   So thrilling, for instance, was his way of telling even the story of Esther that when the climax was reached the audience, that had been listening almost breathless, burst into the wildest applause.

Among the things Professor Moulton said was the following : —

The revised version is one of the greatest steps in the history of literature. It is the first move made to get the book in the right form. For the first time the Bible was translated by men that realized that the Bible is literature.

The reason that the Bible is not recognized in our schools and colleges is that it is not rightly recognized as literature. It is not in literary form. Our literature comes from two sources,— from the Greeks and Romans and from the Bible.

A man is not liberally educated until he is familiar with the classics. Some of those classics are such that if they were printed in plain English they would be seized by the police

The schools and colleges are proud of the father of our literature, the classics, but they disown the mother, the Bible. The literary study of the Bible is distinguished on the one hand from the devotional and theological use of Scripture, and on the other hand from the "higher criticism," which is an inquiry into the history of the sacred writings.

It takes the matter of the Bible as it stands, but endeavors to rescue it from the form in which it is ordinarily exhibited as a succession of pious texts monotonously numbered 1, 2, 3, and to present it in its true literary form as distinct poems, sonnets, dramas, histories, essays, letters, proverbs, speeches, etc.

A good specimen of the different spirit of the two versions of the Bible is the twenty-eighth chapter of Job. In the authorized version this is half isolated sayings, barely intelligible, and half an elaborate question and answer. In the revised version we have a connected picture of mining operations, a gem of description of its kind, and the application of this to the search for wisdom.

First Presbyterian Church.

Practical Conferences.

Conducted by Rev. Charles M. Sheldon.

Topic: *"In the Other Man's Place."*

The First Presbyterian Church was filled; seats, vestibules, and even the edge of the rostrum was decorated with a row of listeners who could not find other seating accommodation. The meeting was a "Practical Talk and Conference." Rev. Charles M. Sheldon, of Topeka, Kan., told of his experience getting a practical knowledge of the world and its workers.

Mr. Sheldon told how he had procured from his congregation permission to take three months' vacation, merely appearing at his church for one sermon each Sunday, and how he put in the time with railroad men, street-car men, professional men, and others, getting in touch with them and inquiring into their intellectual and spiritual life.

"We are in the midst of one of the movements of the age that make for a more perfect brotherhood," he said, in opening his talk. "Christian Endeavor stands for that movement."

He told of the vacation arrangement he had made eight years ago, and incidentally something of the town in which he labored.

"I divided the citizens of Topeka into classes," he said. "Topeka is comparatively a small city. It is called by visitors one of the best cities in the world. There is not a saloon there. There are young men who will vote this fall who never saw a saloon.

"The classes into which I divided the citizens were: street-car men, college students, doctors, lawyers, negroes, railroad men, and newspaper men. I planned to live with each group in turn."

He recited his experience with the street-car men : —

" I wanted to learn how the men lived and where, what they thought about on their trips, whether they cared anything about Christianity, what sort of literature they read, and all such matters. I did n't want to experiment on the men as students of sociology sometimes do — go slumming and write essays. I was animated by an earnest desire to do them good." He told what he found. The Sunday work aroused sorrow in them.

Among the college students he became a student, attended recitations, played ball, and held afternoon conferences with the young men and young women. " I found the students anxious to make inquiries concerning religious matters," he said. " They were interested in questions of duty."

To the college girls he suggested a way to aid in the solving of the servant-girl problem. He proposed to them that after their graduation they go out as servant-girls, get acquainted with the girls in the households of the cities in which they might be, and form associations of the Christian girls and bring them into closer relation with the Christian women who employed them. " And assist to remove," said he, "the stigma from one honest class of labor."

He found the doctors not a promising class.

" I was surprised to find how few cared for religious things. It is surprising that young men are running into the medical profession with no thought of its holy calling."

He said that among the lawyers, when he broached religious questions there was silence and embarrassment. " What a splendid career a lawyer could have if he had a right conception of his place in the world !" said he. " He could make it his business to be a peacemaker, and make a living out of it. There never has been so great an opportunity for a lawyer to serve the cause of civic righteousness as to-day." He told how he invited the lawyers to come and hear him preach about them, and how they came in a body and took front seats, and nodded assent to the lesson he read them.

He canvassed the business men with the question, " Are you conducting your business on strictly Christian principles ? " He said he found but two merchants who were willing to affirm that they were. " There is something wrong there," said he.

He told of the reforms that had been wrought in the colored community in the city of Topeka, how prizes were offered to stimulate civic improvements, and how a college settlement was established. A characteristic sentence was this : —

" You people who live on the avenue try living in cabins of two or three rooms. and see how good Christians you can be."

At the conclusion of Mr. Sheldon's talk on the suggestive theme, " In the Other Man's Place," questions relative to the practice of his preaching were hurled at the popular author.

" Would Christ ride on a street-car on Sunday ? " asked a woman in the audience. Mr. Sheldon said he believed not. He also said that he had an engagement to preach in Bethany Presbyterian Church. "How am I going to get out there if I don't ride on the street-cars on Sunday?" Mr. Sheldon said. A woman suggested a bicycle. The speaker approved the suggestion, but said he'd probably walk, and his statement was applauded.

"Should a hard-working man be a superintendent of a Sunday school and work hard on Sunday?" The speaker said he advised his teachers not to do it, if they could get some one else to act.

"Mr. Sheldon, don't you think it's possible for us to break the Sabbath by having too much service, or preaching, on Sunday?" "Yes, I do," replied Mr. Sheldon, spiritedly. "We should have fewer services on Sunday—one sermon."

Asked as to whether he would have evangelistic service Sunday morning or Sunday evening, Mr. Sheldon replied: "It's just as important to convert a person in the morning as in the evening."

SATURDAY MORNING.

Tent Endeavor.

The Endeavorers at Tent Endeavor, Saturday morning, had another opportunity of demonstrating the fact that no freak of the weather can

An Umbrella Session.

interfere with or impede the progress of the great Christian Endeavor Convention. The big tent was packed again with an ardent crowd of 10,000 delegates.

The services of the morning were conducted along the line of thought, "Saved to Serve," and there were a half-dozen or more excellent addresses upon the theme. Mr. E. O. Excell, of Chicago, led the singing that opened the praise service. Rev. J. Z. Tyler, D.D., of Cleveland, O., presided at the meeting.

Rev. A. B. MacLaurin, of Brooklyn, N. Y., conducted an impressive devotional service, after which the first speaker, Rev. Geo. B. Stewart, D.D., of Harrisburg, Pa., was introduced.

Address by Rev. Geo. B. Stewart, D. D.,

Harrisburg, Pa.

THE JUNIORS SAVED TO SERVE.

Two conspicuous facts characterize the relation of the present-day church to the children. The first is that the church thoroughly believes the children can be saved. It is within the memory of some of us when in certain sections of the church this was not true. Parents and pastors fondly entertained the hope that some day, after the child had grown to young manhood, had learned the ways of the world, had defiled his heart with sin and his conscience with guilt, then, through the blessed work of the Holy Spirit upon his corrupted and polluted life, he might be brought to the knowledge of Christ and consecration to his service. But they scarcely dared to hope that the little child, in the innocency of childhood, with the purity of an unpolluted life, might become and be a child of God.

All this is changed. We now know and rejoice in the knowledge that little children are savable. We do not think less of the value of conversion than our fathers, but we are steadily pushing back into the early years of life the time at which conversion takes place. We do not lessen the radical character of conversion, but we do not believe that the thoroughness of conversion is dependent upon previous experience in the ways of sin. It is not necessary that a life should be given wholly over to Satan in order that it may eventually be wholly given to God. The second birth may be very close in time to the first birth. The regeneration of the Holy Ghost may take place in the heart of the little one who lisps for the first time the name of Jesus. We are quite the more pleased to have our children say they never knew the time when they did not love God and want to serve him than when they tell us of their previous deeds of evil before they became the servants of Christ.

Children can be saved. The little children are being saved. We are laboring to make this more and more possible in the life of the children of our land. We are teaching them to love the Lord. We are teaching them that he loves them and wants them to love him in return. It used to be that while there was some doubt as to whether God loved the good little children, there was no doubt at all that he did not love the bad. We were quite firmly convinced that the two she-bears who tore the forty-and-two children in Elisha's time accurately expressed the feelings, and rightly executed the judgment, God has for bad children in all ages and everywhere. But now we understand that God loves bad children; that in fact his love for the children is not conditioned upon their goodness or their badness, any more than his love of men is conditioned upon their moral character.

The picture of Jesus with the little children in his arms, and blessing them without asking whether they were obedient and truthful and kind, more accurately represents the attitude of God toward them than the two she-bears with their cruel claws. It is impossible for us to measure the distance between that child incident in Elisha's time and that other child incident in Christ's time. The distance in centuries is small as compared with the distance in character. The progress in theology represented in these two pictures is simply incalculable.

Thank God we live in a day when parents can tell their children, whether they are good or bad, that God loves them, and that therefore they are to do their best to be good for their Heavenly Father's sake. They are to love Him who first loved them.

Children can be saved. Children are being saved. The Junior Society is helping in this glorious work. It brings the Saviour very close to the children, and the children very close to the Saviour. The church in many ways is teaching them that God loves the children, and they are learning through many agencies to love him.

The second notable fact is that the church thoroughly believes that the children can serve.

The church has been a little slow to learn this blessed truth and to act upon it. But she is now coming to see it better and better; and with each succeeding lesson the Lord is teaching her that the children have a place in the economy of the church, just as real and important in its way as the place their fathers and mothers occupy. Children, of course, cannot be elders, and trustees, nor superintendents of the sewing-school, or presidents of the Missionary Society; but neither can their parents run errands, take various parts in delightful entertainments, bring children into the Sunday school, distribute the church papers, be hands and feet in multiplied ways for various persons and organizations in the church, as well as the children.

We used to think that children had to be entertained, and the principal work of the church toward them was to entertain them and hold them, or else to fill them full of valuable information with reference to the doctrines, life, and history of the church. But that they could be of any use, that scarcely seemed credible. The best that we could think of the boy was that a man could be made of him; but that he was of any use while a boy, and as a boy, we did not dream.

But now we are using him, and we find him a splendid instrument. In his place he is becoming quite as important and efficient as his father is in his. In many cases far more so. "In his place" and "as a boy" are vital phrases in this discussion. We will fail to get the proper service if we give him a man's work or expect him to do a boy's work in a man's way. I plead for the children that we give them the high place of servants to the King, and make it possible for them to advance his kingdom in their sphere and according to their power. We have much yet to learn in this respect. Every pastor, every Junior superintendent, every Christian parent, ought to be studying the problem, "How To Put the Children to Work." They are servants of Christ. They are valuable servants for the work God wants them to do. There is much work to be done. It is our duty to bring the servant and the work together. It is no small problem, but it is not an unsolvable one if we resolutely undertake its solution. Children are saved to serve as children, and their lives ought to be made as fruitful as possible. They can serve in the home, they can serve in school, they can serve in the town in which they live. They can serve in the church and Sunday school and Junior society. No readier servants can be found anywhere than the children. They are alert, eager, cheerful in their service. A large amount of good material is going to waste which if we were alive to our obligations and our opportunities could be utilized for the service of Christ.

Splendid results would come from such employment of child labor. The children would be happier; their lives would be more fruitful; their training would be more thorough. The church would be more efficient. The home would be more heavenly, and the kingdom of Christ would come more quickly come.

In these two facts of modern church life, we rejoice. Yea, we will rejoice. We magnify them. We earnestly press them on the attention of every one who loves children and loves the kingdom. We proclaim them from our platforms and pulpits. We work them in our societies and churches. The children are being saved by Christ, and the children are serving Christ.

President Jenkins made a most earnest plea for the establishment of the family altar, in spite of the hurry of our too busy lives, and the lack of sympathy at home,— which is often only a veiled hunger for religious fellowship.

Address by President Burris A. Jenkins,

Indianapolis, Ind.

Religion, like charity, begins at home. It is born there. By the side of a little lake at sunset there was a boat just ready to start toward the opposite shore. A group of men were standing round about it, and in the stern of that boat sat a masterful man, with strong face, and yet every look of whom and every gesture of whom was gentleness and kindness. Suddenly there leaned forward out of the crowd one whose face was somewhat scarred with madness just cured; one whose bare arms and legs were torn with the stuns with which he had inflicted himself, and with the bonds with which he had bound him all in vain. This man said, "Master, I will go with thee wherever thou goest." And I can almost hear him now as he said, "I have been with thee through this beautiful day. Thou hast made me free; now let me go with thee forever." Then the Saviour spoke one of those wise and marvellous words of his: "Go back to thy home, to thy father's house, and show how great things God hath done for thee."

Endeavorers, we here at this Convention may have been stirred to the depths of our souls. We may have been set free from some madness. We may have been sitting through beautiful hours at the very feet of the Master; and to us comes the same word to-day that came to that Galilean: "Go back to thy home, to thy father's house, and show how great things God hath done for thee." If here we have gained anything of instruction, if here we have gained anything of enthusiasm, the first place for us to manifest it is in the home; and only as we go back, our lives become increasingly kinder and gentler and truer in the home circle, then all our public praying, all our public speaking, will be but as sounding brass and tinkling cymbal.

These words "family altar" are precisely the arch words, for what does the word "altar" mean but sacrifice? and what does "sacrifice" mean except love? The greatest student in the subject of comparative religions in America to-day declares that altars were erected for the sake of love, and not for the sake of propitiation in the beginning. So that our ancestors, clad in skins as they erected upon the wide plains or in the deep forests the first altars that were made, erected them, not for the purpose of propitiating the anger of the gods, but for the sake of giving out from their lives, toward those beings or that being whom they loved and revered, some token of their regard. Now, if this was true, does it not remain true that the test of sacrifice, therefore, is for the sake of love, and not for the sake of propitiation? And these family altars, unless they be the tokens of love in the home, or self-sacrifice, or willingness to give up with gentleness and kindness, there can be no proper prayer.

Some say that the ring is the token of love. It is not so. Too often it is the token of human ambition. Too often it is the token of love grown cold, or indifference, or hate, even. It is the cross that is the token of love. The altar of sacrifice — that is the true token of love. And only in the homes where the cross and the altar are erected — only there is there any true home life, or home love. And so unless there be these characteristics of family life, love and tenderness, there can be no true family altar. Whether this sacrifice be toward God or toward one another, it is one and the same thing. Love toward God is love toward man, and love toward one's family first of all.

So these two go together,— love and prayer. Where love is dead prayer cannot survive. Where love goes out at the door prayer flies away through the windows. They stand or fall together, one and inseparable. They are reigning together or they are falling together. One is the king, and the other the queen. No queen can reign when her king is dead. Love and prayer must reign together in the home. And if it is true that kindness and gentleness and love slay and choke out wrong in the home, erect the family altar, so is it also true that the family altar can slay and choke out coldness, hardness, and unkindness. People cannot pray together, people cannot lift their hearts up to God together, without drawing closer to one another, and being made gentle toward one another.

I had some friends who started for the Klondike about two years ago. One of them, with whom I was particularly intimate, had been a wild sort of a boy. I knew him thoroughly, slept with him, fished with him, swum with him, ate with him, time and time again. He started for the Klondike in a set of his own company, who went to that far-away northerly region, and no company were better equipped than these boys. They had everything that money could give them, for they were all well to do. Well, this wild boy, who had never been to church for many and many a day, who had not been to Sunday school since he was compelled to go, who possibly had not been to prayer meeting since he was carried there a baby in arms,— this boy, when he came unto the difficulties and dangers of that awful trail, with the winds and the mountains upon the one side, and the precipices upon the other, with the bodies of men and beasts strewn along the way, seemed to be overpowered with the sense of the danger by which they were all surrounded, and he said to them, " Boys, in these times we must not forget God."

Then in the second place, it is said sometimes that we do not meet with sufficient sympathy at home. There is not in our family the desire for prayer. Our parents are not as sympathetic with our religion as they might be. Our children are not so sympathetic with our religion as they might be. Our husbands and our wives are not sufficiently sympathetic. While I would not urge upon any Endeavorer to thrust his religion into the face of those by whom he is surrounded, — religion is not a vaunting ; religion is not for public, — nevertheless it certainly is true that many times those are hungering for some token of religion whom we do not suppose to be. And we shall be surprised sometimes when the swine before whom we think we are throwing our pearls are not swine, but men and women hungering for broader life.

Endeavorers who went to San Francisco two years ago will remember the Union Pacific road as it goes over the great divide and the American desert, past the Sink of the Humboldt and all that section. Well, I rode through there one night on the engine with the engineer. I promised him I would not talk any if he would allow me to ride with him. He said, " It is against the rules." " Well," I said, " I know ; but I will be good if you will let me go." And he said, " All right ; " so I got on with him. And I only broke that rule once, when I said, " What body of water is that over there ? " " No body of water," said he ; " that is a mirage." " Oh," said I. " I can see where the edge of the water comes up on the sand." " No, it is just a mirage ; no water there." As night came on and I turned to go back in the sleeper, I said, " Good night, Captain." and he did not say anything for a moment. He looked into my eyes, that great big six-foot four-inch man, with his eyes looking through those glasses, and his firm jaw as magnificent, and his magnificent figure, and he said to me, " Pray for us, will you ? " I had never seen him before. He never knew who I was. What it was caused him to say that I do not know. I said, " Certainly. Are you a Christian ? " " No, but I once was." And he turned back to his throttle, and I went to my berth and slept quietly and soundly through that night, because I knew that a Christian man was at the throttle there. I believe that a man who needs prayer and feels the need of it and asks for it is close to God ; and we shall be surprised sometimes to find in our own home circle those who never asked for prayer, but who would ask for prayer if we would give them half a chance.

So I might go on. I shall not specify the character of the morning worship. We all know what it ought to be. We all know it ought to have much of song, for song carries a message home where nothing else will do it. A stammerer can get his words out by song when he cannot get them out in any other way. Let us have much of song, much of reading. Of prayer — let us have much of that. Home is the touchstone. It is the place, after all, where our religion is tried ; it is the touchstone for the good of all true religion. Home is the foundation-stone for all the best that is built into our Democratic and Republican and constitutional governments. Home is the centre and soul of our Christian communities. It is the capstone of the arch of all our culture. Home is the tallest building that is erected in all our country. And as the sun rises in the east in the morning, and passes through its course to the west in the evening, the shadow of the home rests upon every other public structure. City hall, court house, state house, lodge buildings, church, and all, are grouped under the shadow of the home. If we have any alabaster box of precious ointment, let us take it home and break it upon the feet of the Saviour there.

"The church is the tree," said the Rev. E. B. Allen, truly, "and the Christian Endeavor Society is only one of its branches. There are not two trees.' Whereupon he went on to urge support of the mid-week prayer meeting.

Address by Rev. Ernest Bourner Allen,

Lansing, Mich.

SAVED TO SERVE IN THE MID-WEEK PRAYER MEETING.

I. *The value of the prayer meeting to the church and the individual; its need, new life.*

A Christian Endeavorer illustrated the subject of self-mastery by the story of a boy who had been taught 1 Cor. ix. 27: "But I keep under my body, and bring it into subjection: lest that by any means, when I have preached to others, I myself should be a castaway." On coming to repeat the verse in public, he said he had forgotten it, but it was something about "*keeping the soul on top.*"

The mid-week prayer meeting is one of the notable and historic features of the Christian church. Its purpose, amid the distractions and anxieties of our busy, workaday life, is to "keep the soul on top." Ever since Jesus Christ gave his life as a ransom for many there has been a prayer meeting in the Church Universal. The ancient landmark has become a bulwark. To remove it would be a sacrilege and invite destruction.

What is true of the prayer meeting as an institution of the church is true of its relation to the individual. It cannot safely be left out of the life. Thomas tried it, we are told, and absented himself from the first prayer meeting apparently without excuse. He may have been unwell. He may have been tired. Perhaps it looked like rain, or a friend dropped in to see him. Possibly the subject was uninteresting, or some one was there whom he did not care to see.

Three great things, says the historian, Thomas missed because of his absence. "In the first place, he missed seeing Jesus; for the Master came to that first prayer meeting and spoke at it. In the second place, Thomas missed the gift of the Holy Spirit which those present received from the Saviour. In the third place, he lost his faith in Christianity. When the disciples met him he had blossomed out into a full-fledged agnostic. He flatly refused to accept their united testimony, and declared that nothing short of full scientific proof could ever convince him of the resurrection. What a price to pay for neglecting to go to one prayer meeting!" The vision of Jesus, the gift of the Spirit, and the positive assurance of faith,—these the disciple loses who neglects the sacred fellowship of the prayer hour. Thomas had to attend the next prayer meeting in order to find what he had lost.

The stability of any institution depends on its getting hold of new life. Without boys and girls to feed its insatiable desire the saloon would fall. The church which does not have steady or periodic accessions will die of old age. The Endeavor society lapsing into sweet and indolent content because of the executive ability of its present membership, and not training others to fill their places, passes into "innocuous desuetude," or something worse. The prayer meeting in which only the saints of half a century unite in tremulous songs of praise will soon pass with its members to join "the choir invisible." What a joy to feel that so sacred and ancient an institution as the prayer meeting, so essential to the individual, has in training a vast, unnumbered host of recruits, whose steady tramp and thrilling cry "for Christ and the Church" shake the very foundations of evil!

II. *Dangers to Endeavor work through professionalism and ignorance; consequent danger, a neglect of the church prayer meeting.*

There are dangers connected with everything good and valuable. Two dangers face our Endeavor work here: first, a sort of professionalism which makes the Endeavor society the specialty, and omits other work in church channels; second, ignorance of the purpose and claim of the church. The emphasis upon two fundamental principles meets these dangers. One is that there shall come a day of graduation into the larger work of the church. For this event no age limit can be set. The character of the individual, the society, and the church must determine. There should ever be conference with the pastor. If any considerable number of mature people remain in a society it is apt to result that the burden of the work falls upon them and those younger are untrained. More than that, the younger ones are insensibly discouraged in accepting responsibility. We may except from this rule societies in communities where churches are small, and where young and old are thrown together more closely. Here local conditions invite the membership of older people. Such societies thrive not on account of adult membership, or in spite of it, but because in the midst of it the youth are being trained, which is the essential thing.

The second principle which needs emphasis is the fact that the church is the tree and the Endeavor society one branch. There are not two trees. Scores of young people are brought into our Endeavor societies who do not know or love the church as an institution. Their first love is a society. To it they are intensely loyal. With it they would abide. Wisely and tenderly they must be taught that the church is the Alma Mater, the fostering mother, and the society simply an obedient child.

III. *The responsibility of the Endeavorer for the prayer meeting because of his training and position.*

Remembering the tendency to pass by the duties of the mid-week meeting and to remain long in the Endeavor society, and realizing that many come into the young people's work who are unacquainted with the church as a home and field for service, let us ask why the Endeavorer should serve the church. What does he owe?

Our heritage calls us to serve. We are

" The heirs of all the ages, in the foremost files of time."

We stand "fronting the dawn" in the unparalleled opportunities of to-day. No generation of young people since Christ walked in Galilee has been so richly equipped, so magnificently trained. This age is ours. "To be living is sublime." *Every* age is ours. History and literature, invention and art, progress and liberty, have poured their priceless store into our lives. Our education has been the freest and fullest. We have seen great uprisings of youth for the flag of our country and for the cross of our Christ. One young man lays aside his pestle and mortar. Another throws the reins over " Brown Bess " and leaves the plow. Still another closes his books, leaves shop and store, school and home, to enter on the sacrificial service of freedom. One goes to Africa to preach the gospel, the other to Santiago to make men free, and which is braver who can tell? The heritage of their heroism is the sweet inspiration of our toil It calls us to royal service. No age has been so prodigal of training and motives as our own.

If you have read " David Harum " you remember how quaintly he declares that " ev'ry hoss c 'n do a thing better 'n' spryer if he 's been broke to it as a colt." And again: " The 's a good many fast quarter hosses: them that can keep it up for a full mile is scurse." In other words, early training brings ease and endurance. Whatever facility in service, whatever capacity for continued toil, the splendid training of our little society affords, we hold it in sacred trust for the church of Jesus Christ. The opportunities of the society work have in-

creased our power. Only yesterday a pastor recommended a young woman as
teacher on the basis of her successful work with her Sunday-school class. You
have been organist and given much time? Yes, and your power has increased
in that service. You owe the increment of power. Mark Twain figures that
one soldier to-day is worth one hundred and forty-nine who fought at Waterloo.
Why? The difference lies in their equipment. More is expected of us to-day,
young people, in the prayer meeting, because of the richer, fuller equipment
which the opportunities of our training have brought us. Who knows more
about prayer-meeting problems than the Endeavorer? In ways to meet and
overcome these difficulties he is prepared. In equipment he is not a flint-lock,
but a rifle! We need him on the firing-line immediately. Experience in the
details of Endeavor work fits him for service in the mid-week meeting, and calls
him to it.

For it is the great law that possession necessitates service. Who knows,
owes. Said Paul, the Tarsan tentmaker, "I am debtor . . . as much as in me
is." "The government educated me and needs my strength. I offer my services until the war is over," wrote Grant when Fort Sumpter was fired upon.
"The reward of one duty is the power to fulfil another," said George Eliot.
After years of training Queen Wilhelmina receives her crown, saying, "Trusting in God, and with a prayer that he will give me strength, I accept the
government." What is that but a Christian Endeavor pledge? What does it
mean to us but that all *our* heritage and equipment are for use? The nobility
of the Christ life was not in its possession of power and purity, but in the fact
that these were given to men. "The glory that thou gavest me I have given
them," he cried, in the ecstasy of joy in service. Whatever Christian Endeavor
has fitted you to do you owe to use and increase in your church home in her
mid-week meeting.

Two questions have been and ever will be asked of Christian Endeavor:
Can it serve the church? *Will* it? These are also questions to be answered
by the individual. Every one concedes our ability, but ability must be wedded
to willingness to be made effective. "Ability is answerability." Because we
can we *ought* and we WILL. Ease, endurance, enlargement, preparedness, every
capacity developed in the Endeavor prayer meeting, we ought to use in the
mid-week meeting. The prayer meeting is an inseparable part of the church.
Its existence is life to the church. We work "for Christ and the Church."
We must not abide too long in our elementary Endeavor training-school. We
must take our places in the active, responsible positions of the church. However much we love the place where we learned to confess Christ and to work
for him, there is no absolution from service in the wider work of the mid-week
meeting. Whether welcomed at first or not; whether misunderstood by old
workers, or lonesome for the old Endeavor meeting, into which we wander once
and again; whether finding our place with difficulty or "enduring hardness as a
good soldier of Jesus Christ;" whether all this and more, or the prompt appreciation of our desire to help and co-operation to utilize it; — *the obligation of
young people to stand by and build up the mid-week meeting of their own
church is imperative because of their training, ability, promise, and the
universal need for their work.* And I expect to see the time when it shall be
no rare thing to step into the mid-week meeting, find an Endeavorer in charge,
and hear a sympathetic pastor calling the roll of graduate Endeavorers who
have "come up higher" in the Master's work and are doing in the mid-week
meeting what they practised in the Endeavor hour.

Dr. Breeden told how to have a good Sunday evening service, emphasizing especially the point, which certainly needs emphasis: "The
minister who fully preaches Christ will create a sensation anywhere."
He urged congregational singing, and quoted with approval the saying
of Henry Ward Beecher, who, when the church put in a hired quartette,

announced solemnly, " The worship of Almighty God will now be suspended while we listen to a performance from the choir. "

Address by Rev. H. O. Breeden, LL.D.,

Des Moines, Io.

THE SUNDAY EVENING SERVICE.

The Sunday evening service is a problem and a prophecy: a problem
which challenges the best thought of the Endeavorer, and which each congregation must solve for itself ; a prophecy of the future strength and usefulness
of the church. If the Sunday morning service is eminently for the spiritual
culture of those who are already subjects of the King, the evening service is
pre-eminently a rallying and recruiting service, where enlistments are made under the Captain of our salvation.

The problem has but two factors. These are, (1) the presence of the people, and (2) the worship of the people.

The presence of the people — how shall we secure it? There are two
methods. First, by personal endeavor and pastoral work. No magnet has
ever yet been discovered with drawing-powers equal to those possessed by
a real, consecrated pastor, who, as Dr. Abbott observes, is "both born and
made ; created to be a personal friend and trained by the school of experience
in the art of personal friendship. " The pastor with quick and catholic sympathies, who loves the little children and shares their frolics, whose heart beats
high with the exuberant hopes of youth, who is eager to share in the struggles of middle life, and who, endowed with prophetic imagination, shares the
calm of old age, will draw people to the sanctuary like a lodestone. If with the
pastor-friend the minister combines the rare qualities of the prophet-preacher
he is a genius, and will require no extraneous methods to fill his house at every
Sunday evening service.

The old hand-picking method is not obsolete. Men must be solicited one by
one. We may talk until the end of the century about the problem, and devise
most ingenuous methods, but no invention will beat this. Besides, if we are
to save people we must know them. We ought to know personally some of
the people about whom we theorize so much, — the poor and the rich, — the
outcast and the *élite*, the dependent, the independent, the sinners in the slums
and the sinners in the palaces. Let us go out after other men —
not men in the lump, but Dives and Crœsus and Lazarus and Jean Valjean
and John Smith and Peter Jones and Michael Hogan.

The second method of securing the presence of people is by advertising.
John Wanamaker pays the Philadelphia *Record* $100,000 for a full-page adver-
tisement for his firm every day in the year save the Lord's Day. He put
$300,000 into printers' ink for his Philadelphia store alone last year. His
profits were $1,500,000. The Pears' Soap people pay *The Ladies' Home
Journal* $3,000 an issue for their full-page ad. the year round. The proprietors
expend a million annually in extolling the virtues of Hood's Sarsaparilla. It
pays to advertise, in the world's business. And in the "Father's business" it
pays to advertise — the *business*, not the preacher ; *the service*, not the servant.
The minister who persistently plasters his own face on every envelope and
letter-head and card and bill-board and dodger will expose himself, and justly,
to the criticism and ridicule of thoughtful people, and be characterized as a
charlatan in Christianity, a mountebank in the ministry. The public have a
righteous protest against putting the gospel of the Lord Jesus on a basis with
Douglass Shoes or Lydia E. Pinkham's patent medicines. But to advertise
the service is different. Let the man be kept in the background, while Christ
and the church are pushed to the front in the newspapers — by cards and bills
and bulletins. The world will never tire of seeing the face of the Master.

Success in advertising depends upon the thoroughness, persistence, and
artistic completeness with which it is done. Printed, type-written, or, better
still, personally written letters, mailed to the straying, to those without relig-

ious affiliation, to students and transients, will yield a fine result. Dr. Russell Conwell counts the mail service a chief ally in the success of the Temple.

A concrete illustration of judicious advertising given in "Modern Methods of Church Work" will enforce my point better than an hour of abstract reasoning. When Rev. Dr. Blank took charge of the Second Church in the city of C — there was practically no evening audience. Within a few months he had an audience ranging from 1,000 to 1.300. How did he do it? He commenced advertising by issuing large numbers of invitation-cards to the church services — some weeks printing as many as 15,000 cards. These were done up in packages of one hundred, seventy-five, fifty, twenty-five, and ten, held together by rubber bands. They were given to the people for distribution. Members were to say as they passed out how many they wanted, and received what they asked for.

The results were immediate. The evening audience individually became interested in the distribution of cards. This at once gave the newcomers something to do and stimulated their interest. The cards were taken to the stores to be wrapped with parcels, carried through the markets and dropped into baskets, and given to the elevator-boys at the hotels.

Is there not increased expense in operating such a method? Yes, and increased revenue through the collections to meet it. The financial problem of a wide-awake church is not how to cut off activities and keep out of debt, but how to increase the efficiency of the church and meet the expenses. God always honors with ample revenue the church which lays vast embargoes of Christlike work upon the conscience and consecration of its members.

But there is prejudice against sensationalism in the pulpit, as well as in advertising. There is indeed a rank sensationalism against which all earnest people protest, which is fitly styled by the dictionary-maker as an effort "to gratify vulgar curiosity:" but real sensationalism is defined as the "presentation of matters and details of such a nature and in such a manner as to thrill" the auditor. In such sensationalism I believe most robustly. And tell me what theme of heaven or earth is so thrilling when rightly presented as the gospel of Jesus Christ, — the glory of his life, the tragedy of his death, the sublime consummation of his resurrection and ascension? The minister who preaches him in his simplicity and fulness will create a sensation anywhere. There is no need to announce a sensational theme. Better a thousand times is it to preach a sensational sermon from a commonplace theme than to make a great flaming announcement and then give a tame, dull, lustreless, uninteresting discourse. Always give the people more than you promise them. Froth and foam and fizz will do for soda-water preaching to the dilettante and the *élite*, but the common people with a great thirst must have the "water of life."

The church of Jesus Christ must have the common people. Every righteous method which promises success in winning them should be used: but it will be a sad and sorry day for the churches when they shall, in mad haste to catch the people, accept the *role* of mere purveyors to the public, competing with one another, — and with the general places of amusement, — placing themselves in a position such that they cannot be surprised when newspapers speak of their congregations as "audiences," their praise services as "musical entertainments," and their prayers as "the most eloquent ever offered to a Boston audience."

The second factor in the problem of the Sunday evening is the worship of the people. What is worship? Is it a synonym for church-going? No; there may be worship without church-going, and church-going without worship. Real worship is higher, deeper, broader, than mere church-going. It is an act wrought at the point where the natural and the supernatural blend, where the sea and the sky meet. The nature of the act is the meeting and the mingling of man's spirit with God's spirit in Godward thought. So when the first factor of the problem is solved, and the people are present in the sanctuary, a problem more complex is on hand,— to transform auditors into worshippers, sinners into Christians. How shall this be done? In all Christendom there are but two types of Christian worship, — the liturgical and the evangelistic. Each of these is the creation of a need of the soul — the answer to a deep and vital sentiment of human nature. The ritualistic churches, with their solemn and impressive liturgy, steadfastly maintain their ideal of worship, and rely upon no other thing to draw and transform the people than the solemnity of a service which in all its stateliness gives varied voice to the emotions of the human heart bowed in awe before its Creator.

In evangelistic worship the elements are more varied. They are six in number; viz., the reading of the Word, the music, the prayers, the offering, the sermon, and the Lord's Supper. The Lord's Supper, by long custom, is now celebrated only in the morning in Protestant churches. The reading of the Word may be dismissed with the observation that the pulpit reading should be soulful, artistic, reverential, and the responsive reading hearty and general. With a caution against long, prolix, and stereotyped prayers, vain repetitions, and an admonition in favor of pointed, special, stately prayers with the merit of honesty and heartiness, they also may be dismissed.

But the offering is also an essential feature, an integral part of the worship, and should be dignified as such in every sanctuary. The blessing of God should be invoked upon every offering — in the presence of the whole congregation. The wise men worshipped the Christ-child by giving unto him gifts, — gold, frankincense, and myrrh. In our enlightened worship of the greater Christ shall we not be as " wise "?

The atmosphere of the Sunday evening service must be genial — the individual members of the church cordial and courteous, with a downright, unmistakable heartiness; with no Uriah Heap hand-shake, but with an affability and a sociability distinctively Christian. It is neither wise nor desirable to go so far in modern days as that church down in Maine which it is said placed a nickel-in-the-slot machine in its vestibule, and when the stranger entered all he had to do was to put a nickel in the slot and a hand would come out and grasp his in friendly greeting. No device ever has been or ever will be invented that will gladden the heart of a stranger like a Christlike personality and a genuinely sympathetic, brotherly heart, always honored of the Spirit in the great work of saving souls.

> " Only a kind word spoken,
> Only a kind look given ;
> But they filled a life with beauty
> And raised a soul to heaven."

A prime requisite for a successful Sunday evening service is a competent and consecrated body of ushers. The doorkeeper in the house of the Lord has a glorious opportunity for service and should magnify his office. Indeed, there is no more important, delicate, difficult, or dignified office in the congregation. The ushers and officers of every church should constitute the real Reception Committee for every service, permeating the body of the congregation with the warm currents of sympathy — a veritable Gulf Stream, whose current is always set toward Christ. The Ushers Association of the Holland Memorial Church, Philadelphia, has published suggestions to ushers so capital that a copy of them should be in the hands of every one who aspires to this service for the Master.

One of the most important and vital elements of the Sunday evening service is music — the absolute essential of acceptable worship. And the choir is an invaluable adjunct to the service. " But," as some one observes, " the choir must not be mere bait for the ministerial drag-net." It must not be perverted from worship to the mere functions of the " puller-in " at a cheap theatre. The natural disposition of Music Committees is to use a choir simply to fill seats — a disposition modified in most cases only by the protest of the minister, who declares it too theatrical to be tolerated. The sanctuary ought to use all the instruments of earth to praise the Lord, but chiefly the human voice; but musicians should render music which will produce worship, and which worshippers can interpret. The New Testament rule is " Let all things be done unto edifying ; " but the most eloquent speaker in an unknown tongue cannot edify. So a prima donna may fill a great building with her wonderful cadences and marvellous trills, and the people may be entertained, but not edified. There is a palpable incongruity between mere entertainment and true worship. A second rule is to "sing with the spirit and the understanding." This rules out all Christless, ungodly singers from the services. Plenty of singers would prefer singing to the honor of Gambrinus in a beer garden rather than the praises of Christ in a church, provided only the pay is larger. What is wanted for the Sunday evening service is not an artistic entertainment by the few, but soulful solos, hearty chorals, stirring gospel songs, and glorious anthems, by the few and many. That was a just rebuke administered by Mr. Beecher in Plymouth Church after the Music Committee had supplanted the great chorus with a quartette of godless artists, when he said, in introducing one of their numbers, "Beloved, the worship of Almighty God will now be suspended for a few minutes while we listen to a performance by the choir."

But all unacceptable song worship is by no means confined to the city church or the Christless choir. The average village or country congregation will furnish an illustration of soulless, unedifying church music fully as disheartening, and no less displeasing to God. But between the cold, unemotional, artistic performance of the professionals, and the careless, indifferent, irreverent, and equally soulless music of churches which take no pains to have God acceptably worshipped in song, there is a happy and golden mean, and Christian Endeavor has discovered it; it is a musical service of sincere heartiness, in perfect accord with the rules of musical science, but full of soul earnestness, and rendered by a consecrated quartette, combined with a large and equally consecrated chorus, and a singing congregation. Such music will sweep the key-board of the soul, and make it resound and thrill with sweetest and sublimest melodies. There is no passion in the human soul but finds its food in music. As Endeavorers let us be wise to find the music that feeds the passion of sincere love to Christ.

Occasionally a special musical service with a programme of solos, duets, quartettes, and choruses is most helpful and attractive, and affords unusual possibilities for good. At such a time the sermon should be abridged to twelve or fifteen minutes, or made replete with musical history or anecdote. The message of the Master may be sung as effectively, and even more impressively, by the average musician than it can possibly be preached by the average minister; but prayerful, spiritual, painstaking preparation is just as essential here as in any other service.

The sermon is the crowning feature in an evangelistic service. A single statement will suffice for that. It must be pre-eminently a gospel sermon. It may be lacking in rhetorical outlines, and deficient in literary embellishments, but if it have Christ for its centre and circumference, its root and its flower, its beginning, its ending, and substance, it will arrest attention and win souls and transform character and save sinners. Let Christ be preached, and the strong will bow their heads, and the simple find their souls strangely thrilled. But Christ may be preached in a variety of ways. The Spirit of the Lord is not straitened as to method.

The illustrated service as a method is as old as God's rainbow covenant. It has the merit of approaching the soul through the eye as well as the ear. Teaching by illustration or pictures "arrests attention at once, concentrates thought, excites interest, and awakens imagination." The stereopticon service illustrating "The Holy Land," "The Life of Christ," or "Pilgrim's Progress," if well managed and effectively accompanied with proper sermon-setting, is a deeply impressive, spiritual, and beautiful service. By it many will be attracted to be entertained who will remain to worship. By it some will be converted, and all will be inspired to holy thinking and Christly living.

The special night service is also proving a most profitable method,— a temperance night, a business men's night, a woman's night, a good-citizenship night, a teacher's night, a children's night, or an evening with the patriots. At such times the presence of the Stars and Stripes, and other appropriate decorations and symbols, will be suggestive and helpful.

Akin to this is the special series on "Problems of Living Interest," which

the best lay minds of the community may be made to preach. A friend of mine
announced a series of eight sermons on vital themes like the following: (1)
"Can a man be successful in business and a Christian?" (2) "What influence in this community is most inimical to our young men?" The pastor secured condensed answers to each query from the most thoughtful people of the
city, and read the best of them in the course of his own sermon. The result
was that the largest auditorium was too small to hold the people, while the service itself was so conducted as to become a converting, uplifting influence upon
every heart in attendance. Such a series has the immense advantage of commanding the sympathy of the press. The reporting of sermons should be
encouraged, not simply to exploit the brilliant sayings of the preacher, but
because "it draws attention to the services, and preaches the gospel over
again."

But after all, one can hardly resist the conviction that the real success of
the Sunday evening service in the last analysis depends, not upon fine music,
song services, elaborate ritual, beautiful pictures. lectures on sensational
themes, or yet upon elegant essays prepared with deliberation, and delivered
with dramatic power, but upon a real representative of the Lord Jesus in the
pulpit, and a body of Christian Endeavorers in the pews, radiating from convenient centres in concentric circles the light and love of the Master; in the
pulpit a prophet-preacher, with the tone of authority, and a spiritual passion, and
in the pews, and in the chorus, enough Christian Endeavor character and consecration to leaven the whole congregation. Bright things, true things, helpful
things, the preacher may say in abundance,— which will instruct the intellect
and touch the emotions,— but the atmosphere of the sermon must be that of
Calvary, opening up the fountains of the heart, quickening the conscience, and
compelling the will to appear before the judgment-throne to hear its decision.
Not mere mouthpieces of the past, but prophets of the present in the pulpit,
and loving Endeavorers in the pews, will fill to overflowing the sanctuary of the
Lord, and demonstrate that those who are "saved to serve" can make the
Sunday evening meeting a "service to some," a holy joy to all, while from
the profounder depths of devoted hearts will break forth the ecstatic strain : —

> "I will worship the Lord in the beauty of holiness.
> I will sing of his name while I have my being.
> Praise ye the Lord."

The Rev. Teunis S. Hamlin, D.D., of Washington, D. C., then read
a resolution which had been passed by the Board of Trustees of the
United Society. The reading of the resolutions received a most hearty
endorsement : —

The Board of Trustees of the United Society of Christian Endeavor, speaking in behalf of over three millions of Americans, solemnly declare their conviction that the seating of Brigham H. Roberts, of Utah, as representative-at-
large from that State to the Fifty-sixth Congress would be, and would be generally understood to be, a condonation of the crime of polygamy, a blow at the
sanctity of the marriage relation, and peril to the purity and integrity of the
family, upon which our civil and religious institutions so largely rest.

We, therefore, confidently call upon our representatives in the National
Congress to rise above all partisan and sectarian and personal considerations,
and in defence of our reputation and character as a law-abiding people, to
deny Mr. Roberts a seat among our national lawmakers.

Dr. Hamlin also announced that a memorial had been prepared, and
that copies of it would be found at all State headquarters. The
Endeavorers were urged to sign the memorial.

The memorial prepared for signature by the delegates is as follows : —

We, the undersigned members of the Eighteenth International Convention
of Christian Endeavor, representing over three and a half millions of Americans,

do most earnestly and respectfully call upon you to use your utmost endeavor and to exhaust all honorable means to secure the prompt expulsion of Mr. Brigham H. Roberts, of Utah, an avowed polygamist, from the House of Representatives, in accordance with the provision of the National Constitution in Article 1, Sec. 5, paragraph 2, which reads as follows: "Each house (of Congress) may determine the rules of its proceedings, punish its members for disorderly behavior, and with the concurrence of two-thirds, expel a member."

We also do most respectfully and most earnestly call upon you to use your utmost endeavor and to exhaust all honorable means to secure the submission of an amendment to the National Constitution to the Legislatures of the several States, defining legal marriage to be monogamic, and making polygamy and polygamous cohabitation, under whatsoever guise or pretence, a crime against the United States, punishable by severe penalties, including disfranchisement and disqualification to vote or to hold any office of honor or emolument under the United States or any State or Territory thereof.

Then followed a season of quiet meditation and prayer, conducted by Rev. John H. Elliott, of New York City, president of the New York State Christian Endeavor Union.

Professor Wells, Managing Editor of *The Christian Endeavor World*, put together a pair of dissected shears, five feet high, divided into nine parts. Did you ever notice the resemblances between our Christian Endeavor pledge and a pair of shears? He found something to fit every part, and nothing left over.

Address by Prof. Amos R. Wells,
Boston, Mass.
THE CHRISTIAN ENDEAVOR SHEARS.

There are only three sentences in our Christian Endeavor pledge. There are only 178 words, and five-sevenths of these are words of only one syllable. When before in the world's history have three sentences gone so far, traversed the globe so quickly, penetrated into so many lands, and influenced so many lives? So mighty are they that it is worth while to study their power. So helpful are they that it is worth while to fasten them into our minds. And so substantial are they that they will not be injured by an undignified comparison, not even if I liken them to a pair of shears! Indeed, there are so many points in common that I think hereafter, whenever you see a pair of shears, you will think of the Christian Endeavor pledge.

In the first place, the pledge has a thumb-hole and a finger-hole. Here they are. One of them is daily prayer; the other is daily Bible-study. Epictetus, that wise old Greek, said that everything has two handles; by one handle you can lift it, by the other you cannot. For instance, you have been injured. "My brother has *wronged* me" — that handle will not lift it. "It is my *brother* that has wronged me" — that handle lifts it easily. And so our pledge has false handles, that will not lift it. "Imitation" is one of them; "whim" is the other. John signs the pledge just because Jim has signed it, and he keeps the pledge just when the notion seizes him. No such crooked handles will fit any fingers that God ever made, not even the india-rubber man's. *No* handles will lift the hard things in our pledge except the Bible handle and the prayer handle.

Yes, and these handles, as you see, are transferable. You can attach them to any heavy weight you please, and carry it as if it were a cobweb. Take a hard day's work; what handles are we likely to fasten to that? This handle: "O dear! how much I have to do!" and this handle: "Ah me! would that my lot were a different one!" And when we take hold of a day with such handles, it drags and it droops, it hangs and it halts, from gloomy morning to discouraged evening.

But fasten to the day our Christian Endeavor handles. Put them on in the Quiet Hour. Seize some winged sentence of Isaiah, some shining thought of Paul's, some golden word of the Master's. In joyous prayer take hold of your Saviour's hands. Ah, that is the way to take hold of your tasks! With these two handles,— Bible, prayer, — accomplishment will be easy; failure, endurable; pain will be borne with patience, and life will be lifted up into the joy of its Lord.

All shears have two blades, and so have our pledge shears. Half of the pledge refers to the society, and half to the church. You can no more work the society half without the church half than you can work by itself one blade of your shears. It is a "shear" impossibility. There are one-legged societies, but they soon topple over. There are one-bladed shears, but they are in the ash-barrel.

Now each of these two blades, the society blade and the church blade, has a long arm and a short arm, just like all other shears. The long arm is a general principle, the short arm is a sample, practical application of that principle. Take first the church blade. The long arm is the general promise, "I will support my own church in every way," and the short arm is the particular promise, "especially by attending all her regular Sunday and mid-week services." It is like a lever. (Do you remember your physics?) You must have a long arm, you must have a short arm, you must have a fulcrum between and muscle at the end; then you have power.

Let us put together these parts of the church blade: the long arm,— general church support; the short arm, — attending the meetings. Please notice that both parts move together. You cannot be true to the great work of the church without being true to the little details of that work. Nor can you be true to the little details without the inspiration of the large ideal. It 's like a political party. You cannot be a loyal Democrat or Republican without, in the first place, believing in the party as a whole, its history and its purposes, and without, in the second place, attending its meetings, its caucuses and conventions, and voting for it at the polls. It 's like building a temple. You need a noble, comprehensive plan, but you need also every cube of stone, every hod of mortar.

It is a grand thing to look abroad over the world and see the church of God rising like the temple of eternity, — here a mountain levelled for a foundation-stone, yonder a poisonous swamp drained dry to receive its masonry; Hindus building at one extreme and Esquimaux at the other; men of all races and a Babel of tongues working upon it in closest harmony; the spacious arches bending above the nations and bridging the oceans in a majestic sweep; course after course of exquisite marble leaping into walls and turrets and towers: and all, under the supreme Architect, hastening toward the time when the world will be one white cathedral, Jesus Christ being the chief corner-stone. Happy are the clear eyes that see this vision!

But not if the vision holds them from the trowel and the mallet. For how is the Kingdom to come? By Abigail Adams's teaching a Sunday-school class, and Benjamin Brown's going to mid-week prayer meeting; and Carrie Conway's telling the pastor that his last sermon helped her, and Dick Dwight's bringing Ed Everett to the Sunday evening service. It is thus that the Kingdom is to some, and not with observation. Do not try to work the long arm without the chort one.

And do not try, either, to work the short arm without the long one. When the church bell calls you from your pleasant novel, say, "Asia is calling!" When your mind begins to wander from the sermon, say, "Yonder stands the King's ambassador!" When the prayer meeting seems long and tedious, say, "This is the council chamber of the Kingdom! the Kingdom! the Kingdom! And I am in the presence of the King!" Thus will you put the long arm with the short one, and thus will the church blade move together, and do its part in our Christian Endeavor shears.

In the same way the other blade, the society blade, is divided into a long arm and a short arm, a general promise and a particular one. The particular promise is to attend the meetings and take part in them, especially the consecration meetings. The general promise is to be true to all our duties as active members.

Let us hold to the short arm, Endeavorers. When absent from the consecration meeting, we have promised to send at least a verse of Scripture. Let us not rest satisfied with that "at least," but let us send eager messages from our hearts. In taking some part, "aside from singing," let us often take the hardest part, do what is most difficult for us to do; not because the dear Lord wants to make our life hard, but because he wants to make our muscles hard, and "soft snaps" never make hard muscles.

And let us hold to the long arm, Endeavorers. "All our duties as active members," — why, that includes committee meetings, and being there on time, and telling the Lookout Committee that the Smitherkins have moved into town, and writing reports — w-r-i-t-i-n-g, and shaking hands with strangers, and being jolly at the socials, and seconding motions, and wearing the badge, and not giving a cent a week when you could just as well give ten, and telling timid Miss Graymouse that she led the meeting admirably, and talking up Christian Endeavor and never talking it down.

Yes, for the long arm means the long look, here as in the church blade. Remember, Prayer-meeting Committees, that noble Endeavorers in Madagascar are joining in your prayers. Look from your monotonous tasks, Lookout Committees, and see the Endeavor hosts of distant Australia! Sing, Music Committees, sing the louder, for China's United Society to hear you. And rejoice, Flower Committees, in your fragrant toil, remembering our Christian Endeavor friends in the Arctics! So will the long look enrich the short look, our humdrum duties will keep step with the mighty Endeavor host; and so will both arms of the society blade move together in the work of the Christian Endeavor shears.

And now we have two blades, useless apart, as the upper teeth without the lower ones. What is the rivet that will join them together? What clause in the pledge binds it all into a coherent, effective force? What but that great first clause, "Trusting in the Lord Jesus Christ for strength"? Ah, here is a rivet that never "works loose," but gets firmer the longer we use it! "Trusting in Christ for strength," hard things become easy, tedious things become alluring, impossibilities discover themselves to be practicable. "Trusting in Christ for strength," we do not seek how little we may do, but what more we may do; we gladly pay more than our share; we seek not the highest office but the hardest task. "Trusting in Christ for strength," we can lead the meeting, though our heart is in our throat and our brains are in our boots. "Trusting in Christ for strength," we can rise in time for our morning talk with him, though all the fiends of sleepiness are perched upon our eyelids. "Trusting in Christ for strength," we can plead with the unconverted, we can give a tenth of our income, we can even fill up the front seats. "Trusting in Christ for strength" — this is the rivet that will bind power to our feebleness and wisdom to our stupidity and zeal to our flagging wills, and make of our Christian Endeavor shears a tool that will verily work.

Now where is the oil for our Christian Endeavor shears? For the closer the shears and the more sharply they cut, the more they need oil if they are to work smoothly. Here is the oil can, — a bicycle oil can, because we must have the very best oil. And what is it? The proviso, twice repeated in the pledge, "Unless prevented by some reason we can conscientiously give to our Lord and Master." This oil is warranted to lubricate the shears so that they may be worked by the weakest and most inexperienced fingers. But let me warn you: to use too much oil on shears is worse than to use too little. Apply this oil of excuses as sparingly as possible, and wipe off all of it you can, or you will soil the fair fabric upon which you are at work.

And now I am sure you have observed something wrong with our Christian Endeavor shears: they are too blunt; they stop short. What will continue them, carry them on and on, so that their sharp points will indicate the great future into which our work extends? Two clauses of the pledge alone remain: "I will strive to do whatever He would like to have me do;" "throughout my whole life I will endeavor to lead a Christian life." These are the points of our shears.

"Whatever he would like!" That carries the lines of our pledge out into every detail of life. Would He like to have me leave the theatre alone? Then I have promised to leave it alone. Would he like to have me vote at the polls only for men that fear God and seek his will? Then I have promised to learn the characters of candidates. Would he like to have me put into my next prayer-meeting testimony the very best thought that study and prayer and Christian living can give me? Then I have promised to get out of the verse-readers' class. "Whatever!" O splendid word of daring and fidelity, well fitted to the followers of Him who lavished upon mankind whatever he had of power and wisdom and infinite love! That word shall complete one blade of the shears.

And to complete the other blade, those magnificent, forward-pointing words, "Throughout my whole life." Once an Endeavorer, always an Endeavorer. You may leave the Society, but you cannot leave your pledge. Your business may call you, but you have agreed to place first of all your Father's business. You may move from home, but the pledge is at home everywhere. You may even die, but your pledge is as good for the next world as for this, since it reads, "throughout my whole life," and you are to live forever — forever.

And how fortunate this is, how blessed, you will not realize until you reflect that, since you have agreed to be Christ's forever, and to do whatever he would like to have you do forever, and forever to support his church of the ages and his unceasing Endeavor, since you are his throughout your whole life, he will be yours. Beside your "whatsoever" he sets his "whatsoever;" and beside your "forever" his "forever," and all the dread empty spaces beyond this earth are filled with his presence, and all the darkness of the hereafter is crowded with his radiance, because here and now you have sealed yourself to him.

Thus the Christian Endeavor shears are completed. And now let us review what has been said by repeating together the Christian Endeavor pledge. Will you not join me in it?

(Audience joined in repeating the Christian Endeavor pledge.)

"Trusting in the Lord Jesus Christ for strength, I promise him that I will strive to do whatever he would like to have me do; that I will make it the rule of my life to pray and to read the Bible every day, and to support my own church in every way, especially by attending all her regular Sunday and mid-week services, unless prevented by some reason which I can conscientiously give to my Saviour; and that, just so far as I know how, throughout my whole life, I will endeavor to lead a Christian life.

"As an active member, I promise to be true to all my duties, to be present at and to take some part, aside from singing, in every Christian Endeavor prayer meeting, unless hindered by some reason which I can conscientiously give to my Lord and Master. If obliged to be absent from the monthly conse-cration meeting of the society, I will, if possible, send at least a verse of Scripture to be read in response to my name at the roll-call."

And finally, what work shall be done by the Christian Endeavor shears? What are they to cut? They are to cut us loose from worldly desires, from greed, from paltry ambition, from envy and covetousness. They are to sever those ignoble excuses, that bind us in swaddling-bands like a babe. They are to cut out our working clothes, and from the stoutest of cloth. They are to cut out our work for us, and give us stints worth the doing. They are to cut flowers for sick-room bouquets. They are to help make national flags and the sails of missionary ships. Sharp edge, steady hand, they are to cut straight to the mark. And while at work upon these earthly tasks, constantly, in some myste-rious way no one understands, they will be at work upon an unseen garment, a robe of light and beauty. It will prove to be our wedding garment, for the palace of the King!

President Turner, of Illinois, told very finely how young people

MEETING JUST ADJOURNED IN ONE OF THE TENTS.

may help their pastor. Among his many forceful sayings, this was the most striking : "Any congregation may get good sermons from any pastor by practising what he preaches. Nothing so stimulates even a Faintheart as the consciousness of having accomplished something."

Address by President A. E. Turner,

Lincoln, Ill.

HOW YOUNG PEOPLE CAN HELP THE PASTOR.

A forceful ethical writer has said that man's true self is the social self. Aristotle seems to have had the same idea when he said, "He who is unable to live in society, or who has no need because he is sufficient for himself, must be either a beast or a god." It is not strange, therefore, that the cry of the average mortal is for help, and that at some stage of his life every man reaches out after a friendly hand. But not until Christ came was the true altruistic philosophy preached and practised. Convicted by his masterly teaching, the self-centred soul began to expand and to yearn for increased influence over other lives. Not nineteen centuries of striving could realize the ideal, however, and it remained for Christian Endeavor to put new meaning into the old inquiries, "How can I help? Whom can I help?" Almost two decades have failed of adequate answer, and to-day we would know "How? Whom?"

I am glad that the question must be raised upon this occasion, for many a devout divine and not a few church courts have put our organization under the ban, because, forsooth, it breeds disloyalty to praying pastors and orthodox pulpits. It means, too, that the ecclesiastical world has moved forward during nineteen years. One can well imagine the consternation of a demure New England congregation of the *post-bellum* period had it been informed by the equally demure minister that "next Sabbath the young people will take charge of the service." A hurried conference of deacons and gentle rebuke of their spiritual adviser would probably have been sufficient to stamp out effectually so heterodox a practice. Twenty years later, in the very presence of that sin we ask, in seriousness, "How can we young people help the pastor?" How strangely the church persevered in its failure to recognize the immense serviceableness of youthful Christianity to every day and generation! Surely it should not seem strange that children of the church, regarded as only to be guarded and guided, grew into irresponsive, ornamental, useless appurtenances of the church, rather than loyal to its interests and pledged to its welfare through early training and active service. The Christian Endeavor gospel is the gospel of apprenticeship, without which there can be no thoroughgoing, adequate effort. There was no little irony in the old-time pedagogue's advice to his pupil puzzled over his first "sum" in "vulgar" fractions: "You would better work it out for yourself. You will get so much more out of it." Young people's organizations in the church have emancipated youthful enthusiasm, directed youthful energy, utilized youthful vitality. The helpless, all-but-useless nursery in the church has become kindergarten, training-school, pastor's auxiliary, well-nigh the church itself.

Young people may help the pastor by faithful and punctual attendance upon the public services of the sanctuary, joining heartily in all parts of the worship, and thus making the hour one of uplift and inspiration to the preacher as well as one of joy to their own souls. The old "standby" in the church who prides himself on having slept peacefully through every service for thirty years does not realize how little nor yet how much he does for the church. A preacher is often heard to say that he will not preach to a lumber-yard, but to my mind it is far more inspiring to speak to inanimate rows of highly polished benches than to face a multitude of emotionless, inattentive faces, upon every lineament of whose faces is written, "I am here to make a record; you say what you have to say, and let us have it done with." Earnest faces of thoughtful young Christians who would know the truth in order to thrive upon it have ironed out many a troubled brow, or sung joy to many a discouraged spirit.

To do uncomplainingly what one is asked to do is often a greater service to the pastor than the taking of a city could be. It is a rare joy to the heart of the leader to realize that every follower accepts service with the confidence that it would not have been required of him had he been unequal to it. In so far as Endeavorers dignify the humble station and exalt the lowly calling they are yoking together a noble aloofness of soul and readiness to serve of which Wordsworth said: —

> " Thy soul was like a star and dwelt apart ;
> . . . . and yet the heart
> The lowliest duties on herself did lay."

One of the loveliest women I know says, " I make it a rule of my life to do cheerfully what others complainingly and grudgingly do." Because of this rule of action she has been a veritable benediction to a toiling and devoted pastor. Perhaps the idea is mirrored in the words of Sophocles : " The end of man is an action, and not a thought." Even eternity, as one has put it, becomes only an opportunity for larger service and more robust effort. "' Thrive and strive ' cry ' Speed! Fight on, fare ever, there as here.' "

A good helper of his pastor should wear a smiling face while living the sermons of every Sabbath. It may be seriously questioned whether the long-faced Christianity of an early day ever helped men to Paradise ; on the contrary, there is little doubt that it was the occasion of innumerable clerical and lay suicides. Too often we neglect to say to our servant of tired brain and fainting heart, " That was a good sermon ; it has helped me, and I pray that it may reach others," and yet no other words could mean so much to him. It is only to be expected that faith is often vain, and preaching vain, also, when those who hear go away straightway forgetting what manner of message they have heard. Any congregation can get good sermons out of any preacher by practising what he preaches. Nothing so stimulates even a Faintheart as the consciousness of having accomplished something. I would have our Endeavorers be walking epistles, known and read of all men.

Liberal giving would convert many pulpit automata into living, moving, striving leaders. Not every preacher's soul is firm enough to resist the taunt, " You are always wanting money," or staunch enough to reform the nature that makes it. The idea of systematic and proportionate giving is fast becoming the idea of loyal Endeavorers. The Tenth Legion enrolls at this Convention 15,000 members after less than two years of effort. Whoever heard of a tither who must say to any call, " I have nothing I can give "? The Lord's box is never empty is the testimony of all conscientious tithers. Help your pastor by setting this good example. Greatly as we have been blessed, surely we cannot do less for Christ's kingdom under grace than did the Jews for the Lord's house under law.

A helpful young parishioner must keep up with the times in matters religious as well as he does in matters secular. The ignorance of most churchmen is a veritable millstone about many a pastor's neck. No enthusiasm can be aroused in denominational enterprises because there is no knowledge on which to base it. I know scores of preachers who, in their efforts to arouse interest, strikingly resemble the whistling coward in the lonely graveyard. This great organization stands for information, intelligence, culture. It proposes that its members shall study the history and achievements of their several denominations. There are those who decry interdenominational organization, and yet I know at least one denomination in which no effort was ever made to teach the church's history to its youth until the Christian Endeavor societies made such study a part of their reading-courses. The reading of one's denominational papers has become essential to good standing in good Endeavor societies. What joy it would be if one could preach to a thoroughly informed people, — a people as well posted in long-suffering, gentleness, justification, faith, regeneration, as in tariff, money, stocks, bonds, finance. The millennium may be confidently expected when the church is versed in creed, in doctrine, in polity, in the things which the church might know.

Every pastor will thrive the better in the purer and sweeter spiritual atmosphere for which the Quiet Hour stands. Given a church which is much in prayer, and you have a church which not only makes the waste places glad by its feeding of missionary fires, but a church which is a joy and consolation to its yearning, soul-saving pastor. Given a congregation of deep spiritual life, and your preacher will be a man of fire. If he does not have the gift of tongues, he will ever after hold his peace. In either case we shall have gained something.

It has often been said that a satisfied church has no future, and it is true because it is true of character. He is greatest among men who can bring to such a church, to such a character, the vision of Browning : —

> " Just when we are safest there 's a sunset-touch,
> A fancy from a flower-bell, some one 's death,
> A chorus-ending from Euripides —
> And that 's enough for fifty hopes and fears,
> As old and new at once as nature's self,
> To rap and knock and enter in our soul."

No altruistic social scheme has yet succeeded fully, because of the innate selfishness of human character. Mr. Bellamy's equality unfolds an alluring prospect, but it can never be realized until the grace of God has free course and is glorified. There is a great gulf fixed between one's care for "number one," which the world calls "business," and the long-suffering which is kind. We shall pass from one to the other by uniting ourselves with others in the pursuit of some worthy end. Experiences must come through which we can

> " welcome each rebuff
> That turns earth's smoothness rough ;
> Each sting that bids nor sit nor stand, but go."

Many a youthful worker who can do nothing which seems to him great may be leaven for the whole lump of careless indifference at home by attending such conventions as this, where, fired by deep-seated enthusiasm, he becomes a very live coal to the smouldering embers in his home church. But there is a host of critics who are saying, " You have too much enthusiasm : " and another host saying, " Your enthusiasm is dying out; you will soon die." To the first I answer, " There is no enthusiasm in a dyspeptic, disordered body ; it is the outgrowth of vigor, energy, power." To the second may be said, as was decided at a recent conference upon the very same question, " Enthusiasm of the baser sort is waning; that of the better type grows stronger and deeper." Your enthusiastic conventionist may now and then draw erroneous conclusions, but can do no worse than the over-lectured seven-year-old Sunday-school boy who, after an oratorical dissertation on the Prodigal Son, was asked, " Now, Reginald, what do we learn from the beautiful story of the prodigal son?" Without hesitation, he confidently replied, " We learn that we ought all be prodigal sons and not fatted calves." Yet there are those who by carrying enthusiasm do greatly inspire and arouse others. And who shall say that the " hewer of wood " and "drawer of water " is of less importance than he who builds a house or erects a fountain? Some must toil and wait.

In answering the question with which we set out, therefore, it must appear to be, after all, not so much a question of what specific steps the young people shall take, but a shaping of their lives in accordance with the Christly model, and bringing themselves into such well-rounded manhood and womanhood in the Master that unconsciously, spontaneously, their lives will bring blessing, joy, peace, comfort, to the heart of the pastor. Some one has said, " That which gives life its key note is not what men think good, but what they think best." It may be added that through no artifice or device or theoretical contemplation of ideals in character is the largest place in God's universe to be occupied, " For in Christ Jesus neither circumcision availeth anything, nor uncircumcision, but a new creature."

In Chickamauga Park a year ago I saw nearly 60,000 boys in blue, many of them from my own State. As I passed among them, wearing the badge of our

Illinois Union, now and then I was eagerly asked, "Are you from Illinois?" and then ringing with earnestness there came always the words, "Oh, I am so glad to see you." I said, "Boys, you seem restless. What do you want to do; go home?" "No! No!" "Well, what do you want?" Their answers thrilled me as I wish they might now thrill you: "We want to get to the front!" Fill your minds and hearts full of the enthusiasm of this great Convention; then go to the front in your home church work, in your Sunday school, in your prayer meeting, in your committee work, in all your work for God, and your pastor will be able to pay to your life and effort the tribute of sincere affection, as well as the noblest praise that can be given any heart,— *he helped me.*

The final address of this most practical session held the attention under circumstances most difficult for listening,— the rain pelting the canvas roof and streaming down through it; the audience crouched under umbrellas. The man who accomplished the difficult feat was Rev. W. F. Wilson, of Toronto, who made a vivacious and wise speech on how the pastor may help the young people. The best way the pastor can help his Endeavorers is by setting them to work. Direction in earnest labor for Christ,— it is this, above all, for which they are hungry.

Address by Rev. W. F. Wilson,
Hamilton, Ont.

HOW THE PASTOR CAN HELP THE YOUNG PEOPLE'S SOCIETY.

Christian Endeavor stands for denominational loyalty and interdenominational fellowship, not only in Christian co-operation but in national citizenship. Hence we meet, as children of the same Anglo-Saxon mother, speaking in the language of Shakespeare and Longfellow, protected by the two greatest flags that ever floated in the air — while we thank God for your great Christian President and our noble sceptered Queen, who, standing together, represent the freedom, culture, commerce, wealth, religion, and manhood of the world.

Nothing equals in importance our young people. Think of the money invested in them, intellect at work for them, time spent on them, and love shown toward them! And is too much being done? No. For in the Young People's societies of to-day the coming citizenship of the world and membership of the church are being trained. Where are the leaders of the dawning century — the merchants and mechanics, teachers and toilers, and physicians and ministers of to-morrow? Why, they march in the young people's organizations of the hour. As they go, the world will swing. They will determine the purity of our national life, efficiency of our public schools, happiness of our domestic circles, and spirituality of our religious institutions. Glorious young people — hope of the world and need of the church! For them our finest buildings are erected, choicest books are penned, best minds are trained, and strongest societies are formed. Thus came the Sabbath school, the Young Men's Christian Association, the King's Daughters, Epworth League, and the Christian Endeavor — all for the young people.

If Columbus added America to the geography of the world; if Washington added the Republic to the nations of the world; and if Wesley added Methodism to the churches of the world; — then Francis E. Clark added the Christian Endeavor Society to the organizations of the world, and now the societies are here by the thousand, and the Endeavorers are here by the million. Wonderful society — born in a Congregational church in 1881, on New England soil, the suns of eighteen summers brighten its path around the world; for the form of its illustrious founder has shadowed every shore, while his impassioned message has echoed over every sea.

Our subject is not, How can the State, press, school, or church help the society? but, How can the pastor?

First. Help by being one of them, as companion, counsellor, and friend — a true comrade, winning the respect, gaining the confidence, and inspiring the enthusiasm of each member. Pointing out the true elements of success, namely, industry, courage, charity, fidelity, purity, and faith, then leading the way; for the general who conquers must lead. Cromwell and Washington stood in the front rank, and glorious victory crowned their efforts. Roosevelt knew his Rough Riders by name, then led them to heroic deeds and splendid conquest. So the pastor who would have his society stand on the summits of service for Christ must know personally its membership and do his best to answer " Present " when the roll is called.

Second. Help by placing before the society its proper work, which is not to study the political questions of the day, solve the theological problems of the church, or answer the great questions of the schools; but to develop intelligent, patriotic, benevolent, enthusiastic, Christlike character. Hence, clear conceptions of duty and plans for service are absolutely necessary to success.

Yes, the great object of the Christian Endeavor Society is to bring young people to Christ, build them up in Christ, and send them out to work for Christ. To this end high ideals must be placed before them. We have missionary heroes, social heroines, and gifted leaders all around us, and while I would not detract from the lustre connected with the names of David Livingstone, Florence Nightingale, or William Booth, yet before all I would place the life and example of Jesus. He possessed an ideal character, proclaimed an ideal message, and left an ideal example; for his star brightens, and his words inspire as never before.

Our age demands manhood. Character is greater than capital; hence we require the priceless principles and promises of the blessed Bible to throb in and thrill human life more than ever. We need the man behind the book. Thus stood Spurgeon, transcendent in power. Thus stand Meyer, Moody, Hugh Price Hughes, Joseph Parker, and J. Wilbur Chapman — conquering by the sword of the Spirit, having for their ideal none of earth, but rather, the untarnished life of Christ, the Redeemer of men.

Third. Help by instruction and inspiration. The Christian Endeavor Society is one of the West Points of the Church of Christ. Here candidates for the pulpit, mission fields, and other centres of religious service and activity are trained. And the church needs well-equipped men — men with convictions, not opinions; views, not visions; facts, not fancies; doctrines, not doubts. Spain had nineteenth-century guns with sixteenth-century men. Give me the first-century Christ with the nineteenth-century Endeavorers, and soon the gospel of Christ will circle the world.

Then, pastor, inspire the society by pointing out new fields for service and new duties to perform. Develop individuality. Remember it was Moses led Israel, Columbus that discovered America, Luther that aroused Germany, and Wesley that awakened England. O for consecrated personality! As the trees make the forest, as the drops make the ocean, and seconds make the centuries, so each Endeavorer has a place to fill and a work to do; and I know it is the prayerful desire of our noble Christian founder that each Endeavorer might be a flaming torch-bearer in the service of Christ, our Redeemer.

Fourth. Help by directing them to the source of all power. The cry of some is, " On to Christ; " but I say, " Back to Pentecost." O the rapture of the Quiet Hour! Thus harness yourself for service; let each life be linked to some noble purpose; then with patience, perseverance, prayer, and power, victory is sure to be yours. This power made Bunyan write, Wesley sing, Summerfield preach, Clark organize, and Bishop William Taylor go around the world preaching Christ. We all need this power — to fire our sermons, spiritualize our worship, deepen our piety, quicken our zeal, and strengthen our love for Christ. Then follows reward.

During the campaign in Cuba a faithful nurse had done heroic duty, but was smitten down with fever. With burning brow, for days she lingered, and then, dying like a conquered queen, she said, " I go to claim my crown." So, fellow Endeavorers, when our work is done, with raptured vision and undimmed faith may we all exclaim, " I go to claim my crown."

The benediction was pronounced by Rev. J. H. Garrison, LL.D., of St. Louis, Mo.

Tent Williston.

While the delegates were gathering at Tent Williston for the morning service some one started that grand old hymn, " I Need Thee Every Hour." Others joined in before the first line was sung, and as fast as the Endeavorers stepped inside the tent they took up the refrain and showed the spirit was strong, notwithstanding the cold wind that swept through the tent.

At the close of the second verse Mr. P. S. Foster, musical director for the meeting, mounted the speakers' platform and announced it was time to begin the praise service. He gave out as the opening hymn " All Hail the Power of Jesus' Name."

For the next ten minutes the delegates filled the tent with mighty melody, Mr. Foster stirring the people into very spirited singing by asking everybody at least to repeat the words and enter into the praise service that way, if they could not sing.

Rev. H. B. Grose, of Boston, Mass., presided and stated that the Convention was a source of astonishment to a certain class of people in Detroit, from the fact that neither rain nor cold winds could keep Christian Endeavorers away from their meetings. Another astonished class were the policemen. He suggested to a policeman Friday that he supposed they were pretty busy Thursday. " Busy ? " said the officer, " Why, what is there for us to do with your people ? "

Rev. M. Rhodes, D.D., of St. Louis, Mo., conducted the devotional exercises.

The Sunday excursion bugaboo stalked into Christian Endeavor circles. Indignation was rampant, and the railroad that had the audacity to announce an excursion for the Lord's Day with the inference that it is authorized by Christian Endeavor came in for a lashing.

President Clark mounted the platform in Tent Williston yesterday morning and said that a Sunday excursion under the auspices of Christian Endeavor is an unheard-of thing. There was a hearty round of applause at this announcement, showing that the large audience was thoroughly in sympathy with the Christian Endeavor idea of Sabbath observance.

The first speaker of the morning was Rev. W. T. Rodgers, of Nashville, Tenn. His topic, " Our Conquering Covenant," was important, for it dealt with the " back bone " of Christian Endeavor. When he said, " Great promises make great men, if faithfully kept," he painted a luminous picture of the significance of the Christian Endeavor pledge to the young people of to-day.

Address by Rev. W. T. Rodgers,
Nashville, Tenn.

THE CONQUERING COVENANT.

One of our Nashville papers related the following incident. A bishop of the Episcopal Church got lost in the mountains of Tennessee. He wandered all day, and near the close came upon the cabin of a mountaineer. He asked for directions, and found that he had gone far from the home of his host and could not reach it that night. The mountaineer offered him lodging for the night, which the good bishop gladly accepted. After supper he asked his host concerning his religion, and was informed that he was an "Episcopalian." The bishop was greatly pleased to hear this, and asked his new friend to what diocese he belonged. "Diocese," said the mountaineer; "I never heard of that before."

"Who is your rector?" asked the bishop.

"Rector," said the mountaineer; "I have n't any."

"That is strange," said the bishop; "you are surely mistaken about being an Episcopalian."

"No, I am an Episcopalian. For a long time," said he, "I was bothered about being a Methodist or a Baptist.— them 's all we have up here,—but last winter I was in Nashville on Sunday and decided I would go to church. The first one I came to was an Episcopalian church. I went in, and the first thing I heard them say was, 'O Lord, we have done the things we ought not to have done and have left undone the things we ought to have done.' That settled it for me," said the mountaineer; "that was just what I had done. I knew from that time that I was an Episcopalian."

Twelve years ago the Christian Endeavor pledge fell into my hands. I read it and re-read it carefully. It captured and captivated me, body, brain, and soul. I said, "I know what I am. I am a Christian Endeavorer." From your presence here I judge that it has captured and captivated you, too. From Secretary Baer's report I learn that it has captured millions. I said, "I will take that covenant; it is just what I need." Then I showed it to others, and they said that it was just what they needed. And almost ere we realized it we had a Christian Endeavor society in that little Illinois town.

After twelve years of experience I thank God for this Christian Endeavor pledge. I believe that it came fresh from the throne of God, and reached us through the brain, the heart, and the pen of our dear brother Dr. Clark. It is from God, and that is one reason that it is a conquering covenant. It has the strength of divinity in it. Covenants are of divine origin. The Bible is full of them. The word "covenant" is used no less than two hundred and eighty-five times in the Holy Scriptures. The first covenant of which we have any record is the one which God made with Noah; and it never rains, until this day, but what God puts his beautiful bow in the clouds, reminding the world that he is still true to that covenant. All the world has heard of the glorious covenant between God and Abraham, which was renewed with Isaac, Jacob, and Israel. Moses was with God forty days and nights when he wrote the great covenant between God and Israel. This is the most solemn covenant of the Old Testament, known as the "Ten Commandments," by which Israel promised obedience and love to Jehovah, and for which God promised blessing and prosperity to Israel.

The Lord delights in covenants. Jeremiah speaks of the mighty God as "a covenant-keeper." In the twenty-fifth Psalm the Lord promises great blessing to them that keep his covenants. Paul declares that Christ is "the Mediator of a new covenant"—"a better covenant" than any of the old covenants, which if we keep means for us everlasting life, but, if we count "the blood of this new covenant an unholy thing," means for us death and sore punishment. We feel that through the Bible we have obtained the divine right to enter into a covenant with the Lord Jesus Christ, and that, trusting in him for strength, we can keep that covenant to the glory of God and the good of humanity.

The beautiful covenant between Jonathan and David was made in the presence of God and received divine approbation. So men have the right to make covenants among themselves. On this right rests the stability of the home, the school, the church, and the nation. Pledges are absolutely necessary for all progress and all safety. Without our great constitutional covenant this nation would become a mob without a guide. No man is compelled to sign it. If, however, he signs it, he is considered a traitor if he knowingly and purposely violates it. The business men of the world could not do business for an hour without a pledge. No true home ever has or ever can be established without a most solemn covenant. The covenanting people of the world have always been the best people of the world. As long as time lasts the dear old Scotch Covenanters will be remembered and the world will ever feel their influence. The church of God is established upon sacred covenants and depends upon the faithful keeping of these for its perpetuity. The foundation of the Young People's Society of Christian Endeavor is its covenant. Say what you please, one thing is certain: that is, you cannot have a Christian Endeavor society without the Christian Endeavor pledge. It is the *sine qua non* of Christian Endeavor. Dr. Clark says, "To speak with all seriousness, so far as my experience has gone, in every part of the world, in every climate, under all circumstances, in all denominations, among young people of every color and condition, I have never known a Christian Endeavor society to long flourish which ignored the pledge, the consecration meeting, or the essential committees. All of the untimely deaths of which I have heard, except those due to ecclesiastical strangling or freezing, can be traced directly to a neglect of these fundamental ideas, which make a Young People's society a Christian Endeavor society."

No one is compelled to sign this pledge. That is a matter of liberty and conscience. We have no king in America, save God, and no slave unless he is a voluntary slave. In matters of pledge-making and religious worship we have that freedom which makes an honest conscience. In religious life we have that latitude which makes a large Christian. We have no pope to bind our consciences — neither to narrow our lives of growth in Christ, nor to curtail our broadest and strongest effort for humanity's salvation. This pledge is a free pledge. The soul that takes it does so of its own accord, "trusting in the Lord Jesus Christ for strength" to carry out all of its great principles in truth, in liberty, and in love. Dr. Conwell says, "I believe that a pledge is a good thing. It makes society safer, it makes mankind purer, it lifts the standard of Christ higher, to take a pledge. It makes men and women. Hence I believe in the Christian Endeavor pledge to speak in the meeting every week, to read the Bible daily, and to trust in the Lord Jesus Christ for strength; it makes men and women."

What the world needs is not more wealth, not more culture (unless it be the culture of Christian education), not more creed, but more heroic and righteous manhood and womanhood, more men and women of Christlike character. I believe this pledge, if strictly kept, will give us such men and such women. It is a conqueror of cowardice and of unrighteousness. This pledge has enabled a million of young people to conquer that enemy of the church known as "indifference." The bane of our churches is the indifference of so many of their members; the bane of our cities is the indifference of their citizens; the bane of our national government is the indifference of the good men who hold the ballot and fail to cast it for righteousness' sake. It has enabled another million to conquer the enemy known as "the man-fearing spirit." It has enabled another million to conquer the church's enemy known as "worldliness." It has enabled millions to overcome the evil spirit of "sectarianism." It has enabled over three millions of young people to overcome, to a great extent, the devil, the great arch-enemy of the kingdom of Christ.

Over 3,350,000 have signed this covenant. What an army! Over 3,350,000 have been united in Christian love and fellowship by this pledge. What a union! Over 3,350,000 have been enabled to make a beautiful covenant with the Lord Jesus Christ by this pledge. What a blessing! It has brought miltions into closer touch with Christ, the source of life, light, love, and power. It has broken down sectarian barriers and united opposing factions into one grand army of consecrated men, women, and children, who are beginning to realize that in Christ Jesus they are one in heart, if not in name. It has emphasized Christ's great doctrine of the solidarity of man. We hold that the right to love and fellowship a brother Christian, whatever be his name, is a sacred right vouchsafed for us by our Lord, the great head of the church. The Christian world is beginning to realize that Christ is more than any creed, and that all who are in him are one in heart, whether one in name or not. This pledge has enabled 3,350,000 young people to emphasize Christ's prayer for Christian unity in the bonds of love. As Dr. Boyd says, " In our judgment the United Society of Christian Endeavor has done more in its short life to break down sectarian barriers, and to draw different denominations together, than all other forces combined during the same period. It does not antagonize the present order. It has no aim to permanently obliterate dividing lines. It seeks no fusing nor confusing of parties or sects. Historic landmarks are undisturbed. It wisely recognizes that enough doctrinal ground has not yet emerged from the sea of controversy for all Christians to stand upon; but it has discovered that while separated by intellectual conceptions of truth, within the heart the same love throbs, the same loyalty to the Master is felt. Forgetting the differences of the head, it seeks to place heart to heart; and on a basis of love and fellowship we stand together, and the will, controlled not by logic, but affection, is harmonized in one sacred vow of devotion to Christ and his church. Whether touched by the hand of confirmation or not, baptized with or into water, to each there was an hour, sacred above every hour, when the Spirit of God came and touched the soul as the breeze touches the cheek in that shadowy hour between the lights. We felt him. He was strangely near and real to us then; we lived, we loved, we vowed,—loved Jesus and vowed loyalty to his divine name and service to his church. That experience has made us one — not one externally, one in that which the senses announce, but really one; one in that inner life, one in the supreme fact respecting ourselves,— that we are the sons of God, and one in Christ Jesus."

This glorious fact Christian Endeavor has proclaimed to the world and has emphasized it by fellowships, hand touches, heart touches, union meetings, state and international conventions, and its great principle of interdenominational fellowship. Without this pledge the nineteenth century would have missed its greatest movement toward interdenominational fellowship and Christian unity. It has enlisted millions in the divine enterprise of world-wide evangelization, and caused hundreds of thousands of dollars to flow into the Lord's treasury for missions. It has enabled the active Endeavorers of the world to win over seventeen hundred thousand of their associates from a life of sin to a life of righteousness in Jesus Christ. *Over seventeen hundred thousand souls converted from Satan to our Lord Jesus Christ!* That victory alone is worth all the effort and all the sacrifice ever made by all of the Christian Endeavor societies of the world. This pledge has made possible the grandest religious movement of the nineteenth century — a movement which, if it should die to-day, would, like Abel, speak to a thousand succeeding generations and influence them for good. I believe, however, that Christian Endeavor is only at its beginning, and on the threshold of its great usefulness. As Bishop Fallows says, " Its interdenominational fellowship furnishes the ground for increase of faith in the triumph of righteousness when it shows not one denomination, but many; not one section of our country, but all sections; not our own continent, but other lands and the isles of the sea; uniting their petitions, their missionary zeal, their means, and their heaven-born enthusiasm for world evangelization."

John Wesley said, " Give me twenty men and I will move the world; but they must be men on fire for God." He got his men, and the world is feeling his power more to-day than ever before. It does seem that with these consecrated millions of Endeavorers we ought to, within the next century, bring Christ to the world and the whole world to Christ. My heart cries out and says, " Myself, my home, my associates, my friends, my neighbors, my country, my world, for Christ." This pledge throbs with this glorious idea. It is a religious covenant. There is nothing in this wide world so powerful as the Christian religion. It has been decidedly the most powerful and beneficent factor in the world's development during the past nineteen centuries. Its gospel is "the power of God unto salvation to every one that believeth." Its Christ is the " Conqueror of conquerors." With its present facilities, opportunities, and resources I see nothing to keep it from sweeping over the whole world within a few decades. And in the success of this great forward movement Christian Endeavor is one of the greatest factors. Its covenant pledge has made it possible for millions of young people to consecrate their lives and service to Christ and the church in such a way as to be powerfully felt for the causes of righteousness, truth, missions, social purity, Christian citizenship, systematic beneficence, temperance, good literature, testimony for Christ, and soul-winning. It has liberalized the hearts of millions, and made thousands of "tithe-givers." It has made millions better church-members, increasing their loyalty to their own churches. It has helped a million young people to do regularly that which they used to do spasmodically, or probably did not do at all. It has given hundreds of thousands a greater hunger for Bible-study and for "the surrendered life" in Christ. It has put millions of young Christians to asking "What would Christ have me to do?" It takes away selfishness and helps us to do things for Christ's sake. It has turned the eyes and hearts of three millions of young people toward Christ with a faith in him which they never had before. It has consecrated their lives to Christ for his use in carrying out his great plan and work of human redemption. Selfishness, covetousness, and laxity in civil and religious morals are the great sins of this age. Against all of these Christian Endeavor is striking heroic and telling blows. It is building up a noble character based upon a profound sense of moral obligation, a true manliness in religious belief, and a heroic faithfulness in Christian testimony and service. It is bringing about a better civil and religious life. "The deepest thing in Endeavor," says some one, "is the surrendered life consecrated to Christ." Life is the sweetest and most attractive thing in the universe. Nothing is so powerful, so unanswerable, as Christian life. Christ came that we "might have life, and have it more abundantly." Christ is "the way, the truth, and the life" of all true Endeavordom. He is the Supreme One of our pledge. He is its "all and in all."

I like this pledge because it exalts Christ. It acknowledges him as the son of God and the Saviour of the world. The Christian Endeavorer who is true to his pledge makes Christ his model. He is the best model the world has ever known. "Trusting in the Lord Jesus Christ"—not myself, not the arm of flesh, not worldly wisdom or wealth, but Christ, is my strength and my salvation. "For strength"—strength is the beauty of youth, the crown of age, the grandeur of an army, and the terror of the tornado. Our strength is from Christ. All power in heaven and in earth is given unto him. Oh, when will God's people realize that their strength is not in money, not in numbers, not in fine church edifices, not in human plans and schemes, not in theological and literary schools, not in bishops and assemblies, but in the Lord Jesus Christ, through the Holy Ghost? These other things are good when vitalized by God's truth and his Holy Spirit; otherwise they are as filthy rags in the sight of Jehovah. Christ! Christ! Christ! He is the watchword and rallying cry of Christian Endeavor. Around him the whole pledge centres. He is its life and its all. He is the world's greatest conqueror; and the man or society that trusts in him need not fear defeat. The power of this covenant is in its recognition of Christ. Take Christ out of our pledge, and it is weaker than a crying infant of a day.

The pledge emphasizes faith in Christ. I like that word "trusting." It is one of the sweetest and most expressive words of the English language. Five years ago a young woman went out from my congregation as a missionary to

Japan. She, with several other missionaries, missed the steamer on which they intended to sail from the Pacific coast, and, being eager to reach their field of work as soon as possible, they sailed on a merchant vessel. On the ocean they were overtaken by a terrific storm, which lasted several days. One evening the captain called these missionaries together and said that his vessel was about to go to pieces, and if the storm continued a few hours longer they would all be lost. He asked them to pray to God to calm the storm. This young woman went to her room. She said, "I had nothing left but Christ, my Bible, and prayer; but I had faith in these." She fell on her knees and prayed Christ to save them from a grave underneath the angry billows, promising him a life consecrated to him on the mission field if he would preserve her and others on the ship. She prayed until something said to her, "Open the Book and read, my child." She threw open the Bible and read these wonderful words in Isaiah: "Fear thou not; for I am with thee: be not dismayed; for I am thy God; I will strengthen thee; yea, I will help thee; yea, I will uphold thee with the right hand of my righteousness. When thou passest through the waters, I will be with thee; and through the rivers, they shall not overflow thee; for I am the Lord thy God." She said that when she read these wonderful words, although the storm was still madly raging, there came to her a peace which passed all understanding. Within an hour there came a sudden and wonderful calm over the ocean. She soon fell asleep, and when she awoke next morning every cloud was gone and the sunlight was giving its good-morning kiss to every rippling wave on the Pacific. Brethren, such faith as that young woman had on the stormy ocean that night is worth more than this world to a human soul. And I believe that the Christ who calmed the troubled sea of Galilee for his distressed disciples also calmed the wild storm on the Pacific Ocean for the faith of his loving child. "Trusting," "Trusting in the *Lord Jesus Christ*," "Trusting in the Lord Jesus Christ *for strength*,"— thank God for a covenant which begins that way! The power is in Christ. Faith is the wire through which it flows from heaven to earth.

Dr. William Patterson says, "Faith is the channel through which God sends his blessings to humanity. We have many statements in Scripture proving this, such as 'According to your faith be it unto you,' 'Thy faith hath made thee whole,' 'All things are possible to him that believeth.' Without faith it is impossible to please God, and without faith it is impossible to accomplish anything in this world for God or our fellow men. It is said of our Lord Jesus himself, that in a certain place he could not do many mighty works, because of the unbelief of the people; and the same thing might be said of many churches and communities in the present age. Too many people are putting their trust and confidence in the things of time, and not in the Lord. 'It is not by might, not by power, but by my Spirit,' saith the Lord, that the world is to be saved. It is only through men of faith that the Spirit will work." Faith is the great lever which God has given to his church, with which it is to move the world. When a man loses faith in Christ, in the Bible, and in the Holy Spirit he loses all.

This covenant pledges one to do something. It means that there are to be no dummies and no drones in Christian Endeavor. Lord Stanley said, "I don't believe an unemployed man can be happy." Burton said, "An idle dog will be mangy; and how shall an idle person escape?" One reason why the churches of the past had so much trouble with their young people was that they gave them nothing definite to do which was worthy of their mettle. Worthy employment is one of the great secrets of happiness, of contentment, of success, and of a pure life. As Christian Endeavorers we enter into a solemn covenant to strive to do whatever Christ would have us to do. We covenant to be something and to do something which is well pleasing to God. Nothing in this world is more blessed than humble, Christlike service. That very thing made the "good Samaritan" one of the most beautiful and lovable characters of the New Testament. It is not what we have, but what we give, that makes our life a blessing to the world. It was not when George Peabody gathered his millions as a banker that his life became a blessing; but when he gave those millions to establish the great Peabody College at Nashville, to establish a great school in his native town, to feed London's hungry poor, and for a great fund for Southern education, his life became a blessing to the world. It was when Edison put his knowledge into a practical telephone that he put all men on speaking terms. Christ is a glorious example of this doctrine. Christian Endeavor translates a life of faith, of prayer, and of Bible-study into a life of Christian service.

This covenant pledges us to a systematic life of prayer and Bible-study. Prayer is the Christian's greatest privilege, and the Bible is his text-book. All great Christians and all great soul-winners have devoted much time to prayer and Bible-study. The Bible is Christian Endeavorers' only infallible rule of faith and practice. Dr. Patterson says, "Now, if any one should ask me what I considered to be the strongest feature in connection with the Christian Endeavor I should answer, 'The place which the society gives *to the Bible.*' So long as a society makes the Word of God its text-book and continues to train young men and young women in the Scriptures, so long will the society prosper and go forth conquering and to conquer in the power of the Holy Ghost, who caused all Scripture to be written."

Ewald says, "The Bible has been the inspiration of that which is purest in literature, noblest in art, greatest in government, most heroic in life, and most blessed in its influence upon the mind of man. Its precepts are pure and practical, and its service is sacred and sublime. It contains all the wisdom of the world." This is wonderful testimony from this great scholar. Christ was a student of the Old Testament. The Gospels show us that he made one hundred and forty quotations from twenty-two of its books. Hamilton W. Mabie says that the Scotch people have read the Bible so diligently and prayerfully for so many generations that they have become an inspired people. I am glad that this covenant has put 3,350,000 young people to reading the Bible daily. This means glorious results for the church of God in the decade to come. As these millions read the Bible regularly, systematically, and prayerfully, they will catch great ideals and receive mighty inspirations which will enable them to overcome in life's battles and to triumph gloriously through Jesus Christ. We believe that Christ is above all conquerors, and that Christianity and the Bible are above all creeds. Malibran said, "If I neglect my practice for one day I feel it; if for two days, my friends notice it; and if for three days, the whole world knows it." I *will* make it the rule of my life to read the Bible *every day.* I cannot afford to do otherwise.

This covenant pledges us to be loyal to our own churches and to support them in every way. Dr. Clark says, "Now this first and general part of the pledge stands for two essential things in the religious life: private devotion, and loyalty to our own church,— private devotion as exemplified by prayer and Bible reading; loyalty to the church as expressed by regular and constant attendance upon her public services."

This covenant pledges the whole life to Christ. It is the covenant of a "surrendered life." That life is the greatest thing which Christ demands of us; and it is what every one can render unto God, be he rich or poor, learned or unlearned. One night the violinist Paganini commenced tuning his violin in the presence of his audience. A string broke, then another, and a third broke. The audience murmured its disappointment. But the great violinist stepped forward and said, "One string and Paganini." Then as the audience listened they heard the music of rippling streams, the soft, sweet sighs of the zephyrs, the songs of birds, melodies low and high, and a mingling of sweet sounds. They went wild with delight when they saw what the violinist could do with one string. A "surrendered life"—with it God can put "a thousand to flight," and with two such souls he can "chase ten thousand."

This covenant pledges us to a life of training for service in the Master's cause. It has put 3,350,000 young people into training for the great battles of the church. Dr. Arnold said, "I rely more on *training* than on telling." Our war with Spain showed the value of skilful training. They say that our guns were no better than those of Spain, but our men outclassed the Spanish soldiers and seamen in skilful execution. They were better trained. The world may well keep its eye on the great Endeavor army now in training.

Without this pledge millions would have missed the blessings of the consecration meeting,— that meeting which has so often brought us close to God and filled us with inspiration and enthusiasm for definite service "for Christ and the Church;" that meeting which has been a great mainspring for Christian activity. It has conquered the indifference of millions and deepened their spir- .itual lives. " This is an age when patriotism, practical benevolence, and enthu- siastic activity are the people's ideals." All of these are furnished to our young people through the pledge. There is something heroic about this pledge which appeals to a true man's heart. It is a covenant of loyalty to the church and to Christ. It is a Bible covenant; a prayer covenant; a working, aggressive, and progressive covenant; a Christian covenant. No one but a Christian can keep this pledge. Once the admirers of Paganini gave him a complimentary concert in which the great violinist was to play. When the time came for a short inter- mission he placed his violin on a table and stepped into the anteroom for a moment's rest. A friend removed his fine violin and put an old one in its place. When Paganini returned he saw at a glance what had been done. It put him on his mettle. He tuned the old violin. The audience wondered if he would get any music out of it. He stepped to the front and commenced playing. He put his whole soul into it. Never before had they heard Paganini play as then. His friends went wild with delight. After a moment, when he came to himself, he placed the old violin on the table, stepped to the front, and as the tears ran from his eyes said, " Friends, you thought the music was in the violin. You mistake. The music is in Paganini's soul." So he who keeps this Christ pledge must have the Christ spirit in his soul.

Some do not believe in pledges. We Endeavorers do. We believe in our pledge, which we have taken gladly and which we keep cheerfully. The pledge fits us and we fit the pledge. In old Saxon times, when a new monarch came to the throne, the nobles came, put their hands into his, and vowed to be his loyal subjects unto death. We have by this covenant put our hands into Christ's hand and pledged that we would trust him and strive to do whatever he would have us do so long as we live.

Some people say that they do not believe in youths taking a pledge, because they are more likely to break it than those of mature years. Such people know nothing of the heroism of childhood. Children are better pledge-keepers than old people; and besides, it is in the beginning of life and not at its close that we need pledges. William Reynolds, who was not much in favor of young people making pledges, witnessed the following and was converted. He said that one day there was a railway accident to the train on which he was travel- ling and many were injured. He was not injured himself, and he helped to carry the injured to homes near at hand. Among others was a little boy about thirteen years of age who was badly injured, and the doctor said that one of his legs would have to be cut off in order to save his life. This would cause the boy so much pain that the doctor poured out some liquid into a glass to give.to the boy to allay the pain. The boy asked what it was, and he was told that it was liquor. He said he could not drink it. They wanted to know why, and he said he had signed the temperance pledge, and had promised his mother never to touch it. " But," said the doctor, " you may not be able to stand this; you may die when your leg has been taken off. Won't you take it?" "No," said the boy, " I can die, but I cannot break my pledge." That is what I would call a pledge victory. No man can become truly great who does not make great and solemn covenants with God and man and then faithfully keep them. Thomas Lynch says, " Till fixed we are not free. The acorn must be earthed ere the oak will develop." The man who has not made a covenant with God is like a pilotless ship without an anchor.

This is a conquering covenant when kept. When one takes it and does not keep it he injures himself and does an injustice to the great Christian Endeavor cause. One of Paul's awful charges against the Gentiles, as recorded in the first chapter of Romans, was that they were "covenant-breakers." Having taken this pledge, let us be true to every item of it, and to the Christ to whom we made it.

Do not change the pledge to suit caviling people. Let us never lower the standard of the pledge to get men into our societies; rather, let us bring them up to the high standard of the pledge. At the battle of Lookout Mountain, the troops were lagging behind in quite a disorderly manner when some one suddenly spied the standard-bearer away on in advance. An officer shouted for him to bring the colors down to the men. "No," he replied, "bring your men up to the colors." The pledge is ideal. March up to it. We must hold fast to our covenant in its integrity, for it has been tried and found absolutely essential to the life of a Christian Endeavor society. It has enabled millions of young people to win glorious victories in the past; it is helping them to make great conquests in the present; it will aid them in the great battles of the future.

In the days of the bloody tyrants of France the boys of Paris got together and marched through the streets bearing a banner with these words on it: "Tremble, tyranny, for we are coming." They did come, and the whole government of France was changed. Listen! I hear the tread of 3,350,000 Christian Endeavorers. I hear them say to the cruel heathen institutions, "Tremble, for we are coming in a world-wide evangelistic effort." I hear them say to the "political boss" and political corrupters, "Tremble, for we are coming with a mighty Christian citizenship." I hear them say to the Sabbath desecrater, "Tremble, for we are coming with the ten commandments." I hear them say to that great blight and curse of our nation, the saloon, "Tremble, for we are coming, and the saloon must go." Mark it! Hear it! "We are coming, and *the saloon must go.'*" I hear them say to narrow sectarianism, "Tremble, we are coming in one of the most glorious interdenominational fellowships the world has ever seen." I hear them say to the dens of gambling, vice, and immorality, "Tremble, for, we are coming in a great crusade for social purity." I hear them say to the arch-enemy of humanity, the devil, "Tremble, for we are coming with our 'conquering covenant' and the 'banner of Prince Immanuel' to fight for the causes of truth and righteousness, 'for Christ and the Church.'"

When the Spanish admiral, Cervera, made prisoner at the sea-fight off Santiago, Cuba, learned that in the battle which had cost him the destruction of his entire fleet, and the loss of all his men, only one American had been killed, and two injured, amazed at this unheard-of disparity, he exclaimed, "It was the will of God!" Christian Endeavor has conquered, it is conquering, it will continue to conquer, because it is the will of God. We are on God's side, and that means victory. God grant us his blessing and wisdom! The Lord Jesus Christ grant us his unerring leadership! The Holy Spirit grant us his baptism of sanctification, inspiration, and power! Amen.

The next speaker, a Lutheran pastor from Kansas City, Mo., had assigned to him a topic dear to the Christian Endeavor leaders,—"The Tenth Legion."

Address by Rev. J. M. Cromer,
Kansas City, Mo.

The Tenth Legion is an effort to bring about a more scriptural practice of the duties involved in Christian stewardship. This subject lies at the basis of man's relation to God. At the beginning God entered into a relation of cooperative partnership with man; but from the beginning man has failed to honor the trust.

God gave man the whole world,—"the earth, the sea, and all that in them is,"—but one little tree, and man robbed God of that. God gave man a nature and a being "fearfully and wonderfully made," requiring only the worship of his spirit, and man has robbed God of that. But man could never rid himself of the God-impressed consciousness of his indebtedness to God. This has followed him both as a faithful reminder and accuser in all his mad career.

Abel offers an acceptable sacrifice, and the blessing of that act abounds unto the family of man to this day.

Out of this consciousness grew a custom of giving the tenth. Older than Moses and the Ten Great Words of Sinai is this law of tithing. It was observed by the patriarchs of many nations. The Phœnicians and Carthagenians sent annual tithers to the Tyrian Hercules. The Lydians gave a tenth of their booty to their gods. The Greeks gave tithes to Apollo, and the Romans to Hercules. According to this ancient custom, Abraham gave a tenth part of his spoils to Melchizedek. No sooner does Jacob arouse from the vision of God's wonderful revelation to him at Bethel than does he most solemnly declare, " Of all that thou shalt give me, I will surely give a tenth unto thee." When Canaan was apportioned no part was given the tribe of Levi. They were to have God's portion, the tenth of all the tribes, and they in turn gave a tenth unto the priests.

Established and enforced by the higher law of God stamped upon the very nature of man, this law has received the additional sanction of God himself, and has always been a part of man's religious observance. Neglect of no other duty has called forth more scathing accusation and condemnation, nor been followed by more dire results in the spiritual life of man.

Under the inspiration of the Pentecostal baptism, no result was more manifest than seen in the voluntary consecration of property. Man never was more spiritual or more Godlike than when he made tangible return to God. And no other duty has been more closely allied with the spiritual life. The grace of giving has been the pulse of spiritual health and strength. When other graces abounded it rose ; when they declined it fell. Hence the ideal giving of Pentecost failed to be practical, because man failed in his spiritual zeal and fervor, and very soon some system was found necessary. Naturally, again, the system of tithes was reinstated. Jerome and Augustine favored it. Councils adopted it, and enforced it at the point of moral obligation, making its neglect a sin. Gregory the Seventh classed it among the most solemn duties.

But the declaration of leaders and the enactment of councils could not thus artificially maintain this grace, which was so closely allied to man's spiritual life. No greater evidence is given of man's estrangement from God than is found in the means resorted to by the church to raise funds to bear the expense of a religion devoid of true spirituality. All other graces could be counterfeited. Hypocritical priests could keep up the appearance of religious life, in their gorgeous robes, long prayers, and high-sounding homilies. A heartless worship, not bearing the image of God, was received at the temple, but the gifts of the treasury must bear the image and superscription of Cæsar. In devotion the church received the lip-service of idolatrous worshippers, but in contributions there must be the authentic signature of the State. Hence when the spiritual life declined, methods and schemes must be invented for extorting money out of uncharitable pretenders. And what made the effort greater, the more false the religion the more lavish expenditure of money necessary.

Then the church began a systematic worship of Mammon. The whole genius of the church was turned into raising funds. An endless catalogue of relics was invented, which were sold to a superstitious people at fabulous prices. Miracles of healing were pretended, for which large sums were demanded. The infamous " rite of patronage " was instituted, whereby wealthy lords and princes were inveigled into building numerous and elaborate churches for the mere privilege of naming those who should officiate in them. Whole nations were received into Christian fellowship upon the most compromising and unscriptural terms, that new tribute might be levied. Masses were invented, indulgences treated, penances proclaimed, the primary object of which was that the coffers of the church might be filled, to support a licentious and luxurious priesthood. Designing priests would appeal to the ignorance and superstition of the rich, persuading them to give all their wealth to the church and enter a life of abject poverty, that the pompous show and splendor of a heartless church might be maintained. Every religious rite had a monetary value, the price of which was in proportion to its importance.

We lose our interest in the grand cathedrals and costly ornamentation and material splendor of the church in these times, because they grew out of the direct worship of Mammon, and are the gilded monuments of a dead spirituality. Every blessing and rite of the church was prostituted to the getting of gain. Thus, according to Paul, when the church was the strongest she was the weakest.

What a spectacle! The church of the living God, whose are the silver and the gold, prostrate upon idolatrous knees at the shrine of Mammon! The church of the self-sacrificing Saviour, who became poor that in his poverty we might have riches beyond measure, Judas-like, selling her Lord for material gain! The loss of spiritual power led to dependence upon temporal power, and opened up all the avenues of corruption and immorality. The prophecy of Malachi has been thundered again and again into the ears of a declining church: "Ye have been cursed with a curse, for ye have robbed me."

During the Reformation scriptural methods were again introduced. Luther could find nothing better than the tithing system, and the peasants of Germany, throbbing with the pulse of a new and more spiritual life, gladly adopted the plan. The same law was again exemplified. With the revival of the true spiritual life came the revival of the grace of giving.

No more striking instance of this fact can be found in the history of Christendom than in the revival of missions which grew out of the Reformation, and which became world-wide in their operation. A new spiritual baptism solved the problem of church finances. The church was never advanced with more zeal and success, and upon more scriptural grounds.

There was no force of arms compelling the confession of unwilling captive nations, save the sword of the Spirit. There was no conquest of territory save that of the heart. There was no burden imposed save that of the cross, which now became the symbol of a new creation. There was no tax levied, for with true apostolic zeal men gave up all and followed Christ. There were no gorgeous temples built, for the Holy Ghost now took up his abode in the sanctified heart and body. Immanuel, God with us, became the name of the Most High. There was no elaborate ritual, nor gorgeously bedecked priests, for with a broken and a contrite heart men worshipped God according to the dictates of their own consciences. There was now no unholy compromise between Church and State, for that which truly belonged to God was enough, without bartering with Cæsar.

But we have come to a time of great activity in the church. We stand upon the threshold of a new century, with faces all agleam with new hope for the coming of the King. You represent an army 3,350,000 strong, gathered for the evangelization of the world, standing with the sword of the Spirit drawn to strike down the legions of Satan. And yet we are only beginning to grasp the full meaning of our mission.

That was a bold act of brother Amerman, of New York City, when he organized the Tenth Legion. It was an heroic effort to get at the real pulse of the spiritual life of Christian Endeavorers. Nothing is more reliable as a test of the sincerity of this whole movement. The splendid success of this plan has proven that the Endeavor movement has not been mere sentiment, but that we have been in earnest in our efforts to advance the kingdom of Christ. A deep spiritual meaning has been given all the magnificent demonstrations of the past; for, after all, the practical test of our religion is, How much will we give to advance it?

Nothing could be more timely. Wise men have become alarmed at the rapid increase of wealth; and Christian people have their share. What does it mean? That they shall give as they have been blessed. The world has never been so open to the entrance of Christian missionaries. What does it mean? Wealth increases with opportunities to use it for God and humanity. How plain! For years we have been praying for the falling of the walls of China. God has answered our prayers. That vast Empire is on the verge of disintegration. Are we ready to "enter, in the name of the Lord?" God has placed us in the Philippines. The West has been called back to the East.

The Star of Empire has made his circuit. What does it mean? Who does not understand it? Wealth; the dismemberment of the vastest heathen empire of earth; a strategic point or vantage-ground from which to operate;—how plain!

God never spoke so plainly to us as a nation as to-day. Who will not answer? We have freed Cuba. We will civilize the Philippines. But does it not all mean the Christianization of China? No other nation of earth was prepared to answer this call. As a nation we represent the highest type of Christian civilization. We have no complicating alliances with foreign powers. But have we the spiritual force to carry on this great work? What thought has been made more prominent in Endeavor circles than that of consecration? Has it been for naught? Aye, we had not thought God was going to trust so much to our care.

We represent the advanced guard of the Christian forces to-day. The church has come to look to us for a watchword and a battle-cry. Shall it not be "China for Christ"? Has God himself not indicated this?

My friends, no one subject so measures and comprehends the whole cause of Christian progress as the one question of Christian stewardship. No one duty gives the Christian such a full exercise of his spiritual gifts. We have the ability. We have the pressing need. Have we the willing disposition?

Never before has Mammon been so strong as to-day. He is the gilded god of the closing year of the nineteenth century. He is the Jupiter of modern times. He rules the world. Money-making has become a science and a disease. We do not consider money as a talent to be used, but as a god to be worshipped. Man has robbed God from the beginning. This is his chief danger to-day. No progress can be made in the spiritual life, in the conversion of the world, until we break down the altars of Mammon. Here is a rival god unworthy our worship, threatening to supplant the King of kings.

What are we doing? Let us look about us, and through our churches. Never before have the calls for money been so urgent at home and abroad as to-day. And again we have gone to inventing schemes and methods to raise money. We have not so much preached Christian stewardship, and sought to lay the foundation of a true character for benevolence for all time. We have been too much pressed for this. The process was too tedious and slow, and we lacked faith in it. We, too, have been afraid of encroaching upon the sphere of harmony. Hence we have invented the church fair. The good women spend one dollar for material, and one dollar in hard work upon a fancy article, and sell it to the ungodly rich for a dollar and a half, thus making the rich richer, and the church poorer. We have gotten up spectacular tableaux, concerts, and sociables, with their catch-penny devices to extract money from the uncharitable *without hurting.*

We have not so much concentrated our energies upon the great scriptural doctrine of stewardship, and tried to arouse the conscience of Christian wealth, so that it will purge itself of its idolatry and lay all on the altar of Christ, as we have given ourselves to schemes. We have aimed rather at the non-churchgoer. We have given great suppers, and gorged our own stomachs, for Christ's sake, at twenty-five cents a gorge, just to get some hungry and rich outsider to pay twenty-five cents for a fifty-cent meal. And this we call raising money for the church.

Imagine David rising from his knees, when he had prayed, "What shall I render unto the Lord for all his benefits toward me?" and calling together a lot of the old priests and scribes, and their wives, to arrange for an old folks' concert, something like they used to give when down in Babylonish captivity, to draw in a few of the Philistines and make a few dollars for *David* to pay *his* debt to *God!* Or think of Paul, when he had fully recovered from that midnight vision, in which he heard the call from Macedonia to come over and help them, calling Silas and Timothy together, and saying, "We must go over into Macedonia, and we must have some funds. Silas, you remember how you saved that Jerusalem church and got it on its feet. Suppose you try the same plan here. You and Timothy call the old folks together and teach them how to give the Deestrict Skule. Silas, you can be the 'school-master,' and Timothy, you can be 'the little twin brother.' Then Timothy, you remember what a success you had over at Lystra with the *Peak Sisters.* You might import a few of them, and get our young people here to join in giving that. All Troas will turn out, and we can set sail *at once* for Macedonia!"

What a travesty this would be upon the gospel! And what will more mar the history of our great age of evangelization than just these things? Nothing can be more humiliating than for the church of Christ, for which Paul suffered, and Huss burned at the stake, and Luther faced the devils of Rome, to humiliate itself in this manner. This is not the Spirit's plan. David arises from his knees, and says, "I will pay my vows *now* unto the Lord." Paul goes forth "*immediately*" from his vision, having faith to believe that with the call will come the means to obey. God holds the challenge constantly before us: "Prove me now herewith."

May the Tenth Legion consume the whole church, and rescue God's footstool from the rule of Mammon, and drive out all practical unbelief, and hasten the coming of our Lord

"I Hope I'll Jine de Band" was then sung in tuneful jubilee style by the Hampton Institute Quartette of colored songsters. In order to permit the rendition of an encore in response to the long-continued, insistent applause, President Clark, who appeared later on the programme, consented to give up enough of the time allotted to him in order to permit the quartette to sing again.

Chairman Grose said, "I thank God that the Christian Endeavor is an international, interdenominational, inter-racial, interesting organization, and everything else that is good and begins with 'inter.'"

Rev. Cornelius Brett, D.D., of Jersey City, N. J., conducted a testimony meeting on the tithing movement. He asked those present to tell of their experiences in this line, and as many responded as there was time to hear. Among the more interesting declarations that were made as to benefits received from giving a tenth of one's income to God are the following: —

"I did not think my salary was large enough for me to give a tenth of it and support myself and wife; but I did it, and my salary was increased that year from $500 to $990."

"I've been giving a tenth for two years. My salary has not been increased, but I'm going to give the tenth as long as I live."

"I've been blessed in every way."

"Giving one-tenth leads me to long to give more."

"Students in our society who do not know where the money is coming from to defray their next year's tuition are giving their tenth."

"Our members who give their tenth are our most spiritual members, not because they give their tenth, but because they realize that they are stewards of God."

"I don't think that it is giving. It is only paying back a part of that which we owe."

"If you give a tenth out of a small salary, I find that the nine-tenths will stretch."

"I find the Lord is the best banker. Ordinary bankers pay but three per cent, but he pays one hundred per cent."

A voice shouted, "That's so."

"A mission accommodating eight hundred people was built in our city by systematic giving."

"My wife, my mother, two of my children, my two nieces that live with us, and myself each give a tenth. Our baby will do it when he gets old enough. I recommend it as a family affair."

Dr. Brett said, "If you've been blessed you want your friends to know about it. I can say that I have been wonderfully aided by the tithing plan."

A heavy rain began to fall. The tent leaked, and nearly every one in the audience who had an umbrella raised it. The sight was novel and amusing.

President Clark then gave a brief address upon the Quiet Hour.

Address by Rev. Francis E. Clark, D.D.

This will be largely a meeting of testimony. Your voices are better than mine. I would have been glad to give all my time to my friends from Hampton Institute had it not been that this question so important, this matter of such vital moment to Christian Endeavor, required that I should hear from you. Will you be ready in two or three minutes with your testimonies as to what the Quiet Hour has done for you?

Just a word about its influence upon the movement. Mr. Grose has said that it is the missing link of this century. It is the thing that we need. I believe it with all my heart, in this bustling, hustling, rushing, roaring century: in these years when business is to the front and meditation is to the rear; in these years when it is so hard for us to find a moment to go away by ourselves to talk with God; in these years when meditation has become a lost art, as some people have said. But we need to go back, we need to have something or other to bring us to this condition, that we do not spend all our lives, or the best part of our lives, in the crowd, in our business, in the rush and roar of the world, but see to it that the best part is spent alone with God, that there is something above the material, above the intellectual,— the spiritual, which must be cultivated in the moment of quietness with God. This is the thought of the Quiet Hour, and its influence on Christian Endeavor I cannot begin to tell you all. I have felt it everywhere, in every convention of all this year, from the Atlantic to the Pacific, from Manitoba to Oklahoma, in every State and Province and Territory that I have visited; in talking with tens of thousands of young people; in opening my mail every morning and finding there testimonies of the glad Comrades of the Quiet Hour. Better than all, I hope I have found something of the blessedness of it in my own life; and I am sure, as I look into your faces, that they reflect something of the blessedness that has come into your lives. Christian Endeavor is stronger to-day, far, far stronger, because of this intangible something which we call communion, devotion, meditation, thought, talk with God.

Just one word of caution. Ours is not the quiet hour of the ascetic; it is not the quiet hour of the monk in his cell; it is not merely the rapt vision of the mystic who never uses what he finds at the throne of God; it is the vision of those who use all that they get there in work among the people whom God has given us to serve. Bishop Whipple, at the convention in Florida,— that grand missionary among the Indians of Minnesota, of whom you know, whose name is fragrant throughout all the world,— said, at the Christian Endeavor Convention a year ago, "We must reach both ways,— one hand up to God to take his hand, the other down to our fellow men to take their hands; and when we reach those up and down, and hold his hand and the hand of our brother who needs, then we are in the right place." The thought of the Quiet Hour is that we reach up to God in order that we may afterwards reach down to man and help him. It is preparing for service; it is putting on the panoply for work; it is pressing ourselves for more strenuous effort; and it is getting the blessing which we will give. It is not simply the vision on the mount; it is the vision that we get that we may use in our future life and work.

This question is often asked,— and let me try and answer it that you may answer it for others,— What is the necessity of an organization? Why are we banded together? Why do you advocate the Comrades of the Quiet Hour? Why is it necessary to enroll our names? Just this: it makes it tangible, definite, particular; it gives us something to preach, something to talk about; it makes it definite for our own hearts. I have kept the Quiet Hour a great deal better since I have said to my heart, I will do it, and since I signed my name to the covenant that I would, and I think you will find it so; and then through our conventions, in our States, in our papers, everywhere, we can project it, talk about it, make it definite, bring others into the covenant, tell others what was done for us, and make it something that will be definite for them as well; and so — though I do not insist that this is the only way — I think it will help you, and think it will help many others, if you will sign your name as one of the Comrades of the Quiet Hour. You will receive, if you will write to the United Society in Boston, the blanks and the covenant card, which you will keep, and we will record your name with the thousands of others who are thus enrolled, so far as their names are concerned, and in a better way are brought heart to heart as they come to the throne of God morning by morning.

Now, dear friends, what is your testimony? We have a few moments. We will begin over here, and then come to this side of the desk. How has the Quiet Hour blessed you? Will you rise and speak loudly, so that we can all hear.

The following are some of the responses from those present : —

" It helps me to easier overcome the temptations that beset me during the day."
" It fills my heart full of sunshine day by day."
" It has helped me to be patient in time of trial."
" It has increased my longing to be like Christ."
" It has drawn me nearer to my Saviour."

President Clark asked, " Has it added to your inward joy and peace ? If so, will you raise your hand ? "

A great many hands were raised. President Clark then said : —

I am sure that the great many of you would, if there were time, compare your own personal experiences. It has added to your joy and peace, I am sure. Are there those on this side who can say the same thing? Has it brightened your life? Has it irradiated the day? Has it added to your joy, your inward joy, your peace of mind and quiet rest? If so, raise your hands. (Many hands were raised.) I am glad to see the hands go up in such numbers. Now give your personal testimonies in regard to this.

" It has given me new strength for every new hour."
" There is something sublime in the thought that in this great universe which God rules, he has time to listen to our hearts in our meditations, and that joy comes to us from him in the Quiet Hour."
" It enables me to recognize and appreciate the fact that God is with me."
" I have felt that unless in the morning I have the touch of God on my heart the day does not go right."
" It is a source of inspiration never before experienced."
" I have been able, through the Quiet Hour, to settle the important questions that are before me in the duties of the day."
" I could not live without the Quiet Hour."
" It has strengthened me for the labors of the day, and it has brought me in closer contact with Christ."
" My life would never have been anything of satisfaction to myself or blessing to others had it not been for the Quiet Hour."

In conclusion President Clark said: —

Now let us bow our heads and enjoy for the moment this Quiet Hour with God. We can have it here as well as in our own rooms. Look up into God's face for a moment, dear friends, while you look with bowed head downward, and with closed eyes lift your hearts to God. Practise the presence of God for a minute here. Say to yourselves once more, God is here, God is here in this tent by my side; listen for a moment to his voice; say to him, Lord, what wilt thou have me to do? Let us all say it together very softly: Lord, what wilt thou have me to do? (The audience joined softly in this aspiration to God.) Now listen to his voice of suggestion. He will tell you, perhaps; he will surely tell you if you are ready to receive the message. Lord, teach us, we pray thee; tell us thy will; show us thy way; cleanse us from our sins; help us to put ourselves to one side; help us to trample upon selfishness: help us always, trusting in thee for strength, to do whatsoever thou wouldst have us do; and may we listen for direction and guidance day by day ever more carefully and intently from on high, for Jesus' sake. Amen.

There was a warm-hearted friend of young men on the platform, Rev. Hugh K. Walker, D.D., and God used his splendid voice, fine physique, and magnetic personality as a trumpet-call to young men to preach the gospel, in an earnest address, " Young Men Called to Preach."

Address of Rev. Hugh K. Walker, D.D.,
Los Angeles, Cal.

If my topic was "Young Women Called to Preach" I would have a great many more people interested in my talk than I will have in the topic, " Young Men Called to Preach ; " but that reminds me that occasionally honor is given to woman that does not properly belong to her. That seldom happens, but sometimes happens. For example ; in connection with the Resurrection, it is said that woman was the first herald of the gospel. It is a very common thing: " Woman, the last at the cross, the first at the sepulchre." I have not been able to understand how woman was the last at the cross, because I am sure John, a young man, was at the cross about as long as anybody, and he was not a woman. I am sure that the first herald of the gospel was not a woman, for if I reason aright it would be implied that the first herald of the gospel was a young man. In the sixteenth chapter of the gospel of St. Mark we read that when the women came to the sepulchre early in the morning they saw a young man sitting at the head, clothed in white raiment, and he followed them to go and tell the disciples. "Jesus is not here; he has risen from the dead." And so some of us here are authorized by this incident to go and tell the disciples that Christ is risen. I think from my understanding that it may have been an angel; but it does not say so. But I believe it was a sure-enough flesh-and-blood young man, as well as I could tell. But grant it that it was an angel, I want to impress upon you the fact of the significance that a young man was called to proclaim the risen Lord.

Now, this morning, I want to emphasize the fact why the young men are called to preach, rather than young women. I am not opposed to women talking as much as they please. They are born to talk, as well as to rule. They are both teachers and ruling elders — and by the way, most of the teaching in the Sunday schools of this country has been done by women ; nine-tenths is done by women. I am not here this morning to emphasize the fact that women never ought to preach. I have had the privilege of listening to many preachers, Parker, Farrar, Talmage, Hall, and a great many others ; but I want to say to you this morning I was never so thrilled in all my life, never so uplifted to noble deeds and aspirations, as when listening to the silver voice now stilled, the voice of Frances E. Willard, God bless her. But I am here this morning to state that so far as we have any scriptural warrant, young men are called to preach, and we are not required to explain why. Why God chooses a certain man rather than another man is something I do not know. Paul, for example—he was an uncertain fellow and was apathetic so far as his inclination toward the gospel was concerned; but here is one reason I want to give you why young men and not old men, and not women, but young men, were called. The young man was especially called because there never was a time when vigor was demanded more, when physical strength, as well as mental acumen, were more demanded, in order that men might know the gospel and understand the truth of God's Word.

Expansion is in the very air. I do not believe there has been a speaker in these tents who has not referred to expansion or imperialism, or to Dewey or Sampson. The fact is,—and I am glad of it,—I come from the Pacific slope, where they are all imperialists, politically and ecclesiastically. My boy, when he went to Occident College last fall, came home after he had been there a time, and the first thing he did, after he got home, was to say, "Mamma, I am not going to school unless I put on long trousers." Well, there was objection; but by and by she said, "I will go down-town and get you a pair of long trousers;" and so with a few tears she brought the trousers home. He had outgrown his knee pants. Uncle Sam is like that big boy; he has outgrown his knee pants, he is in long trousers. There never was a time in the history of the world when strong men, physically, intellectually, and spiritually, were needed more than now to proclaim the gospel of Jesus Christ. That is why, it seems to me, the young men of the country are needed. Young men are the ones who should carry the gospel. Some magnificent preachers are called later in life; but if you are ever called, young men, the clarion voice that calls you will not be mistaken.

Another question I will ask is, What young men are called to preach? I want to tell you that not all of them are called. A good many of them answer when somebody else is called—I may be one of them. If all young men were called to preach, there would be nobody left. A man is called to be an usher as much as to be a preacher, and it calls for more religion, too. These men who have attended the great crowds here need more religion than any of the speakers on the platform, and more than any of you down there. But the ushers ought to be called, and set apart, and ordained, in a sense, to do the work they are to do. So there are really a great many useful offices you may occupy outside of that of the preacher. Not all young men are called on to preach. Some of them are, and they ought to be the very choicest of young men,—young men who have virtue in the broadest sense, not in the sense that it is ordinarily used; men who have toughness of fibre, who stand all things. If a man thinks he is going to the ministry in the way he would go to a picnic, he is going to get left. If he thinks he is going for pleasure, he is greatly mistaken. It means powerful exertion, instead of diversion. In addition to that he has to have a powerful voice, especially if he ever speaks to Christian Endeavorers under such circumstances as these. But after all he must have spiritual conviction. He must know and see what is right in spite of all things that may be wrong. He must see beyond the things that are seen to the things that are unseen, and, with splendid optimism and splendid faith, say, I will fight the good fight for Jesus and his Word. Just make up your mind if you come into the church to crook and turn you will be left alone. You will have to move effectively, and with a purpose, or your congregation will move out; but if you teach the gospel of faith and sunshine the people will stay with you all the time. The only thing I object to in that hymn "Let a Little Sunshine In" is that word "little." Let a lot of sunshine in.

I want to say that this Christian Endeavor movement has produced a seriousness on the part of young men as no other movement I know of has in the world. There are more young men, in my judgment, who are struggling with this call of God at their hearts than ever before. Edward W. Bok may be a good editor for *The Ladies' Home Journal*, but I do wish he would let the young men in the Sunday school alone; and I say he is mistaken in his estimate of them. What about the Brotherhood of Andrew and Philip? What about the Young Men's Christian Association, with their phalanxes of noble young men?. What about the Baptist Young People's Union, with their thousands of members? What about the Epworth League, with its tens of thousands of consecrated young men? What about the Christian Endeavor, with its scores of thousands of young men? No; they have been doing the young men injustice. They have been claiming things that are untrue. They are not saints or angels, but they are lots better to-day than they used to be. They have struggles, and they have heartaches, and they have temptations; but I want to say that the young men of to-day are more serious than their fathers were, more earnest along certain lines than the men who went before them. And I am not disparaging the older men; I know they are sincere, I know they are honest, but there is a seriousness in the minds of men to-day such as you never saw before.

I want to tell you what I believe was the reason for putting this topic on the programme to-day. A good many young men are trying to get out of doing their duty. They are called to preach, but they are satisfied to be simply Christian Endeavorers and associated with Christian workers. That is glorious; but the most glorious work in the world is the preaching of the gospel, and don't let anything stand between you and the first best thing.

And now, beloved, let me say in two minutes what I have to say. Where are you to preach? Anywhere that God calls you. The choicest young men and women that I know are those who are engaged in telling the story of Jesus and his life. They are not the poorest sticks; but they are the blessed men and women whose hearts are on fire with Jesus, and are giving to-day more in proportion to what they have than any other class. Talk about the Tenth Legion! They give all they have, some of them. It would have been impossible for our boards to have gotten out of debt were it not for the fact of the consecration of these devoted missionaries to the cause to which they are called. Our best young men and women have gone across the seas. I want to say to you, You must go anywhere, everywhere.

"Wheresoever thou sayest, I will go. I will follow thee, whithersoever thou sayest." So may God help you to enter this blessed work, to go where Jesus wants you to go, and to say what he wants you to say.

A topic well calculated to pique curiosity was that of Prof. Graham Taylor, "Self-Consecration. To Whom? For What? Answer." He characterized the idea that a man may have a personal religion for his own exclusive enjoyment as the most anti-Christian and atheistic notion in existence. A man has no more religion that he has relations with his fellows. Perhaps no better definition of consecration was ever given than this: "You cannot be set apart to Father God unless you take part with brother men. That kind of consecration is the dynamics of the nineteenth-century Christianity."

Address of Prof. Graham Taylor,
Chicago, Ill. I

The presence of Christ seems to awaken the expectation of the people. The existence of a church arouses expectation of its service. The announcement of a consecration meeting from within awakens in the dullest heart some ideal, an idea of what that consecration ought to mean. Our great American writer Hawthorne once said that Christian things were like stained-glass windows; they were to be seen only from within. That depends on whether you look at them from the daylight or the dark. At night you can only see them from without, as the light streams through into the darkness of the outer world. Among those who are without it has been my fortune to have my lot cast for many years, with those who are without, with the dispossessed, the disinherited, those who are aliens from the church, the commonwealth, and strangers to our ecclesiastical arrangements; and as I have swung from the citadels of faith in evangelical seminaries to my home, which has been made for years among the great unchurched multitude of the wage-earning classes, I tell you, my fellow believers, you need to test consecration even by the need that is seen of it without; for sometimes it seems to me as if those without have a more constant and a more practical conception of what the Christian life is for, of the seriousness and of the tremendous obligations of setting up to be a church, a soul-mothering, life-saving service in the world, than we who are so often likely to take these matters as matters of course.

Seen from without in the mighty strife of life, where the great needs of the world are felt in the struggle between the everlasting right and the never-ending wrong,— of which we hear, after all, very little within the charmed circle of our protected lives,— we know very little indeed of the things that are about us. Let me say that the need of the hour is for a new consecration; that the need of the hour is for a new oath of allegiance to the King and to the kingdom. And yet that new consecration is as old as Christ's own. That new oath of allegiance is as old as that which he took for us when upon earth. Let me read what is said in the Epistle to the Hebrews of Christ's own consecration: "Both he that sanctifieth and they that are sanctified are all one, for which cause he is not ashamed to call them brethren." And when he entered within the pale in that holy of holies of life, and re-consecrated himself for the service of Christ, what were his words? "I sanctify myself, I consecrate myself, for their sakes." Consecration was the test of Christ's sanctification; service was the test of his consecration. "For their sakes" was the motive of his giving himself up ever, renewedly, to God.

Now there is a conception of consecration which has very largely prevailed which is not the whole of its truth. It is the conception of setting self apart to God. But these words about Christ's own consecration show that he who sets himself apart to God tests it by taking part with his fellow men. Consecration to the father of God is tested by taking common part in the common cause of fellow men. Now let us bring Christ's consecration of self to that test. Do we wonder, then, that at childhood, when the boy begins to ask, What shall I be? he was taken up to the temple-crowned mountain with his parents, and, losing him, they returned to find him in the school of the rabbis; and in answer to the mother's question, "Why hast thou done this?" this child of the Father declared, "Did you not know, mother, that I must be about my Father's business?"

There was a setting aside of self to the Father. What was the test? He went down with them to Nazareth and was subject unto them; and for eighteen years in the family life he devoted himself to taking care of the younger children, and to service in Joseph's carpenter-shop; to loyalty to his family, to the village school, to the young craftsmen of the city — tested for eighteen silent years setting apart to the Father. There was no secular apart from the religious. If consecration to God meant his union with man, it was tested by his taking part in the family, in the school, in the village life, in the shop life of eighteen silent years — a sanctification and dedication for the service of the world. But the time came when the forerunners of heaven sounded over the land, and out from the obscurity of those eighteen years he came, with the throngs whose life he had shared, up to the valley of the Jordan. There the heavens were opened. There voices that sounded from beyond the stars spake. There he was baptized of the Spirit, he was set apart to God. But the man that administered to him the consecration oath said, "Why comest thou to me, when I have need to be baptized of thee?" Listen to how he took part with fellow men, so he should subordinate himself to an inferior in the requirements of the service: "Suffer it to be so, now, for so it becomes us to fulfil all righteousness." Set apart by the sanctification of the Holy Ghost, he took part in the offices, he baptized for the first year of his ministry. He was the assistant of the forerunner, following in his wake, leaving the field alone to him when there was a quarrel between the disciples of John and his own. "Suffer it so

now to be; subservient I will be." The Lord of all took part therein to show
that he was set apart by God.

And once more, as he enters within the vale in that last intercessorial
prayer, he began to look out upon the pathetic hopelessness of man. Think of
his being the Son of Mary — and recognizing the yearning heart for brotherhood, facing the God before whose throne he was, he started to pray. In between
him and his Father seemed to be a broad gulf; and not for his own sake, for
his own soul's sanctification, and looking around upon the pathetic helplessness
of man, he said, "Father, I seek sanctification myself." The old theologian
who said, "To be religious you must think of yourself and Almighty God as
the only beings in the universe," gave utterance to the most anti-Christian,
unjust thought that any man could utter. There is no such thing as individual
religion. Religion is a social bond. It means, if it means anything, relationship — nothing more, nothing less; and Christ's religion is the progressive relations, is the ideal relationship to God as Father, to man as brother. You and
I have no more religion than we have relationship. Songs and hymns and
Bibles are all expressions for that real, vital relationship that we have to the
Father God and brother men. There is a good deal more talk about religion
than there is religion itself. It is the religion of worship that is the only real
religion, and if there be not a new note of reality struck in religion, if somehow
or other we cannot fill the old words with new meaning, if somehow or other we
do not fill the empty phrases with new meaning, the world will not believe in
the reality of religion, or in our consecration thereto.

Now let me say that after nearly fifteen years' residence among the unchurched classes, especially among the American working men and those of
foreign extraction, there is really no antipathy to religion, to the real thing;
but I cannot begin to describe to you the depth of alienation, or bitterness of
antipathy, to the church. The separation is almost impassable in the whole
of the areas of laboring life. A gulf seems fixed, across which nothing but the
brotherhood of the human heart can ever span the chasm; but, thank God,
one touch of that human brotherhood will somehow put to flight the prejudices
and prepossessions of years of antipathy.

I wish I could take you into some scenes I have witnessed. Let me
describe one of them. It was a meeting of one of the more radical groups of
workmen gathered in Chicago; it was under the roof of my own house, only
two years ago. A socialist had just been speaking when a man arose at the
rear of the audience and said. "I am tired of hearing this Golden Rule talk to
American workmen. It is a lie. It is a dream of a Hebrew madman," said
he. "It has never been true, and it will never be true. The survival of the
fittest is the law of nature. Competition is the law of trade. The biggest dog
gets the biggest bone. Might makes right. Stand not back for the weakly.
Trample on the man that is down if he stands in the way of your progress."
I had never seen that audience startled before. There was an ominous silence,
and again to the forefront came the socialist. He said, "Men, I thought that
man would say that the Golden Rule was a lie after he got started. I have
been reading in Drummond," he said. "that there is something else than the
struggle for self; there is struggle for the life of the soul." He said, "That
man's evolution must have been arrested at the hyena;" and then, with tears
in his tone such as few orators possess to grace the platform, he spoke to the
boys, and he said, "Men, I am no Christian; I am none of your churchmen;
but," he said, "it was to get the beast out of all of us, that is in that man
over there, that the Carpenter of Nazareth came and hung on the Cross of
Calvary." And he said, "It makes a fellow's heart break to think that he had
to die for the like of a thing like that." And I tell you, and it is the truth, even
if you think I am optimistic, that there is more religion in many of these gatherings everywhere than there is in many of our institutions. The footfall of the
Holy Ghost is far behind us, thank God; for if it were not our gospel would be
small enough compared with the great world.

Let me say that in song and story, in working men's discussions, at anar-
chist meetings, in the depths of out-of-the-way places, I have yet to hear but

two men who ever attacked the Creator, or what they thought to be the purposes of Jesus Christ. It is a name still above every name in almost every
quarter, however far out of the way, that I have chanced in yet — in the depths
of underground Chicago, even. Christ's name is upon every tongue, and men
are still saying, Praises to his name. "If Jesus Christ was a man, and only a
man, I say that of all mankind I will cling to him, and to him will I cling
alway. If Jesus Christ is God and only God, I swear I will follow him through
heaven and hell, on earth and on sea, and through the air." That is Richard
Watson Gilder's new oath of allegiance for men who look at Christ from the
human or denominational side; but let me say that that new oath of allegiance
to be registered to the King is to be tested when we get together out of this
Convention by the interest we take in fellow men. Ah, men and women, there
are certain tests which come in a tremendously practical way, in almost overwhelming form, to show whether we mean what we say, or whether we are not
what we seem to be to ourselves. Try the beatitude test. We say we believe
in Christianity as a rule of faith and the rule of practice. I ask my own heart
and your hearts to-day, Do we really believe in it as a rule of practice, do we
really believe in it as a rule of faith, do we really believe that the gospel is a
lovable principle? I am prepared to believe that the faith in the gospel, as a
thing to live by to-day, and to work by in the shop and in the newspaper office,
where Sheldon raises the question, What would Jesus do? has hardly yet
gotten hold of our churches. Are we prepared to believe that the gospel is a
practical thing to live by, to do business by, to run newspapers on, and to conduct the relationship between mistress and maid? There is where the test of
our consecration comes. And I want to ask that test to be the test of the
beatitudes.

"Blessed are the peacemakers, for they shall be called the children of God."
Blessed are the peacemakers! How does our consecration stand that test when
the Filipino is as much a child of the Father as are the men that are shooting
them to death? I wonder how we can say, "Blessed are the merciful, for they
shall obtain mercy" in the competition of trade, when it means that our com-
petitor will be crowded to the wall? I wonder if we can stand the test of
Christ's rudimentary ethics, the Golden Rule? Will you tell me how we can
do business in Chicago on the stock exchange and in the wheat pit, and do
unto others as we would be done by? Will you tell me, in competitive trade,
how you can love your neighbor as well as yourself? I tell you that we have
got to either lower the ideal of Jesus, or we must raise the standard of practice.
For one, let me say that if you believe in the rule of the gospel as a rule of
practice, then compel your children to act in diametrically opposite directions
from which their inclinations will take them. Let me say there must be one of
two alternatives chosen. Keep the flag up to the masthead, swear new allegiance to the idealized Cross, and be willing to give yourself up to self-sacrifice, and float on; or pull that flag down to somewhere near the level where it
belongs. The consciences of Christian people cannot much longer stand the
strain which is the very crucifixion of the church's life. I am no pessimist,
but I vow before God and you, my brethren, to-day, that I had rather, in any
Christian institution in which I have anything to do, have the thing sink and
go down with the flag at high mast than to float on any kind of bottom with
the flag at half-mast.

I would to God that I could make you hear the mandatory, imperative
consciences of the great working classes of America. They are more alert, I
want to tell you, than the consciences of many men in the pulpit or in the pews.
There is an everlasting right and a never-ending wrong with which these men
are face to face that we hear too little about whenever they come to church, if
they ever do, or even in the consecration meetings of the Christian Endeavor
society; and we must take part with fellow men if we are to be set apart to the
Father God, and there is no alternative but actual consecration. Christ cannot
save part of a man. You cannot have a saved soul in a lost body. You must
be saved entirely, if at all. The consecration that is called for, then, is the
solemn setting apart of our efforts to God's service for fellow men. Give;

give; and in a church that is thus set apart the men are going to love their gospel, or else give it up, and there is a consecration there that will have a dynamic force that will move heaven and earth. What is the new sacrifice, the new oath of allegiance to Christ? It means the Cross — not the cross that is a crowning ornament on top of church spires, or the trinket on our watch-chains; it means that you shall take up your cross and follow Jesus.

You need not fear annihilation, for Jesus, in the words of the Epistle to the Corinthians, said, "I will go myself that other men may take hold of me." He gave up that other men might share, and humbled himself, and he became obedient unto death and even unto the death of the cross; therefore highly exalt him. Are you holding on to yourselves, are you holding on to your prestige? Are you holding on to a little separation idea of sanctification when the great race calls you? Are you with your fellow men? Have you your shoulder under the workman's burden? Do you care whether that mother with sick children cannot go to church, and is compelled to stay at home with her children because of her duties? Can't you stay with her children and let her have the opportunity she desires? Are you willing, instead of saying, "Throw out the life-line," are you willing to live where the life-line is slimy and stand in mud up to your hips? I tell you the chorus evaporates, and it becomes a solo where I see the life-line thrown. Are you willing to change your home to a place where you can get the most out of it, and where the neighborhood can get the most out of it? Are you doing any of this missionary work? This is the kind of consecration that takes a family from the pleasant suburb and moves it into the centre of a city, to where the streets are filthy. How do you stand on this question of the test of our consecration? Let us take part with our fellow men, to show that we are set apart to the Father God in the spirit of Christ. "For their sakes I sanctify myself"— not for my own sake; not for my own soul's salvation's sake. And if one does that you need not fear; you will not annihilate that self of yours. You will be dead; yes, but you will be doing the Master's work. And then when he gathers us to the dark continent, then David Livingstone will appear with Christ in glory; when the sufferings of the human race are taken into account, Florence Nightingale will appear; when the prison doors are opened and the prisoner is released, John Howard will come from the heart-break into which he went in life. Are you faithful enough to realize that death of self so that you may appear in the newness of life, the life of glory that can come only by service and the service of sacrifice? Would to God that I could put my hand, with yours, in between the pierced hands and swear over again our new allegiance, and say with infinitely greater meaning than ever was put into words before, "Long live the King. The King lives. Let the King live. Long live King Jesus."

At Northfield, several years ago, a telegram was sent to Japan, and back over the wires came a message which has rung in my soul ever since. "Make Jesus king." And before the Father of us all let us lift high to heaven the hand, as we take that new oath of allegiance: "Make Jesus king"

The benediction was pronounced by Rev. Canon J. B. Richardson, of London, Ont.

First Congregational Church.

The Romance of the Bible.

By Prof. R. G. Moulton, Chicago, Ill.

The First Congregational Church was filled by Endeavorers to hear Prof. R. G. Moulton, of Chicago, give an address on "The Romance of the Bible." The wealth and beauty of Professor Moulton's description are unexcelled, the vividness of the scenes he portrayed was remarkable, and the attention of every auditor was held from the beginning to the end of his talk. He said in part : —

The literature of former times was at first a spoken one, and only gradually, as the knowledge of writing became more common, did these thoughts come to be written. When the time came for putting thoughts in writing, the Romance languages were the ones generally used by scholars, and the name comes from that. It has later taken on another meaning, and that is picturesque.

Both history and romance deal with facts; the one with events that appeal to the sense of record and explanation, and the other to the sense of imagination and fancy, or to the sense of satisfaction. The latter is romance.

Is the Bible narrative a story of history or romance? There is no better way to learn for yourself than to read the Book of Genesis. When you come to the story of Joseph you have ten chapters devoted to this great personality. What is this? Much of it can be classed under romance rather than history.

There is a picturesque background to the historical narrative. There are the dreams, which we call miracles; and the great mutations of fortune — a change in a single day from the prison to the palace. Then the ambiguous or ironical situations are numerous. Joseph recognizes his brethren, but they do not recognize him. This is a double situation, and no modern novelist has developed his story better. Not in a sportive manner, but in all seriousness, was the event chronicled. Next comes the greatest of all these elements of story — Providence and its intervention. Joseph shows his brothers that all was for the best, and that the removal of the family to Egypt was a part of God's plan. The migration was the last chapter of the story.

As in the story of Joseph, so with many others. There is a great necessity for a differentiation between history and story. Both may be fact, but they must be understood. Look through a microscope and you see the object much enlarged. You are not deceived, for you realize that the object is not viewed with the naked eye. The microscope serves a purpose, and so does the romance in the Bible.

With the exception of the stories of the Bible, all great epics are in verse. The " Iliad," the " Æneid," and " Paradise Lost " are in verse, while the nearest approach in the Bible is a mixed epic. This is a kind of prose that breaks into verse at the proper place.

Every form of literature is represented in the Bible, with the possible exception of humor. It does not belong to Oriental life, and that is the manner to account for its omission. The one exception, where there is deep humor, is in the story of Samson. To my mind, the book is humorous throughout. Samson is sportive, as is shown in such instances as the riddle, the foxes, and the wedding feast.

Samson's irritability breaks out at the wedding feast; he propounds a riddle. A wager of thirty changes of raiment is made. Samson did not play fair, as he based his riddle on exclusive information, but the Philistines were not fair either. They appealed to the young wife, and she used woman's strongest weapon, tears. Samson lost, but, in the end, the loss was with the enemy, as he killed thirty of them and took their clothes with which to pay the wager.

A story of constructive imagination, with a beautiful literary atmosphere, is that of Esther. This is the greatest story in the Bible, and has never been surpassed. The scene is laid in a distant country, the surroundings are sumptuous, and the gorgeous details are beyond the grasp of the imagination. In secular or religious literature there is no character that surpasses that of Esther.

SATURDAY AFTERNOON.

At Belle Isle.

Saturday morning's rain was the clearing-up storm, and fairer weather for an outdoor meeting was never known than that which greeted us on lovely Belle Isle. The crispest of breezes swept over the island from the broad river on either side. Crowded ferry-boats, street-cars, and omnibuses delivered great throngs, and went swiftly back for more. Grass, flowers, trees, were shining after the storm. Soon the bright dresses and bright eyes and flashing ribbons were to be found everywhere along the wooded walks. The little ponies and their dainty car-

The Out-Door Meeting on Belle Isle.

riages were a great attraction. Bicycles were darting everywhere. A group of Georgia delegates sang "Dixie" with superb enjoyment, and swung us all along with them. Happy groups here and there were merrily chatting. A quartette of cornet-players began to play lustily. They were seated on a freshly made platform, and speedily drew the delegates together about them. There were at least five thousand of them in that island audience.

Under the spirited direction of Chairman Clark, of the Music Committee, a medley of patriotic songs was sung with a vim. There was prayer by Rev. William Bryant, editor of *The Michigan Presbyterian*, and much applause greeted the Peace Memorial as it was read by Rev. Charles M. Sheldon.

Christian Endeavor Peace Memorial.

To the Senate and House of Representatives of the United States of America :—

We, whose names are affixed hereunto, are members and friends of the Societies of Christian Endeavor, numbering in this country over 40,000 organizations, with more than 2,500,000 members, and in foreign lands over 14,000 organizations, with nearly 1,000,000 members. It is the sense of our world-wide fellowship that impels us to this memorial. Canada, Great Britain, and Australia contain hundreds of thousands whom we have come to honor and love as brethren. Among the Hindus and Persians, the Chinese and Japanese, the natives of Africa and Madagascar, the republics of South America, are large numbers who are thus closely knit to us. Our comrades in Christian Endeavor are found in France, Italy, Germany, Russia. Switzerland, Turkey, Greece, Norway, Sweden, Holland, Denmark, Austria, Belgium. In Spain itself, our foe in the late war, is a rapidly increasing number of them, and Christian Endeavorers were found in each of the opposing armies.

In view of these facts, we wish to express our abhorrence of war and our solemn conviction that it is the duty of every civilized nation to do all in its power toward making war impossible. We wish to record our desire for the speedy establishment of an international tribunal of arbitration.

We wish to show our interest in the international conference to discuss this matter proposed by the Czar of Russia, and to urge that our country act promptly upon the proposals of that conference. And especially we desire by our signatures to appeal for the immediate consideration of the question of arbitration between this nation and Great Britain, that the Anglo-Saxon race may become united in the interests of peace and good-will.

In presenting this memorial we are emboldened by the assurance of a cordial reception on the part of large numbers of our legislators, and we are confident that the Congress of the United States of America will in the future, as in the past, prove true to the largest sentiment of humanity. May the divine blessing attend your deliberations !

Then came the stirring addresses. Dr. Hill spoke for the United States as Dr. Hill alone can speak,— witty, wise, winsome. At the close of his oration he asked for a show of hands, and many hundreds gladly committed themselves to these three promises of peace : that they would never henceforth think meanly of a person who differed from them in his religious faith ; that they would have peace with those that differed sharply from them along political lines ; that they would try to gain the peace of God, the most beautiful peace of all.

Address by Rev. James L. Hill, D.D.,

Salem, Mass.

This scene recalls to my mind another of long ago. It was just after the War of 1812, and another war with Great Britain was imminent. Our great country was almost impoverished, having only a short time before come out of the War of the Revolution. The great question of the hour was whether the United States should be plunged into another bloody war. Commissioners went across the water to try to decide whether it should be peace or war. There was no submarine cable at that time, and the people had to await the return of the commission to find out the news. The country wanted peace, and every nerve was strained to know the results of the conference. A noble ship, the *Fearnaught*, sailed into New York harbor with every rope strained and every sail filled. She was gaily caparisoned, and it was known that she carried important tidings to the people of the country. Mammoth crowds went to the wharf eager for the news. One man leaned far out over the prow of the boat and cried out one magic word that threw New York into convulsions of joy. That one word was "Peace." The news spread like wildfire into every street in the great city, and there was no sleeping that night. Persons embraced each other, for they knew from what they had been delivered. Until a nation goes down into the very hell of war once, she does not know the true meaning of that one word "peace."

It is a great pleasure this afternoon to remember, when we are striving to walk in His steps, to follow Christ, to do as he would do, that we are still honoring the Saviour, God's gift to man. When we get his last expression as divulged to the human mind, when we come to this consummate expression of the Christian heart, we shall have not gone beyond the point forever glorious. He is Immanuel, the Prince of Peace; and inasmuch as we become members of the Society of Christian Endeavor by so much are we the heralds of peace.

I would like to ask my friends if they will some time place themselves at a street-corner in some great city, and study the people that go by. Of course, I would not want to take a company like this, for you all read one thing in your favor; but some time, on a busy day, when men are rushing right by on the grand thoroughfares of the city, notice these. Here comes a man; you will find intellectual brightness expressed in his face. There comes another man; you will find earnestness, resolve, and purpose in his face. That next man you will find with a great deal of business expression. You will find a high form of business energy. Another will have an intellectual cast. Another will look like a philosopher; but there is one thing you have not been able to find upon American faces of late, and that is an expression of peace, the peace of God, a submission to the will of God, acceptance of the will of God. I want to say to my friends right here now that I count one of the great blessings of this Convention that some of us are permitted to sit at the feet of a very holy man, who is eminently so,— I refer, of course, to Dr. Chapman,— and learn the blessings of peace. God grant that we may not go forth from this place without having in our hearts a benediction of peace, the peace of God that passeth the understanding of the world.

The sending of that commission over to The Hague represents the latest and best development of the human mind. This expression of peace to-day will be counted as one of the great blessings of this grand Convention. God grant that we may not go from it without peace in our souls.

The only way for a nation to enjoy the spirit of peace is to be led by the Spirit of God. We have come to a new day. The forces of the young people are beginning to assert themselves in no uncertain way. I often wish that I were young again, that I might live with you young folks through your day; that I might see the epoch of history that you help to make. There never has been such an era in history as you will see. Mammoth problems will confront you, and it is a blessing that you can enter the next century with a spirit of peace surrounding you. I have now three questions to ask you, and I wish you to answer by the uplifted hand : —

How many of you young people will resolve that you will never think meanly of a person that differs with you in religious doctrines? (Nearly every hand in the vast assemblage was raised.)

How many of you will resolve to have peace with all others as regards your political preferences? (There was the same showing of hands.)

How many of you will try to have peace with God and have your sins forgiven? (There was a unanimous reply.)

Rev. James Mursell, of London, said Amen to the Peace Memorial. He especially urged the truth that "the cause of peace is most likely to be achieved among the nations of the world by real and deep concord between America and Great Britain," and was cheered superbly by both Americans and Canadians when he said, "We in England feel that the bond which binds America and England together is a great deal closer than the bond which binds us with any other nation in the world."

Address by Rev. James Mursell,

London, England.

I consider it a very high privilege to be allowed to speak before so great an assemblage, bent on the consideration of so important an issue. I am greatly rejoiced that the Christian Endeavorers of this country have drawn up and presented such a beautiful memorial. As an Englishman, as a man, as a Christian, I say " Amen " with all my soul. In Europe, the necessity of peace is pressing on the lives of the people more heavily than in this country. We of England live too near the continent to detach ourselves from its movements and feelings. Europe is to-day an armed camp. For years it has waited for a voice to speak. For years Europe has been afraid that the voice would say " War." To our great delight it said the magic word " Peace."

In this conference at The Hague a mighty problem is being considered. Even if all the aims of the Czar are not achieved, much good will be done. It is almost certain that international arbitration will be an accomplished fact. While we shall in time expect to get disarmament, we believe that the present conference has taken a long step in the right direction. A few years ago there was a great question between America and England. It was over the Venezuelan matter. At that time all the newspapers in the country were talking of war. On one certain Sunday, when everything looked dark, there came a voice. That voice said, " Peace." Mainly because of the influence of the Christian people of the land the war cloud was lifted and the shame of the vision of a conflict between America and England passed away forever.

But peace, sweet and sacred as it is, may be bought at too large a price. Then the sweetness vanishes. We of England followed carefully the progress of the Spanish-American war. We prayed for righteousness to prevail; and when the tyranny of Spain was wiped off the western hemisphere, and liberty, that great goddess of beauty and right, settled down upon the stricken islands of the sea, we thought that righteousness had conquered. Tyranny has no place on our doorstep. We know that the victory has been given of God. We hope that the past has been buried forever and that America will spread her beneficent institutions over the islands of the sea. God speed you in your great task.

The Christian Endeavorers of every land are for peace. When I came to this platform I was glad to see the Union Jack and the Stars and Stripes draped side by side. The cause of peace is most likely to be achieved by the two nations so largely concerned, America and Great Britain.

The other day, as we crossed the Atlantic, we celebrated the Fourth of July upon the *Teutonic*, and we had sports upon the deck; but I somewhat regret to tell you, although perhaps with a little secret pride in my own heart, that American independence has disappeared on the Fourth of July, at all events so far as the *Teutonic* was concerned, because in all the sports, or most of the sports, Britain overcame America. When the prizes were distributed, Mr. Pollock, having the matter in his hands, spoke some words in the same sense as those to which I have given utterance, and an American gentleman very ably replied. Yet in my own mind there was an element of disappointment, because he seemed to speak as though Britain was only one of many other nations with which America might, if they would be friendly with her, also be a friend. Now we, at all events, in England feel that the bond which binds America and Britain together is a great deal closer than that which binds any other two nations together. I am glad, by the heartiness of the applause with which you greet that sentiment, to believe that that gentleman, though he may represent an element in American society and in American politics, does not at all events represent the whole of it, but that there are in this land thousands and thousands of Christian men and women who feel the same; who believe that blood is thicker than water, and who, though they still make reference to the glories and the shames — glories for you, shames for us — of the war more than one hundred years ago, still have forgotten, at all events so far as any bitter feeling is concerned, our wrong, and are prepared to go with us into the very van of the advanced of nations, and, by God's help, stand shoulder to shoulder, with heart beating true to heart, to say that while America and Britain are strong and blessed by God with an influence among the counsels of the earth, peace, so far as they are concerned, shall be maintained by every just and righteous means.

Australia was represented by that zealous Endeavorer, Rev. Joseph Walker, of Queensland. He gave some amusing examples of American brag and bluster which had been inflicted upon him (making, however, the most delicate reference to them), and warned us to mind lest in teaching patriotism we foster the spirit of war.

Address by Rev. Joseph Walker,
Queensland, Australia.

I am glad, Dr. Clark, to speak to my fellow Endeavorers for Australia. The home where I am staying has been almost like an inquiry-office since I came to Detroit. Many friends have friends in Australia, and have been wanting to know something about them. I am glad that I have been able to put some on the track of their friends. Others I have not been able to help in that direction. I have been asked a good many things about Australia, Dr. Clark, since I came to Detroit. A young lady said, "Do you have churches and congregations and Sunday schools like we have in America?" "Well." I said, "we have Sunday schools, very large ones, and the Sunday school connected with my church in Ipswich — built, may I tell you, to replace one that was swept away by the great flood in 1893 — is the largest Sunday-school building in Australia. It is a large hall, seventy by forty, and has twenty-two separate class-rooms, and the Christian Endeavor room is the largest and brightest and best of them all. There is one thing I would like to say," I replied. "We have congregations; and among the congregations that I have visited in the States on Sunday mornings since I came, I have not seen one with a larger congregation than that I love in Ipswich, Queensland. I have seen one night congregation very much larger, and that is the one in Mr. Moody's church in Chicago."

Now, we grow some things in Australia. One of the speakers has referred to one of the States that makes even feet grow. Shall I tell you a story of that city of Ballarat to which Dr. Clark has referred, and where I have spent nearly thirteen years of a very happy life. When Dr. Clark was there there was a parliamentary representative of Ballarat who had represented it almost from the beginning of its history. He was known as Major Smith, and the major and his feet were remarkable throughout Australia. When he was minister of education, on one occasion, he had to go to open a State school at a distance, and at the terminus of the railway they were keeping holiday. and every kind of vehicle was pressed into service to take the people some miles away to the school opening. The minister of education was later than was expected, and when he arrived there was n't a vehicle of any kind to take him, and only one horse in the township, and that was said to be one that no body had ever tried to ride, — a splendid goer in the shafts, but nobody had ever tried to ride it. The major said. "I must go." With some difficulty they got a bridle on and a saddle on. Then the major put one foot in one stirrup and threw his leg over the saddle and put his foot in the other. and it ,is said his feet cast such shadows that the horse thought it was in the shafts. and took him to his destination in safety. Now, Detroit is about the best-known place in Australia, and it is best known because of the marvellous newspaper stories that are put in our Australian papers. If Detroit can beat that that I have just given you from Australia, I would like to see it.

Now, will you permit me, in a more serious mood. I have had a passionate love for America ever since I was a boy. I heard Henry Ward Beecher in that memorable meeting in Manchester in 1864. and it was one of the red-letter days of my life. I would like to tell you about it, if time permitted. I was a minister, a young man in the north of England, at the time of the cotton famine, and I helped to give American benefactions to some of the poor toilers in the cotton-mills of the North. I have had a strong, deep interest in America all my life. I have been looking at your cities for the last five weeks. I have been visiting some of your institutions. I have been watching, with a kindly interest, many things in your States. May I just say that I think I see just a little danger? May I venture, Dr. Clark, to point it out? I am sure you will take it kindly. I do not know how my brethren from Scotland and England are; but I have seen the Union Jack so seldom that I could hardly describe it accurately. I have seen hardly anything else but " Old Glory" since I landed in San Francisco. Now don't make any mistake. It is a splendid thing, by object-lesson, to teach your young people patriotism. But there is a danger near to our very best things, and mind lest in teaching patriotism you foster the spirit of war. I went to a summer picnic at Chicago last Monday week. There were four thousand people at that picnic, on the *Christopher Columbus*, and about one thousand people had to be shut off, that could not get on. There were many things about that picnic that pleased me very much. I was talking with one and another; and I was talking with a good old Methodist body, a good old Methodist sister on board that boat. And if you could have heard her talk about America! I happened to suggest that Great Britain was a great power. "Why," she said, " if it ever comes to war between Great Britain and America, Great Britain, why, she will be wiped out before she knows where she is at," said this old Methodist sister. Now, I think I saw in that, and in some other things, just a trace of your danger.

May I tell you another Australian story or two in closing? When I first went to Melbourne, in '65, I had a man in my congregation who was always asleep, nearly, and he sat by the boys, and after he had had a good nap and waked up, he would give the nearest boy a good slap, as a kind of salve to his own conscience for going to sleep. I said to him one day, " Why do you sleep in this way during the service every Sunday? I am ashamed of you." " Well, Mr. Walker," he said, " they tell me I was born asleep, and it was half an hour before they could wake me up after I was born, and I have been sleepy ever since." Well, what could you say to a man of that kind if he did sleep through the sermon? But this is the point : when he awoke, instead of hitting himself for sleeping, he hit somebody else. Now another time I was in the western district, that probably Dr. Clark visited when he was in Australia, and while staying there for a day or two, the squatter told me of his cook, a marvellous character. He said, " Now, Charley, whenever he makes a mistake, he does n't growl and grumble at somebody else, but he does something else. The other day he was baking an apple-pie, and he had taken an apple-pie out of the oven. Some of the juice, like your maple sugar very hot, came onto Charley's fingers, and he dropped the plate very quickly. What did he do? I have known many a man, if his fingers were burned, it would have been a bad matter for his wife that day. Charley doubled his fist and gave himself one in the right eye and then one in the left, for being so stupid."

Now, Dr. Clark, if we Americans and Australians will just keep ourselves right, and bring ourselves in subjection, that will be better for us. You have heard from the dear old Motherland. We love Britain as you love America. God pity the man who does not love his country. Next to God, our country; and what Great Britain wants, what Australia wants, what I believe America wants, is this : the men to live for their country, opposed to everything that is mean, everything that is impure, everything that is unjust, and in God's name and for Christ's name to live for the peace of those that love us, for the welfare of our country, for the glory of God, and for the coming of his kingdom. I referred on Wednesday night to the fact that with the two banners always intertwined, and the English-speaking races animated by the fear of God, nothing, I believe, can disturb the peace of the world. God bless you, make you peace-loving, God-loving, and help us that we may try to save this world that Christ came to redeem.

Rev. W. F. Wilson spoke for Canada. He brought together the noble picture of Queen Victoria attending religious worship as the first act of her jubilee, and President McKinley earnestly seeking God's guidance at the outbreak of the Spanish war, and declared that as long as republic and empire have rulers that pray we need have little fear for their peace and prosperity.

Address by Rev. W. F. Wilson,
Hamilton, Ont.

We have heard a good deal of England, and a good deal of Australia, and a good deal about this great republic. We have not heard much about old Ireland yet, and that is my country. The fact is, I am an Irishman, improved by being born in Canada. We have some great things in Canada. The north pole is there, when it is found. We have the Klondike, a great many Americans there — more Americans than Canadians. The senior senator of this great State was born there, Senator McMillan, and the honored founder of our society is a Canadian by birth. We want to claim good things when we have an opportunity. I am an optimist. I believe this is the best day of the best week of the best month of the best year of the best century this old world has ever seen. I believe the world is growing better. I believe the nations are coming together, and no two peoples have made such advances during the past decade as have the two great Anglo-Saxon peoples represented on this platform this hour. We are in a beautiful city. We are in a paradise grove. We have on this platform the chief magistrate of this city, a man that honored us, eloquently and warmly; and if I were an American and lived in Detroit next fall I would give him a good ballot if he would run for office again.

Now I want to tell you a secret. I am an EpworthLeaguer of Christian Endeavor. I was located in the city of Peterboro a few years ago, when I pronounced a marriage of the Epworth League and the Christian Endeavor, and like all the things that I do, and all the persons whom I marry, they have gotten along splendidly in Canada from that hour to this. And I hope, Dr. Clark, that the spirit may broaden and deepen until every young people's organization on American soil has federated with the Christian Endeavor Society.

Now we are Anglo-Saxon. I said this in the tent, and I say it here. We honor the great President of this republic over in Canada. As an object-lesson for the world, in the time when this nation of 70,000,000 of people, and the welfare of the bravest and fairest of your land, was in the balance, your chief magistrate, with heavy heart, I have no doubt, and yet strong faith, repaired to the place of prayer with reverent brow to talk with God. After sixty unparalleled years of reign, the noble woman whom we honor queen, last June, a year ago now, went to the house of prayer, the first act in that great and noble gathering, to commemorate her rule of sixty years. I say, sir, long as the republic has a man that prays, long as the empire has a ruler that prays, we need have little fear for the peace and prosperities of these great peoples.

In the sixteenth century the Spanish Armada was destroyed in English waters. In 1898, the first day of May, your noble admiral finished the job. We heard that gun in Manila Bay. It thrilled through our hearts as it thrilled through yours. And, when we heard of that marvellous victory,— I believe of Almighty God,— without the loss of a single life under the Stars and Stripes, we said, "All hail, all hail! May these guns echo, and the brave boys in blue fight, until the superstition of centuries is swept from the isles of the sea."

I want to say that in Canada, as citizens in Canada, as Christians in Canada, as young people, we are one with you in this great republic. We are one with you, sir, to keep sacred the Sabbath Day — not merely as a day of worship, but as a day of rest, a day of meditation to the toilers of this republic; and it is our right and our place to maintain it for them. We are one with you, sir, to maintain the restfulness of the Sabbath. We are one with you to improve the efficiency of the public school. We are one with you to close the saloons. We are one with you to maintain the sacredness of the home. We are one with you to keep pure the ballot; and we are one with you to maintain the priceless principles of peace. We are one with you; and I hope and trust that we shall go home from this Convention,— the Australian yonder across the mighty seas to his home land, my friends from England and Scotland to their home land, the missionaries yonder to the far-off empires of the East, and those of us representing every State in the Union and every Province of the Dominion,— we shall go back home and do our best to make the year upon which we have entered one of the very best and brightest in the history of our great organization. So that, as we approach the century, whether we be in London at the great convention, or whether we stay at home to man the posts until our leaders return, we shall do our best to make this year one of the very best and brightest in the history of our great movement.

Now, Mr. Chairman, my friend from Australia said he despised the man that did not love his country, and so do I. I am British from hat to heel, and I am going to remain British, and we in Canada are going to be British; but we are going to live in peace and harmony side by side with you, and I would like the privilege to-day, I would like the privilege on this eighth day of July, a foreigner, living under another flag, to ask you to join with me and give three rousing cheers for the noble man who sits in the White House at Washington.

Then Dr. Hill led in three cheers for Victoria, three more for McKinley, three for Dewey, and three for Christian Endeavor, and, to crown all, three for Mayor Maybury; for, as Dr. Clark told the audience, never before has the Convention city's chief official shown so hearty interest in a convention. Mayor Maybury not only greeted us on the opening night and gave us all official aid, but he attended the meetings, went to his own denominational rally (the Episcopal), and had even come out with us to Belle Isle.

Of course he was compelled to make a speech, and it was a good one — especially valuable as calling attention to the fact that the island was a spot consecrated to peace in the old Indian days ; no drop of Indian blood was ever shed there. He had himself watched the island for twenty years, had never heard a profane word there, had never seen a blow struck, and the cells of the station-house near by were never occupied. And verily, Belle Isle, the Isle of Peace, received a new consecration that afternoon to that great cause.

Address of Hon. W. C. Maybury,

Mayor of Detroit, Mich.

Those of us who had our own way about the place of being born were born in the city of Detroit; and, although we are very proud of it, we are very glad to welcome those who were unfortunate enough to be born elsewhere. Therefore our affection takes in Australia, England and Ireland and Scotland, and the British possessions. Now, my dear friends, you have been standing a long time, and I am a sort of a conscripted soldier this afternoon. I came here to follow my official family, and I saw them making in this direction, and I think it is the part of the good father to go where the children go. Hence I came here, and I found you engaged in an excellent work: and I get up here now to endorse it, and to say to you that the spirit of this afternoon is entirely consonant with the feelings in my own heart.

I want to say one word to you that will have a local application. Let me approach it in this way. You know that One who spoke as man never spoke before, as man will never speak again, uttered words that you and I remember and reverence. He said, in answer to those who gathered about him, and to whom he had talked about the coming of certain great events, who asked, "But, Master, when will these things be?" he said to them, "When you see the fig-tree about to blossom, you know that summer is nigh at hand." And so I say to you, when you see the premonition of these things, lift up your heads, ye nations, for you know that the time of your redemption is drawing nigh. A little less than a year ago there came, as a flash of lightning out of a clear sky, a message. It came from the most unexpected source. It came from the representative of one who inherited the name of Czar, a name so terrible to the liberty-loving of the world heretofore, and it said:—

"To the peace-loving nations of the world: Let us come together, disarm our soldiers, and get upon a peace footing."

In answer to that call of the Czar there is gathered to-day in the most peace-loving part of this world, old Holland, upon the banks of The Hague, the representatives of the nations of the earth. Now does not the word of the Master come back to the nations of the earth and say, "When you see these things come to pass, lift up your heads, for the day of your redemption is drawing nigh," just as clearly as when he said to them, "Ye know that when the fig-tree is about to blossom the summer is nigh"? So, in these strange and remarkable events, do we see coming that for which we all pray, universal peace.

Now I want to show the local part to you. You are gathered this afternoon in a peculiar spot, and peculiarly devoted to the spirit for which you have assembled. The Indian tribes of this great Northwest had a love for peace in certain localities, and the consequence was that there is not an island along the shores of those rivers and lakes but was held sacred by the Indians to peace, and although the battles between the Sioux and the Hurons, the Ojibways and Pottawatomies, were incessant upon the mainland, so much so that they really decimated each other, none but the warlike Sioux continued to be fighters, and went to the far West. The others found bloody graves here. Yet, upon this island, under whose trees you are gathered, history tells there was never shed one drop of Indian blood; and add to that that for twenty years, since this beautiful park has been under the control of the city of Detroit, visited by thousands and hundreds of thousands of people, I have been a close observer of what has been going on upon the island, and I say to you I never heard a profane word uttered; I never saw one blow struck. We have near-by a station-house, but I say to you that its cells are never occupied. Close by is a little sanitarium supplied with that which will help those who meet with accidents; or those who faint here, or are met with sudden sickness. You will find kindly care in that part of the station, but you will find no prisoners in the cells. Therefore, I look with great significance, my friends, not only upon the spirit of this meeting, but upon the fact that it is held on a spot devoted and sacred, even by the savage, to peace.

Deafening applause followed the speech of Mayor Maybury, and the great meeting closed with a benediction pronounced by Rev. Dr. John Henry Barrows, president of Oberlin College.

SATURDAY EVENING.

The State delegations and their untiring hosts met face to face, under a score of church roof-trees, on Saturday night. Never was service more loyal than that which the young people of Detroit, of all denominations, cheerfully and magnanimously gave their guests; and never was appreciation more generous.

The attendance at many of the rallies taxed Detroit's large churches to the utmost; at most of them refreshments were served, and in all of them the decorations were beautiful, and in some cases lavish.

Bits of Interior Decoration.

SUNDAY MORNING.

The Sabbath dawned as lovely as a day in heaven. To many thousands it *was* a day in heaven.

The most wonderful meeting of the entire Convention, the most remarkable and blessed meeting, was the Quiet Hour on Sunday morning. Tent Endeavor was crowded with a vast multitude. The women first, and then the men, repeated together that psalm which had come to mean so much more than ever before. Mr. Smyth sang "The Inner Circle ": —

> " Have you heard the voice of Jesus
>   Whisper, ' I have chosen you '?
> Does he tell you in communion
>   What he wishes you to do?

Are you in the Inner Circle?
Have you heard the Master's call?
Have you given your life to Jesus?
Is he now your all in all?"

Then began Dr. Chapman's Spirit-filled pleadings. There might come forth from this Convention a character that would outshine in beauty, peace, and power anything the world has yet known. "We have only to let the Lord lead us. Yes, it might be through the valley of death; it would be *through;* we should not tarry in it. Stop seeking for power, for peace, for sinlessness; seek him. Be his bond-servant. Live for three days in that thought, and on the fourth you will walk with him as naturally as you breathe. God will not hold back from you a single bit of his blessing if he can only trust you, if he has all there is of you. Will you surrender utterly to him? Will you do it to-day?"

It is impossible to describe the scene that followed Dr. Chapman's quiet invitation, given to all who wished from that moment to live the yielded life. There was no urging, no excitement. The seats in front had been left vacant. Promptly, from platform, press table, choir seats, the myriad benches of the audience, the multitude pressed into those waiting-places of pardon, peace, and power. There could not have been less than three thousand souls. It was a second Pentecost. Hundreds were weeping, but silently. Benches were shaken by some strong man's emotion, but there were no outcries. Only whispered prayers and suppressed groanings, audible enough in the ears of God. And as these three thousand, repeating after Dr. Chapman strong words of surrender and determination, found during his closing prayer the joy of the surrendered life, the angels in heaven must have sent up a hallelujah chorus around the throne of God.

This meeting was a magnificent prelude to a magnificent day. One hundred and seventy different preachers were heard in the regular church services. Not a man among them but was famous in his own denomination, and many of them have world-wide reputation. The churches were crammed to the walls, with people standing in every vacant place, crowding the pulpit stairs, the edges of the platforms, sitting on tables and on the floor. The closing moments of each evening service were most solemn and uplifting consecration services.

Dr. Chapman's Quiet Hours with God.

Christian Endeavor could have discovered no more suitable and inspiring opening for the first full day of the Convention than a Quiet Hour meeting Thursday. The great Armory was crowded in every seat at the very start, with a reverent company of morning-faced Endeavorers. "Blessed Assurance," the first hymn sung, under the skilled leadership of Mr. H. G. Smyth, of New York, was a true augury of the entire series of glorious meetings.

"O Thou who wast here before we came," rose Dr. Clark's opening prayer, "thou who wilt abide here when we go, reveal thyself unto us, we pray thee, and help us to realize, as we have never realized before, thine abiding presence." That was the key-note of these Quiet Hours.

One never knows just when Dr. Chapman begins his morning talks, for they are ushered in with no pompous prelude; but the first thing we know, every ear is intent and every heart is responsive to the piercing truths presented. This year's Quiet Hours were based upon the twenty-third Psalm, its verses being treated, day after day, under the attention-holding heads: "Possession," "Position," "Promise," "Progress," "Provision," "Prospect." The first day emphasized the great thought that Christ, in his fulness of blessing, can be with us in all the details of our daily lives. "I find," said Dr. Chapman, "that it is not a good thing for me to say, when I rise in the morning, 'I am going to live this whole day with Christ;' but it is a good thing for me to say, 'I will live with Christ till ten o'clock;', and then at ten o'clock to say, 'I can live with him till noon.'" With such pungent, practical expositions the meetings were crammed, up to the Sabbath climax.

Such was the interest that the stock of Dr. Chapman's "Secret of a Happy Day," containing his talks, was sold almost as soon as it was offered. This book may be had of the United Society of Christian Endeavor for fifty cents, post-paid.

SUNDAY AFTERNOON.

Westminster Church.

A Great Sabbath-Observance Meeting.

Westminster Presbyterian Church was thronged to the steps, while dozens craned their necks to peep through doors and windows to catch some of the emphasis which Dr. McAllister, Mr. C. N. Howard, and Hon. John Charlton, M. P., laid on Sabbath observance. It looked as if one of the tents would have been none too large for those who wanted to get in.

Treasurer Shaw presided, and Mr. Foster led the spirited singing. Dr. Wayland Hoyt, of Philadelphia, conducted the devotional exercises.

The first speaker, Rev. David McAllister, D.D., LL.D., of Allegheny, Pa., is a veteran and staunch defender of the Sabbath, a Covenanter of the Covenanters, a denomination of stalwarts for Sabbath observance.

He believes that it is in the home that the Sabbath is most imperilled. There is one little section of Scotland which has furnished in the past century ten times as many statesmen, authors, poets, ministers, as any like extent of territory, and that section is noted for the strict observance of the Sabbath in the family.*

"The side door of the saloon is the front door of hell," Mr. Shaw declared in introducing Mr. C. N. Howard. president of the Prohibition Christian Union.

---

* Note. — We regret that through some error Dr. McAllister's address was not reported.

Address by Mr. C. N. Howard,

Rochester, N. Y.

THE SIDE DOOR; CAN IT BE SHUT?

Well, according to this issue of the Rochester *Morning Herald* of December 26, it can be shut, was shut, and on the authority of the press, remains shut. And this in a city of 200,000 inhabitants, with six breweries that produce more than 25,000,000 gallons of beer a year, and more saloons in proportion to the population than New York or Chicago. Rochester, N. Y., once owned by the rum power in the sense that a hen owns an egg before it gets into the nest; where a man was elected mayor the sixth time successively because of his liberal Sunday policy; where the chairman of the Executive Board was a rum-seller; where the president of the Common Council was a rum-seller; where the city's representative at the State capitol was a rum-seller; where, of the seventeen members composing the Grand Jury, eight of them were rum-sellers; — here, in this city, where public sentiment once permitted this deplorable situation, on the unanimous testimony of four daily newspapers, the side door was shut, and no one ever contradicted the newspapers. The police said so; the police never lie. I said so, and if that is not conclusive, a reporter, a reporter for a New York newspaper, made a personal investigation and pronounced Rochester the dryest spot this side of the Sahara Desert. What further need have we of witnesses? How was it done? It was brought about by the Prohibition Union of Christian Men,—an organization of all honest saloon-haters, embracing men of every political faith and religious creed, with a white flag upon which is inscribed in black letters : "In the name of Jesus Christ as King, the liquor traffic must die." It has only one department, agitation; and it agitated Rochester. It held mass-meetings that for enthusiasm and numbers were new to Rochester and are unknown elsewhere. It packed Music Hall to the roof with men; it held a hundred mass-meetings in fourteen months, and raised $3,000 to carry on the work. This it did, believing that Nestor was right when he told the generals of Greece that "the secret of victory was in getting a good ready."

While this thing was going on, the press called "time." Our name and watchword expressed what we were after,— prohibition absolute, for every day, for all time; but the press, less inclined to fanaticism, less disposed to wild-eyed schemes of reform, called "time." The press said, "Be practicable; enforce the laws you already have; get prohibition one day in seven before you ask for the other six; shut the side door." So far, so good.

The side door ought to be shut. How was this to be done? Few cities there are that have not tried the experiment. Law Enforcement Leagues have been organized, Committees of One Hundred have been named, Societies for the Suppression of Vice, all have lent a hand. Good men have acted as spies on saloon-keepers; they have peeped through drawn blinds, entered back doors, fouled their own mouths, and themselves violated the law in order to get evidence. They have hired policemen and done the policeman's work. They paid taxes to support the government, and organized a private machine to do the government's work. All of this has been done, and much more. But so did not we. We answered the demand of the press. We said, "The purpose of this organization is not to enforce laws, but to awaken such a righteous public sentiment as will compel the public officials, sworn and paid to do the work. to do it." We said that a people who were taxed to send men to their State capitol to make laws, and taxed some more to support a municipal government and pay a police department to enforce them when made, ought not to be obliged to organize and support by private contribution another government to do the work of perjured public officials and lazy policemen; that with the ballot in the hands of the people, such a necessity was a blot on our civilization; that it was, and is, a tremendous indictment of American citizenship: and that when a public official refuses to do his sworn duty the practicable thing was, not for the citizens to do his work for him, but — to kick him out. These are quotations from the address following the demand of the press.

Well, if so did not we what did we? We called together a strong committee of representative business men and preachers, called upon our chief executive, and addressed him in most vigorous language, calling attention to his oath of office, which had been violated from the beginning of his administration, showing that the law was being violated, insisting that it could be enforced, holding him individually responsible in the matter, and demanding as the servant of the people that he do the work, or the people expect to know the reason why.

The mayor went from the presence of that committee to a meeting of the Police Commission, of which he is the head, and an order was issued to the police department commanding the strict enforcement of the Sunday law that same night. So far, so good.

We then sent out a call for the members of the Prohibition Union of Christian Men to meet at the Y. M. C. A. Hall for practicable business. Now there is a text for another discourse. What is the practicable business of the Christian citizen in the presence of an open Sunday saloon? Our invitation read: " We want to see every man who is ready for practicable business in this fight against the saloon." Now understand me — not to play spy on saloon-keepers; not to peep over transoms; not to sneak in the back way, or any other way, and sample the dregs of beer-glasses in order to get the kind of evidence that it takes to convict a rum-seller — for it takes more evidence and better evidence to convict a rum-seller than it would require to hang every preacher at this Convention. Let a man be seen going into my house, and after two hours let him be found there with his body full of lead, and unless I can prove an alibi or give a minute account of where I was and what I was doing for every minute of that time, there is danger of my being hanged. But let a sober boy go into a saloon, and after two hours come out with his body full of whiskey, maudlin drunk, and that kind of evidence would n't count. You might even follow him in, you might hear him call for whiskey, you might see it handed over the bar, you might smell its fumes, and the victim might be your own son, but your evidence would n't count. Let no decent man engage in such tom-foolery as that. So did not we. Our request was for men who would act as superior officers, as high privates of the police force, and report to our organization the number of every officer who failed to suppress open violations of the law. Three hundred men responded to that invitation, two days before Christmas, on twenty-four hours' notice. So did we; and with what result. Let the infallible public press tell the tale.

In big black type across the top of five columns devoted to the story: " Not One Oasis in the Dry Desert of Rochester! Front door, side door, back door, all shut. "

Hear, then, the conclusion of the whole matter: the side door can be shut. The side door *never has been shut.* Every city that has attempted to shut it has abandoned the job. St. Louis tried it. Omaha, New York, Cincinnati, Chicago, Buffalo, cities East and West, North and South, large and small, and with one result. — failure, failure, failure. And it never was shut in Rochester. Did n't the Rochester papers tell the truth? No. Did n't the New York reporter tell the truth? He never saw the Sahara Desert. Did n't I tell the truth? I never said the side door was shut.

I did say that the front door on Sunday was shut, and it has remained shut; but the front door of hardware stores next door was open; the front door of groceries next door was open; the front door of adjoining barber-shops was open, and men were shaved a dozen times in a day; and side doors all over the residence district were open — open to the knowing knock and the familiar voice. Letters giving the saloon and the hour poured in upon me. I was invited to private views from across the street or an adjoining house to see the procession. Men in our own factory, living all over the city, said they could get all they wanted; and these people told the truth. They could A man going in for a drink was warned that he might be seen and subpœnaed to appear before the Grand Jury as a witness, and he answered, " Do you think I would give away my friend? " No, he would n't. He would perjure his soul before God before he would turn State's evidence against the man that sells him rum.

Men and women of America, hear me! The side door never has been shut, and it never will be shut so long as we legalize the open week-day front door. And the same thing is true of every prohibitive feature of a license law. No law that says you may sell a man until you make him drunk can be enforced that makes it a crime to sell him after he is drunk; no law that makes it legal to sell a man over twenty-one can be enforced that makes it a crime to sell him at twenty; and no law that makes it legal to sell strong drink throughout the six days of the week can be enforced that makes it a crime to sell on the seventh. You might as well propagate the smallpox throughout the week and expect to quarantine it on Sunday as to encourage and legalize the sale of strong drink throughout the week and expect ten million men to go dry or drink stale beer on Sunday. We will never have an ideal dry Sunday until we have an ideal dry Monday. We will never, never, never, shut the side door until an aroused Christian citizenship shall wake up to the awful fact that, bad as it is for bad men to violate the law that shuts the saloon on Sunday, it is infinitely worse for good men to consent to the law that opens it on Monday. This is the message — I believe — that God would have me proclaim to-day: the only solution of the side door is no front door; the only solution of the Sunday saloon is no Monday saloon; the only solution of the saloon problem is no saloon. Anything that stops short of that is treason to the country, treason to humanity, and treason to the cross of Christ. Let this great army of the living God lift up the watchword of the Prohibition Union of Christian Men: " In the name of Jesus Christ as King, the liquor traffic must die," and we will put a lock on the side door that will exhaust the genius of perdition to pick. It is in the power of this mighty organization to forge that lock.]

Mr. Howard is a slender, pale-faced man, whose energy in speech, as well as in organizing men, is simply tremendous; and his conclusion, " In the name of Christ, our King, the liquor traffic must go, " swept irresistibly over his audience like a whirlwind.

" This is a great nation, " said Hon. John Charlton, of Ontario, " but no nation is great enough to violate the laws and live without the blessing of God. " Horace Greeley called the Sunday newspaper " a social demon. " The speaker went farther than that, and characterized it as " the Antichrist of America. " He spoke in behalf of the white slaves of America, more than a million men who come to Saturday night tired, but are compelled to hand their consciences over to the keeping of their employers, and force their tired bodies to go to work on Sunday morning.

Address by Hon. John Charlton, M. P.,

Lynedoch, Ont.

What the Sabbath May Do For Us.

Dim and far seems the period when God created the heavens and the earth. With that act of creative power is associated the creation of man in the image and likeness of God. This early dawn of the history of our race is marked by the paternal care of the Creator in establishing the twin institutions of marriage and the weekly day of rest, the latter being blessed and sanctified by divine observance.

These two institutions were not designed to be of transient character, but were permanent arrangements designed for and necessary to the well-being of man. The obligation to observe this Sabbath of rest was in due time formally promulgated as a part of the Decalogue. It was no mere Mosaic observance or ritualistic ceremony designed to pass away with the ending of the covenant of works, but was to continue from the commencement to the end of time.

In entering upon inquiry, "What may the Sabbath do for us?" it is proper to glance for one moment at what the observance of the Sabbath has done for man. It has been in all the centuries since Christ purchased our redemption a day of rest and gladness to the Christian. It has marked the weekly pauses in the moil of labor and toil, and is the visible reminder of a higher destiny and higher aspirations for man. Its observance has been a fountain-head of Christian development and influence. It has been a dispenser of choice blessings to nations, communities, and individuals. The degree of its observance marks accurately the measure of favor which God has bestowed upon nations, and the commonwealths which have most closely complied with the requirements of the fourth commandment are those which have progressed most rapidly and stand forth as shining examples of the favor that the obedience to God's commands will win for nations.

As to what the Sabbath may do for us, the garnered store of blessings which its observance has already conferred upon man may properly give indication of what the continuance of such observance will do for the present and the future.

It is a feature of human history that as nations grow powerful and wealthy there is a tendency to lapse from the condition of virtue and virility which marks the earlier stages of their career. History furnishes a melancholy list of defunct empires, which have risen, flourished, possessed commanding power, and have then declined and fallen a prey to conquering foes, and internal corruption and decay.

To-day the United States is one of the great world powers. Its growth has been phenomenal; its wealth is boundless. The sources of its power are deep and strong. Its career thus far, especially since the abolition of slavery, has been one in which the requirements of the Divine Ruler have been fairly well observed. There is a manifest tendency now, however, to depart from the old lines, the old restraints, the old observances, and the Puritan fear of God as the Ruler of nations. Let it never be imagined that the nation is so strong or so great as not to need God's blessing, or to depend upon God's favor, or that it can with safety defy his commands.

Canada Sent a Prominent Member of Parliament, the Hon. John Charlton.

In reply to the question, "What may the Sabbath do for us?" I would say it may and will, if it is faithfully observed, keep the Christian life active, trustful, and aggressive, ready for the Master's work, and anxious to perform his requirements.

It may and will, if properly observed, bless the toiler with the rest which nature requires that he shall enjoy, and will bring him under elevating and refining influences which are not the attendant of any other condition of life.

It may, and will. exercise the most potent and desirable of sanitary influences by promoting public health, cleanliness, and self-respect. The laborer who observes the Sabbath, who attends church and Sabbath school with his family, who washes off the grime and soot of the week-day toil, appears in clean and respectable garments, and enjoys all the elevating influences connected with the privileges and associations of the rest-day, furnishes an example which conveys its own lesson, and it is not necessary to enlarge upon the valuable sanitary and healthy influence which the observance of the day exerts.

Its proper observance may, and will, develop and continue in existence through the land Christian homes, which are the educating schools of good citizens, the antipodes of the rumshop and the slum, and are the bulwark of the State.

Its observance will promote temperance, good morals, social purity; and in all respects named, the fruits of its observance are of a character not only to warrant but to demand the interposition of the strong arm of the civil law to secure to the community these priceless blessings.

Its due observance will be a powerful factor in promoting material prosperity and material development. Sabbath-observance lands are the richest of all lands. Sabbath-observance communities are richer than those tolerating the desecration of God's day. As a promoter of material development and national wealth, Sabbath observance exercises a most potent influence.

Its observance will secure the acknowledgment of the rights of conscience, and the boon of religious liberty. Without the properly secured observance of this day, the laborer may, and will, be forced to work against his will. His conscientious scruples will be violated, and his enjoyment of religious privileges will cease.

Proper observance of this day will make free men of millions of white slaves who now labor on the railways and other public works, and are unable to command a rest-day, or any of the enjoyments or privileges connected with the day; who reach home Saturday night too tired to continue their labor, and who go forth to their labor Sunday morning because they are too poor to quit.

The proper observance of this day would abolish the American Sunday newspaper. Horace Greeley declared that the Sunday newspaper was a social demon. To-day it may be termed, with truth, the Antichrist of America. Recently an attempt was made to establish two Sunday newspapers in the city of London. The five million inhabitants of that great metropolis of the world did not furnish a constituency sufficient for their support, and they died a natural death. May it be a death without resurrection.

In the United States the Sunday paper seems to have firmly established itself. It goes without saying that it is a violator of God's law, and naturally it is the enemy of that law; its influence is deplorable. It keeps the public, or at least that portion of the public that patronizes it, in the deeply worn rut of worldly thoughts, purposes, and employments, and most effectually secularizes the Sabbath. It is the foe of sound literature, whether religious or otherwise. It is trivial, superficial, and immoral in its character and tendencies, and steadily lowers the public taste. Beyond question it imperils the future of the State, and is calculated to emasculate the moral sense of the citizen. Its influences beget contempt for the higher law. It attacks, by example, if not by teaching, the sanctity of the Sabbath. It laughs to scorn the precept "Righteousness exalteth a nation." The Christian sentiment of America should be directed with firm and relentless purpose to the destruction of this instrument of evil.

The task, of course, is a gigantic one, but if the professing Christians of the United States were true to their duty it could be accomplished. Let every man and woman in the United States who professes the name of Christ refuse to buy or read a Sunday paper, let every Christian business man in the United States refuse to advertise in a Sunday newspaper, and its publication would be rendered unprofitable very speedily. With the accomplishment of this would come the end of the evil.

We should ever bear in mind that no law of God is designed for the purpose of oppressing or injuring man. Every one of his commandments are designed for the good of human beings, and not one of these commands can be broken without serious consequences. God's Sabbath law is designed for and will certainly secure man's moral and religious advantage. The Sunday law of the State is designed for and will secure man's social and temporal advantage. Christianity and the higher type of modern civilization are inseparable. All that is good, pure, and desirable in the civilization of the nineteenth century is the direct outcome of Christianity.

We stand upon the threshold of a new century. We look back over the annals of the one just about to close, and while there are many things to mourn, there are many things also to give encouragement and hope. It has been a wonderful century. Great material progress has been made; spiritual and moral progress also is a feature of the age. The Christian philanthropist and philosopher may mourn over many things, but may rejoice over more. As we enter upon the new century, a great problem meets us: How are we to ennoble the future? How are we to elevate mankind? How are we to make the world a higher, nobler, and more congenial home for moral and intellectual beings? The necessities that confront us are imperative. We must reach the toiling millions, the great hosts that man our fleets, till our fields, run our factories and our railways, fill our counting-houses, and prosecute the multiform processes of our industrial life;—these must be reached. The life of the nation, the interests of the race, the requirements of God, demand that this shall be done. How is it to be done? God's Word will give the answer, and point out the course to pursue. We must pursue that course courageously, ceaselessly, and with a sense of the obligation to God and our fellow man resting upon us.

The great army of young Christian workers embodied in the organization known as the Society of Christian Endeavor are standing upon the threshold of a field where mighty opportunities open. The future beckons to you. The world waits for the fruits of your efforts. Never lose sight of the great fact that a desecrated and dishonored Sabbath is the enemy of Christian progress, the assassin of Christian life. Go forward, not in your own strength, but in the strength of Him who moveth us to serve; strive to do what his law requires of you; and may your influence be blessed for the good of the nation, for the good of humanity, and for the glory of the kingdom!

Woodward Avenue Baptist Church.

The Women's Meeting.

There was such a grand rush for the women's meeting that it was early reckoned a high privilege to poke one's nose within the door. The women would have filled one of the large tents. They overflowed into another church, filled the audience-room, and the overflow meeting had to overflow.

Mrs. F. E. Clark, the presiding officer, and her staff of speakers had barely room on the platform to turn. The press tables were completely swallowed up in gay shirt-waists and muslins, and the reporters scribbled standing, kneeling, any way they could. Mrs. J. Walker, of Queensland, Australia, conducted the opening devotional exercises.

Mrs. J. L. Hill, Salem, Mass., equal to and ready for any emergency, took charge of the overflow meeting. The speakers, as fast as they finished one meeting, were hurried to the next.

The first speaker, Mrs. C. Scott Williams, of Mexico, with rare skill in description, made her hearers see the daily life of Mexican women as if thrown on the screen of a biograph. She introduced a Mexican maiden, who sang a Spanish song that helped to plant in the hearts of all present a more loving thought for their Mexican sisters.

The life of women in China was seen through the eyes of Miss Caroline E. Chittenden, Foochow, China, who represented the first Christian Endeavor society organized in China. There was a little bit of Orientalism before the speaker's eyes. At the suggestion of Mrs. Clark, a hundred or more young ladies who had been standing in aisles sat gracefully down on the floor, as Chinese girls sit in meeting.

Miss Jessie Ackerman, speaking for the women of Asia, said, "The greatest discovery of the nineteenth century was woman's discovery of herself."

Address by Miss Jessie Ackerman,
Chicago, Ill.
THE WOMEN OF ASIA.

In expressing the possibilities of women in the future, Miss Willard was wont to say, "The greatest discovery of the century is, woman has discovered herself." While this is a truism concerning the English-speaking women, it is a pitiful fact that more than half the women of the world are so far from having discovered themselves that the task of even aiding to this end seems almost hopeless. The women of many parts of the world are so deeply intrenched behind the mighty and almost unsurmountable obstacles of time-honored customs and ancient superstitions that even the approach to them is often cut off, and contact with them is among the impossible things.

More than one-half the women of the world are matters of merchandise. In the Orient every man buys his wife just as he does his buffaloes or oxen, and has just as full and complete control over her movements as he has over his beast. Among the lower classes she becomes the hewer of wood and the drawer of water, is harnessed to the plow with the buffalo, breaks stone in the quarry, and becomes the bearer of burdens beneath which a beast would almost sink. Besides physical burdens, she is degraded,— even the highest caste women, in every relation of life, — without even the distinction of a soul. She is wholly uneducated, and the passing of days that marks time can in no sense be termed life; it is merely existence.

In India the degradation on the part of women is more marked than in China by reason of the very early period at which a girl's earthly destiny is sealed. In Siam a woman is branded, just as we brand cattle. A mark on her wrist indicates what branch of the imperial family she belongs to. While visiting that country I was granted an audience with His Majesty the King, who received me in the greatest possible state. In referring to the degraded condition of his women, he brought forth as clever an argument as I have ever heard. The king is a "muchly" married man, having forty wives, sixty children, and 1,500 women in his harem, each woman having a slave. When the great gate closed upon me I found myself in an enclosure where there are three thousand women who never go out. In speaking of the lack of education of his women, the king argued thus: "You know with education there always comes culture and refinement. If I educated my women I would educate them into a state of discontentment, for they would want many things that it is impossible for them to have." While this is a clever argument, the king knows that if his women were educated it would be impossible to wall high enough to keep in three thousand educated women. When he asked me what was the secret of England's greatness, and America's greatness, my reply was: "Two things. First, we worship the true and the living God; and next, our women are educated; and any nation whose God is the living God, and whose women are educated, must rise, and all the powers of darkness could never keep them down."

While the condition of these women is lamentable in the extreme, their slavery is scarcely to be compared with the condition that exists among the women of Greater India. In this latter country, when a girl is born and reaches the age of two or three months she is at once betrothed to some male child in the vicinity, and so binding are these relations that they are regarded as sacred as marriage. If the boy dies the girl is branded as an outcast, and is ofttimes thrown into the dirt heaps or ash piles, for a superstition prevails among the people, who believe in the transmigration of souls, that when she lived on earth before she must have committed some horrible sin, and as a punishment the male child dies. The most dreadful fate that can overtake a woman in India is to be known as a widow. So great is the degradation that in years past it was a frequent occurrence that a widow would throw herself upon the burning funeral pile of her husband, preferring to suffer the agony of this horrible death rather than live and endure the degradation attached to widowhood.

It cannot be said that the condition of India women has been altogether improved by contact with the Western world, although it is the boast of the Christian nation that conquered these people that they did so in the name of progress and Christianity. They have failed to exemplify the teachings of the Founder of our faith in their relation toward them, and as a result the women are ofttimes degraded below the level to which heathenism alone has reduced them. In connection with the British army in India, regulations forbid eighty-eight per cent of the soldiery marrying, and in lieu of wives, undertakes to supply the army with native women, and a system has been introduced by which the native women are being debauched shamefully.

In addressing a vast throng of native men in Central India, on "What the Gospel Has Done for Women," at the close of the address an educated Indian asked if he might make a few remarks. He was invited to the platform, and the substance of his address was as follows: "We are looked upon by people of the Western world as both ignorant and pagan, but we have never known a heathenism so dark as to degrade our women by law." When the meeting was over I asked him to more fully explain his statement, and he said, "It is a matter I cannot explain to you; but I refer you to the cantonment, where you will find quarters in every barracks for native women." And when regiments are moved from place to place women are moved as part of the army equipment, and the heathen round about look upon this as part of our religion, and one of the factors of Christianity.

The season of Quiet Communion with God, which followed, was conducted by Mrs. J. W. Baer, of Boston.

To the women of America Mrs. Howard Ingham turned her face, because woman, in this country, is the key-note of society. Her words were a revelation of the unused powers of American womanhood. Such meetings are of vast importance in inspiring Christian women to rise up and use that power.

Address by Mrs. Howard M. Ingham,

Jefferson, O.

WOMAN'S WORK FOR HER COUNTRY.

Admiral Schley, in a recent address, declared he had but just learned how America had grown such a mighty nation; that the fundamental principle of its growth was its respect and love for women. "The man who serves best behind the guns," he said, "is he who has the best woman serving behind him." In this terse sentence, it seems to me, is expressed the highest duty and profoundest responsibility given to women,—the duty and responsibility of standing for and leading up to the noblest and truest ideals in individual and in national life. It is a solemn fact—an almost terrifying fact—that the tone of social and national life is that which woman gives it. She strikes the key-note; and whether it be low and base, or whether it be high, sweet, and pure, the whole of society becomes attuned to her note as completely as do all the diverse instruments of a great orchestra breathe forth the exact pitch of the leader's own.

A profound student of social life was lately commenting upon the improved conditions visible in a certain city; and, like Admiral Schley, he attributed the change to the stand which women had taken. Women were holding up a loftier standard, he said, requiring of themselves and of men a nobler, truer life. Faults and vices once overlooked or condoned were now condemned; and because women required this loftier standard, men were reaching up toward it. and all society was finer, nobler, and sweeter.

It is in the light of these facts that I would speak to you, sister women, of the possibilities and consequent duties open to us in behalf of our country. We are American women, with hearts full of love for our native land. The sight of our starry banner makes all our pulses thrill with purest emotion. We would die for our country, would we not? But the great Commander bids us do a yet nobler thing,—to live for our country; so to live and act and work that we may help her to achieve the grandest destiny ever proffered a nation.

It was "in the fulness of time" that God discovered this great continent to the nations across the sea. From among them all he gathered those who were to possess it. He planted them here, built them round with freedom and riches and opportunity. He moulded and blended, protected and blessed, them until they became this mighty nation. For what? For their own sakes? That they might selfishly and self-glorifyingly enjoy the riches of this splendid inheritance and count it all their own? Indeed, no; but that America might be the joy of the whole earth; the champion of the wronged, the strength of the weak, the teacher of the ignorant, the saviour of the lost, the splendid living embodiment of all that is noble and Christly, and so might lift the world toward God. Not for herself — ah, no ! — but for the world's sake, is America so richly blessed; not for selfish satisfaction, but to give herself as her Lord and King gave himself, for the world. She caught a glimpse of her divine destiny when, a year ago, she struck the fetters of despotism from our Cuban neighbors, and found how sweet it is to give self for others.

But how fully is she fulfilling the divine purpose toward the weak nations of the earth? Is she setting them the example of pure government by free men? In part, yes. But what shall we say of the abuses that darken our great cities, and make our municipal legislation too often the scornful astonishment of the world? Is she so training her own people in honesty, sobriety, and purity as to make them a fit model for all people to pattern after? In much, yes. And yet, alas, for the moral laxity, the active moral poisons, that in too many places imperil the very existence of our nation and the souls of our people ! Is she generously holding out to weak peoples a high ideal of national life, and the blessed treasure of Christ's pure religion? In a measure, yes. But what shall we say of the destruction we are sending them, too? Look over the seas at this moment, and see the terrible shiploads of intoxicants we are speeding away to every one of these weak child-peoples ! See Alaska's untaught tribes, needing protection from appetite and vice, stripped by our very last Congress of their blessed prohibitory law and tossed, helpless, to the wolf of the rum power. Remember how we have deluged Africa with rum ! See Cuba and Porto Rico and the Philippines already invaded by the brutal drink system ! Think you that God, the Father of all these poor children, will permit this great nation he has so heaped with blessings to destroy his helpless ones? Nay, verily. One thing is certain. No half-drunken nation can ever carry out God's purpose toward the world. The world he gave himself for will be saved, and some great nation will be the chief instrument in its saving; but it can only be a nation itself saved from vice, and so prepared to give others protection and help. "If thou altogether holdest thy peace at this time," said Mordecai of old to Persia's young queen, "then shall deliverance arise to the Jews from another place; but thou and thy father's house shall be destroyed." "If thou, strong young America, whom I have guarded and enriched," says the King eternal, "wilt not make thyself the blessing of the earth, still all the nations shall be mine; but thou, for thy recreancy and self-love, shall be destroyed." And so to our America, as to Queen Esther of old, comes the necessity of choice. Which shall it be, O great, fair country, — a future of lofty, generous work for the world, and so the building up for thyself the noblest national life, or the brutal selfishness that for present gain in silver and gold sells to vice and destruction the dependent and helpless, and hurls thyself from the noblest height possible to a nation? Which shall it be, life or death; God or Mammon?

What have we, sister woman, to do with the answer America shall render? Much; a work to rouse the noblest activity of every maid and matron in the land. We have an influence that shapes destiny; we can so mould public sentiment and public conscience as to ensure the victory of righteousness. "He who makes public sentiment," said Lincoln, "goes deeper than he who enacts statutes or pronounces decisions." There is no evil so strong that the earnest, concerted effort of American women could not overthrow it.

Especially should we give our strongest work to overthrow the drink system. There are other evils in the land; alas, yes ! but beneath and above and around them all, the soil in which they take root, and the air they breathe, is the evil of drink. This it is that is destroying our own people, laying its blighting curse on six hundred thousand new victims every year; filling the land with insanity, idiocy, pauperism, and crime; predestining helpless children to moral weakness and vice; dotting our country all over with almshouses, prisons, and jails; robbing children of their birthright, society of security, men and women of home, happiness, and heaven; pouring out to destroy our very own more money every two days than we give in a whole year to save the world! This it is that makes America's destiny tremble in the balance. This conquered, all minor evils would slip easily from her erect majesty.

We Americans pride ourselves on the number and extent of our philanthropies. Their number is almost incredible; their cost in labor and money is enormous. But if the drink traffic were abolished there would be no occasion for these philanthropies. Just now the cities of Washington and Baltimore, led by men of noble benevolence and wisdom, are establishing a Junior Republic, modelled upon that splendidly successful work at Freeville, New York, in which a vast number of boys from the New York slums have been trained to a noble manhood. It is a glorious thing to do; but if there were no drink habit there would be no slums in New York nor Washington nor Baltimore; no ill-born, untrained, vagabond youth needing such help as this. And so with all our philanthropies and the most of our municipal and national burdens. Free her from the drink system and its fearful effects on men and morals and finance, and how America would soar!

What can American women do along this line for their country? These two things assuredly: first, they can set themselves as an immovable rock against the whole drink system, attuning their own personal habits, the administration of their homes, and the entertainment of their guests to the key of total abstinence,— and society would follow this behest,— and secondly, they can set themselves to the building of a dominant public sentiment for temperance. It must be not an unreasoning prejudice, but a sentiment founded on positive truth. Hence women must know many things; the incontrovertible facts concerning alcohol, and its effect on the individual and his posterity, upon society and the State; the awful cost of intemperance, and the far-reaching destruction it continually works out.

Knowing these things, we should teach them. The children should be so grounded in these truths that they can never forget; the young people must know the facts and their own consequent responsibility. The citizen-body must be reached with the same irresistible logic, and every stratum of society leavened through and through by the knowledge of the great national danger. This universal education will inevitably mould the laws; but we, in conjunction with the brave men of the temperance reform, can hasten this result by keeping even now a close watch on the elections in city and State, and urging the acceptance in every party of such candidates only as are true temperance men. We can watch legislation, and secure the framing, and the passage, too, of such bills as will effectually suppress the giant evil. We can stimulate the enforcement of righteous laws when once secured; and so, all along the line, by tact and earnestness, can exert a saving influence.

The effort that accomplishes these results must be the concerted efforts of the women of the nation. It must be bound by no limits of denominational or partisan affiliation, and it must be for the one single purpose. "Exclusiveness of purpose," said Napoleon, "is the secret of great successes and of great operations." *All* women for this *one thing* is the need of this critical hour — undenominational, non-partisan, sharply specialized, determined work.

O that all women, our country over, forgetting every difference of church or political party or social station, might bind themselves together in a holy alliance, nation-wide and millions strong, for the freeing of our land! How soon the battle would be won!

What can you do, young women of this great organization of Christian Endeavor, to bring this result? I know you have your Temperance Committees; but have you grasped the critical necessity for strong work? Are you clear-sighted enough to look away down through and beneath the multiform evils of society and discern the root iniquity from which they spring? Are you strong-hearted and enduring enough to grapple with this iniquity? Are you ready, at this Convention, representing as you do every section of the land, to declare yourselves from henceforth actively and unalterably against the cruel drink traffic that menaces the very existence of the nation? Looking upon the young strength of this splendid company, I covet it for this great, critical struggle. In Christ's name and our country's, I beseech you, give yourselves for this most desperate strife.

The degradation which Mormonism forces on women was not overlooked. Mrs. Teunis S. Hamlin, of Washington, D. C., made a telling plea against the seating of Congressman-elect Roberts, and every woman's hands and eyes applauded.

The Light Guard Armory.

The Marvellous Men's Meeting.

The Armory, with its three thousand chairs, was absolutely filled with men. As may easily be imagined, the finest singing of the Convention was heard from those five regiments of men, led by Mr. Smyth. The Hampton Institute Quartette entertained and inspired all by their singing. Mr. Baer's talk was intensely earnest. He described most powerfully his emotions when, in company with Dr. Chapman, he first saw Munkacsy's "Christ on the Cross." His application was pointed and brief.

Address by Rev. J. Wilbur Chapman, D.D.

He shall be driven from light into darkness and chased out of the world. — JOB xviii. 18.

The text is chosen from one of the most remarkable books in the Bible, the principal character of which is Job, and he is a real character. It is a striking text, and yet gives a perfect picture of Satan's treatment of man when once he is under his control.

We are in darkness by nature. First, we are slaves, and no galley-slave was ever more truly in bondage than we to sin. Second, we are like lepers, and Naaman himself was not more hopeless. Third, we are dead in sin, and therefore helpless.

In our darkness, by the spirit of God, light begins to break in on us, and generally in the following order, First. Impressions come to us that we ought to be better. We are resolved that the church shall receive our attention and support. Second. We are filled with a longing desire to be free from sin, and this grows into a hope that some day we may be saved. Third. Finally we are determined that the whole matter shall be settled. We are sick of sin.

Then it is that the devil begins to drive from the light into the darkness. This is the teaching of Scripture. First. He meets our impressions and puts every obstacle in the way. Second. He meets our longings for freedom by declaring that we are free. Third. He meets our determination to be saved by congratulating us and telling us to wait for feeling, or until we grow better, or declares that there is time enough. Fourth. Then he drives us, and no foe is so relentless. He uses conscience as a whip. He brings up our old sins and by them makes us afraid.

Then, finally, he chases us out of the world. Have you ever noticed the difference between the end of the just and the unjust? It is plainly written in the Bible. Concerning the wicked we are told, "There shall be weeping and wailing and gnashing of teeth." Of the judgment we are told, "The earth fled away and there was found no place for them," and again we are told that "they shall stand naked and open before Him with whom they have to do." Concerning the righteous it is said, "Enoch walked with God," and as Dr. Andrew Bower has said, they walked so far that God just took him home. Elijah was translated, and in a chariot of fire swept into the presence of God. Tradition says that God kissed Moses to sleep, and buried his body where no man could ever find it, while Paul faces martyrdom with the shout, " I know whom I have believed."

Dr. Chapman's address to the men was a terrible picture of the effects of sin. It was a fearful presentation, with lightning flashes from many a ruined, hopeless life the great evangelist has seen. "O our God," he prayed at the close, "save us from the awful end of sin. Blessed God, make this the hour of all this Convention when our hearts may be made clean. Our blessed Father, we could crucify the Son of God afresh by just keeping these sins in our hearts. Help us to be free from sin to-day. My God, begin with me ; go through my heart. And search every man in this building. And do it now."

Then followed a testing-time of great power, and a yielding-time of rich fruitage. By word of mouth and by rising, practically all in the room gave in their allegiance to the Master. By lifting the hand, scores of these asked special prayers for their salvation. To these were given cards that they might fill out, and receive further help from the pastors of Detroit.

SUNDAY EVENING.

Consecration Meetings.

The consecration service is the "crowning meeting" in all Christian Endeavor conventions. Sunday night there were thirty-one such services, in as many different churches. The object of the service is to bring the members and all who participate to a realizing sense of what it means to be one with Christ.

The churches were overwhelmingly filled for these consecration services. Following is a list of these important meetings. It is manifestly impossible to give reports of these blessed meetings.

BETHEL CHURCH (Napoleon and Hastings). — Opening Exercises by Rev. R. F. Hurley, D.D., Pastor; Addresses, Bishop Alexander Walters, D.D., Jersey City, N. J., and Bishop B. W. Arnett, D.D., Wilberforce, O.; Consecration Service conducted by Rev. James L. Hill, D.D., Salem, Mass.

FIRST CONGREGATIONAL CHURCH (Woodward and Forest). — Opening Exercises by Rev. Nehemiah Boynton, D.D., Pastor; Address, Rev. W. W. Boyd, D.D., St. Louis, Mo.; Consecration Service conducted by Mr. Robert E. Speer, New York City.

FOREST AVENUE PRESBYTERIAN CHURCH (Forest and Second). — Opening Exercises by Rev. James M. Barkley, Pastor: Address, Rev. Wm. Patterson, Toronto, Ont.; Consecration Service conducted by Rev. Arthur J. Smith, Savannah, Ga.

WESTMINSTER PRESBYTERIAN CHURCH (Woodward and Parsons). — Opening Exercises by Rev. John Brittan Clark, Pastor; Address, Rev. M. Rhodes, D.D., St. Louis, Mo.; Consecration Service conducted by Rev. John Pollock, Glasgow, Scotland.

CASS AVENUE M. E. CHURCH (Cass and Selden). — Opening Exercises by Rev. E. J. Baskerville, Pastor; Address, Rev. W. F. Wilson, Hamilton, Ont.; Consecration Service conducted by Rev. J. F. Cowan, D.D., Boston, Mass.

FIRST PRESBYTERIAN CHURCH (Woodward and Edmund Pl.).— Opening Exercises by Rev. William Beatty Jennings, D.D., Pastor; Address, Rev. A. C. Kempton, Janesville, Wis.; Consecration Service conducted by Treasurer William Shaw, Boston, Mass.

FIRST BAPTIST CHURCH (Cass and Bagg).— Opening Exercises by Rev. Chas. A. Fulton, Pastor; Address, Rev. John Henry Barrows, D.D., LL.D., Oberlin, O.; Consecration Service conducted by Mr. D. B. Eddy, Leavenworth, Kan.

WOODWARD AVENUE BAPTIST CHURCH (Woodward and Winder).— Opening Exercises by Rev. Donald D. MacLaurin, D.D., Pastor; Address, Rev. Andrew B. Chalmers, Saginaw, Mich.; Consecration Service conducted by President Francis E. Clark, D.D., Boston, Mass.

WOODWARD AVENUE CONGREGATIONAL CHURCH (Woodward and Sibley).— Opening Exercises by Rev. Herman P. DeForest, D.D., Pastor; Address, Rev. Teunis S. Hamlin, D.D., Washington, D. C.; Consecration Service conducted by Rev. W. F. McCauly, Dennison, O.

CENTRAL M. E. CHURCH (Woodward and Adams).— Opening Exercises by Rev. J. M. Toburn, D.D., Pastor; Address, Rev. J. E. Pounds, Indianapolis, Ind.; Consecration Service conducted by Mr. H. B. Gibbud, Springfield, Mass.

CENTRAL PRESBYTERIAN CHURCH (Farmer and Bates).— Opening Exercises by Rev. Marcus Scott, Pastor; Address, Rev. Wayland Hoyt, D.D., Philadelphia, Pa.; Consecration Service conducted by Rev. A. L. Geggie, Truro, Nova Scotia.

FORT STREET PRESBYTERIAN CHURCH (Fort and Third).— Opening Exercises by Rev. John Reid, D.D., Pastor; Address, Rev. Hugh K. Walker, D.D., Los Angeles, Cal.; Consecration Service conducted by Secretary John Willis Baer, Boston, Mass.

JEFFERSON AVENUE PRESBYTERIAN CHURCH (Jefferson and Rivard).— Opening Exercises by Rev. A. H. Barr, Pastor; Address, Rev. Chas. E. Jefferson, D.D., New York City; Consecration Service conducted by Rev. James Mursell, London, England.

SECOND AVENUE PRESBYTERIAN CHURCH (Grand River and Second).— Opening Exercises by Rev. C. E. Bronson, D.D., Saginaw, Mich.; Address, Rev. F. D. Power, D.D., Washington, D. C.; Consecration Service conducted by Mr. Frederick A. Wallis, Hopkinsville, Ky.

SCOVEL MEMORIAL PRESBYTERIAN CHURCH.— Opening Exercises by Rev. J. D. Jeffrey, Pastor; Address, Rev. W. F. Richardson, D.D., Kansas City, Mo.; Consecration Service conducted by Rev. Ernest Bourner Allen, Lansing, Mich.

TRUMBULL AVENUE PRESBYTERIAN CHURCH (Grand River and Trumbull).— Opening Exercises by Rev. Henry T. Miller, D.D., Pastor; Address, Rev. Geo. B. Stewart, D.D., Harrisburg, Pa.; Consecration Service conducted by Rev. J. M. Lowden, Olneyville, R. I.

CALVARY PRESBYTERIAN CHURCH (Michigan and Maybury Grand).— Opening Exercises by Rev. Wm. H. Shields, Pastor; Address, Rev. Allan B. Philputt, D.D., Indianapolis, Ind.; Consecration Service conducted by Rev. W. T. Rodgers, Nashville, Tenn.

MEMORIAL PRESBYTERIAN CHURCH (Clinton and Jos. Campau).— Opening Exercises by Rev. W. J. Darby, D.D., Evansville, Ind.; Address, Rev. George E. Soper, St. Paul, Minn.; Consecration Service conducted by Rev. F. S. Hatch, Monson, Mass.

CHURCH OF COVENANT (Russell and Napoleon).— Opening Exercises by Rev. George B. Crawford, Pastor; Address, Rev. Joseph Walker, Queensland, Australia; Consecration Service conducted by Rev. W. I. Chamberlain, India.

IMMANUEL PRESBYTERIAN CHURCH (Porter and Boulevarde).— Opening Exercises by Rev. Wm. H. Clark, D.D., Pastor; Address, Rev. E. W. Clippenger, Warrensburg, Mo.; Consecration Service conducted by Rev. Clarence E. Eberman, Lancaster, Pa.

BETHANY PRESBYTERIAN CHURCH (Champlain and Seyburn).— Opening Exercises by Rev. W. D. Sexton, Pastor; Address, President Burris A. Jenkins, Indianapolis, Ind.; Consecration Service conducted by Mr. C. V. Vickrey, Bartley, Neb.

UNITED PRESBYTERIAN CHURCH (Grand River and Alexandrine). — Opening Exercises by Rev. Wm. H. Vincent, D.D., Pastor; Address, Rev. M. F. Toxell, D.D., Springfield, Ill.; Consecration Service conducted by Rev. A. C. Crews, Toronto, Ont.

SIMPSON M. E. CHURCH (Grand River and Bagg). — Opening Exercises by Rev. Chas. W. Blodgett, Pastor; Address, Bishop Samuel Fallows, D.D., LL.D., Chicago, Ill.; Consecration Service conducted by Rev. Jacob W. Kapp, D.D., Richmond, Ind.

MARY PALMER M. E. CHURCH (Champlain and McDougal). — Opening Exercises by Rev. Joshua Stansfield, Pastor; Address, Rev. H. O. Breeden, LL.D., Des Moines, Io.; Consecration Service conducted by Mr. S. J. Duncan-Clark, Toronto, Ont.

CENTRAL CHRISTIAN CHURCH (Second and Ledyard). — Opening Exercises by Rev. Chas. B. Newman, Pastor; Address, Rev. F. A. Noble, D.D., Chicago, Ill.; Consecration Service conducted by Rev. Clarence A. Barbour, Rochester, N. Y.

PEOPLE'S PLYMOUTH TABERNACLE (Trumbull and Baker). — Opening Exercises by Rev. James McAllister, Pastor; Address, Rev. Asher Anderson, Meriden, Conn.; Consecration Service conducted by President A. E. Turner, Lincoln, Ill.

BREWSTER CONGREGATIONAL CHURCH (Warren and Trumbull). — Opening Exercises by Rev. Theo. D. Bacon, Pastor; Address, Rev. W. N. Yates, Philadelphia, Pa.; Consecration Service conducted by Prof. James Lewis Howe, Lexington, Va.

ST. PAUL'S MEMORIAL EPISCOPAL CHURCH (Woodward and Hancock).— Opening Exercises conducted by Rev. Rufus W. Clark, Rector; Address, Rev. Canon J. B. Richardson, London, Ont.; Consecration Service conducted by Rev. Floyd W. Tomkins, D.D., Philadelphia, Pa.

HIGHLAND PARK PRESBYTERIAN CHURCH (Highland Park). — Opening Exercises by Rev. Perry V. Jenness, Pastor; Address, Rev. J. H. O. Smith, Chicago, Ill.; Consecration Service conducted by Rev. J. V. Clancy, West Medford, Mass.

GRACE REFORMED PRESBYTERIAN CHURCH (Finley, near Jos. Campau).— Opening Exercises by Rev. Charles W. Brugh, Pastor; Address, Rev. David McAllister, D.D., LL.D., Allegheny. Pa.; Consecration Service conducted by Rev. Samuel McNaugher, Boston, Mass.

The Windsor, Ont., Meeting.

ST. ANDREW'S PRESBYTERIAN CHURCH. — Opening Exercises by Rev. J. C. Tolmie, Pastor; Address, Rev. J. Wilbur Chapman, D.D., New York City; Consecration Service conducted by Mr. H. H. Spooner, Bull's Bridge, Conn.

MONDAY MORNING.

Tent Williston.

When the Endeavorers came together in Tent Williston on Monday morning it was raining in torrents, but Dr. Hill was chairman, and his sunny sallies soon drove the clouds away. He said that since he had come to Detroit he had gained a new sympathy with Noah. He advised us to hold a convention in Dakota, where they greatly need such storms as attend us. More seriously, he prayed that "as the rain cometh down," so " might the word be that goeth forth out of God's mouth, that it might prosper."

Dr. Hill called on all the Sunday-school teachers and church officers in the tent to stand up, that the missionaries might see some of their Christian Endeavor supporters; and there was scarcely a person that remained seated. A second striking exhibit was made when he called for the home missionaries, and got them on the platform, introducing them to the audience by name. There were about sixty of these heroes, and they came from all frontier parts of the United States and Canada.

Rev. Eben Herbert, of Hammond, La., conducted the devotional exercises. The singing was led by Mr. Foster.

In his unique manner, Mr. Hill spoke of the home missionary and his trials and triumphs. Of his own experiences, he had many amusing incidents to tell, which were generously applauded.

After the Hampton Institute Quartette sang the song embracing the sentiment: "Jesus Christ is the first and last man, and no man works like him," Mr. William Shaw, the business manager of *The Christian Endeavor World*, made a plea for increased support of the publication, and also of the United Society's printing department. Following Mr. Shaw, the colored quartette sang their farewell song: "In Egypt's Land."

"Our Country's Many Problems," "Our Country's Greatest Peril," "Our Country's One Salvation,"—that was the stirring outline of the session; and these great themes were treated in masterly fashion by Dr. Boyd, of St. Louis; Mr. Howard, of Rochester; and Dr. Jefferson, of New York.

Dr. Boyd had time to discuss only immigration and the negro problem; but he spoke strong words on both, and especially on the latter subject, showing fairly both sides of the dark picture, pleading for more adequate protection against the evils handed down to us from the dreadful slave days, and also for the severest penalties against "the diabolical crime of lynching.

|Address by Rev. W. W. Boyd, D.D.,
St. Louis, Mo.

My brothers and sisters, I am here under orders to speak on our country's many problems in thirty minutes. It reminds me of Sidney Smith's criticism of the modern traveller, who he said was very much like the man who professed to tell you all that was going on inside a house because he had time to count its windows. Some of our modern lecturers might well take as their subject "Three Minutes in the Crater of Vesuvius," and an account of its effects upon the organ of circulation. This habit of getting great subjects and crowding them into a few minutes is rather distressing, both to the audience and the speaker; but our noble secretary evidently thought that the preachers needed a lesson in the art of condensation. A ministerial friend of mine was going home from church one Sunday night, after having preached an interminably long sermon, when his wife in a very gentle manner upbraided him for it. "Oh, my dear," said he, "I fear you do not desire the sincere milk of the Word, that you may grow thereby." "Oh, yes, I do, husband," said she, "but it is a custom nowadays to use condensed milk."

Now that is what you are going to get,—condensed milk. I wish it were cream. For one to go through our country with his eyes opened and his ears shut he would see so many and marked evidences of prosperity that he would have but little fear for its future; but if he were to go through the land with his eyes shut and his ears open he would be assailed by so many cries from so many different directions that he would feel that our institutions were trembling to their fall. Now we must go through these thirty minutes with both our eyes and ears open. The problems are legion: social, religious, educational, industrial, ecclesiastical, theological, national — a list of them would exhaust the thirty minutes. We must then exclude all problems which the State can solve alone, and all problems which the church can solve by itself, and speak only of some which must require for their solution the united co-operative action of both government and applied Christianity. And the very first problem is that suggested by the chairman, the problem of imigration.

This is a question not peculiar to America, but certainly no nation has such a problem of imigration as the United States. I want to say here at the start that we want all Christian imigrants of every nation, tribe, and people under the face of the whole heavens, whatever their nationality is. It is not a question of nationality at all; it is a question of character; it is a question of ideas. Eighteen million foreigners have imigrated to this country since 1820 — not all of them Christian Endeavorers. To-day they constitute one-fifth of our population. The value of each immigrant, from a commercial point of view, is estimated at $1,125; but the vast benefits accruing to the country from this imigration, which alone has made the rapid development and productive power of the United States the miracle of civilization — this is beyond compute. Many of these imigrants are friends of law, of government, and of religion. Very many are our best citizens. They bore our standards to victory in the Civil War and in the late war. I want it distinctly understood that I am not speaking this morning about the better class of imigration; but many of these imigrants are not of that character.· The vast majority of them are not. They are clannish. They hold false notions of liberty. They are indifferent, rationalists, sceptical, in matters of religion, and they therefore constitute a menace to our American ideals. Though constituting but one-fifth of our population, they furnish more than one-half of the inmates of our reformatories, over one-third of our convicts, and very nearly three-fifths of the paupers in our almshouses. Within the last decade, too, a great change has come in the quality of our imigration, and a change for the worse. Formerly the average imigrant was among the most industrial class from the community which he came, but within the last ten or fifteen years it has not been so. The majority of imigrants have not come from Great Britain and Germany and Norway and Sweden. Now Italians, sixty-three per cent of whom can neither read nor write, Poles and Hungarians and Japanese and the lower element of the Chinese, have come to our shores without the slightest indication of taking a permanent residence here, but content to live at the very lowest level of life if they may get enough money to return to their native land and spend the remainder of their days in ease.

Now this mass of illiterate imigration is not distributed through the whole country. It has settled into great cities, and has become the fruitful source of nearly all municipal corruptions. Mr. Bryce is right when he says that the one conspicuous failure of the United States is the government of our cities. It is admittedly the weakest point of our community. Now the corrupters of our city politics may be the bosses, the saloon politicians, the ward heelers; but back of these some very eminently respectable citizens, and church-members even, who find that they can get franchises and other favors they need from the city government with a much less outlay of time and money by bribery than by uniting with the better class of public servants for our city government. I say though the corrupters of politics are these, yet their vocation would be gone were there no people to corrupt. Now this lower class of imigration supplies the easily corruptible mass of voters. Eighty per cent of the population of New York City is foreign; therefore Tammany Hall is possible. Seventy per cent of the population of a western city is foreign; and therefore, a most corrupt Republican machine runs the town. It is not a question of politics after this date.

People will unite in city government irrespective of national considerations. It is simply a question of spoils in the city government, and their whole power resides in this low mass of imigrants. Nay, more, wherever you find a large proportion of the population in great cities composed of this class, there you will find low moral and political ideals, and wide-open, desecrated Sundays, and a lack of administration of criminal law, with its consequent harvest of murder, burglary, and footpads and nameless crimes. My friends, the welfares of the great centres of population of this country hang upon the quality of the imigration.

There is also an industrial danger in this matter of imigration. Machinery makes it possible for cheap labor to undersell skilled work. And so we have in manufacturing towns of our country the survival of the unfittest. Irishmen drive out Americans; French Canadians drive out Irishmen; Poles and Italians drive out French Canadians; and the Lord only knows what is coming to drive out these. Now in the coal-mining districts of Pennsylvania, and in some of the districts of Illinois, the native-born and the naturalized laborer is being driven out by these foreign imigrants, — a class from which you can neither expect national patriotism or a sense of civic duty. Now I contend these are great perils. They put a tremendous strain upon all our institutions of industry and government and religion. And yet, dear friends, there are some counteracting tendencies. Fifteen per cent of this imigration falls out by death and return; so that the ratio of percentage of foreign-born and native population is steadily diminishing. And then again, the second and third generation of the better class of imigrants, through public opinion as voiced in the press, the pulpit, the platform, and the factory, gradually shake off all Old-World notions, and adopt American ideals; and the public-school system of the country, and the Sunday-school system of the country, complete this work of transformation. A careful English writer and a student of our institutions has said that what strikes the traveller and what the American delights to point to him is the amazing solvent power which American institutions, ideas, and habits have over the newcomers from the Old World; and he adds this encouraging judgment. He says, "I 'venture to believe that the moral and religious atmosphere into which the settlers of the old country come will exercise greater power over them in assimilating them to American ideals than they, in their racial qualities, will exercise in changing it." That certainly is a glorious thing if it be true. But there are three lines along which I think this problem must be solved. First, we must maintain our simple, original American ideals, by the force of an aroused public sentiment, at their highest point. The best element of this country must not yield the ideas upon which thus far the destiny of the nation has advanced. Secondly, the government in its national authority must pass adequate laws and execute them to shut out from this country the pauper and vicious classes of Europe. We are perfectly willing to have America as an asylum for the oppressed and down-trodden of all nations, but I do not think we ought to be asked to turn it into a poorhouse and prison or a madhouse. And thirdly, the church must convert the whole power of a combined and quickened Christian, as realized in this Christian Endeavor movement; must put its whole force to bear upon the stranger within our gates, to win him to the love and service of Jesus Christ. And here is the need, the imperative need, of home missions.

Now the next problem is a very delicate and intricate one: the race, or the negro problem. I want to say I am an orphan, born in the State of New York, educated in the State of Massachusetts, having lived some years in the State of Missouri, was sent seven years out of the Union on a vacation by my church to the State of New Jersey, but have returned again to my first love: so I want to discuss this question fairly, and without the prejudice of a section. Now these are the factors in this problem. About one-eighth of our people, eight million, are negroes. In the eight States lying nearest the Gulf these negroes increased during the decade of 1880 to 1890 at the rate of nineteen and one-tenth per cent; while in the rest of the South the rate of increase was only five and a half per cent. This shows that the centre of negro population is steadily moving southward, and that the natural home of the negro, therefore, by the ordination of God, must be in that low and warm climate. Another factor, the relative proportion between the negro and the white, is steadily changing against the negro. In 1790 the negroes were nearly one-fifth of our population; in 1881, one-seventh; 1890, less than one-eighth. In one hundred years they had relatively decreased from one-fifth to less than one-eighth. Even in the eight black States the increase of the whites from '80 to '90 was ten per cent greater than the increase of the negroes; so that we may conclude from these figures that the negro is a relatively diminishing element in this problem. The third fact, their industrial condition, is complex. Any man who makes a general statement about the industrial condition of the negro is an ignoramus or a fool. It changes with every changing locality of the country. There can be therefore no deduction of a general sort. Everywhere throughout the South they are the poorest and the socially lowest stratum of society. They furnish nine-tenths of the unskilled labor; comparatively few of them are skilled workmen. In rural districts the vast majority are ordinary laborers. An increasing number, however, are working small farms that they own. And there is a great ray of hope. In cities they are improving industrially because they have to work for a living and are coming in contact with the whites constantly. Many in the cities are becoming well-to-do, and some of them are rich; but in localities outside of cities, needing to work but little and left to their own resources — my brothers, I speak the truth when I say that they are in danger of lapsing in barbarism.

Now this is one side of the problem and it is the black side. But let us look now on the other. Certain very definite influences are at work. First, schools in elementary education since their emancipation. The negro has made the most marvellous and wonderful progress of any race merging from barbarism. Their desire for education is pathetic. They have got the idea — I am talking now of the great mass of negroes, not of our Northern negroes, not of the more intelligent ones in the South,— but the great mass of negroes in the South have got the idea somehow that the white man gets the ability to live without working with his hands through his knowledge of books. And they believe thoroughly that if they can get the same book knowledge they will be saved the awful grind of manual toil. This is a stimulus, therefore, to them to improve every opportunity, so that from the year 1877 to 1889, while the white pupils in the country schools of the South increased seventy per cent, the colored pupils increased one hundred and thirteen per cent. In higher education, 25,000 schools, a million and a half of people in them, is a wonderful development, and since 1876 over $80,000,000 has been spent by the North and the South in this matter of negro education. Let me say it to the credit of our Southern people, over fifty millions of which have been raised by the South through taxation. Now what would go far, I think, to solve this problem of the negro is that in all our effort to educate them, together with the academic training we give, we should also put, as the basis of it all, an industrial and a manual training. Teach them the dignity of labor, as has been done at Hampton. You saw before you to-day four of the noble students of Hampton. During the years that institution has been in existence five thousand negroes have been educated to use their hands and their brains, and have been sent out to be the healers of their people throughout the South.

Now another powerful influence in moulding the negro is religion. They are extremely responsive to religious appeal, though large numbers,— I am sorry, as it is true in the North,— with large numbers religion is purely emotional and often divorced from morality. Nor did the long years of their bondage teach them truly the distinction between *meum* and *tuum*. And we must remember this,— that almost all races that have emerged from low conditions of civilization have done it through a long period of time, and this emergence has been gradual. These people were lifted out of their bondage by a stroke of the pen. But the government made a mistake — you will pardon me if I say it made a mistake; but it will not be liable to repeat the mistake in the case of the Philippines — when they put into the hands of this race all of the privileges and franchises of the freest government known on the globe. We here find the most serious of all this terrible trouble in the South. My friends, I have but a moment more, but I want to call your attention to the industrial problem, the problem of the family and home; but I do want to say this, too: that you people who come from the North ought to clearly understand that in this matter of the negro problem there are two sides. There is not a white man in the North who, if his wife or daughter were outraged by a beast, would not inevitably and instantly revenge it; and yet the time will come, and must come, when governments, unless it be a rope of sand, shall step in on the one hand and punish crime, and on the other stop and punish with the severest penalties this diabolic matter of lynching. The solution of the negro problem rests in the application of the great truths of Christianity both to the black and white. The dear brethren and sisters of the South must think and dwell more upon these two great facts that are the substantial and underlying facts of Christianity; namely, the fact of a common nature, and the fact of a common relationship to Jesus Christ, who died for all. Here is the cement of love that ultimately will settle this question. Legislation cannot do it, but Christianity can and will, if we have patience, forbearance, and the grace and spirit of God.

Mr. Howard's address was a temperance whirlwind. He is a little man, but a giant orator. How the ringing sentences flashed from their scabbards! — "Shall we postpone the destruction of the saloon till, as some say, we can find a substitute for it? As well shut up the churches till we have found a substitute for the devil." "Shall we license the saloon? As well expose your baby to disease, and than spank it for having the measles. As well expect to cure consumption by levying a tax on microbes." "Shall we wait and discuss? Would a man stop to bait a mouse-trap while a burglar was firing the house?"

Address by Mr. C. N. Howard,

Rochester, N. Y.

The Nation's Greatest Foe.

The American people are face to face with a mighty problem. It is not, What shall be done with Cuba or the Philippines? but, How shall we restore to the people the right of self-government in the United States? It would seem that democracy had given place to rumocracy. The American people have abdicated the throne of government to the saloon. Red-handed anarchy spits upon our laws, insults our flag, robs our homes, curses our motherhood, and damns our children, while we are pouring out the nation's treasure and offering our sons to the god of war to shoot the Declaration of Independence into the hearts of the insurgents at Manila.

We are sending our young men half way around the globe to teach the half-breeds of the far East respect for law, and allow rebels against the flag, rebels against our laws, rebels against our homes, to walk the streets of our cities, infest the camps of our soldiers, smite with moral paralysis our public officials, and furnish opinions for the national government. National expansion is demanded, and the first cargo of American products to follow the flag is a train-load of Milwaukee beer. Bishop Thoburn of the Methodist Episcopal Church is on the ground, and writes from Manila, " Every alternate place of business is a liquor-shop. Drunken soldiers meet me everywhere, and it is painful to remember that many of them have come from Christian homes and have been thrust into the very jaws of temptation." God pity the boys in Manila if, in addition to the bullets of the enemy and the tropical climate, they are to be deluged with beer. And pity their mothers.

At home, in spite of the law of Congress as plain as language could frame, so understood by the leaders in both Senate and House, accepted by the press, and Grigged to death by a jugglery of words that is an insult to common sense, the canteen continues to pour hell down the throats of the boys in the army. Ten thousand people cheered the boys of Rochester the day they marched away to battle at their country's call. Ten thousand gathered to welcome them back. Who was missing? Private Kelley, who was killed by a fellow soldier in a drunken row at the canteen! Sergeant Edwin Stuart, once the slave of strong drink, but living for several years a sober life with his family at Fort Portland, where the canteen was not allowed, is transferred to Fort Hamilton, with head-quarters next door to the canteen, succumbs to temptation, suicides after a debauch, and leaves his wife and two little boys, whom I found in wretched poverty, a legacy of $18 in overdrawn beer checks on the canteen. At the hand of one man God will require their blood. Not satisfied with young blood, this demon demands his pound of flesh and pound of gold from the old veterans of '61, who, housed in homes provided at the people's expense, weakened by old age and ill-health, are surrounded with dives and made the prey of the highwaymen and the harlot. For example, at the Soldiers' Home at Leavenworth there are 2,500 old soldiers, old men of feeble mind and broken-down health, wards of the nation, drawing pensions for services rendered the flag. Here, adjoining the home, in violation of the law, is a nest of twenty joints known as The Klondike, run by a gang of criminals who entice these old men in to maltreat and rob them. Old soldier after old soldier has been murdered in those dens for the little pensions paid them by the government. The day I visited that town, on June 8th last, one old comrade in a drunken frenzy murdered another in one of those law-defying dens, and the governor of the home appealed to Governor Stanley in behalf of these wards of the nation — and appealed in vain. Such facts are almost enough to drive patriotism from the heart. Shame on the government! Shame on the people! And as for Governor Stanley, he ought to suppress the whiskey rebellion at Leavenworth, or be sent to the penitentiary as an accomplice to the crime.

The immoral condition of our great cities is a blot on our civilization. The saloon runs the caucus, names the candidate, robs the public, and spits on the law. I read an interview with a New York millionaire the other day in which he emphasized the fact that nearly all the men of affairs, successful business men, and men in professional life in our great cities were boys that came from the farm or were reared in the small town. He lamented the fact that rich men's sons reared in the city seldom amounted to much; and he wondered why. Well, if the poor old innocent does n't know, I 'll tell him the reason why. It is because the moral tone of our great cities is so low, vice is so open, so alluring, so tempting, the saloon, with the gaming-table in the rear and the scarlet women upstairs, is so numerous, that it is almost impossible to raise a boy in the city without sending him to hell. God pity a tempted boy that walks the streets of an American city after the fall of night!

Down in the slums of New York goes a mother's boy — penniless, ragged, dirty, drunk. Down he goes, lower and yet lower. Debauch follows debauch, until the delirium seizes him; crime follows crime, until the penitentiary shields him. Then he hears the story of the Christ. Out of the slough of despond, out of the pit of perdition, the love of Christ digs him. Clothed and in his right mind, he testifies for the Master. For four years, in mission and music hall, he preaches Christ to lost men. Last November he came to Rochester and told a thousand men that the title of " B. A." after Bernard Rielly meant " Born Again." Where is he to-day? His body lies buried in the Potter's Field of St. Louis. He disappointed an audience at the Y. M. C. A. on Sunday, and died in the pauper's hospital of alcoholism the next day. Slain by rum!

War has slain its thousands; rum has slain its tens of thousands. Cut the usual estimate in half, and it would require one hundred whole trains, ten cars long, with sixty dead bodies in every car, to carry the remains. It would make a funeral procession, hearse following hearse, from Detroit to Dubuque, and fill a trench with dead bodies, end to end, sixty-eight miles long. To simply state the case is to answer the question. Why multiply examples? The saloon is the nation's greatest foe because it murders its citizens in cold blood; because it destroys the character of its citizens, the units upon which the national structure rests; because it fosters ignorance, immorality, and crime, which sap the vitals of the nation, and means death to a democracy founded upon the virtue and intelligence of its subjects; because it defiles the ballot, entrenches the boss, defies the law, and impoverishes the people. It is a crime against the State, a crime against humanity, a crime against God. It has opened dens of anarchy; schooled our young manhood to a life of sensual indulgence, personal impurity, and profanity; sickened the public conscience with its daily horrible detail of debauchery, deviltry, and crime; blocked the wheels of every righteous reform; paralyzed industry; crucified labor; defeated the church, outraged the heathen, and blasphemed the Almighty.

These are the facts about the country's greatest foe, and it would be adding crime to crime to simply state them and offer no remedy. The mighty question that should engross the head, the heart, and hand of the Christian citizenship of America is not, What is the country's greatest foe? for on that thoughtful men are everywhere agreed; but, What shall be done with the nation's greatest foe? Shall we take a revenue from it? Shall we engage in what has been proclaimed from pulpit and press as God's Holy War to break the yoke of oppression and set at liberty them that are bruised, and assess the devil's business to pay the bill? Shall we subscribe to a system that, during peace or war, proposes to bottom the revenues of this Christian nation on a barrel of beer and whiskey? Our revenue system is founded upon the avarice of the people, and is a curse to the nation.

It was avarice that led King Midas, to whom was offered whatsoever he wished, to choose the golden touch; who found himself naked, for it changed his garments into threads of gold; starving, for the food became metal in his mouth; dying of thirst, for his lips turned the water into a solid mass. One kiss turned his sweet child into a gold statue. In an agony of despair he besought the gods to remove the curse, and, instead of the golden touch, he asked for a cup of cold water, a cluster of fruit, and the love of his child. Let the nation learn that on every dollar that the liquor traffic pays into the public treasury there is human blood, human sorrow, human nakedness, human hunger and death, and the avarice of the people that reconciles them to this iniquity will yet bring upon us the curse of heaven to teach us the lesson that "better is a little with righteousness than great revenues without right."

What shall we do with the nation's greatest foe? Shall we delay doing the right thing about it, as some contend, until we find a substitute for it? Of all propositions proposed, this is the most childish. A substitute for the saloon! A substitute for the gambling-hell! A substitute for the house of shame! You might as well close up the church until you can find a substitute for the devil! The only substitute for slavery was liberty. The only substitute for disease is health. The only substitute for wrong is right. The only substitute for the saloon is — *no saloon.* Give the homes of the country a chance, and we will not need a substitute for the saloon.

What shall we do with the nation's greatest foe? Shall we regulate it? Shall we say, "You may keep open all the week, but you must close on Sunday"? "You must not sell to an Indian, but you can debauch our white men"? "You must not sell to a man that's drunk, but you can intoxicate a man that's sober"? "You must not sell after midnight, when the people are in bed, but you may sell after they get up"? "You must not sell to a man after he gets into the penitentiary, but may make a criminal of him, send him there, and sell him after he gets out"? The biggest farce outside of perdition are the laws on the statute-books of America that were passed to regulate the saloon. You might as well propagate the smallpox throughout the week and attempt to quarantine it on Sunday; you might as well expose your baby and spank it for catching the measles; you might as well try to regulate consumption by a tax on microbes.

The license laws of America are the biggest humbug that language ever framed into law. Under them a mother's boy is not safe until after he gets into the penitentiary. Regulation will plant a saloon opposite the factory, on every corner of the main street, and next door to a boys' home; burn out his manhood, school him in crime, and send him in to State's prison; and after bolting the ponderous door, stands upon the threshold with colossal mockery and says to the liquor traffic, "Thou shalt not come in." In the name of God, unbar the door; swing it open wide; let in the rum-seller; let in the saloon; let in the brewery; let in the distillery — now then, swing to the doors; make sure the bars; train on the guns, and let the laws of this Christian republic proclaim in thunder tones, "Thou shalt not come out!" Away with all this tomfoolery about regulating deviltry, and raising the price of sin that grace may abound, and estimating the power of the law for righteousness by the price charged for an indulgence; it is unmanly, un-American, and un-Christian.

What shall we do with the nation's greatest foe? Shall we compromise with it? Shall we say, "We can't get what is right, therefore let us demand something less that can be had"? Well, you would get a good deal more by demanding all than you get by surrendering half before you make any demand at all. The most demoralizing thing on earth is a compromise with wrong; and it is as cowardly as it is demoralizing, and as devilish as it is cowardly. The man that talks about compromising with principles of morality is a moral monstrosity.

Napoleon shortened the stature of the French people two inches by choosing all the taller of his thirty million subjects and killing them off in war. Horace Mann says that the forehead of the Irish peasantry was lowered an inch when the government made it an offence punishable with imprisonment and death to be the teacher of children. And when a Christian man consents to compromise with such a fearful iniquity I believe that his moral character shrinks in the presence of God.

The framers of the Constitution compromised with slavery in the colonies, and their children paid billions of treasure and half a million lives for their folly. Thomas Jefferson emphasized the declaration that "all men are created equal" by a clause in which he defined the words "*all men*" to include all men, black or white, bond or free; and this clause was dropped out by the Continental Congress to avoid giving offence to the slave-holders. They imagined the question would settle itself. They thought it could be hid by their failure to mention it in the Constitution. But brave John Randolph said, "Sir, I know there are gentlemen who think this unhappy question of negro slavery, which the Constitution has vainly tried to blink by not using the term, should never be brought to public notice. Sir, it is a thing which cannot be hid. You might as well try to hide a volcano in full operation." But the devil of compromise had done its work, and it took blood to erase the stain. A nation that compromises with the liquor traffic is building a volcano under the liberties of its people; and as God lives, the day of eruption will surely come, and the longer the delay the deeper the stain and the more blood it will take to wipe it out. Away with all suggestions of compromise with this diabolism of the devil. You might as well ask the dove to compromise with the hawk; you might as well ask the lamb to compromise with the wolf; you might as well plant a snowball in January and expect to reap a toboggan-slide in June, as to hope to reap righteousness by a compromise with iniquity.

A compromise that leaves one saloon leaves one too many, and a compromise that gives us 200,000 saloons in America to-day is a disgrace to our civilization, a crime against the people, and an insult to the throne of God. And no amount of money paid into the public treasury, and no kind of legislation that provides for its continued existence, and no questions of political expediency, and no love for political party, ought to reconcile the Christian conscience of America to the legalized whiskey traffic for another hour. If this is the nation's greatest foe, it is the nation's greatest question — and it ought to be given first place. To turn aside from this overshadowing evil to consider the questions of tariff, finance, trusts, expansion, great as they are, is like stopping to bait the mouse-trap while a burglar is firing the house.

It is high time for some kind of an organization to teach the people that lesson, — to teach them that the free coinage of boys into drunkards, of men into maniacs, of homes into hovels, is a bigger question than the free coinage of silver; that protection to the homes of the nation is a bigger question than the amount of tariff that shall be assessed on a barrel of axle-grease; that the destiny of the liquor traffic at home is a larger question than the destiny of the nation beyond the sea.

If America is to fill her divinely appointed mission as the civilizer of mankind, if she is to carry the blessings of liberty and self-government around the world, we have got to raise the standard of public life at home. I doubt much our success in bettering conditions abroad until we change them at home. I see little hope of changing the conditions at home until the church of Christ takes a definite, positive, and aggressive hand in the fight. Let us sever notice on the statesmen of the day, on the political parties that boss the statesmen, on the boss that bosses the political parties, and the people that submit like dumb dogs to being bossed, that our votes cannot be had for any other issue unless it includes the abolition of the saloon. I commit you to no political party. I do commit you to the principle of local, state, and national prohibitory law — as the only solution of this modern monopoly of abomination in harmony with the Word of God and the Constitution of the country that guarantees life, liberty, and the pursuit of happiness to all the people, and the right to destroy, debauch, and damn to none; and standing on that declaration, to go where it leads as straight as a lightning-rod points toward the sky.

The brewers' national organ says, " If we find that one political party is against us, we must support the other. Self-protection must be our only guide. Beer first, and then politicians." That is good gospel for us. If you find the first party opposed to your demands for the prohibition of the saloon, support the second; if you find the second in league with the saloon, support the third; if, for conscientious reasons, you are unable to support that, make one of your own. *First right*, then politics. *First God*, then politicians. On such a platform as that the Christian citizens of America could shake the throne of perdition. There is enough moral dynamite in this single gathering to blow up the rum power within the lives of men whose heads are already gray.

There are, no doubt, more than a thousand preachers at this Convention. No other profession can gather together into one convention a body of men that will equal the brains, culture, personal integrity, and moral power of a thousand American preachers who are ministers of the gospel of the Son of God; and if they only knew their power and used it without fear or favor to glorify God in the service of the people, they could build a railroad to hell and send the rum power home on the first train. Daniel Webster said, "There is not a monarch on earth whose throne cannot be shaken by public opinion." America is ruled by public opinion, and one hundred thousand preachers, backed up, as they would be, by two million men from the pews, could whip into life a public opinion that would demolish the throne of the rum power inside of ten years. God wake them up to their divine opportunity and their awful responsibility ! The Christian church could confer no greater blessing upon mankind, or bestow any greater honor upon her Lord, than by doing that.

" Thy kingdom come "— that was the prayer of Jesus. " Thy kingdom come " — that was the mission of the Son of God. " Thy kingdom come "— that is the mission of his church in the world. Not to take men to heaven; but to bring heaven to men.

How to live before how to die.
How to walk before how to fly.
How to lose before how to gain.
How to fight before how to reign.

" To heal the broken-hearted; to preach deliverance to the captive; to set at liberty them that are bruised "—and that means war against every institution that defiles, degrades, and enslaves men ; war against every institution that bruises the bodies of little children and breaks the sacred heart of women; war against sin, war against oppression, war against Satan. " And there was war in heaven. And the great dragon, that old serpent called the devil and satan, was cast out." I go in for a war against the saloon devil in the United States !

"And there was war in heaven. And Michael and his angels fought." Let the saints of God upon the earth stop making faces at the saloon-keeper, stop framing indictments, stop passing resolutions, and *fight*. Fight—with the weapon that God has placed in the hands of every Christian citizen, and we can cast the rum devil off from the earth. Onward, Church of God in the United States; onward, Young People's Society of Christian Endeavor; onward, Epworth Leagues; onward, six million Christian voting men; onward, twenty million Christian women.

"*And I saw heaven opened, and behold a white horse; and he that sat upon him was called faithful and true, and in righteousness he doth judge and make war.*"

"*His eyes were as a flame of fire. . . . He was clothed in a vesture dipped in blood; . . . and the armies which were in heaven followed him upon white horses; . . . and out of his mouth goeth a sharp sword that with it he should smite the nations: and he shall rule them with a rod of iron: and he treadeth the winepress of the fierceness of the wrath of Almighty God.*"

"*And he hath on his vesture and on his thigh a name written, King of kings and Lord of lords.*"

In the name of Jesus Christ as King, the liquor traffic must die.

Dr. Jefferson carried the great session to a climax with an oration full of thought and power. Of course the "one salvation" he proposed for our country is the religion of Christ. "What our nation wants is not more money, more arts, more science, but *more men*."

Address by Rev. C. E. Jefferson, D.D.,
New York City.
OUR COUNTRY'S ONE SALVATION.

You know what it is before I tell you. Peter divulged the secret over 1,800 years ago, when he said in the city of Jerusalem, "There is none other name under heaven given among men whereby we must be saved." He was speaking to Jewish rulers and leaders and scribes, but he spoke as the representative of humanity. He used a personal pronoun which took in the world,— "whereby we must be saved." That "we" is one of the largest pronouns in the New Testament. It swept out beyond the borders of Judea and took in Samaria and Greece and Rome; and stretching itself outward, it covered the Barbarians and the Scythians and far-away people dwelling in the uttermost ends of the earth. Peter not only spoke for all humanity, but for all time. His thought swept out across the centuries, embracing all kingdoms and principalities and powers, all races and nations and tribes; and coming down to the nineteenth century, it takes in the republic of the West. So that Peter's words translated into the vocabulary of to-day are: "There is none other name under heaven given among men whereby America must be saved."

Mark that word "must." It has an arbitrary and peremptory sound. But that is not peculiar to St. Peter; that is not an illustration of Hebrew narrowness and bigotry; we catch that same tone all through the discourses of Jesus. Listen to him as he says. "This is the stone which the builders rejected; the same is made the head of the corner. He that falleth on this stone shall be broken to pieces; but on whomsoever it shall fall, it will scatter him as dust." The Son of God has said that there is but one way that leads unto life, and that all other ways lead unto death. "No one cometh unto the Father but by me." "No one knoweth the Father save the Son and he to whom the Son shall reveal him." "Agonize to enter it at the strait gate, for many shall seek to enter in and shall not be able." So thoroughly was this thought burned into the marrow and blood of the apostles that they all felt just as the writer to the Hebrews felt when he wrote: "How shall we escape if we neglect so great salvation?" Christianity is not Christianity if we drop out the word "must." Jesus used it himself. He taught his disciples to use it. It is a word which God

THE PEACE JUBILEE AT BELLE ISLE.

uses when he speaks to his children. The laws of religion are as inexorable as the laws of mathematics or physics. There is only one remedy; there is only one physician; there is only one foundation-stone for men and for nations. There is only one salvation whereby we must be saved. All this is as true of nations as it is of men. Nations, like men, have their responsibilities and their duties. To each nation, as to each individual, is given a task, a trust, a work. Nations, like men, live under law. Obedience brings life. Disobedience brings death. Retribution does not come so soon to a nation as to a man, but it comes. God is long-suffering, but he never spares the guilty. As Anne of Austria used to say, "He does not pay at the end of every week, but he pays." He is the maker of the universe and the ruler of it, and he has marked the road along which a nation's feet must walk, if it is not to be humiliated and over-whelmed.

> "Though the mills of God grind slowly,
> Yet they grind exceeding small;
> Though with patience he stands waiting,
> With exactness grinds he all."

Whenever we speak of salvation we take it for granted that there is a pos-sibility of being lost. But can America be lost? We do not like to think it. It seems preposterous! After such a past, could America be cast away? After the sacrifices of the Pilgrims and the heroism of the Puritans and the daring and achievements of the heroes of revolutionary days? Surely the nation whose foundations were laid in tears and blood, and whose entire career has been marked by the bloody sweat of men, cannot be permitted to perish from the earth.

> "We know what master laid thy keel,
> What workmen wrought thy ribs of steel,
> Who made each mast and sail and rope,
> What anvils rang and hammers beat,
> In what a forge and what a heat
> Were shaped the anchors of thy hope."

And knowing this, it seems incredible that America should ever be in danger.

We look round about us, and on every side there are marks of national prosperity and progress. What an age it is we are living in, and what a coun-try! Innumerable nations have longed to see the things which we see, and were not able. No other century since time began has ever made so many in-ventions and discoveries. It was only yesterday that the untamed forces of nature came trooping out of the wilderness of matter, looking up into man's eyes to find out what he wished to call them.

In our day the elemental forces of the universe have grown tame and docile, and man uses them at his will. No other century ever saw a railroad-train or a steamship. No other century ever used the telegraph, the telephone, the graphophone. The people of no other century ever struck a match or saw an electric light. No other century ever took a photograph or used a typewriter. No other men since the world began ever were able to see through a human body, or were able to tear to pieces the flaming atmospheres of the stars. With water our servant and steam our slave, with the winds our drudges and electric forces our fiery hoofed steeds, with the rivers and tides and constella-tions all fighting for us, with the vast and mysterious forces of God's universe making obeisance to us, surely we are safe against every danger and able to conquer every foe.

The future only deepens our conviction that America is safe. We cannot think of the map of the earth with America blotted out. We cannot think of the family of nations without our republic standing in the midst, beautiful and triumphant. The future needs us. The Orient stretches out her arms to this young nation of the West, asking for culture, law, religion. The weary and oppressed in every land turn their eyes toward our flag. For uncounted thou-sands of years humanity travailed in pain to bring forth the principles for which our flag floats, and lives of innumerable martyrs have been built into the foundations of the institutions which are our glory and pride. America lost! We cannot think it. We say with the poet: —

> "Sail on, O Ship of State,
> Sail on, O Union, strong and great,
> Fear not each sudden bound and shock;
> It is the wave and not the rock.
>
> "It is but the flapping of the sail,
> And not a rent made by the gale.
> In spite of rock and tempest roar,
> In spite of false lights on the shore,
> Sail on, nor fear to breast the sea;
> Our hearts, our hopes, are all with thee,
> Our hearts, our hopes, our prayers, our tears,
> Our faith triumphant o'er our fears,
> Are all with thee, are all with thee."

But we cannot rely altogether on the testimony of the past. Greece had a mighty past, but Greece perished. We cannot rely on the evidences of the present. There was a time when Rome was mistress of the world, and evidences of might were so abundant that men dared to call her the eternal city — but Rome fell. We cannot build upon our hopes, for hopes often come to naught. The only thing which standeth sure is the Word of the Lord. Nothing is eternal but his judgment throne. It is eternal truth that righteousness exalteth a nation and sin is a reproach to any people. It has been decreed, and the decree can never be changed, the wicked shall be turned into hades, and all the nations that forget God. No nation is ever out of danger; but from the highest pinnacle of prosperity and fame there is a road which leads to death.

That our nation is sick everybody is agreed. A great host of doctors have gathered around her, and every man of them is ready to write a prescription. It is intensely interesting to listen to the remedies which are vociferously proposed. There is a pandemonium of conflicting voices. One says, We must have a new industrial system; the old order is rotten and ready to be burned. Socialism in some form or other is our only salvation. Another man says, We must have a new system of taxation. The present system is unjust. Give us an equitable system of taxation and present troubles will disappear. Another man says, We need a new political party. The old parties have outlived their usefulness. They are antiquated and corrupt. They are run by demagogues who care nothing for the people. Give us a new political party pledged to great reforms, and all will go well. Another man says, Give us a new financial system; the present system places us at the mercy of the lords of money. Give us more silver and more greenbacks and prosperity will rush in like a flood. Others say, Give us larger markets. Let us push our way into foreign lands. Let us back up our pretensions with a mighty army and a mighty navy, and become a great world power. Another man says, Give us more education. Let us build more schoolhouses. Let us instruct the masses in science and literature, and crime will diminish and the future will be safe.

But alas, these panaceas are only superficial. Not one of them goes beneath the surface. They do not reach the roots of any of our ills. What this nation needs is manhood — the manhood which is exemplified in Jesus of Nazareth. There is no other character under heaven given among men whereby we must be saved. Is there an evil which Christian manhood will not cure? Is there a problem which Christian manhood will not settle? Is there a danger which Christian manhood will not enable us to escape? Is there a demon or a dragon which Christian manhood cannot trample into the dust? God give us men!

> "God give us men! A time like this demands
> Strong minds, great hearts, true faith, and ready hands;
> Men whom the lust of office does not kill;
> Men whom the spoils of office cannot buy;
> Men who possess opinions and a will;
> Men who have honor, — men who will not lie;
> Men who can stand before a demagogue
> And damn his treacherous flatteries without winking;
> Tall men, sun-crowned, who live above the fog
> In public duty and in private thinking."

What are we going to do with the liquor traffic? Our nation is putting into its mouth an enemy which steals away men's brains. We spend more for alcoholic drinks every year, than we spend for meat and bread and clothes; more than we spend for churches and for schools. The havoc wrought by alcoholism is indescribable and beyond calculation. Ceaseless processions of paupers and lunatics and imbeciles and criminals move out from the doors of the saloon, and what is our remedy? Somebody says, More legislation. Legislation is good, but it is not enough. Nothing but a spirit that will lift men above the lusts of the flesh is capable of casting out so great a demon.

What are we going to do with our cities? They are growing larger every year. Streams of population from the four ends of the earth keep flowing into them. Every city is a menace to the welfare of the nation. All our great cities are politically corrupt, — the most corrupt cities in Christendom. At the top of society thousands live in luxury. At the bottom of society other thousands starve and rot. Dives dresses in fine linen and fares sumptuously every day, and Lazarus curses because he gets nothing but crumbs. What are we going to do with our social separations and gulfs that divide different classes of men? How are we going to bridge the chasms? Somebody says, By legislation. Legislation is good, but it will not reach the heart of the trouble. Our redemption lies in a reconstructed manhood. Unless we have men with the sympathy of Jesus of Nazareth we are lost.

What are we going to do with capitalism? It is growing with the years. The wealth of the nation is being gathered up and concentrated in a few hands. Out of the industrial river great corporations emerge, swallowing up the smaller corporations that preceded them just as the seven kine in Pharaoh's vision ate up the seven that had gone before. What shall we do with our corporations and trusts? Somebody says, Give us new legislation. Legislation is good, but it is not enough. Love alone is sufficient for these things. Love is the only fire hot enough to melt the mountains of gold now held by the rich, and to set it flowing in streams which will gladden the earth. What can stay the madness of greed, and what can check the insanity of avarice, but the spirit of the man who announced and lived the Golden Rule?

What are we going to do with militarism? — one of the blackest demons that ever came up out of the pit. Having desolated the Old World, it is now endeavoring to find a foothold in the new. For more than a quarter of a century the military establishments of Europe have been growing larger and larger, impoverishing the people, till only recently the Czar of all the Russias cried out in a voice that startled the nations, "Is there nothing we can do to save us from going over the precipice?" But notwithstanding the awful experience of Europe, notwithstanding mighty nations have been brought to the verge of bankruptcy, and a spirit of discontent and bitterness has been generated in the hearts of the masses which threatens to burst into flame and burn up the very framework of society, we have editors and politicians and leaders who say we ought to follow the example of Europe and cover the ocean with our battle-ships, and build up an army which will awe the world. What shall cast this demon out? Certainly not arguments, for militarism is an insanity that cannot be argued with. This kind of demon goes out only by prayer and fasting. We need a change of heart. Nothing will save us but the vision of that man who never strove or cried aloud in the streets, who would not allow his followers to draw a sword, who rode into Jerusalem on the day of his triumph on the back of an ass, and whose loftiest title is — Prince of Peace.

What are we going to do with political indifferentism? Our problems are growing increasingly complicated, but men are too busy to attend to their political duties. Thousands of our citizens never attend a caucus or a primary. Thousands never vote at all. While good men busy themselves in making money, bad men run the political machine, working themselves into office. What is the remedy? Shall we confess that government of the people by the people and for the people is a failure and ought to perish from the earth? No! We need a change in the hearts of men. Give us the self-sacrificing spirit of the Carpenter of Nazareth; give us his courage and his enthusiasm, and we will enter the desecrated halls of the republic and drive the rascals out.

What are we going to do with scepticism? Millions of our people are living without hope and without God in the world. There are millions who never enter the door of a church. There are millions who never pray. In an age of unbelief it is not surprising that every heathen superstition and every crazy speculation should number its devotees by the thousand. Mormonism and Buddhism and Theosophy and Christian Science—these are a few of the modern manifestations of the spiritual disease of the century. No matter how silly the superstition or preposterous its claims, it finds enthusiastic and devoted defenders. Who shall deliver us from these superstitions and errors? He who is the sanest man who ever lived, the man who said, "You shall know the truth, and the truth shall make you free."

We have an abundance of everything in America but manhood. We do not need money. We have more gold than any other nation on earth. We are piling up wealth faster than any nation has done it since time began. But a nation's life consists not in the abundance of the things which it possesses. Men have died on the Yukon trail with their pockets filled with money, and nations have gone down to ruin with their treasuries filled with gold. We do not need anything which nature can give. Our natural resources are boundless. Our rivers are broad and deep; our fields are fertile; our forests are illimitable; our mines are inexhaustible. No more beautiful country ever lay beneath a flag. But the King of heaven takes lands away from those who do not use them for his glory. We have law in abundance. Legislatures and Congresses have been endeavoring for more than a hundred years to work out into statutes suitable for our condition the everlasting principles of justice. We have great court-houses and wise judges, but the law cannot save us. Thousands of men and women are murdered every year under our flag, and millions of money are stolen every year by American men. We have ability; no other nation has ever had more. We have an intellectuality that sounds the depths and scales the heights and dares all things. We have a genius for invention, and have placed our feet on the neck of the wild forces of nature. But we have not yet subdued our own spirit. We have extensive, varying, enormous knowledge. The wisdom of the centuries and the continents is garnered in our great libraries. Our schoolgirls go beyond Solon and Solomon, and our college graduates know a thousand things of which Plato and Aristotle never dreamed. We have a great past. Heroes and saints in shining galaxies look down on us, encouraging us, inspiring us. We have a great opportunity. We can blaze the way along which the nations are to travel out of their darkness and trouble into the golden age. Shall we seize it? Shall we use it? Not if we rely on knowledge or law or money or force. America's one salvation is obedience to that man who was crucified upon the cross, and who now, enthroned in the heavens, is King of kings and Lord of lords.

Tent Endeavor.

The heavens were very generous with their moisture before the Quiet Hour closed on Monday morning; but, true to its record, Tent Endeavor was full.

Rev. C. E. Bronson, D.D., of Saginaw, Mich., conducted the devotional exercises, and Mr. Excell had charge of the singing. Dr. Clark, who presided, introduced severally the twenty-eight foreign missionaries present, each one responding in the native tongue of the land whence he came,—Japan, China, India, Brazil, Korea, Cuba, Mexico, Africa, Persia, Turkey, and so on through a long list.

President Clark said:—

There are a number of people now coming to the platform to whom you will give the Chautauquan salute. They are our missionaries, they are our warriors, they are our generals upon the foreign field; they come from all parts of the world; they represent all denominations. I am going to introduce them to you, and I am going to ask them, as they come to the front, to give you some greeting in their own language, or some verse of Scripture in their own language; and whether you understand it or not, it does not make much difference, but I want you to hear their tongue. I wish there were hours and hours for this service, but we have had to crowd everything in our crowded Convention, and we must run on time, even in this. This is Rev. Elwood G. Tewksbury.

Mr. Tewksbury ascended the platform, and was saluted by the audience with the Chautauquan salute and applause.

President Clark: Mr. Tewksbury is a missionary of the American Board in North China.

Mr. Tewksbury spoke a few words of greeting in Chinese.

President Clark: And now will you salute Miss Annie Lincoln Forest, of the Methodist Protestant Church, who has been five years in Negauye, Japan.

Miss Forest was given the Chautauquan salute and applause, and sang in Japanese, " Nearer, My God, to Thee."

President Clark: Now you will salute Rev. and Mrs. James L. Fowle, of Turkey; and let me tell you a little story at the beginning. Mr. Fowle, Mrs. Clark, and I took a long journey of two weeks across Asia Minor, from Tarsus, the old

A Corner in the Missionary Exhibit.

city of St. Paul, clear to Constantinople, in one of the two or three wagons there are in Turkey in which civilized man can ride. Mr. Fowle took this long journey across the mountains there, seven days to the seashore, to get us and take us to his own home in Cæsarea, and then across to Constantinople. I want you to give Mr. and Mrs. Fowle a greeting, and he will say two or three sentences concerning the work which he loves.

Mr. and Mrs. Fowle were loudly cheered, and were saluted with the Chautauquan waving of handkerchiefs.

Mr. Fowle spoke some words in the Turkish language, and then said : —

Those of Cappadocia and Galatia salute you in the Lord. When I left to come to America, a little more than a year ago, our few Endeavorers especially requested that I should bring their greetings to all the Christian Endeavorers I should meet in America. I am very glad indeed to be here this morning and to give you these greetings. When I return I hope you will allow me to take your greetings to them. Endeavor has not done much in Turkey yet, but it is not the fault of Endeavor. It is not the fault of Endeavorers, it is the fault of environment; but the time is coming, mark that, when Endeavor shall win that land, as it has won other lands.

President Clark: Now we will see Mr. and Mrs. G. L. Wharton, of India, of the Foreign Christian Missionary Society, who were my kind hosts two or three years ago at a delightful convention held at their station.

Mr. Wharton: In the name of the United Societies of India, Burmah, and Ceylon, I give you their hearty salaams as sent by our Allahallabad Christian Endeavor Society last January.

President Clark: Now, the Rev. George R. White, missionary to the Indians of Brazil, of the South American Evangelical Mission, will appear before you.

Mr. White: I could greet you in Portuguese, which is the language of Brazil, but I am unable to speak the language of the Indians, in whose behalf I ask your prayers. There has never been any Protestant missionary gone to preach the gospel to the two and a half millions in the interior of Brazil. They need your prayers. Pray for them.

President Clark: I now introduce to you a missionary of the Christian Missionary Alliance in Shobara, Japan,—Miss E. Barnes.

Miss Barnes saluted, and she spoke in Japanese.

President Clark: Now from China we will be greeted in the Chinese tongue by Dr. Butchard, of the Christian Hospital of Loo Choo Foo, China.

Dr. Butchard spoke in Chinese.

President Clark: We will now see a medical missionary. The medical missionaries are among the heroes of the world, as are the evangelical missionaries. Dr. George E. Crosier, of the Baptist Missionary Union.

Dr. Crosier: I am told, friends, that it rained six months during the whole year out in Assam; but it has not rained showers of blessings, as we are enjoying here. I am simply going out there this fall to give them the showers of blessings.

President Clark: We will excuse him, then, for not talking in his own language. Now I introduce to you a missionary of the Reformed Church of America, Miss Nellie Swama, of Amoy.

Miss Swama spoke in Chinese, and then said:—

That is the message given me by an old woman of seventy-two, meaning, "When you return to your country, greet the Christians there for us, and thank them all for sending us the good tidings."

President Clark: I do not suppose there ought to be any nepotism in such a Convention as this, or anything that can be laid to special friendships of the past, and yet it is a peculiar privilege to me and an enjoyable one. I will now introduce to you an old college classmate of 1873, of Dartmouth College, a dear friend of mine then and ever since,—the Rev. James H. Pettie, of Yokohama, Japan, a missionary of the American Missionary Board.

Rev. Pettie [after greeting the audience in Japanese]: I feel a little like Dr. Jekyll in the Jekyll-Hyde combination. It might be better to call it Dr. Shakel. In the first place, I stand here as the representative of the thousands and millions of Shintooists. The Shintooists believe in the old national religion of Japan. The particular sect of the Shintooists whose yellow gown I wear are in a part of the country the name of which means hiding or lying in the mountains, because they hie to the mountains and live there in communion with the spirits of their gods. But the time has come when the thoughtful Japanese rejects Shintooism. Why? Because, among other reasons, there are too many gods. What do we want with eight million little gods? And they hear about the great God; and although they take the longest name in one god they have, yet in these hurried days they want a shorter word than that, as well as one that means more. So while they have worshipped the sun heretofore,—every morning many loyal Shintooists go out and look at the sun, clap their hands and worship it, shaking this rattle which I now shake [shaking rattle] to call the attention of the sun god or goddess,—and if they go to the little shrines, shaking this to wake up their sleeping gods, still I say the day of Shintooism is passing by. And now we come to the gorgeous apparel of the

Buddhists. [The speaker took off the garb of the Shintooist and appeared in the dress of the Buddhist.] The Buddhists are the most aggressive religionists in Japan. Buddhism is more or less believed in by the great bulk of the Japanese, and it may be said perhaps to be the only true religion outside of Christianity that is worthy the name of religion. Buddhism was a thousand years old when it went to Japan, and it has had its hundreds of years of service there; but Buddhism, too, is passing away. Some one has said that Japan is a nation seeking a religion. The statistics in three of the schools of higher education in Japan a short time ago showed that out of 4,098 there was one Shintooist; there was one Confucianist, fifteen Buddhists, four Christians, and then by far the larger numbers were, some sixty atheists, — sixty students in three of the higher schools in Japan said they were atheists, — while the remaining 282 classed themselves as agnostics, a small number, however, refusing to commit themselves. Think of that! Out of the old religions, only one young student in those three schools dared called himself a Shintooist, and only fifteen Buddhists. Is not that a nation seeking a religion?

[The speaker then took off the Buddhist dress and appeared in his own proper attire.]

And now that I am clothed and in my right mind, I feel better before you. I am glad to state to you that although Christianity is only one generation in Japan, it is reaping its great fruits there. Forty Christian Endeavor societies of Japan salute you. And not merely are they doing their own work, but they have put Christian Endeavor ideas and methods to quite a large extent into many churches where there are no Christian Endeavor societies. A nation that in one generation has been brave enough to pull itself out of the crumbling ruins of its old crumbling civilization, and to establish new foundations, and has tried to build a new palace, and is still trying, is certainly to be congratulated and helped. There are 41,000 Protestant Christians in Japan to-day, — 110,000, if we include the Catholics, — and if we say there are 200,000 people in Japan who believe more in Christianity than in any other religion, we, I think, would be stating what is true, and the work is still going forward. They have their beautiful little poems to their favorite cherry blossom, that is the flower that teaches every Japanese heart. There is a little poem I will close with that expresses just the situation in Japan : —

> "Thou distant hills where the cherry-trees bloom,
>   The breezes waft hither their peerless perfume."

President Clark : I now introduce to you Miss F. Rica Straffer, of Louisville, Ky. She is going to Korea in the fall. She is not acquainted with the language yet, but she will say a welcome to you in English.

Miss Straffer : I have not any welcome to say to you, dear friends, but I do want to ask this: that as I go out into the work to which I feel Christian Endeavor has sent me, I want to know that I will have the prayers of all the Christian Endeavorers both in this country and in other countries.

President Clark : Mr. H. B. S. Beakes, of Japan, who represents the Reformed Church of America in that country, will now greet you. Give him the salute.

Mr. Beakes : Brother Chapman has said a great deal to us about the comfort there is to us in the first verse of the twenty-third Psalm, and you can even get a great deal of comfort in saying it in the Japanese language. [He repeats this in Japanese.]

President Clark : The Rev. A. Mazaroni, of Havana, Cuba, represents the Gospel Alliance Church. He will give us a few words in Spanish.

Mr. Mazaroni spoke somewhat at length in Spanish.

President Clark : A missionary from Mexico comes next,— Miss Jennie Wheeler, of the Presbyterian Board. She speaks the same language you have just heard.

Miss Wheeler : God be with you until we meet again. [This was repeated in Spanish and English.]

President Clark: Dr. and Mrs. Thompson, of the East Central African Mission, of the American Board, I have now the pleasure of introducing to you.

Both Mr. and Mrs. Thompson spoke in an African language or dialect.

President Clark: Do you know what they said then? They said, " We greet you all, Christian Endeavorers." I now introduce to you another of my kind hostesses, who made my ways very pleasant while in India,— Miss Barber, of Owgong, Central India, of the Friends' Mission. I think she speaks Indee, but you will know when you hear it.

Miss Barber says a few words in a foreign language, and then proceeds : —

Salaam; that means " peace " and everything good that a Hindu could wish; and I just want to say that I entertained Dr. Clark in India by starting out to take him on a buggy ride, and a woman came in front of the vehicle and was hurt, and we were so delayed that it made us late to get into the second-class coach at the station; but he taught that woman what kindness was, because he gave her as much money as she earned in a month; and that was the royal entertainment, or part of it, that we gave Dr. Clark, so I know you will appreciate our kindness to him. So again I say, Salaam, and close by saying what our boys that we took in the famine, five hundred of them, always say, which means " Glory to Jesus Christ, glory." [Miss Barber repeated the words in Hindu.]

President Clark: How much do you think it was that I gave that woman for being run over by our team? It was one rupee, thirty-three cents, and Miss Barber says that would keep her for a month. I now introduce to you Miss Kimball, representing the United Presbyterian Church, from India.

The lady introduced bowed, and greeted the audience in Hindu.

President Clark: Here is one that all Endeavorers will give a special greeting to, for she was one of the first Endeavor missionaries,— Miss Coleman, of Illinois, of the American Presbyterian Mission, of Deradoo. India.

Miss Coleman : I will tell you what we say to the little children in India when we say the text, " Suffer little children to come unto me," etc. I will say that text in Hindi. [The speaker does so.] I want you to particularly think of the little girls in Hindustan. There are forty millions of widows over there, and a great many of those,— eight millions of them,— are under eight years of age. I want you to particularly think of the very little girls in India. As I go back I want to take your greetings especially to the girls in our Endeavor society in India.

President Clark: Miss M. G. Dean, of the Presbyterian Corps of Arraroom, Persia. She sailed first in 1868, and will sail again for the same station this month, on July 29.

Miss Dean spoke in Persian, saying in that language, " Blessed are the pure in heart, for they shall see God." She also said, " And do pray for the women and girls of Persia, that they may become pure in heart, and have some of the privileges that we have been enjoying during these days."

President Clark: I now introduce to you Miss Esther B. Fowler, of the American Board Mission, from Shanapore, India.

Miss Fowler: I represent two Christian Endeavor societies of Shanapore, India, and they wished me to bring their greetings to you.

President Clark: Another of my kind hosts, this one from Japan; I wish you could have enjoyed the same generous hospitality that I did. This is the Rev. Otis Carey, of Japan, of the American Board.

Rev. Mr. Carey: O-hi-o — that means good morning.

President Clark: Miss Jane R. Whetstone, of the Methodist Protestant Corps, of Japan, another missionary doing splendid work, that I personally saw. And I will ask Miss Annette E. Lawrence, of the same corps, to come up at the same time. Give them greeting. Both of these are of the Methodist Protestant Corps.

Miss Lawrence said a few words in Japanese, which we translated as follows: "We congratulate you Endeavorers because you are here to-day."

President Clark: Miss Mary Leach, of the Canadian Presbyterian Mission She expects to go to India next year. She is almost there, so we will give her a salute.

Miss Leach: There was a man sent from God whose name was John; the same came for a witness. I like to read that verse in this way, "There was a woman sent from God, whose name was Mary Leach; the same came for a witness." I am going to be a witness in India, God willing.

President Clark: Rev. E. A. Smith, of the German Evangelical Mission, of Malapar, East India.

Mr. Smith said a few words in Hindi, which he translated, "Christ, the victor all over the world, to him glory and honor."

President Clark: Miss Patton, of the American Board Mission in Western India.

Miss Patton said a few words in Hindi, which she said were, in English, "Peace be with you. O my brothers, O my sisters, pray for us."

President Clark: Rev. William I. Chamberlain, of the Reformed Church, from Southern India. I want you to give him, too, one of your heartiest salutes, for he was Christian Endeavor's first friend in India, and has been one of its staunchest friends ever since.

Mr. Chamberlain: [Mr. Chamberlain said a few words in Hindi.] In behalf of twenty thousand Christian Endeavorers and of five hundred societies in India, I give you greeting this morning; and in behalf of three hundred millions of the people of India, seventy millions of young people of India, I beseech and bespeak your kindest and continued interest, so that India shall join the great possessions around the world, Orient and Occident clasping hands, and shall be lifted so close to the bosom of God that it shall hear the beatings of his heart, and shall march on with the Christian nations throughout the ages.

President Clark: Rev. Scott C. Williams and Mrs. Williams, from Mexico. I want you to give them your hearty greetings. They were others of my kind hosts who made my journey pleasant. They are of the Presbyterian Board.

Mr. and Mrs. Williams were heartily received.

Mr. Williams: Mr. Moody declares that the two disciples who went out from Jerusalem on the Resurrection morning were Cleopas and his wife; whenever you read Matthew xviii. 19, remember that Mrs. Williams and her husband believe those words mean us, too.

President Clark: I now introduce to you Caroline E. Chittenden, of the Foo Chow Mission, of the American Board, a Christian Endeavorer before she went out, and one all the way through.

Miss Chittenden: I am very glad to read to you a word of greeting sent by the First Provincial Union in China, including the first society in the Empire.

President Clark: Now, dear friends, has it not been a blessed half-hour that we have spent together in listening to these friends and seeing their faces and rejoicing in their prosperity in the work God has given them to do? I will ask Dr. Teunis S. Hamlin, of Washington, to lead us in a brief word of prayer for our friends from whom we have heard in their world-wide field of activity.

A living panorama of the world's degradation without Christ was painted by Rev. A. McLean, secretary of the Board of Foreign Missions of the Christian Church. It was a masterly focusing of facts, the concentrated essence of all the missionary libraries, volumes boiled down to pithy sentences that stirred deep pity for the world's great need.

Address by Rev. A. McLean,
Cincinnati, O.
THE GREAT NEED OF MISSIONS.

The non-Christian nations need schools, sanitation, good government, the sewing-machine, the printing-press, the telegraph, the newspaper, and other helpful agencies; but more than any or all these do they need to be brought into right relations to God. Of the many things they need to live a complete life, this is the chief. Some of these nations have elaborate religious systems and ethical codes; they have art and philosophy; they have elegance and magnificence; but none the less do they need the gospel. This is as true of the king and the noble, of the Brahmin and the Mandarin, as it is of the coolies who serve them. It is as true of the rich man, who dresses in purple and fine linen, and fares sumptuously every day, as it is of the beggar at his gate. All have sinned and come short of the glory of God. All are shut up under sin and are liable to punishment. All alike need to be washed, to be sanctified, to be justified by the Lord Jesus, and in the Spirit of our God.

Nineteen centuries have passed since Christ was born, and only one-third of the race is even nominally Christian. Nine per cent of all the people on the globe are Protestant, fifteen per cent are Catholic, and seven per cent are Greek. The Protestants number 137,000,000; the Catholics, 215,000,000; the Greeks, 95,000,000. The Mohammedans number 200,000,000; the Buddhists and Brahmins, 672,000,000; the Jews, 7,000,000; and the Pagans, 125,000,000. At the present hour there are more than 1,000,000,000 souls without an adequate knowledge of God or of the gospel of his Son. Not only so, but the non-Christian part of the population is increasing at an appalling rate. There are 250,000,000 more in this class than there were when William Carey sailed for India a century ago. The annual increase is equal to the number that have been won since the modern missionary era began.

Taking the field in detail, we have the following: Africa has an estimated population of 190,000,000; the Protestant communicants number 140,000, and the adherents 800,000. China has a population of 400,000,000, and has 85,000 communicants. Japan has a population of 42,000,000, and reports 40,000 Protestants, 22,000 Greeks, and 40,000 Catholics. India has a population of 287,000,000, and has 235,000 communicants and 750,000 adherents. South America has a population of 37,000,000; of these 15,000 are Protestant communicants. In the Pacific there are thirty-eight groups containing 2,000 islands, with a population of 10,000,000. Fourteen groups have been evangelized; the communicants number 58,000, and the adherents 225,000. The Turkish Empire has a population of 33,000,000; the missionaries in Turkey report 13,000 converts. There are in the churches in the West Indies 113,000 members, while the adherents number 300,000. Madagascar reports 231,000 adherents, and Ceylon 68,000. Korea has a population of 15,000,000, and has 1,000 baptized believers. In Java, Sumatra, and Borneo good work has been done, but the converts are not numerous.

China has one convert for every 5,000 of her people; Japan has one for every 1,000; India has one for every 1,200; South America has one for every 2,400; Africa has one for every 1,357; Mexico has one for every 738; the South Seas have one for every 172; Korea has one for every 15,000. Some fields have hardly been touched. This is true of Anam, with a population of 20,000,000; of Afghanistan, with a population of 8,000,000; of Arabia, with a population of 10,000,000; and of Thibet and Mongolia. In the fields that have been entered there are wide areas that have few or no missionaries. In one district in Northern India there are 23,000,000 people, and only two missionaries. In the Soudan, with a population of about 80,000,000, there is no missionary. Three-fourths of the people in Japan have never heard the gospel. It is estimated that 35,000,000 die annually in regions where Christ has not been named.

The church sends 6,096 male and 5,751 female missionaries to evangelize the vast populations of the non-Christian world, and pays $16,000,000 for their support. England has a population of about 35,000,000, and has 50,000 ordained ministers. The United States has a population of about 75,000,000, and has 120,000 ordained ministers. In this country we have one minister for every 750 people; in the mission fields there is one ordained missionary for every 200,000. Now, as in Christ's time, the harvest truly is plenteous, but the laborers are few. The need is infinite; the supply is infinitesimal.

There is no hope for the nations in the non-Christian faiths. They do not reveal God or tell how he may be approached and served.

Hinduism is a vast system of compromise. To protect itself it becomes all things to all men. It includes atheism, monotheism, polytheism, pantheism, and demon worship. It denies personality to God and responsibility to man. Whatever is done is the result of Fate. Sin is ceremonial defilement, and consists in eating beef and in touching forbidden objects. Hinduism concerns itself about caste and about paying due regard to the Brahmins. There is no inconsistency between devoutness and the most flagrant immorality. There is no sense of shame over falsehood or uncleanness. Under Hinduism the people are noted for their superstitious beliefs and their corrupt practices.

Buddhism has no Creator, no Saviour, and no Helper. Though it began as atheism, it has temples to the gods of wind and of thunder, to the gods of the sun and moon and stars. Its avowed policy is that of scuttling the ship and leaving society to sink beneath the waves. Buddhism has not checked polygamy or polyandry. The Buddhist hopes to lay up merit by buying fish and putting them back into the water, or by buying birds and setting them at liberty. Buddhism has no gospel for humanity; it is the religion of despair.

Confucianism emphasizes the relation between father and son, between husband and wife, between king and subject, between elder and younger brother, and between friends. China's greatest sage had nothing to say about man's relation to God. He could explain neither life nor death. Confucius was the original agnostic. His system tolerates polygamy and sanctions polytheism. The Confucianist does not pray for a clean heart and a right spirit, but for riches, honor, and good luck.

Five times every day Islam declares there is only one God; but the God of the Koran is a stern and unbending and unloving despot. He exacts obedience from his creatures, and promises them sensual joys in return. Islam has its rites, ceremonials, prayers, alms, fastings, and pilgrimages. At the same time it is destitute of any provision for human redemption. Purity of heart and life are foreign to its teachings. Islam depraves the home and thereby depraves the race.

Paganism has no message of hope and good cheer for those who sit in darkness and in the shadow of death. It has temples, idols, fetiches, priests, sorcerers, and rain-makers. It cannot tell the troubled soul how he may find pardon and peace and eternal life.

There is almost nothing in the non-Christian faiths that makes for righteousness or social well-being. They have been weighed in the balances, and have been found wanting. After a test lasting for millenniums, we find that darkness covers the lands, and that gross darkness covers the peoples.

Africa is a den of desolation, misery, and crime. Bloodshed abounds, Satan is supreme, the darkness is darkest. The slave-trade and intertribal wars devastate the land. In the Congo Free State alone there are twenty million cannibals. Neesima, when asked as to the leading defects in the Japanese character, replied without a moment's hesitation, " Lying and licentiousness. " In Japan immorality is legalized and made a source of revenue. Some one else has summed up the characteristic faults of the Japanese as "conceit and deceit." Shintooism and Confucianism and Buddhism have left the people very much as they found them.

In China every man is for himself. Because of this there is no public spirit and no patriotism. State and military secrets are sold by those in high position. China has a vast population and raw materials in great abundance, but there is no national strength and no progress. Her armies and navy and fortresses went down before the attacks of the Japanese, as a child's house of cards goes before a storm. The Chinese are a nation of liars. Justice is bought and sold like any other commodity. The filth of a Chinese city is something to be imagined rather than described or experienced. It is boundless, endless, and sublime. Every street has a cesspool or a dumping-ground of filth.

In the temples of India are found cows and monkeys as objects of worship. Under every green tree, and on every high hill, and along every road, are seen the emblems and instruments of idol worship. The bulk of the population lie down hungry every night in the year. Periodic famines cause millions to perish. Caste curses the land. There is no mutual confidence and no cooperation, and consequently no prosperity. One of her own most enlightened men has said that no country on the face of the earth suffers less from political evils and more from self-inflicted or self-accepted, and therefore avoidable, evils than the Hindu community. One of her prophets has said that Hinduism has filled the capitals of India with the most rotten superstitions to be found in the world. Among the evils of India are untruthfulness, dishonesty, and perjury.

In the South Seas, where the gospel has not been accepted, the club of the chief is the sole law of the land. Infanticide is so prevalent that two-thirds of the children are buried alive or are strangled in infancy. These islands are notorious for their tyranny, their superstitions, their absence of the very idea of morality, their profligacy, robbery, thievery, and perpetual reign of terror.

The Sultan of Turkey is the spiritual head of two hundred million souls. It is said of Islam that it has either found a desert or created one. The evils of this system are polygamy, divorce, violence, intolerance, slavery, and sensuality. The government of the Sultan is evil, oppressive, and corrupt. It is getting worse and worse all the time. The Turk has been in Europe four hundred and fifty years, and is still an alien and barbarian. The Greek and Armenian massacres are chargeable to the Sultan, who is spoken of by his sycophants as the finest Pearl of the age and the esteemed Centre of the universe.

In Persia it is said that lying is rotting the country. The Persians tell lies before they can speak. Curzon says, " I am convinced that the true son of Iran would sooner tell a lie than the truth, and that he feels twinges of desperate remorse when on occasion he has thoughtlessly strayed into veracity."

There is nothing in any of these faiths to regenerate and perfect the race. Not that they are wholly false and bad. In every system there is some truth. It could not exist and endure otherwise. In non-Christian lands one finds here and there gentleness, refinement, hospitality, generosity, friendship, and domestic fidelity and affection; but these graces are found among a very small number. Their possession is the exception and not the rule.

Where the gospel has not gone woman is degraded. Mrs. Bishop says that the non-Christian faiths degrade her with an infinite degradation. They dwarf the intellect and develop the worst passions of the soul,— jealousy, envy, murderous hate, intrigue. All Hindus are agreed on two things: the sanctity of the cow and the impurity of women. The laws of many say, " We may trust deadly poisons, a swollen river, a hurricane, beasts of burden, a thief, a savage, a murderer; but a woman, never." In Africa ten large beads buy a cow, five buy a woman. In some parts of the continent she eats with the dogs. When a girl is born in China poor parents say, "She must be fed, clothed, betrothed, wedding presents must be made, and when she has children of her own more presents must be given." To escape all this outlay she is exposed or drowned or poisoned. In the South Seas, when a girl is born, men say, "She cannot poise the spear, or wield the club; why, then, should she live?" In some parts of India, one-third of the girls born are secretly destroyed. John Williams says that in some places in the Pacific islands the women were not allowed to enter the temples. The pigs might, the women could not. The pigs were not regarded as so great a pollution as men's mothers and wives and daughters. In India there are 25,000,000 widows. Of these 13,000 are under four years of age; 78,000 are under nine years of age; 200,000 are under fourteen. A widow is obliged to shave her head, to give up all jewels and ornaments, and to eat only once in twenty-four hours. Her dress is a badge of disgrace and shame. There are in India 128,-000,000 illiterate women. Six in one thousand can read and write. In Japan one marriage in three is followed by a divorce. Cameron describes the burial of an African chief. A river was turned from its course and a huge grave dug in the channel, the bottom of which was covered with living women. The dead body was supported in a sitting posture by his wives. The earth was shovelled in and the women were buried alive, after which the river was allowed to resume its course. According to Bainbridge there are 300,000,000 women living in the Buddhist hope of being born again a man, and not a toad or a snake; 90,000,-000 more are living in the most abject slavery of mind and heart to their Hindu lords; and 80,000,000 more in the Moslem harems, unloved and uncared for but as tools of lust, and in the certainty of being superseded when the charms of youth are gone. The degradation of women is, as Dennis has said, the sign and shame of the non-Christian religions.

Poverty is another evil. In India the average income is less than ten dollars a year. The money-lender charges exorbitant interest. It ranges from twelve to seventy-five per cent. In Turkey the tax-gatherer can take what he pleases. The people have no redress. The nerve of enterprise is cut. There is no inducement to industry and economy. If one is prosperous he is certain to be robbed and may be strangled or shot. China has people who live on grass and roots and bran. If a sick dog or donkey or mule should die, the neighborhood has a feast on his carcass. The Chinese are kept poor by their superstitions. They are afraid to mine for coal lest they should disturb the great dragon that supports all things. They must not build railways for the same reason. So it costs them ten times as much to send their produce to market, and ten times as much to get the commodities they need, as it should. The Chinese are kept poor by their gambling habits. They risk lands, houses, wives, children, and their own liberty on the throw of dice. Drummond saw an African chief buried. All his effects were deposited in the grave with him. They consisted of his bow and arrow, his pipe and clay bowl. In Africa he says one stick sharpened makes a spear, two sticks rubbed together make a fire, several sticks tied together make a house. These people create little; they consume little.

In the non-Christian lands there is small regard for human life. In Borneo no one is allowed to marry till he can show a number of heads he has recently struck off. In Assam a native is not considered a man until he has imbrued his hands in human blood; whether in peace or war makes no difference. A Kaffir chief said, "When the word of God came among us we were like beasts. We knew nothing but war and bloodshed. Every man was against his neighbor. Every man tried to destroy his brother." In some of these lands human sacrifices are offered to avert some disaster or to secure some boon. They are offered in time of drought to secure a harvest, or in time of war to secure victory. In the lifetime of one king in the South Seas 2,000 human beings were offered to his idols. If a house is to be built for the royal family, or if a canoe is to be launched, if war is to be declared, if a chief is sick and likely to die, or if a new chief is to be elected, blood must be shed. In Alaska, when there was an epidemic of grippe, men and women and children were sacrificed to appease the demon who was the cause of the sickness.

Travellers and experts tell us that in the dark lands of the earth sin is enthroned, deified, and worshipped. Crime and shame and sorrow are everywhere. These lands are a waste, howling wilderness. The people are without hope because they are without God. One tells us that the whole continent of Asia is corrupt. "It is the scene of barbarities, tortures, brutal punishments, oppressions, official corruption. There are no sanctities of home, nothing to tell of righteousness, temperance, or judgment to come, only a fearful looking for the future of fiery indignation from some quarter, they know not what; a dread of everlasting rebirths into some forms of obnoxious reptiles or insects, or of tortures which are infinite, and which are depicted in pictures of fiendish ingenuity." Another says, "Paint a starless sky; hang your picture with night; drape the mountains with long, far-reaching vistas of darkness; hang the curtains deep along every shore and landscape; darken all the past; let the future be draped in deeper and yet deeper night; fill the awful gloom with hungry, sad-faced men and sorrow-driven women and children; — it is the heathen world, the people seen in vision by the prophet, who sit in the region and shadow of death, to whom no light has come, sitting there still through the long, long night, waiting and watching for the morning."

There is no hope for the race in education, or in commerce, or in civilization. The world by wisdom did not and cannot know God. There is nothing in firearms or in fire-water to redeem the peoples. Civilization may refine, it cannot regenerate. The nations need the engineer, the social economist, the humanitarian, the moralist; but more than all these they need the evangelist. India has in her pantheon 333,000,000 gods, but India's supreme need is the need of Christ, who is able and eager to save. China worships the dragon; she pays tribute to the spirits of water and of air. She spends $400,000,000 a year on idol worship. China needs Christ to bid these evil spirits depart, and to fill her marts and her homes with prosperity and righteousness and peace. Africa is stretching out lame hands toward God. This is her deepest need, her divinest hunger. The Dark Continent needs Christ to dispel her darkness and to give her the light of life. The acceptance of Christ as Saviour and Lord makes all things new. He causes the wilderness to blossom like Eden, and like the garden of the Lord. Under his beneficent reign the nations rejoice in liberty, and justice, and progress. The gospel is all-sufficient and alone sufficient to save from sin, and to perfect the individual, and thereby to perfect society. By regenerating human nature it changes customs, and conduct, and literature, and legislation, and jurisprudence, and art, and ideals, and everything else. There is salvation in Christ, and there is salvation in none other; for there is none other name given under heaven and among men whereby we must be saved.

Mr. Eddy, the Kansan of the Yale Mission Band, summed up the resources with which this need is to be met. He spoke of the inventions that facilitate intercourse. When his brother was married in India, at four P.M. he received the telegram announcing it at half past three. Our speech travels around the world faster than the sunlight. Speaking of the men who are ready to meet this need, he told of one young college graduate who took three prizes on his commencement day, and who afterwards spent three years in special preparation, and was offered a fine business situation, but went to a foreign field at five hundred dollars a year, with the understanding that if he was not a success, in a year he would be recalled, with four of the best years of his life torn out; that was the kind of material that Christian Endeavor was asked to put itself behind.

Address by Mr. D. B. Eddy,
Leavenworth, Kan.

You have sometimes seen a full-rigged ship built up from a small piece of wood, and the boast of its maker has been that his only tool was a knife. You have read of a prisoner making his way to freedom through iron bars and solid walls with an ordinary rusty nail, or piece of broken glass. The point worthy of notice is this: that great work has been done with few resources. How much of the glory we give Lincoln and Garfield is due to the fact that we have in mind the rail-splitter and canal-driver? We have the right to expect from men to whom much has been given that much shall be required. You and I, on this tenth day of July, 1900 years after our Master lived, are under a measurably greater burden of responsibility than ever was Philip or Barnabas. From added resources comes an added responsibility. Great resources given you mean great results demanded.

We may take a short inventory of the stock intrusted to us for our work the coming year; and in order to do this, will you merely close the doors of your lives for a few moments in quiet, and decide whether or no we have used the great God-given resources of our lives ; and, if you find the message is to you, that, redeeming the past failure, we shall use them, lest at the end we throw back into God's face the drained dregs of an empty life. For our memory's convenience, will you note under four heads the great resources entrusted to us. First of all, notice the means that God has given us, the manifestation of his will, that this world is to be won, and won now. It needs but a single word to mention the American inventions to-day, which is a mark of God's will, sign-posts that bless the way of conquest for Christ. Steam, the railway, the press, the telegram. have made a neighborhood of the world. I well remember this last winter reading a telegram of my brother's marriage in India at half-past three, when the marriage had occurred at four o'clock. Telegraph is faster than the sun. San Francisco will gossip to-day over the back gate with Shanghai of political upheavals, of riots. of plague and famine. But write large in the letters of your memory that these inventions of to-day, as truly as Lazarus in the parable, have brought to our gates these millions — laid at our gates, full of sores and demanding to be fed from the crumbs that fall from our loaded tables. And will you notice in a single suggestive word that God has opened before us the door, in the political opportunities of the day. England's army is in India, in China, up the Nile, in South Africa, in the islands of the sea, and bowed under the white man's burden of responsibility. Yours and mine are increasing daily. Under Commodore Perry in Japan, under our growing influence in the South America republics, in the islands of the east and the west, the political opportunity has opened the door in answer to our prayers. "See, I have set before thee an open door which no man openeth, and which no man can shut. " Let us take this old message to Israel and apply it to ourselves.

Will you notice a thought that is most stimulating to those who like to trace out such things. — that in the history of the ages the intellectual life has been developing and expanding. from the first days. in which the savage hunter of some aboriginal tribe, skulking through the bushes, marked every other human being as his deadly enemy, to be slain on sight — from that time, with the broadening horizon of the family under his protection, with the broadening responsibilities connected with his tribe, or his clan, to the day when nations were at peace with the heathen, but at war with all thought, Greece called a stranger on her shores the barbarian, Rome used for a stranger the word " hostis," and it is their word also for deadly enemy; the stranger without the gate is the enemy against whom we war in the struggle for existence; but notice, under God's mercy, nations are as individuals. The development has gone on, in alliances for offence and defence, until you and I are living in a time, under a heavy burden of responsibility, when our Congress passes a bill to relieve the famine of India, when one nation wars against a second for the sole benefit — at least ostensibly — of an oppressed third, when, even now, we pray for the gathering met to discuss the possibility of peace.

Bear in mind that the intellectual life has but kept pace with the widening spheres of influence. It is no surprise that the religious life and the expansion of the church have been especially blessed of God. We can hardly even picture it in the imagination now that young William Carey was insulted for daring to suggest such a thing as the demands of the heathen upon the church, and called a miserable enthusiast, and by the greatest critic of his age, that dreamer of dreams, who dreamed that he had been dreaming. In this scene of missionary interest and enthusiasm, we cannot even picture it; but even now we notice the change in public opinion, for your presence in your society from which you have come,—that pastor who does not do his duty in this regard, that church at home becomes the object of our earnest prayers; if they deny the claims of the heathen world, on account of the pretension of the need at home, we pray for them that the broad Christ love may come into their lives, with all its fulness of blessing. But above all this, in our religious life, we have seen the new generation of Christians raised in the church of Christ, that, if it will, can solve the entire problem. Before the generation has passed, the dearest, the sweetest story ever told can be rung into every home, into every village and place in the world, if we will.

Fellow Endeavorers, think what is the object of our gathering in this Convention. What is the aim of the world and the literature of the time; of your Social Committee? What is the purpose of the Endeavor movement itself? Is it that we have come here to prove our loyalty to Dr. Clark? Is it that we gather here in convention to stimulate our own lives, in order to live more worthily of the Master? Yes, but immeasurably more than this. We are called in Christ to win a world, and nothing less. Pray, then, and work, lest our enthusiasm and energy, instead of being of God, directed against the sin of the world, should roll back upon itself until the wonderful possibilities pouring out upon this great movement have accomplished their purpose. But pray that we may be guided aright, lest we divert the stream into unwise ventures. Thank God that the movement so far is directed toward the winning of the world! It is not enough that God has blessed us with our American inventions, our political purity, our religious expansion. He has poured upon us one other great resource,—the men, the men who shall bear the message. See them! More than ten thousand knights that are laboring in other fields, heroes of Christ, standing in your place, in your stead. The missionary call comes feebly to some; but if you had a brother in India, and if you receive the month-old letters, telling of fever-stricken cities, of the plague-ridden districts, of the stifling heat, of the sickening sights that meet their eyes upon the streets—if you could read between the lines of the overwork and sleeplessness in carrying out the burdens that we have laid upon them, God pity us, if there was one of us that has a little spark of manhood in him, if he did n't carry out his burden of responsibility toward those great heroes of Christ who have been given us by God, by whom we are to stand.

There is a regiment recruiting that has n't been deaf to the call in this country. Thirty-five hundred young men and women in the country have signed this card: "It is my purpose, if God permit, to become a foreign missionary." A regiment, a host of young men and women, called of God to serve him in the world! Don't misunderstand this in a personal way. These men are your responsibility, your great resource of God. We must stand behind them.

Not long ago, in Chicago, in a great meeting in the Auditorium, the name of one of a class was read as the prize-winner, at which time the place rang with his name. Two days later, after a talk with Mr. Vickrey, in Chicago, he was on his way to New York with thirty other men to take a competitive examination to serve God in India for four years at a salary of $500,—pledged to be unmarried for that time,—and if at the end of that time he was not successful in the work, to be returned home, the best four years of his life torn out of his life-work. Fellow Christians, that is the material we are standing behind. An old classmate of mine who broke the record in his studies has devoted himself to the cause. That man has a large salary waiting him if he will go into medicine, but he likes the salary of $500, and he will leave the wage if you will stand behind him. God grant that no society here should turn from these young student volunteers, with any thought that they are not called of God, or that you are not responsible for them. It would be sad indeed if we did not have the privilege of joining with them in working in their fields.

But God has given us three great resources, and these are ours to use for those who have gone to the front. I mean our money,— our money; the wand of magic that can transfer your energy, and your talk on the typewriter, into thousands of pages of Christian print. You who are clerks at the desk, you who are measuring pounds and yards, spend two hours a day in sending something to the men and women of India — the magic wand that will transfer your society into a missionary field representing you. Behind him you stand. Oh, this next year, in your society, let your offerings be, not in the copper-hued thing taken from the mite-box on the back table, nor in the silver stream bubbling in its flow, but in its place let the stream be steep and bright, reflecting the gold of its source, the sun. Oh, is it impossible? There are difficulties in the way. We can say, like Caleb and Joshua, that though the children of Anak hamper us, though there be walled cities, we will go up against them. It shall be our place at home to bring an offering unto the Lord, that shall be worthy of the great cause. " The silver and gold are mine, saith the Lord." It requires, then, that we should lay hold of the last great resource, and give God's mite. " It should not be according to your ability, but according to the power of his might; with the means, the money, the might of God, we will give, these are all ours." " All silver and gold are mine, saith the Lord, and all that is thine is mine, saith Christ," and " All things are yours in Christ Jesus," saith Paul. Will you give, then, to lay hold upon your inheritance? They are ours, and all that Christ has given to us is our right in God.

For a few moments our lives have flowed together in this place, and perhaps we are to drift away and see God's love bound only by the tie that binds. But before we separate, let us unite our hearts in a motto that shall stay with us.

Back under a haystack five men met for shelter from the storm. They adopted, in answer to the convictions of one of their number, a motto, " We can do it if we will. We can do it if we will." That is a motto that is worthy the history of missions. Two years ago, in an annual meeting held by the Christian Student Federation, they were grouped about a map of the world. There were represented there thirteen nations and five continents, which knew best the work that was to be done, and the rafters rung with the enthusiasm of these young Alexanders, who planned to take a world. They said, " We can do it if we will." O fellow Endeavorers of America, of the world, God has written large in our history the words, " We can, we can." Will you? Will you? Will you? By the outpouring of the young life of this organization; by the thousands of young men who are in the fields even now, who are spending their lives abroad; by the memory of David Livingstone, dead, upon his knees in that open sore of the world; by Patterson, drifting out at sea in an open boat, with his dead face staring into the face of the one whom he loved; by Keith Faulconer, the best stenographer, the best bicyclist, in India, in Arabia dead; by that host of men who came to us when we were in the shadow of death; by Augustin; by Boniface; by that earlier band who went out into the world; by Barnabas; by Philip; by the young student of Tarsus, who ran the race, who finished the course; by them all, for the sake of Him, will you say, We will, we will, we will? If you will, bow your head, and in quiet tell the Lord Jesus that without count of the future, to the best that is in us, and out in the borders of the tents, and in the halls all over the land, let us do it. Will you bow your heads and tell Christ?

Then followed a blessed season of quiet meditation and prayer, conducted by Rev. Arthur W. Spooner, D.D., of Camden, N. J.

Dr. Clark, in introducing the next speaker, said : —

If the young people of the world had the choosing of their missionary commander-in-chief, I am not sure but what the election would fall upon Mr. Robert E. Speer, of New York City. Our leader in missions is the one who can lead us nearer to God and open our hearts widest toward our fellow men. Mr. Speer will speak to us this morning on " Missions, the Great Blessing," the closing exercises of our morning session; and you will not be averse to hearing before he appears before you that three days ago he was elected one of the trustees of the United Society of Christian Endeavor to represent the Presbyterian Church.

Address by Mr. Robert E. Speer,

New York City.

It is only possible to understand the blessing of missions to the world as we understand what Jesus Christ himself is to our own hearts. If Christ is lovely to us, if he is the loveliest to us, we may be sure that Christ alone can be lovely to any man, and Christ alone be the loveliest to man. I am not sure it will be possible for us this morning to understand much of the great blessing of missions, for the simple reason that it is impossible for us to understand much of what Jesus Christ himself is to our own hearts. We were born into his love, we grew up to love him with the very first words that dropped upon our ears from a mother's lips. The very atmosphere of our life is thrilled through with the influence of Christ. The humblest and most commonplace blessings of every day are Christ's gifts to us. It would be the sheerest impossibility in any one of us here this morning to begin to define what Jesus Christ is to us, and what Jesus Christ has done for us. If we could this morning strip off from our lives everything that Christ has brought into them, then we should begin to understand something of that great blessing. If we could tear out of our homes all the influences of Jesus Christ in their establishment, if we could go down deep into our own hearts and root out of the tendrils of our hearts what Jesus Christ has entwined there, and have left nothing but the dead, scarred wreck, then we could understand something of what it means for Jesus Christ to come into our lives and into our work; and we shall only begin to understand the great blessings of missions when we come to understand, first of all, what life is, destitute of Christ.

Thousands of poor, benighted people are living to-day in hopelessness because they have not heard his voice; they have not heard the voice of Christ saying unto them, " Let not your heart be troubled. You believe in God, believe also in me. In my Father's house there are many mansions; if it were not so, I would have told you, and if I go, I will come again and receive you unto myself. "

And so we live not in a world of hopelessness, but in the word and love of Christ. What Dr. McLean was telling this morning of the destitution and the fear of the heathen world is every word true. They will tell you in the Punjab that their only worship is the worship of graves and the fear of devils, and three-fourths of mankind are living in a perpetual atmosphere of fear.

There are three great elements in religion. The element of independence, the element of accomplishment, and the element of progress. It is not to be denied that every religion teaches man to be dependent, and every religion, save Christ's, teaches him to be so dependent as to live in constant and mortal fear. We live where Christ Jesus has spoken by his angels to man, " Be not afraid, I bring you glad tidings of great joy; " there is nothing to fear. We live in a world of ignorance save where Christ has gone.

When that great man in China, Li Hung Chang, not long ago was appealed to because of the overflow of the Yellow River, he went into the temple and worshipped a snake that some one of the priests had brought there. When we consider this, we can have some idea of the ignorance, the superstition, the puerile fear, in which a multitude of 400,000,000 of living souls are living.

A friend from Korea was telling me the other day of the destruction last month of the only street-railway in Korea. There had been no rains for a long season and the people blamed the absence of rain upon the disturbance of the spirit by the railroad. A man was sent up on the mountains to pray and manufacture rain, and the people gathered and tore up the rails from the ground and fell upon all the cars and made a bonfire of them, because they feared that the railroad running through the streets had been the cause for two months of no rain falling upon their land.

And so, friends, tear out of the life the courage, the confidence, which Jesus Christ has brought into it, and you can understand what it means to have Christ come into fear-stricken, hopeless lives and bring all that is high, all that is infinite, of the blessing of his love.   Christ seals a thousand fountains of sin, he opens a thousand fountains of joy.   Wherever in this world he touches, this love blazes out with the blessing of his Father.

I have been speaking as though this world of ours was made up of men with hopelessness, fear, and ignorance.   When I think thus I think pityingly of the world, but when I think of my wife and my little child, my heart nearly breaks over the thought of the multitudes of women and children that are without Christ.   We live not in a world of men; we live in a world of women and little children.   Two-thirds of the heathen of the world is made up of women and children.   We get ourselves into the way of thinking and speaking as though men made up this world.   I care very little what becomes of the men of this world.   A man is a master of his own sufferings all the world round. He is the master, too, of the sufferings of the women and children, and it is to

A Fourth-of-July View of the Tents.

the women and children in the world that my heart goes out; and I think of that little Babe that lay in Mary's arms in the manger, who brought peace and love to all the earth.   I say we live in a world composed of two-thirds of women and little children, and they speak to us the truest message as to the blessing that Christ brings into our lives.

One of the speakers this morning said that there were eight millions of widows under eight years of age in India, and my mind went back to a scene in a little Moslem house where we stayed one night.   We made our beds in a little gray dirt in a hut in the village.   The woman of the house stood looking on.   She had never seen such wealth and treasure.   When at last my friend got out of the bottom of his saddle-bags a red counterpane made up of squares and laid it over his cot, the poor old woman, with barely an interest in life, stroked the squares gently with her hand.   She turned to him and said, "Where did you get that counterpane?"   "My wife made it," said he.   She pointed to the room in which the ladies were, and she said, "Is your wife in there?"   "No," said my friend.   "Are both his wives?" pointing to me. "No," he said, "only one of them.   It is the custom of our religion never to have more than one wife; it is not so with your religion, is it?"   "No," said she.   "How is it in your home?   Is there more than one wife here?" said he. "No, there is only one now," she said, "but another is to be brought next week."   "How will your life be after that?" said he; "what is your life here in your home?"   "Ah Shaibs," said she, and the tears came stealing down upon her furrowed cheeks, "Ah Shaibs, our life is hell."

My friends, their life is hell, the life of three hundred millions of our fellow creatures.   If you will not take it from me, when you go home read the best tract I know of on the subject, by Rudyard Kipling, "The Enlightenment of Paget," and read there his own judgment. "What is the matter with this land," he writes, "is not in the laws political, in things growing out of their civil conditions; the real secret of their corruptions here roots itself back in their treatment of the family. One-half of the population of this land is shut out of its right. The foundations of their life are utterly rot, bestially rot." I am interested, not in behalf of the skin-scarred man, I am interested in behalf of the women and little children; and as you men love your mothers and wives and sisters at home, as you men love the little ones who have nestled in your arms, I entreat you to remember that this love is born of Christ, and that these great multitudes of the earth are waiting for the coming of Jesus and for the same blessings that have made our lives rich.

A friend of mine told me the other day of a telegram received from Missionary Peat, in Eastern Arabia. Last year I was kneeling down by a little cot in a Presbyterian hospital in New York, with a last prayer for a dying missionary lying there, and another prayer for a new missionary who was going out to his field. The telegram the other day informed me of the new missionary's death. There rose up before my mind the scene in that station wherein he was alone. Just two years ago I landed there from a ship, and one of the men there showed me his household. His household consisted of eighteen little black boys, gathered from all parts of Africa, brought there in a slave ship. The British Consul had gone out one night alone, with revolvers in his hand, had captured the ship, and had turned these little boys over to my friend to be trained. I asked him if he knew where they came from. Well, he said he was very anxious to find that out one day, so he asked them. One of them said he had come from the shore of a great sea. "Was it good to drink?" said the man. Yes, it was good to drink, and he thought the name sounded like Nyanza. Another came from the bank of a great river as large as the ocean; the name he thought was Zambesi. Another came from a mountain, and my friend looked it up and it was in the west of Africa. These eighteen little fellows had been pilfered from most all over Central, Eastern, and Western Africa. I looked upon each one, and each had a little scar on his cheek about the size of a half-dollar. I asked my friend, "What is that?" "That is the brand of the slaver's iron," said he, "just as they brand wild cattle upon our Western plains." And there they sat, the eighteen little fellows, gathered out of all Africa, learning of Christ. "When I first got them," he said, "they huddled together like a little group of rabbits in the centre of the floor. They would not speak a word, would not let me come near them. They would shrink close together, and it took me nearly a month to win their confidence and love." They all sat around on their little forms and sang the song that I suppose Dr. Clark has heard all over the world, and I think no words ever sounded sweeter as they came from their lips,

> " Jesus loves me, this I know
> For the Bible tells me so."

Nowhere else had they learned it. They had lived in a life of superstition and hate. Can you think what it meant, that into their lives came Jesus Christ? And so we can never understand the great blessing that Christ brings until we can see that there are no homes in Christendom into which he has not come.

My friends, we have in our power in the Christian faith the only force that can bring a blessing to the world. Nothing but the blood of Jesus Christ can cleanse us from sin. Nothing but the blood of Jesus Christ can cleanse the world from sin. Did it never strike you that every heathen city as soon as it becomes holy is happier than it ever was before, and more healthful? The very foulest ceremonies in these places are carried on in the name of religion. Only Christ cleanses life. Has it never occurred to you that only Jesus Christ can build the foundations of a true society?

I think one of the most ludicrous and yet one of the most pathetic sights of our day is Elizabeth Cady Stanton, with her ilk, reviling Christianity because, forsooth, Paul forged manacles for the hands of women. I tell you what woman is Christ has made her. And all that woman has Christ has given her. The world in which she lives Christ has made. All its sweetness, all its love, all its glory, are Christ's gifts to us. People talk to us now and then about nice things in non-Christian religions. It is enough for me to remember that every one of these religions but one was here when Jesus Christ came. I raise no question of comparative religion. Jesus Christ settled that question for me. When, 1,800 years ago, God tore apart the home in heaven and gave his only Son, that he might die upon the Cross of Calvary for mankind, that was enough for me. Once and for all he pronounced every other way of access to him, except Christ, futile and vain. When Jesus Christ said, "I am the way, the truth, and the life, and no man cometh unto the Father but by me," he made proof plain to us, not alone what his gospel was to us, but what could be found in the world for his gospel to do.

When, a generation ago, troubles arose in India, there were found those who were asserting that it was not Christianity, but it was the British government that held India; but a noted Hindu said to them, "Who is it that rules India? Not Lord Lytton, or Sir Frederick Haines on the battlefield; not politics nor diplomacy. Christ rules British India. The British army does not hold it. If any army deserves the honor, it is the army of Christian missionaries headed by their invisible captain, Jesus Christ."

There comes back to me at this time a visitation to a temple in Northern Korea, which I made a few years ago. The grass had grown up between the stones, the bars were thrust through the locks. We sought admission. At last a tawdry priest came to let us in and show us the idols and the empty jars, and we asked him if any one came there to worship. "No," he said, "ever since this Jesus religion came to Northern Korea they have lost interest in the temple; they come no longer to worship here." My friends, even now, the hands upon that cruel tree, extended wide, are gathering to the Son of Man the joys past and that are to be. And we now understand our dead Christ when we look upon that that influenced him, and see what he would like to do for the whole world.

I may not close without saying a word about the blessing that awaits us if we will fall in line with Christ's will. There is no blessing apart from sacrifice, and I do not see why the Christian church should not gain that blessing, as well as those who seek it for lucre's sake. The railroad in Africa, just completed, cost $12,000,000 and 4,000 lives. More than twenty human lives have been laid down upon every mile of the Congo Railway. On that railway more human life has been sacrificed than has been sacrificed in Christian missions from the days of the Apostle Paul to this day. Are we to say that we are to permit human sacrifice for gain which we are not willing to sacrifice for Christ? Friends, our personal life will never rise up into the fulness of Christ's desire until we have learned his secret of large service.

MONDAY AFTERNOON.

Tent Endeavor.

The Junior Rally.

A great company of human faces is always more eloquent than any words, and no group of faces is so eloquent as the faces of children. There were thousands of these sweet human flowers in Tent Endeavor on Monday afternoon, ranged in the front seats, and banked upon the platform in the loveliest of choirs. Around the tent stood people as many deep as they could see or hear.

Canada presided over the rally in the person of Rev. William Patterson, of Toronto; and Australia led the devotional exercises in the person of Rev. Joseph Walker, who gave the message of Australian Juniors to the Juniors of America,—"We want the children of the

The Juniors' Jubilee.

whole world for Jesus Christ." It was Detroit's turn next, and Miss Austin welcomed them charmingly, the hundreds of Juniors on the platform emphasizing her greeting with the waving of handkerchiefs and flags, and a shrill and hearty cheer.

Address of Welcome by Miss Elizabeth E. Austin.

Detroit, Mich.

Dear friends, you have been welcomed to our city by officials, pastors, and individuals, yet we feel it is incomplete without our Juniors' welcome. It gives me great pleasure to extend to you from all Juniors in Detroit a hearty welcome. We have been preparing for you and this is our day. Take back to the boys and girls in your society and neighborhood our message of love. Tell them, though separated, we are being trained together by our Master for service by and by.

Among the most carefully preserved instructions to the Jews of old was that command of Jehovah to "diligently teach the children." Jesus Christ, our Lord, distinct from all other teachers, emphasized the importance of childhood. The proof of Peter's love for the Saviour was asked in the feeding of his lambs. His miracles included children, and the embodiment of their characteristic qualities is given as a test of divine love. God has used the trusting child in the turning of a nation's fate.

As we draw near the time when our Lord shall come again, the need for careful lives is apparent. How shall coming years be saved from threatened ungodliness, with attendant despair, if the boys and girls are not taught the inevitable love and laws of God. Well done, this solves every vexing problem of our age.

What a privilege is that of a Junior worker! You may have about you those whose mothers, like Hannah, have lent them to the Lord as long as they may live. It is your privilege to be the Eli to whom Samuels shall come not yet knowing the Lord; his word not yet revealed to them. Oh, be faithful in your directions to answer: "Speak, Lord, for thy servant heareth." Then will Samuels grow and the Lord will be with them. Make the first thing in your Junior work a passion for souls. Seek an attitude that will ever invite a seeking Samuel.

Fill the craving mind of Juniors with Bible stories. Let Bible heroes be their silent guides. At this age, when memory acts at its best, store it with God's precious Word. Encourage the memorizing of hymns of devotion and praise, from which they can draw in old age and times of sickness. Equip them to reach out the hand of sympathy and counsel with "It is written."

In this feverish age of rush the lesson of preparation is one hard to learn. Forty years for Moses. John the Baptist "grew and waxed strong in spirit and was in the desert until the time of his shewing in Israel." Christ was apart from public service thirty years before his ministry, and he the Son of God. The daily submission to the divine will, the practice of losing our lives for Christ's sake, the seeking of opportunities for service, will secure an attitude that God can use to the enlargement of soul. Train them to rejoice in the balance given to lives through trial as does an artist in the harmony of light and shade in a perfect picture. The sheltered tree in the pleasant valley is left for the weather-beaten, storm-proven one on the hill-top when the keel of a ship is to be chosen. "Success is nine-tenths drudgery" 't is said, and we must be trained if we would excel. Lead your Juniors in seeking joy rather than happiness — joy in the exercise of unselfishness. Let their activities find pleasant employment in lightening the burdens of the weary and contributing to the welfare of the unfortunate. Our Junior Arsenal is a revelation to us all as to what can be done. May it prove an inspiration!

And now, dear fellow workers, rest in the Lord. "Laying aside every weight and sin that doth so easily beset us, let us run with patience the race that is set before us." Ours is a great privilege. The sacrifice of trifles is not much to ask. We have not to do with results. They belong to God. Let us all appropriate the abiding presence of the Holy Spirit. He will exercise in us the power of choice. He will provide a patient spirit. He will enthrone the soul. Our hearts shall then be filled with love which shall appear unto the world, as Drummond so beautifully writes of the thirteenth chapter of First Corinthians, in the spectrum of a perfect character: patience — love suffereth long; kindness — and is kind; generosity — love envieth not; humility — love vaunteth not itself, is not puffed up; courtesy — doth not behave itself unseemly; unselfishness — seeketh not her own; good temper — is not easily provoked; guilelessness — thinketh no evil; sincerity — rejoiceth not in iniquity but rejoiceth in the truth.

> I look to the sky at evening,
> And out of the depths of blue
> A little star, we call it,
> Is shining faintly through.
> Little! He who looks from his throne
> In the highest place

Sees a great world circling grandly
The limitless realms of space.
So with our life's deep purpose,
Set in his mighty plan,
What to us is weak and little
To him is great and grand.

Cosmopolitan Juniordom was also splendidly illustrated by the exercise, "World-wide Christian Endeavor." This was an intensely interesting review of Christian Endeavor history, presented by the Juniors themselves. They came up two or three at a time, or in larger companies, each representing the origin of the movement in some country, or some remarkable Christian Endeavor fact from some part of the world. The children would give a sentence or two, their clear voices ringing out with a will, and Dr. Hill, in his jolly fashion, telling the rest of the story. Two youngsters from Maine proudly bore a picture of Williston Church. The Canadians carried a great, green maple-leaf. Hawaii showed a leaf of a scrap-book, because Christian Endeavor sprung from one of Dr. Clark's articles a Hawaiian missionary pasted in his scrap-book. China marched proudly under her yellow banner. The Pacific islands sailed along with a dancing little missionary ship. How pretty the girls looked, with their gay sashes, and how manly the boys, you must be left to imagine.

Appropriate songs came in here and there,— "Our Mission Ships Are Sailing," "The Canadian Song," and the like. Some of these were in foreign tongues, and the German song was by some German children of Detroit. A great map of the world stood on a lofty platform; and, as each country came to the front, a busy Junior boy stuck red Convention seals on the proper points of the map. Any amount of curious and inspiring information about Christian Endeavor was packed into this capital exercise.

Rev. Floyd Tomkins's talk to the children was as bright as a dollar. He took the fingers of their hands, and made them spell "Jesus" on them. Then the fat, jolly little thumb was made to stand for "Joy;" and the index finger, pointing upward, was made to stand for "Eternal;" and the highest and most important finger meant "Salvation;" and the ring finger, which is so hard to move alone, but must move with the others, meant "United;" and the twinkling little finger meant "Social;" and these words together spell "Jesus" with their first letters, because they show what kind of persons Jesus wants us to be.

A fit close was the beautiful salute to the flags. A long line of boys with uniform caps stretched across the platform. Two cornetists played spiritedly, and at the proper bugle-call there was raised to the top of the tent a long string of flags of all nations. The boys saluted with their caps at the same time. A fitting close was this to one of the most interesting and instructive Junior rallies ever held.

First Presbyterian Church.

What is said to have been the largest open conference held in any of the churches during the Christian Endeavor Convention was the one in the First Presbyterian, Monday afternoon. It was on " Prison Work," and, in addition to the hundreds there and turned away from the doors, the sympathy of thousands behind the gates of prisons was with the meeting, as was shown by the greetings sent from many of the State penitentiaries. Under the leadership of Mr. E. O. Excell, that familiar Christian Endeavor chorus, " All the way, all the way, for I have the Saviour with me, all the way," was sung while the audience was becoming seated and others were making themselves comfortable in the aisles and in the rear of the seats. Mr. Frederick A. Wallis, of Hopkinsville, Ky., presided over the large gathering. Mr. Wallis is an active worker in the prisons of his State, and is at present the superintendent of the Kentucky Christian Endeavor prison work. Prof. James Lewis Howe, of Virginia, led in prayer, after which Dr. Jennings, the pastor of the church, conducted the devotional services.

President Clark was then introduced by the chairman, and the greeting of the president of the United Society was heartily received. The features of the meeting were the practical conference conducted by Mr. Shaw and the address by Dr. Chapman.

Address by Rev. J. Wilbur Chapman, D.D.,

New York City.

" In prison and ye visited me."

It has been stated that no work is more full of discouragement than that of special service in the interests of men and women who are in prison. That there are some discouraging features all will agree, for this is true of every form of Christian work ; but it is my purpose to show the bright side of the picture and present, if I may, that which may serve as an inspiration to the Endeavorers who are engaged in this particular form of service.

Whatever other interpretation may be given to the twenty-fifth chapter of Matthew, this at least is true : there is a special blessing promised to those who minister to the unfortunate and the suffering ; and particularly is this true when the suffering ones are his own little ones.

A Russian soldier called out on picket duty left the barracks so hastily that his greatcoat was forgotten. The cold, biting winds of winter cut him through and through, when a Russian peasant passing by said, " I will soon be home, take my coat." But hurry though he did, he was overpowered by the cold, and under the touch of pneumonia, came to the very brink of eternity. He came back, as it were from the skies, and said, " I have had a vision, and have seen Christ ; and strangest of all, I saw that greatcoat of mine, and when I asked him what it meant he said, ' I was naked and ye clothed me.' "

Then it is true that you could not, with a desire to glorify Christ, give a cup of cold water, speak a word of cheer, or lift a brother's burden that you did not touch him. This is certainly true of prison work.

But note the encouragements : —

First. There is no story of sin that can be told behind prison doors that does not have its counterpart, and its accompanying story of forgiveness, in the New Testament.

Is it theft charged against the prisoner ? Then read the story of Zaccheus, and forget not to read that when he confessed himself a sinner then Jesus went with him to his house and his whole house was saved.

Is it adultery? See the picture of the woman at his feet, and his stooping to write her forgiveness in the sand. Or see Mary Magdalene with loving lips and hands pressed close against the bleeding feet of Christ, and remember she was forgiven the "scarlet sin."

Is it base denial of Christ? Then look at Peter, who denied him thrice, and remember Mary, who came from the tomb where she had seen her risen Lord, and bore from him the invitation to his disciples to meet him — and Peter's name alone was mentioned, as if he feared his denial might make him afraid to meet him again.

Is it murder? Then come with me outside the city of the king, climb the hill until you come to Calvary, and hear him say who hangs upon the cross,— when they who put him there have done their worst, have driven nails through his hands and feet, thrust their spears through his side, and mocked him in his dying agony,—"Father, forgive them, for they know not what they do." And remember that the murderers of our Lord could have been forgiven if they would. It is true that Calvary is hardly a hill outside the city gate, but faith makes it the highest mountain in all the world; for never has there been a mountain from which you could so nearly see into heaven, so plainly hear the angels' music, or so fairly see into the heart of God, as from Calvary.

I pray you remember, all of you as you go to work with prisoners, that there is written in the New Testament a story of forgiveness for every prisoner you will meet, however dark his deed may have been.

Second. Remember the literature given us from prison cells, and then take hope that you may be the messenger of peace to some one who might set the world on fire for God, prisoner though he be. It was when he was in prison that Paul wrote Colossians, which speaks of our risen Head; Ephesians, which tells of the body, which is the church; Philippians, the key-word of which is "*rejoice*," and records the glad experience which may be ours when we know that he is our head, we are a part of his body, and live accordingly.

It was when Savonarola was a prisoner that he wrote his matchless comment on Psalms xxxi, and li.

It was while Francis Baker was a prisoner in the Tower of London that he wrote the hymn "Jerusalem, My Happy Home."

Most of the letters of Samuel Rutherford were written from the Aberdeen jail, John Bunyan wrote "Pilgrim's Progress" while in Bedford jail, and Adoniram Judson wrote his thrilling letters from a Burmese prison.

How true it is that if one has Christ filling his soul

> "Stone walls do not a prison make,
>   Nor iron bars a cage!"

And you who form the noble army of Christian Endeavorers, go with Christ for every discouraged, downcast soul.

Third. There is still another encouragement in the remarkable transformation of many who have been in prison. In a western city a Christian Association secretary found a young lawyer in prison, completely disheartened. He was a drunkard. No one believed in him; every one had cast him off as hopeless. This secretary, with love in his heart, told him of Christ, assured him that there was forgiveness for him; and to-day he is an honored minister of the gospel. The age of miracles is not past.

Remember Jerry McAuley. He had served three terms in Sing Sing prison, was a poor, old river thief, hopeless and helpless; yet when he died it was asserted by New York's leading minister that no one had ever exerted a wider influence for Christ than he in all the city.

There is not in all the prisons of the land to-day a character too hardened or too sinful for Christ to transform. Let this inspire you.

There are some reasons why the work should be hastened:—

First. While in prison there is a rare chance to place in the hands of prisoners good literature, and thousands have been saved in this way.

Second. If the work is not accomplished while in prison the case is almost hopeless; for if one is without sympathy during all his term he comes forth with spirit broken, feelings hardened, a menace to society, and useless to himself and the world, so far as any good is concerned.

What if there are discouragements? "If God be for us who can be against us?" Let it be known in every prison that wherever a Christian Endeavorer is found there is one who will not give the prisoner up.

There died the other day in Boston an old woman whose story was pathetic. She had fallen from sheer weakness at the steps of the hospital and was carried into the building to die. The nurse who won her confidence drew from her this story. Some years before her son had left his home on the Pacific coast, and did not tell her where he was going nor when he would return. She had immediately converted all her property into money and started in pursuit. She had visited every large city and had gone always to two places,—the police court and the hospital,—her thought being that in one of these two places he might be found; but the search was hopeless. She had reached Boston, and had fallen in her task. When told that she was dying she whispered to the nurse attending her, "Some day he may come in here, and if he does I want you to tell him that there were two that never gave him up,—God, and his mother," and she was gone.

Let it be known in every prison in the land that no matter what sin may have sent the prisoner there, there are two that will never give them up,—God and the Christian Endeavorer.

May God's richest blessing be upon this great work, and upon this Endeavor movement, which grows larger and better with each passing year!

St. Paul's Memorial Church.

Missionary Workers' Conference.

Conducted by Mr. D. B. Eddy, Leavenworth, Kan.

That the Christian Endeavorer is full of missionary zeal and believes in the evangelization of the world as one of the chief problems confronting Christian effort to-day was demonstrated by the large attendance at St. Paul's Memorial Chapel. The building was crowded at the special missionary conference on practical methods for missionary committees and workers.

After a praise service and prayer, Mr. D. B. Eddy, of Leavenworth, Kan., one of the members of the Yale Mission Band, opened the conference by suggesting the following methods for perpetuating missionry interest.

First, a development of prayer life. Second, a missionary library in each society. Under the head of study, with the above, was suggested the maintenance of regular missionary meetings, and the conference discussed various ways of conducting the same.

The missionary study class, as suggested by the Student Volunteer Movement, was also recommended.

The subject of giving was then discussed at length. Miss Ella MacLaurin, of Boston, related several of her experiences along this line, and referred to a lady from Buffalo, who had been influential in raising, not only $500 to support a worker in the field, but had also, in this way, raised $3,000 on a church mortgage. She recommended the "forward movement" which embodied a plan of supporting some particular worker by a society or church.

Rev. C. H. Hubbell, of Cincinnati, made the following suggestions:—

"Have prayer for the grace of generosity; study of the Bible concerning missions; use of missionary charts; correspondence with missionaries; live missionaries to talk to the society; have a volunteer go from the society; give people facts; ask and expect; give yourself; push the Tenth Legion, and get sight of the missionary, Christ."

Mr. C. B. Vickrey, of Bartley, Neb., also of the Yale Band, then gave an exhibition of "tools" used in promoting missionary zeal. He also called attention to the remarkable missionary exhibit of St. Paul's Church, comprising a large library of one hundred and fifty volumes, fifty of which are now in use, a large assortment of missionary maps and scrap-books.

Mr. Robert E. Speer, secretary of the Presbyterian Board of Missions, said : —

"There are many people who learn, but fail to do. Some of these plans look quite smooth, but will not work without effort and disappointment. Take prayer, for instance. We can begin that to-day. Put your quiet hours into the busiest days, as Christ did. It is easy to give, if you want to. Begin reading now.

"In regard to 'going,' we are seeking men now to fill several vacancies in large fields, and can't find them. We want fighting men."

The conference closed with the benediction.

MONDAY EVENING.

Tent Williston.

There were crowds without and crowds within the tents long before the hour for opening. Inside, they were singing State songs — different songs in different parts of the tent, but that did n't matter; outside, they were wishing themselves in.

There were glorious doings awaiting all who were fortunate enough to get in. The first instalment came in the form of a batch of telegrams,— an answer to President McKinley's cordial message of greeting received early in the Convention; telegrams of greetings to, and replies from the Peace Commission at The Hague, and Lord Minto, Governor-General of Canada; and a telegram to Her Majesty, Queen Victoria.

The spirit with which the audience entered into this interchange of courtesies by lightning was delightful, and the episode was happily closed by singing the national airs of America and Great Britain, and "Blest be the Tie."

The message from The Hague had a jubilant note, which capped the climax. It read: "American Commission to the Peace Conference sends sincere thanks for message, and congratulates you and all friends of peace on the great success achieved, providing for a permanent tribunal of arbitration."

This was the first publication of the glorious news, and it fell upon waiting ears like an echo of the angels' song twenty centuries ago.

In the introduction of the Committee of '99, the best committee of arrangements an International Convention ever had, Chairman Strong thought he had the laugh on Dr. Boynton when he introduced him as chairman of " The Weather Committee ; " but Dr. Boynton neatly turned the tables by reciting some lines born of Convention weather : —

> " O the weather!
> Blow the weather!
> It upsets our plans altogether.
> But whether it 's cold,
> Or whether it 's hot,
> We must weather it, whether or not."

Then came the roll-call of States. Here are some of the most striking responses. Illinois's large delegation waved flags as they sang their State song to the tune of " John Brown's Body." " Maine, the mother of Endeavor, will follow her well-known child, and keep on going and growing," was the motto of the Pine-Tree State, and right lustily did they sing their song to the tune of "Tramp, Tramp, Tramp." "Blest be the tie that binds," sang Delaware's two delegates. "That 's a good motto for any couple," said Dr. Clark. "Tennessee for Christ " brought up such delightful memories of a year ago that the audience applauded to the echo. The familiar and popular " Maryland, my Maryland " was started by a colored man, whose strong, melodious voice rang out above all the rest.

Miss Antoinette P. Jones appeared for the Floating Endeavorers, and led by Mr. Excell, the whole audience sang a stanza of " Jesus, Saviour, pilot me."

Japan's five representatives sang a stanza of " All hail the power of Jesus' name " in Japanese.

In introducing Bishop Vincent, Dr. Clark suggested that no one could more fittingly receive the Chautauquan salute, and no one ever did receive a more generous, white-winged welcome. His sermon on " The Value of the Unit " was the very message that was needed to clinch all the good impressions that had preceded it. He said, "If I had entertained any doubt of the value of these great mass-meetings, the magnificent demonstration which I have seen here to-night was sufficient to banish it." The bishop was all too brief for his appreciative audience, but the address was so packed with the highest truths, illustrated with rare tact and projected from a warm heart, that all will treasure it through the coming year, and strive to apply it in personal work for the salvation of others.

Address by Bishop John A. Vincent, D.D., LL.D.,

Topeka, Kan.

Mr. Chairman, Ladies and Gentlemen : I am profoundly impressed with the significant and far-reaching influence of the Young People's Society of Christian Endeavor, as illustrated by the great meeting just now closing. The Christian Endeavor represents a large idea. It represents a Christian idea ; it represents a catholic idea, for the perfection of Christian unity you illustrate in your gathering and your movements generally. I believe in denominations ;

I believe in the unity of denominations under the domination of a single thought, the thought of Christ; under the control of one mighty force, the love of Christ. It is to-night too late for me to say all that is in my heart to say concerning this association. My heart is in full sympathy with it, with the noble work it has accomplished, and the larger work which lies before it. I am confident that the great movement is prophetic, and that the foundations are laid — but the superstructure is yet to be erected; and as I have listened to voices from various parts of our own land, and various parts of the Old World, to-night, pledging States and communities and nations to the service of Christ, my heart has been filled with the enthusiasm which the hour and the Convention have kindled.

I have, however, but a single message to convey to you. I do it with difficulty; the hour is late; the audience is in danger of being restless; but I have my watch within sight, and I assure you that I shall not trespass beyond the time which has been assigned, and I shall even limit that.

We are living in an age of great mass movements. We believe in large churches, great choirs, eloquent preachers, great conventions, mammoth Sunday schools. We do things on a large scale; and we are in very great danger of forgetting a law which I desire to-night to emphasize, and that is what I call the law of the unit. Our work on the mass is of no avail unless we take one soul at a time, and develop in the individual life, which the mass so magnificently might represent. I look upon the Sunday-school work with great interest; but I have been very much afraid of the tendency to superficiality in Sunday-school work. I watch now and then, or did in the other years, in general review in a Sunday-school session. I remember the superintendent who said to the school on the occasion of a visit from a distinguished gentleman, a Sunday-school worker in New York, "Now, children, we want to-day the recitation of the golden text. All together:" and about twenty-five of a school of five hundred recited the golden text. "Ah," said the superintendent, "that will never do; certainly our friend from New York will have a very false idea of the efficiency of our Sunday school with a recitation like that. Now together;" and then about one hundred recited the golden text. The superintendent was still dissatisfied, and protested against the insufficient answer, and with especial appeal secured from the vast majority of the school the recitation of the text. Whereupon he said, "That is worthy of you; see, my dear friend from New York, how well we do our work." What a piece of fraud the whole thing was! I know a student accustomed to the methods of secular schools must have felt the contrast between the methods of the Sunday school and the methods of what we call the secular school. I wish to insist that in all our work in the church, and in all the educational departments of the church, in pastoral service, in public ministry, we must put emphasis on one at a time; — the unit — the unit should be our aid in all our endeavors.

I certainly believe in small churches. We have a protest everywhere against the multiplication of churches, and the Christian church is condemned because, in a single community, there are eight, ten, or twelve different denominations. Now, I presume I shall differ from a great many of the good people who are now within the sound of my voice when I say that we do not, on the whole, have too many denominations, nor too many churches. I put emphasis on the value of small churches. A man said to me, several years ago, concerning a city in Dakota, "Here we have a town of so many inhabitants, and yet in this town we have fifteen churches — fifteen churches in a town like this!" Said I, "Who proposed to build the churches? Did the denominations here represented propose it?" "No;" he said. "In fact, the real-estate agents proposed it. The real-estate agents, when they develop a town, always look ahead, and form an estimate as to what the town is to be in the future: and such is the high tribute they pay to our Christianity that they say civilizations cannot succeed unless the church lays hold; and we give you lots for that purpose, we help you to put up buildings, and therefore the twelve or fifteen different churches in this little Dakota town." "Well," I said, "suppose that on next Sunday morning, a bright and beautiful June morning, all the people in the city, this particular city, should decide to attend church; who could go to church? Have you church accommodations for all the people who ought to be in the sanctuary next Sunday morning?" He made a rapid estimate, and he said, " I declare, we have n't church accommodations now for the people who might go to church in this town." Said I, " Now you build five or six more churches, and be ready for that touch which shall come from the Spirit of God awakening people to a sense of their responsibility and calling their attention to their obligations to attend God's house on God's day."

I have said I sympathize with small churches. I sympathize with small churches because small churches are more likely to secure attention to the units, and the man with his little congregation of one hundred or one hundred and fifty, with his faithfulness to his one hundred in pastoral service, in the study of individual needs, in going to their homes, in training their children, in ministering to the sick, in winning to Christ the individuals that compose his little church and congregation, will find one hundred and fifty people all that he can well handle in legitimate pastoral work, which accomplishes most in the building-up of a church.

I insist that the emphasis upon the law of the unit will guarantee a church an amount of pastoral oversight, and a larger number of individuals surrendering to Christ. This law of labor for the unit is the law of life. A dentist takes one at a time; a doctor deals with one at a time; a life-insurance agent takes one at a time, and he takes him over and over again, until he secures him; a railway conductor in a car passes through the crowded car and has no thought about the mass, but he says, " Your ticket if you please. sir; " and he examines the particular ticket and looks at the man, and puts a little ticket — that annoying thing that conductors will do — puts that little slip. to remind him, in the hat of the passenger; and so he goes through, becoming acquainted with the individuals. until the right sort of a conductor will stand at the end of the car and tell you where every man and every woman is going to. Conductors study units. The teachers who do their work well study units; the lawyers who are worthy of anything study and make for units. "Excuse me, sir, but you have repeated all your arguments during the last thirty minutes; you had finished your plea thirty minutes ago." He said, " Yes, I had, and I had won all but one man, and I had to secure him; and I had to repeat over and over again, and now I have him; and I could show you," he says, "how from the beginning of my argument I have taken two men at once, and then one, the third, and then the fourth, and then the fifth, and the sixth, and at last I had on my hands the twelfth juror, and I worked for him until I secured him. "

Bishop Vincent Won All Hearts.

The Bishop of London, one day, in addressing a class of candidates for the ministry, said to them, "Gentlemen, the one great thing you need as effective ministers is to reach individuals. " He said, " When I place fifty or sixty jugs together, and then take a pail of water and empty that pail of water over those jugs, into each jug will go a few drops; but if I want to fill the jugs, I take a jug at a time, and fill it. " It was a homely illustration for the Bishop of London to use, but a very good illustration.

The Roman Catholic Church — that organization of such immense power in this country, and concerning which I should like to say a few things to-night which I shall not say — the power of the Roman Catholic Church is in her emphasis on individuals. her looking after the units; and her confessional is one of her mighty agencies by which she controls the multitude through her care for the individual.

Now, pastoral work is one of the most important departments of Christian activity. I address, I trust, a large number of ministers to-night, of all denominations, and I wish to emphasize the vast importance of supplementing earnest pulpit endeavor with faithful pastoral service. I address a large multitude, running into thousands to-night, of Sunday-school teachers. Class work is valuable, but the care through the week of the individual pupil is worth more than the general teachings of a half-hour in a class on the Sabbath Day. And when ministers have opportunities to reach individuals whom affliction confines for a time to the home, then they have the opportunity of their pastorate. Tom, yonder, met with an accident; his limb is broken; he is shut up for six weeks or more in the home; he is a fellow who cares very little about religious matters, and never goes to church; but when the minister finds out that Tom has been floored and has been held for a time for his service, the minister calls on Tom day after day, ministering to him, counselling with him, reading him the news, delighting him, winning his confidence and his affection. What wonder that before the weeks have passed the fast friend of Tom is the minister and the fast friend of the minister is Tom?

I hold in my hand a very remarkable letter, a letter which I received during my administration in one of the Eastern conferences of the church which I represent. I must read it to you. I have had it printed in exquisite style,—printed in the very highest style of the art, by an association that devotes itself to printing on hand-made paper, in the most careful fashion,—because I said that the letter deserves being put in the best possible form. The writer supposed that I had episcopal administration over the conference to which her church belonged. I had been the bishop of that conference the year before; she took it for granted that my administration continued, and she wrote this letter. It is a letter written by a woman who washes for a living. When I read the letter I said, "That puts me in mind of the style of Abraham Lincoln." When I read it to one of the most distinguished scholars in the country, he said to me, "That puts me in mind of Bunyan's 'Pilgrim's Progress.'" And I will read it to you. It tells a volume by way of illustrating the doctrine of the unit, which I desire to-night to fix upon your thoughts. The letter reads as follows:—

Dear Sir: I hardly know whether I ought to do this or not, but I do not see how it can do any harm, that is, if you will be kind enough not to tell any one that I have written, as some of our good people might think, perhaps with truth, that one who could not help any more than I can had no right to say anything; but I do want our minister to stay another year, and I suppose if you say he has to come back for another year he will come. If I thought he would dislike to come I would not write this; but I was talking with him about it, and I did not think he would feel very badly if he were sent back. I am a poor woman, trying to earn a living for mother and myself by washing. I am really not strong enough for the work, and I get so discouraged sometimes that it seems as if I had about as well give up everything: I feel as if God did not care what became of me, and Brother —— will come in and talk a while, and pray with us, and somehow we feel better and stronger, and as if God did care a little, after all. Brother —— does care for poor people; some of our ministers do not. I speak from a sad experience of a time when I was ill for many months, and hoped, day after day, that the minister would call, but he never did. Mother is over eighty years old, and cannot get out to church, and is so glad to have our minister call; and we know that Brother —— will. Won't you please send him back? He is a good man, and when I hear him in the pulpit, or anywhere else, I feel more like trying to be good myself; and it will be one good thing in a hard, dull life to know that for one year more I can have him for our minister. There are some that do not like him; but I think there are more that like him than there are that do not.

I really thought when I read that that if St. Paul were to go to some churches as pastor he would not be liked.

I do not know that you will be the one to decide this year; but I did not know to whom to write, and if you can send him back please do, unless you can see that it will not be best. And once more I ask, please don't let any one know I have written this letter, and then it can do no harm, if it does no good; and if you think I have taken a liberty in writing, please excuse me.

There is the very soul of pastoral responsibility set forth by a plain, everyday woman, who knows from experience what it is to have one of God's ministers go into her home and contribute, by faithful pastoral service, to the wellbeing of that home. I plead for the care of the unit in all our great work.

Do I believe in such a mass-meeting as this? If I had before any question as to the value, every shadow of doubt or objection must have vanished before the magnificent demonstration of to-night. But, with all the glory of the Christian Endeavor, with all the power of eloquence in pulpits in great cities, with all the millions of people listening to charming music and held spellbound by the eloquence of gifted men,— we need with it all the fidelity which sends one earnest soul to another earnest soul pleading, edifying, comforting, inspiring; and if we did our duty as pastors, as Sunday-school teachers, as church officers, as members of the Society of Christian Endeavor, to the units with whom we come in contact, the magnificence of our work would be incalculably augmented.

Do you remember, too, that this law of the unit is the law of the divine in its operation? Do you remember that Laodicean church? That was a curious church. It was a church that said, "I am rich and increased with goods and have need of nothing," and it knew not that it was miserable and poor and blind and naked. It was the church that was neither hot nor cold, but lukewarm. Do you know the reason? Because Christ was on the outside of it. It was a Christless church. It was to that church that he said, "I stand at the door and knock;" and when he came to prescribe the method by which he should enter the church, what did he do? He said, "If any man will open the door, I will come in to him, and will sup with him." Christ's indwelling in his church is in the units who compose the church; and the best work we can do is in the building-up of individuals.

Allow me to say two things more, and then I shall relieve your patience. I was once on the Juanita River in Pennsylvania, about forty years ago, on a hot August night, in a Methodist Church that was crowded to suffocation, and everybody was restless, and the preacher had a very responsible bit of work, which he certainly appreciated. He weighed quite three hundred pounds, although he was a comparatively young man; he was in a state of embarrassment and perspiration; he suffered intensely, and the people kept coming in and going out; and at last, taking a long breath, and wiping his ample brow with a red silk pocket-handkerchief, he said, "Brethren, I am a travelling preacher, but I do hate to preach to a travelling congregation." I sympathized with my brother of forty years ago. The two things I wish to say to you are these; let us recognize more than we have done the family as the social and church unit. Let us work more for the building-up of godly homes where children are individually studied by their parents, and where the law of the unit has full sway. And lastly, let us make the study of the individual, and the application of whatever gospel we have to them, the great work of our lives.

I have no sympathy with a gospel of mere culture. I have no sympathy with science and literature and art and the knowledge of history, as a means of bringing men to God, or of building men up in God; but I believe in culture and its place in the development of the units that make up the church. I have a theory that there are about four stages. My Unitarian friend, as a rule, begins with culture. I end with culture. The first step we should take as evangelical Christians is to emphasize the doctrine of sin. The curse of our age is the disposition on the part of certain schools of thought to depreciate sin. We need no gospel at all if sin does not exist as a fact, as a tendency, as a habit, as a stain, as a bondage; and therefore the first thing we need to do with the units we would save is to impress upon them the reality of sin. Secondly, we need to emphasize the reality of restored harmony with God. Thirdly, we need to emphasize the possibility, as Dr. Chapman said so eloquently yesterday morning, the power of the divine grace to save us from the dominion and the love of sin. Now, when I get a congregation, a church of units, hating sin, assured of divine acceptance, possessing the power which the divine grace gives, I want to open to every one of these units the splendid possibilities of culture which our civilization places at our command; and we need to build up a church of earnest, positive, spiritual, consecrated personalities, every one the temple for the indwelling of the Holy Spirit.

I close by reading about a little society which my colleague, Bishop Mallalieu, says he has organized. I hold the card in my hand, and reading it, I shall bid you good-night:—

THE ONE AND ONE SOCIETY.

No officers, no meetings, no dues,

Motto: One and one make two.

SCRIPTURE.

And ye shall be gathered one by one (Isa. xxvii. 12). For no man liveth to himself, and no man dieth to himself.

PLEDGE.

Unless unavoidably prevented, I will attend every one of the preaching services in .... Church. I will attend at least one social meeting each week. After each sermon, at least once during the week, I will speak to some one of some good or helpful thing contained in the sermon last heard. Once every week I will invite some one, not a churchgoer, to attend public worship in .... Church. Before each service, or at its close, I will speak to one stranger, at least, one word of welcome. At one o'clock each day I will offer a prayer for the blessing of God on all the members and on the pastor of .... Church.

Signature........ ....

Let us live for the unit, that we may win millions to Christ.

Closing Words by Dr. Clark.

Just this closing word. Take this Convention home with you. New responsibilities are yours. You have more to account for before the throne of God than when you came. Unless you Endeavorers who came to this meeting are more consecrated and faithful hereafter, you have lost your opportunity and God will hold you responsible.

Take this meeting home with you. You cannot keep it to yourself and remain guiltless. Take it to your society. Take it to your church, your village, your city, your State, and make this country a better country because we have held our Eighteenth International Convention of Christian Endeavorers.

Bow your heads a moment in silent prayer for God's blessing upon each other (pause); upon the people of Detroit, pray for them (pause); for the republic of the United States and the Dominion of Canada, pray for them (pause); for President McKinley, and the Governor-General of Canada, and the Queen of Great Britain, pray for them (pause); for all the rulers of the world and for all the people in all the earth, pray for them (pause); for our kind hosts who have opened wide their doors, pray for them (pause); for the committees and singers and the ushers, and all who have contributed to our happiness, pray for them (pause); for all Endeavorers, and for all kindred societies of young people, pray for them (pause); for our churches and friends, for our associate members, for all, pray (pause).

O God, hear us, bless us, keep us, save us; send us home to live for thee as we have never done (pause).

Now with our heads bowed let us repeat the Mizpah benediction, and then, as we remain seated, sing one verse of "God be with you till we meet again," and go home singing all the way on the cars. Now all together, the Mizpah benediction: "The Lord watch between me and thee when we are absent one from another."

And now I pronounce the Eighteenth International Convention of Christian Endeavorers adjourned without date.

Singing of hymn, "God be with you till we meet again."

Tent Endeavor.

As usual, the massing-together of the State delegations for the first time during the Convention made the scene in the tents just before the beginning of the closing sessions one of abounding jollity. Impromptu State calls were the order of the day. California would pipe up :—

> " Who are — who are — who are we ?
> We represent Californee! "

Then Colorado would roar out : —

> " Pike's Peak or bust, Pike's Peak or bust,
> Colorado! Colorado! Yell we must."

From Pennsylvania would come the response : —

> " Way up! Way up! We 'er not late.
> Nine hundred strong from the Keystone State."

The various delegations, State and national, were divided between Endeavor and Williston. Placards showed the Endeavorers where to go, and they had to " move up " many times before they all got in.

" Finally," was Mr. H. B. Gibbud's word in conducting the devotional exercises in Tent Endeavor, " finally, brethren, be strong in the Lord." And to point out the way, the noble choir sang most nobly Gounod's beautiful anthem, " Send out thy light and thy truth; let them lead me."

Some final figures were given by Secretary Baer. The total attendance of delegates, including the Detroit young people, had been about 28,000. There had been held 150 meetings, attended by an aggregate of 298,500 persons. This does not include the sixty-six evangelistic meetings, with an estimated attendance of 15,000, and with about one hundred professed conversions.

Rev. Teunis S. Hamlin, D.D., speaking for the Board of Trustees, read the following resolutions, which were endorsed by the entire audience rising: —

Resolutions of Thanks from the Board of Trustees of the United Society of Christian Endeavor.

We ask the Convention to heartily join with us in rendering devout thanksgiving to Almighty God for our safe and happy coming to, and sojourn at, this Convention; for the instruction and spiritual uplift that he has vouchsafed us; for the delightful Christian fellowship and hospitality that we have enjoyed; and for the inspiration that we shall carry to our homes, and that we shall try faithfully to use in his service, and in the service of our fellow men.

We but feebly express our earnest gratitude and sense of obligation to the citizens of this noble, beautiful city; its pastors and the members of its church es and of its various societies kindred to our own; its police; the motormen and conductors of its street-cars — when we say to each one of them, " I thank you." And to the chairman of the Committee of Arrangements, Mr. W. H. Strong, as well as to each of his able and efficient assistants, to every one who has made our stay here a delight, each of us says most cordially, " Your energy, industry, fidelity, courtesy, and Christian kindness have won our hearts."

We deeply appreciate, too, the concessions of the railroads and steamboats, and the thoughtful carefulness of their employees. And we especially prize the generous treatment accorded us by the local papers and by their obliging and industrious reports, and by the agent of the Associated Press — all whose generally accurate, sympathetic, and helpful reports have done so much to spread the influence of the Convention.

These six July days in Detroit will be a precious and cherished memory while life shall last. The acquaintanceships — may we not say friendships? — here formed will be sacredly prized. The spiritual impressions here received will be henceforth a part of our Christian characters. We earnestly wish and devoutly pray that we may leave with you as rich a blessing as we shall carry away. May the Eighteenth International Christian Endeavor Convention prove to us all a long forward step in the Christian life, an ever fresh and joyous memory, an unfading inspiration in service, an honor to our common Saviour and Lord.

The Purpose Meeting was something new in Christian Endeavor. As each State was called, its president, upon the platform, expressed the desire of his union for the coming year. Usually he bore in his hand the handsome State banner,— Pennsylvania's blue and red, Maryland's orange and black, and so on. His delegation then rose and gave their message in concert, a stirring song or a noble Scripture motto, or both.

The presidents' watchwords for the new year were inspiring. Hear a few : — Pennsylvania : "Dictate no terms to Providence ; accept the service offered you, high or low, far or near, then burn to the socket." Alabama (the words of General Wheeler): "I will not retreat in the presence of the enemy, but will press forward until our banners are perched in victory over the enemy's trenches." Oregon : "Watching, praying, working." Missouri : "More of Christ in me, in order to save the soul that is nearest me." New Hampshire : "Raise the standard." West Virginia : "Grow and go." Minnesota : "Lord, teach us what is truth and what is duty, and give us the courage to do our part."

The choice of Bible mottoes was often interesting. Nevada's was : "The wilderness and the solitary place shall be glad ; and *Nevada* shall rejoice and blossom as the rose." "Let us not be weary in well doing," etc., was a favorite verse. Vermont : "As the mountains are round about Jerusalem," etc.

There were many beautiful songs, especially the State songs of Kentucky, Texas, Missouri, New Hampshire, and Minnesota. New Jersey gave us, for the first time, her new and beautiful State song, written by Dr. Spooner. For Colorado, Miss Marion Cordingly, of Denver, sang most delightfully "I'll go where you want me to go." Detroit, sitting in the host's place at the rear of the audience, sang with fine effect the noble Convention hymn, "The Son of God goes forth to war."

California's word was for discipleship and fruit-bearing. New Jersey adopted Nevada and stood up with her two delegates. Utah made an earnest plea for help against Mormonism. New Mexico's one delegate also asked help for her "foreign country."

The tent was surrounded with a wide ring of people, the canvas sides being raised. Hearty rounds of applause greeted each delegation, those that rose in hundreds and thousands, those that rose in ones and twos. It was a scene of splendid enthusiasm.

The climax was reached in the introduction of the three delegates from Great Britain,— Rev. Messrs. Tresidder, Pollock, and Mursell. They stood up together and sang a song right manfully,—" Britain for Christ."

> Britain for Christ. Hark, the challenge resounding,
>   High over mountain and valley and plain,
> All the dark forces of treason confounding,
>   Christ is advancing to conquer and reign.

> Rally, Endeavorers, swell out the chorus,
> Trusting in God and renewing your cries,
> Bright gleams the banner that 's marching before us,
> Claiming the victory, Britain for Christ.

Then Secretary Baer put his arm around two of the trio and pushed in the line, and at this the audience vigorously gave the Chautauquan salute, then applause and applause, "God save the Queen," "America," "Blest be the tie," three cheers for the Queen, "We 'll expect you all in London,"—why, the very tent-poles swayed with shouts.

At a word from Mr. Baer, and in deep contrast to the cheering and applause that had greeted the others who came before the assembly, all heads were bent in an attitude of prayer, as Rev. J. Wilbur Chapman, D.D., stood before them to make the closing address. He prayed for the blessing of God upon the gathering in his name. "May the Holy Ghost fall upon this assembly. Come, Holy Spirit, descend upon us, and prepare us for the proper reception of the graces which God is about to shower upon us."

Address by Rev. J. Wilbur Chapman, D.D.,

New York City.

OBEDIENCE AND POWER.

There was a man whose right hand was withered.— Luke vi.6.
And looking round about upon them all, he said unto the man, Stretch forth thy hand. And he did so: and his hand was restored whole as the other.— Luke vi.10.

This is one of the seven miracles of our Lord, performed on the Jewish Sabbath. The other six were as follows: the demoniac of Capernaum (Mark i. 23); Simon's wife's mother healed of a fever (Mark i. 29); the impotent man by the side of the pool (John v. 9); the woman with the spirit of infirmity for eighteen years (Luke xiii. 14); the man with the dropsy (Luke xiv. 2); the man born blind (John ix. 14). And in all these our Lord reveals himself to us as a helper in every need.

There are those who are living lives in which they are controlled by the flesh as truly as the demoniac by his evil spirit; those who are made miserable by the fever of the world life as certainly as Peter's wife's mother; those who are bound by evil habit, as was the woman with her eighteen years' infirmity; and those among us who are blind to all the beauties of the life of blessing, who live themselves with the glories of a better life just within their grasp, and comprehend it not. All such need not a better environment, for Adam and Eve had the best environment the world ever saw, and failed; not strength of will, for mere strength of will is the secret of failure in many lives; but they need Christ, "who of God is made unto us wisdom, and righteousness, and sanctification, and redemption" (1 Cor. i. 30).

It is a very significant thing to me that in his miracles and teachings Christ fully establishes his ability to help in every form of weakness. He met the insane man in the tombs, and restored his reason. For us he gives his own mind: "Let this mind be in you" (Phil. ii. 5), says Paul. He gave Bartimeus his eyesight; put back in place the ear of Malchus. In Decapolis, he met the one whose tongue was tied that he could not speak, and he touched him, and his tongue was loosed, and he spake plainly. In Capernaum a man who was a helpless paralytic was let down through the roof, and Jesus said, "Arise, walk," and immediately he went forth. So that disease which touched the mind, the ear, the lips, the heart, the feet, the whole body, fled before him. Even death met its conqueror, and the daughter of Jairus, the son of the widow, and Larazus of Bethany came forth from the embrace of the last enemy that s to be destroyed. Thou shalt indeed call his name *Wonderful*.

There are special moral deformities which some Christians have, such as defective vision, imperfect tempers, faulty habits. To all of you who are weak, I submit him as your strength.

But of all the miracles, the one most helpful to us to-day is this one where the withered hand is made whole. There are many fine touches in the picture of the story.

This is one of the silent looks of Jesus. Mark and Luke both describe his look of anger and grief when he said nothing. When men speak we can answer them, but there are looks of men that make us afraid. What of the look of Christ? "He looked with anger, being grieved."

The anger of malice — who cares for it? The anger of abused pride — who heeds it? The anger of selfishness — who would pay attention to it? But when grief is turned to anger and love is changed to wrath it is time to tremble; and yet beyond doubt he looks upon many of us who have been the recipients of the best gift of heaven,—we who have had all that all the saints in all the ages have had, and with it have become saints, while we are still standing with dumb lips, deaf ears, closed eyes, and withered hands,—he must look with both anger and grief, because we will not be as he would have us.

The three evangelists, Matthew, Mark, and Luke, give the story, but Luke alone tells us that it was his right hand that was withered, which is easily understood, for Luke was a physician, and must be exact in his description. Tradition says that he was a stone-mason. Of this we are not sure, but he needed his hand, and Christ met his need — *he always does.*

This man with the withered hand is a perfect illustration to-day of all those who really are the children of God and yet for some reason are shorn of power and all but useless in the great work of our Master. Whatever interpretation may be given to the miracle for the unsaved, this at least is permissible: he is an illustration for the child of God, in that he had life, but was without the fulness of life, and therefore without power.

He was in the *synagogue*, and he knew that Jesus was to come there. He did what was always done in the New Testament days, by the lame, the halt, and the blind, or their friends; he put himself *in the way*, where Jesus was, and He did all the rest. Alas, many a feeble Christian has failed just here.

The withered hand was useless. This disease had its origin in a deficient absorption of nutriment. For some reason the blood pumped into all the parts of the system from the heart was hindered here; the bones were there, the finger-nails, the skin for a covering — but the hand itself was useless, because withered. There was the presence of life in the body, but none there.

When he obeyed the command of Christ, the result was wholeness, and the effect of wholeness was power. "Stand forth," said the Master, and he obeyed. "*Stretch forth thy hand*," and again he obeyed, doing an apparently impossible thing; and when he showed his willingness by his standing, Christ put the strength in his shoulder and the miracle is wrought.

These three points are for us in our weakness, and in our search for power.

First. *Put yourself in the way of blessing.* You never will until you feel your need. I am talking to you as a child of God; my message is not to the unsaved. I believe God's plan for your life can be nothing less than ultimate likeness to his dear Son. I presuppose that you have failed in other days; my message has nothing to do with the professedly sinless.

I am sure that you are sick of a life of compromise. O that your need would draw you to Christ to-day! There are certain tests by means of which you may be sure of your need: (*a*) occasional or frequent indifference to the claims of Christ and the demand of a holy life; for you are called to holiness; (*b*) occasional or frequent spiritual unrest; for to suffer thus when he said, "Peace I leave with you," "And lo I am with you alway," is alarming; (*c*) occasional or frequent failure in the same sin. To lose one's temper continually is a clear indication that you are not appropriating Him who is the secret of victory over every sin. Like the man with the withered hand, we have in the fact of our regeneration everything to show forth His power. We have spirit, soul, and body; but O how we need Christ in control of it all!

These are a few of Andrew Murray's steps to blessing and victory: First, there is such a blessing to be had. Second, it is for me. Third, I have n't got it. Fourth, I am very hungry for it. Fifth, I am prepared to give up everything that clashes with it. If you can breathe an Amen to this, then put yourself in His way, and claim what is your birthright privilege as a child of God.

Second. There are certain helps to be obtained as you go:—

(1) If you would meet him, then familiarize yourself with the Word of God, particularly with the Epistles; for here you will find God's plan for your life in minutest detail, and here you will see Him like whom you may become.

(2) Get alone with him, and tell him all your failings; spare not yourself in any way; tell him your name, even if it be Jacob; tell him your faults, even if they be many; tell him your hopes and desires, that you may be filled with himself.

(3) Put yourself in the way of his purpose. Would you know what it is? Read the Epistle to the Ephesians: "He hath chosen us in him, before the foundation of the world, that we should be holy, and without blame before him in love" (Eph. i. 4); and again, "Ye shall receive power" (Acts i. 8). The Holy Ghost stands related to the believer in a threefold way. "He dwelleth *with you* and shall be *in you*" (John xiv. 17); but there is yet another relationship of the Spirit, described by the words, "Behold I send the promise of my Father *upon you;* but tarry you in the city of Jerusalem until ye be endued with power from on high" (Luke xxiv. 49); and "Ye shall receive power after that the Holy Ghost is come *upon you*" (Acts i. 18). (a) He was *with us* when he convicted us of sin. (b) He was *in us* when we were regenerated, or born from above. (c) He is *upon us* when we yield unreservedly to him and he perfectly controls us. And this coming upon, or filling with, the Holy Ghost is to every believer in his Christian life what the word of Christ was to the man with the withered hand.

Third. The Christian who is without this touch of God is useless practically, so far as service is concerned. Men often speak of being filled with the Holy Ghost, as if it were a desirable thing yet not indispensable. In the estimation of many, to hear their testimony, you would think of it as one of the luxuries of the Christian life; when, indeed, without this touch of God one is like this man with the withered hand. No act of service is with power, and no Christian should perform the slightest act of service until he is definitely filled. If the Apostles of Jesus Christ, the chosen men, those who had walked and talked with him, and had felt the uplifting influence of his wonderful presence; who knew of his miracles and were witnesses of his resurrection; whose memories were stored with precious promises, which they had heard him speak;— if they must tarry to be filled with the Holy Ghost, how dangerous it is for us to begin any service without the Holy Ghost resting upon us. No Christian can live as God intended he should if he is a stranger to this manifestation of the Holy Ghost.

Since it is the Spirit who makes Christ real, and so strengthens us in him that victory over sin is possible; since he produces the fruit of the Spirit, imparts spiritual vigor, teaches how to pray, comforts, guides, and makes true worshippers of us all; then may God pity us if we have neglected putting ourselves in his way who waits to give power in the place of weakness.

There are certain reasons why so many of us are without power, all of which we find illustrated in this story:—

(1) The man's hand was withered, because there had been deficient absorption of nutriment. And you are powerless because you have not appropriated Christ. He is yours, but you have not used him. There is no favoritism with God. "Just as the spring flowers, the sunshine, and the pure air are as free to the beggar as to kings and queens, so God's abundant grace is for every one, and there is nothing that any one has ever had which you may not have if you will. The same stream is passing your door, but you have not used it; the same electricity is in the air, but you have not cared to appropriate it. The same grace that made a Luther, a Knox, a Lattimer, a Havergal, a Spurgeon,

is for you to-day." Alas, you are living the withered-hand life, when all the power of the Almighty is waiting to help you.

(2) There may be some special way in which you have hindered the life of God in you. There is a story in the Old Testament which is a good illustration here (1 Kings xiii. 4): "And it came to pass when King Jeroboam heard the saying of the man of God, which had cried against the altar in Bethel, that he put forth his hand from the altar, saying, Lay hold on him, and his hand which he put forth against, dried up so that he could not pull it in again to him." The prophet of God was prophesying against the King's wickedness, and he (Jeroboam) put out his hand to stay that divine plan and his hand was withered. How many there are to-day in the church — men and women — who are certainly saved and yet powerless! May it not be because consciously or unconsciously they have hindered the working-out of the plan of God? How may we hinder him?

(*a*) By grieving his Spirit. In Eph. iv. 30, Paul says, "Grieve not the Holy Spirit of God;" and then follows immediately the injunction, "Let all bitterness, and wrath, and anger, and clamor, and evil speaking with all malice, be put away from you." And remember always that the things which grieve the Spirit are the unholy things *allowed* in the life. Temptation is not sin; yielding is.

(*b*) By quenching the Spirit. In 1 Thess. iv. 19, Paul says, "Quench not the Spirit," and the word primarily means "to put out a fire;" in another sense it means to resist any effort. When the Holy Spirit is spoken of as a fire, it is his purifying and cleansing power presented to us. If, then, I resist his work of purification, I quench him. If I refuse to allow him to touch one part of my nature, I quench him. To hold on to one sin is dangerous for the Christian, and however small that sin may be, it was just such a small beginning that has lost the soul of many a man. If you own a piece of property a mile square, with the exception of one little piece of ground in the centre, which is my property, I can compel you by law to give me the right of way to my property through yours. And if one part of your heart has not been yielded to Christ, then Satan, whose property it is, can compel you again and again to give him the right of way to it. And you have wondered so many times why you have failed! This is the reason: you have not WHOLLY SURRENDERED, and Satan has therefore had the right of way too frequently.

(3) When the man with the withered hand obeyed Jesus his hand was made whole; and be it remembered THAT POWER IS ALWAYS LINKED TO OBEDIENCE. "There is not the slightest reason in the world to-day why you should not know and enjoy as much of God's love as any one else; the only lack is that somewhere in your nature there is a paralysis." What you need is to link your nature to that of Christ, your risen Lord. You may do that now; it is not necessary that you should wait. Paul says, in Romans vi. 13, "Yield yourselves as instruments of righteousness;" and the tense of the verb is the imperative, "Aorist," the meaning of which is something like this, "*This ought to have been done; now do it.*"

The result will be glorious. What came to Isaiah, as he stood on the highest step of the temple at the gate beautiful, when he said, "Woe to me, for I am undone," and then shouted in ecstasy, "Here am I, send me"? When God called for service is the thing for which I plead. What came to Joshua, the High Priest, when he stood clothed in filthy garments, and the Lord said (Zech. iii. 4, 5): "Take away the filthy garments from him; and unto him he said, Behold I have caused thine iniquity to pass from thee, and I will clothe thee with change of raiment. And I said, Let them set a fair mitre upon his head. So they set a fair mitre upon his head and clothed him with garments"? This is the burden of my plea, that men might cast off old habits like filthy garments, and let God clothe them with his own nature, setting upon them the fair mitre, like the special gift of the Holy Ghost. And what came to Jacob, supplanter and cheat, as his name would indicate, when he came to be Israel the Prince, with God? And men, this is the truth for which I contend, — the old Jacob nature put under foot, the new life in Christ given the pre-eminence.

And what came to Peter, the fisherman, the coward, the deceiver, the profane man, the false friend, who was made the Peter of Pentecost, the rock, the hero, the man crucified with the head down? For this I stand: it matters little what material we bring to God; if only he is given the right to mould it, the transformation will be glorious.

"Whatsoever he saith unto you, do it." Obey at any cost. If it cost you humiliation, obey; if it should mean crucifixion, still obey. Make the wrong in your life, so far as you have injured others, right; if this be possible, and he will tell you if it is, confess every known sin; hold nothing back from him. Step out on his promises, and claim from him the gift of power. Take the last two steps suggested by Andrew Murray: —

(1) I do now yield myself to God, that I may receive the special promise of the Holy Ghost.

(2) By faith, I now receive him. He is the light; he will drive out the darkness.

"Stand forth," I hear him say it, as to the man with the withered hand. "Stretch forth thy hand." He speaks once again to you; if you will obey he will make you whole. And this is the secret of power.

Finally, some earnest words from Secretary Baer, and a last word from the blessed Book : " Depart ye, depart ye, go ye out from thence, touch no unclean thing ; go ye out of the midst of her ; be ye clean, that bear the vessels of the Lord. For ye shall not go out with haste, nor go by flight : for the Lord will go before you ; and the God of Israel will be your rearward."

Mizpah.

" God be with you till we meet again."

And the greatest of Christian Endeavor Conventions was ended.

Those Wide-Awake Junior Workers' Conferences.

No brighter, more practical, more eager, and thoroughly enjoyable meetings were held during the entire week, than the Junior workers' conferences. No better Junior superintendents are to be found anywhere than those that led these meetings,— Miss Haus, Mrs. Wood, and Mr. Bray,— while in the pews — when not on their feet with some bright and helpful remark — were Mr. Atkinson, Mr. Shannon, Mrs. Clark, Mrs. Hill, Miss Kay, Miss Le Barron, and scores of others quite as efficient.

The most practical topics were discussed in that most practical way, a series of open parliaments. From all over the large auditorium, with not a vacant place, the suggestions and testimonies came in swift flashes. "Make it a privilege for the boys to join. Keep them on the waiting-list awhile." "Let the feminine superintendent get a masculine assistant to hold the boys. Pray till you get him." "Use postal-cards to ask the Juniors to do certain work for the meetings. They will do twice as much as you ask them to do, and be so proud!" "Appoint the unruly members to posts of responsibility." "Laugh with them once in a while." "Divide the society into four armies,— United States, Cuban, Porto Rican, Philippine. They will enter into a struggle to see who can win the banners of the other armies by getting the most new members, and the victor in twelve contests will be entertained at a 'banquet' by the others." "Do not think that Junior meetings must be held on Sunday. Train the Juniors to put their religion into all the week."

That was the sort of work done at these brisk conferences.

Junior Workers' Reception.

In the Junior headquarters Friday afternoon there stood a line of ladies elect — Miss Austin, president of the Detroit Junior Union, Mrs. Clark, Mrs. Hill, Mrs. Lathrop, and others — to receive the faithful Junior workers from all over the world. It was an encouraging prophecy for the future of Endeavor that the church parlors were thronged until elbow-room was at a premium by the brightest men and women whose lives are consecrated to the service of God in service of boys and girls.

Professor Moorehead's Bible-Studies.

No teacher of the Bible in this country is more honored and beloved than Prof. W. G. Moorehead, of the United Presbyterian Theological Seminary at Xenia, O. His books, and his work in Mr. Moody's schools and at Y. M. C. A. conventions, have greatly extended his influence. He is the picture of a Christian scholar, with his keen, kindly face, his spare form with its slight stoop, and his alert, thoughtful manner. It was a delight to watch the crowds of young people thronging around him to tell how he had helped them, or to ask for and receive a luminous exposition of some perplexing Bible passage.

The beautiful First Presbyterian Church was thoroughly filled at his very first lecture and at every subsequent meeting. His style was quiet, instinct with poetry, alive with practical helpfulness. His illustrations were genuine illuminants. Though he could treat only sample portions of Scripture, he made the Bible a new book to many hundreds. Such a course of Bible-study, so enthusiastically attended at an hour that meant much self-denial, is an evidence of the earnestness of our pledge to read the Bible every day, and is one of the most cheering features of our conventions.

Dr. Moorehead Is a Masterly Bible Teacher.

Prof. H. L. Willett's Daily Bible-Studies.

Professor Willett Was an Effective Bible Teacher.

Think of a thousand busy people from all parts of the world meeting for an hour daily to study the Bible !

Probably there is not in America a finer teacher of the prophetical books than Prof. Herbert L. Willett, of the Chicago University, and the number of Endeavorers who took advantage of such an opportunity was limited only by the seating-capacity of one of the largest churches in the city. Enthusiasm for the Bible ; that 's the word. Not hand-clapping over it, but delving into its treasures.

There was a printed syllabus for each lesson, and a blackboard was freely used. It is estimated that the Bibles brought into actual use in this Convention in searching the Scriptures would fill a car.

The Old Testament prophets will go home on the train with many delegates, living characters for the first time in their experiences.

Mr. Gibbud's Evangelistic Conferences Were Most Practical.

A Daily Personal Workers' Training-School.

Conducted by Mr. H. B. Gibbud, Springfield, Mass.

A man who is helping scores of young people to get a working knowledge of the Bible, Mr. H. B. Gibbud, of Springfield, Mass., was a great blessing to the Convention. Every day he packed his hour full of best things. Here are some of them : "People say they have n't time to read the Bible. The book of Ephesians can be read through in ten minutes; some of the shorter books in five minutes or less. One business man kept a Bible on his telephone, and whenever he rang a man up, he always got a message from God first."

Mr. Gibbud's style is so pithy and bright that it is no wonder that the largest church auditoriums in Detroit were crowded by those anxious to learn how to win men. As all-night missionary in the Bowery, New York, Mr. Gibbud worked out the practical methods he teaches. His work is doing much to stimulate the formation of training-classes for preparing the average Christian to win souls by the use of the Bible. He showed how any one may become familiar with his Bible, as a brakeman is familiar with the stations along his line,— by going over the road every day.

When the average Christian becomes as full of his Bible as the miller's coat is of flour, he will, like the miller in a crowd, leave his mark on every one he touches.

The Evangelistic Meetings.

Arranged by Rev. P. V. Jenness, Detroit, Mich.

The evangelistic work of the Convention was better done than ever before. Preparation had been made longer beforehand. Throughout the year the local committee, headed by Rev. P. V. Jenness, had been in correspondence with active evangelistic workers in different States. These workers had been gathering their bands, learning who would attend, and drawing into the work whomever they could hear about whose services were likely to be helpful.

A very elaborate programme of meetings was carefully laid out, sixty-eight meetings in all, at twenty-nine different places. The volunteers from the Endeavorers gathered in Detroit were even more in number than could be effectively used.' In street-car barn, jail, house of correction, dry-goods stores, great factories, at the wharves, in public squares, in hotels, the meetings were held. At each of them there was much singing, and there were many testimonies. Cards were distributed which, when signed, were statements of a surrender to Christ ; and many of these cards were signed.

Each party of workers that was sent out was placed in charge of a guide, armed with full printed directions, with two blanks for duplicate reports, a stamped return envelope, a supply of song leaflets, and of inquirers' cards.

Take as a sample of the work these bands accomplished, the following incident. It was at the jail. The Massachusetts company, under Mr. Washburn's leadership, was singing and testifying in one of the corridors, the prisoners crowding eagerly to the bars, sulking in the corners, or pacing nervously up and down. The Endeavorers began to sing, " I 'll go where you want me to go, dear Lord." But, thought the leader, that is n't exactly the song for these prisoners, some of whom are doubtless thinking that they would be good men if they could only be set free to go where they would; so he had them sing it, " I 'll stay where you want me to stay, dear Lord." Then the Endeavorers were asked to kneel, and make that song their personal vow. They all did so; and while they knelt, with bowed heads, the prisoners were asked to take the same vow by kneeling down. About twelve of them did so, and the scene was one to melt even the hardest heart.

In all, nearly one hundred of these meetings were held, attended by 15,000 people. And numerous conversions were reported.

Two Fascinating Exhibits.

In one of the recitation-rooms of the handsome new high-school building was a creation of Mr. Merritt B. Holley's brain, which delighted thousands of visitors. It was a Christian Endeavor museum, which has engaged Mr. Holley's spare moments for ten years, and which rivals Dr. Clark's collection.

You might begin with A, and go through the alphabet, and find something curious and instructive beginning with each letter. There are autographs, badge banners, convention souvenirs, diagrams of Junior plans, the evolution of *The Christian Endeavor World*, flags of all nations, gavels, etc.

Then you might go through the list of nations, and find that all had paid tribute. At his home in Traverse City, Mich., Mr. Holley keeps it in a room called " Holley's Den ;" and, augmented by the treasures rare and odd that have recently flowed in, it added a unique and piquant feature to the Convention.

Cass Avenue Methodist Episcopal Church.
Junior Headquarters.

Another magnet whose drawing-power never lessened during the week was the exhibit of work by and for Juniors, at the Junior headquarters. The fairy fingers of hundreds of children had helped to furnish the decorations for the walls, load the tables with bright handiwork, and drape the doorways fit for a royal palace.

Imagine a portière of crimson paper poppies, made and strung by the deft hands of the children! Then there were

A Bit of the Junior Headquarters.

maps, scrap-books, banners, quilts, dressed dolls, and other creations of beauty by the Juniors, in this enchanted place. One little girl with the Massachusetts party had alighted with the others for lunch at Syracuse, N. Y. Returning, she saw the train leaving the station, as she thought for good. "Oh!" she cried in distress, "bring back my Junior dolly!"

On other tables were specimens of programmes for many interesting kinds of Junior meetings.

The Convenient and Splendid General Headquarters.
All Sorts of Aids.

Detroit's famous high-school building was generously tendered by the authorities to the committee for general headquarters during the Convention, and was crowded with interesting booths. Facing every one as he entered was the exhibit of the United Society of Christian Endeavor, never before so helpful and attractive, and never before so well patronized by earnest workers, who found there everything they needed to aid them in their Christian Endeavor labors. The ever-popular "Tom" Wainwright, of Chicago, was in charge.

Then there were booths for various young people's and denominational papers, the Colportage Library, Detroit souvenirs, the Bible Society, Cuban Industrial Relief, and many other good causes. A room was set apart to a very valuable exhibit of helps for the study of missions, prepared by the indefatigable Yale Band. There were graphic charts, instructive maps, libraries of missionary books and pamphlets, exhibits of literature from the mission boards of different denominations, relics from mission fields, and many other helps for live Missionary Committees.

Greetings From and To the Great Convention.

EXECUTIVE MANSION, July 4, 1899.
Rev. Francis E. Clark, D.D., Detroit, Mich.:
On the occasion of the Eighteenth International Convention of your society, I desire to express to you my cordial interest in its work, my best wishes to those assembled with you in convention, and my earnest hope for the continuance and increase of the great results which the efforts of the Christian Endeavor Society has achieved. WILLIAM MCKINLEY.

DETROIT, July 8, 1899.
To President William McKinley, Washington, D. C.:
Twenty-eight thousand American and Canadian Christian Endeavorers assembled in international convention received with hearty enthusiasm your kind message, and pray for God's richest blessing upon you, your administration, and the great republic of which you are the chief magistrate.
FRANCIS E. CLARK, *President.*
JOHN WILLIS BAER, *Secretary.*

DETROIT, July 8, 1899.
To His Excellency, Lord Minto, Ottawa, Canada:
The Christian Endeavorers of Canada and America, in international convention assembled, representing two and one-half millions of young people, are drawing closer the bonds of international fellowship, and pray for God's best blessing upon yourself and your great dominion.
FRANCIS E. CLARK, *President.*
JOHN WILLIS BAER, *Secretary.*

Francis E. Clark, Esq., President International Convention of Christian Endeavorers, Detroit:
His Excellency, the Governor-General, desires me to express his warmest and most sincere thanks for your very kind and cordial message of good-will to himself and the Dominion of Canada. MAJOR DRUMMOND,
Governor-General's Secretary.

DETROIT, MICH., July 8, 1899.
To Her Majesty, Queen Victoria, Windsor, England:
Tens of thousands of Canadian and American Christian Endeavorers in international convention assembled in Detroit rejoice in your long and glorious reign and pray God's constant blessing upon you. Thousands of Endeavorers next July will cross the ocean to convention in London with love and reverence in their hearts for you. FRANCIS E. CLARK, *President.*
JOHN WILLIS BAER, *Secretary.*

11 July, 1899.
Lieut.-Colonel Sir Arthur Bigge is commanded to express the thanks of the Queen for the kind message of congratulation which the president of the International Convention assembled in Detroit has forwarded to Her Majesty.

DETROIT, July 8, 1899.
American Peace Commission, The Hague:
Twenty-eight thousand American and Canadian Christian Endeavorers now assembled in international convention, Detroit, represent two and one-half millions enthusiastic for peace and arbitration. Great peace meeting held. All wish you Godspeed. FRANCIS E. CLARK, *President.*
JOHN WILLIS BAER, *Secretary.*

41 SGRAVENHAGE.
Clark, President Christian Endeavor Meeting, Detroit:
American Commission to the Peace Conference sends sincere thanks for message and congratulates you and all friends of peace upon the great success achieved, providing for a permanent tribunal of arbitration.
WHITE. *President.*
HOLLIS *Secretary.*

Term of One Year from July 5, 1899.

ALABAMA — Rev. O. P. Spiegel, Birmingham.
ARKANSAS — Rev. J. H. Curry, Russellville.
CALIFORNIA — Prof. James A. Wiles, San Francisco.
COLORADO — Mr. William E. Sweet, Denver.
CONNECTICUT — Mr. H. H. Spooner, Bull's Bridge.
DELAWARE — Rev. W. L. S. Murray, Ph.D., Wilmington.
DISTRICT OF COLUMBIA — Mr. A. L. Dietrich, Washington.
FLORIDA — Mr. C. Arthur Lincoln, Winter Park.
GEORGIA — Rev. Arthur J. Smith, Savannah.
IDAHO — Rev. R. B. Wright, Boise.
ILLINOIS — Mr. A. E. Turner, Lincoln.
INDIANA — Rev. Jacob W. Knapp, D.D., Richmond.
IOWA — Rev. C. W. Sweet, Des Moines.
KANSAS — Rev. A. M. Reitzel, Hutchinson.
KENTUCKY — Rev. A. Judson Arrick, Louisville.
LOUISIANA — Mr. F. F. Morse. Jennings.
MAINE — Rev. Ellison R. Purdy, Portland.
MARYLAND — Mr. W. O. Atwood, Baltimore.
MASSACHUSETTS — Rev. Franklin S. Hatch, Monson.
MICHIGAN — Mr. C. D. Harrington, Grand Rapids.
MINNESOTA — Rev. George E. Soper, St. Paul.
MISSISSIPPI — Mr. John A. Stinson, Columbus.
MISSOURI — Rev. E. W. Clippinger, Warrensburg.
MONTANA — Mr. G. H. Wilson, Bozeman.
NEBRASKA — Rev. John Hood, D.D., Beatrice.
NEVADA — Rev. A. J. McMurtry, Cannonville.
NEW HAMPSHIRE — Mr. Allan M. Wilson, Manchester.
NEW JERSEY — Rev. Cornelius Brett, D.D., Jersey City.
NEW MEXICO — Mr. J. E. Wood, Santa Fé.
NEW YORK — Rev. John H. Elliott, New York City.
NORTH CAROLINA — Rev. A. D. Thaeler, Winston.
NORTH DAKOTA — Mr. N. B. Fitch, Casselton.
OHIO — Rev. A. C. Miller, D.D., Plymouth.
OKLAHOMA — Rev. T. H. Harper, Newkirk.
OREGON — Rev. A. J. Montgomery, Oregon City.
PENNSYLVANIA — Rev. Clarence E. Eberman, Lancaster.
RHODE ISLAND — Mr. Robert Cushman, Pawtucket.
SOUTH CAROLINA — Rev. W. L. Walker, Piedmont.
SOUTH DAKOTA — Miss Flora Margaret Wilson, Sioux Falls.
TENNESSEE — Mr. W. L. Noell, Huntingdon.
TEXAS — Mr. H. H. Grotthouse, Dallas.
UTAH — Mr. Harry N. Tolles, Salt Lake City.
VERMONT — Col. E. G. Osgood, Bellows Falls.
VIRGINIA — Mr. W. R. Kennedy, Lexington.
WASHINGTON — Mr. H. J. Fries, Tacoma.
WEST VIRGINIA — Rev. I. A. Barnes, Morgantown.
WISCONSIN — Mr. F. R. Barber, Warren's.
WYOMING — Mr. Robert Lawson, Cheyenne.
CANADIAN COUNCIL — Mr. G. Tower Fergusson, Toronto.
BRITISH COLUMBIA — Rev. W. B. Cumming, Nanaimo.
HAWAII — Prof. Theodore Richards, Honolulu.
MANITOBA — Mr. A. H. Bailey, Winnipeg.
NEW BRUNSWICK — Prof. W. W. Andrews, Sackville.
NORTHWEST TERRITORIES — Mr. A. H. Smith, Moosomin.
NOVA SCOTIA — Rev. William Ainsley, Halifax.
ONTARIO — Rev. Elliott S. Rowe, Toronto.
PRINCE EDWARD ISLAND — Mr. W. C. Turner, Charlottetown.
QUEBEC — Mr. W. L. Shurtleff, Coaticook.

Number of Societies Reported July 1, 1899.

United States.

	Young People's.	Junior.	Intermediate.	Mothers'.	Senior.	Parent.	Total.
Alabama	159	48	5				212
Alaska Territory	10	1					11
Arizona	19	3					22
Arkansas	130	35	4				169
California	715	599	126		3		1,443
Colorado . . .	214	114	8	1			337
Connecticut . . .	530	227	15		2		774
Delaware	77	32	3				112
District of Columbia .	83	60	8				151
Florida . . .	143	65	2				210
Georgia	174	38	5				217
Idaho . . .	61	24	1				86
Illinois	2,056	1,054	76	33	1		3,220
Indiana	1,407	622	58				2,087
Indian Territory	46	19	1				66
Iowa	1,322	604	38	1	1		1,966
Kansas	1,036	448	22	11			1,517
Kentucky	355	109	10	1			475
Louisiana	50	12	1				63
Maine	658	215	12				885
Maryland . . .	396	142	7	1	1		547
Massachusetts	949	529	43	2	2	1	1,526
Michigan	1,081	521	48				1,650
Minnesota	566	320	33		1		920
Mississippi . . .	73	22			1		96
Missouri	863	483	20		1		1,367
Montana	52	27	1				80
Nebraska	595	255	18	2	1		871
Nevada	11	6					17
New Hampshire . . .	310	134	6		3		453
New Jersey	845	469	24	4			1,342
New Mexico	27	7	1				35
New York	3,144	1,423	59		2		4,628
North Carolina	273	69	7	1			358
North Dakota . . .	112	54	3				169
Ohio	2,471	1,031	73	4	1		3,580
Oklahoma Territory .	182	30	1				213
Oregon	326	144	8	1			479
Pennsylvania . .	3,751	1,575	107	8	6		5,447
Rhode Island .	141	71	9		1		222
South Carolina . .	87	14	1				102
South Dakota	189	79	4	1			273
Tennessee	379	159	10				548
Texas	466	248	32				746
Utah	39	28	2				69
Vermont	311	146	4	1	1		463
Virginia . . .	258	44	3				305
Washington	281	105	9				395
West Virginia	253	55	2				310
Wisconsin	531	269	22				822
Wyoming	21	5	1				27
	28,228	12,793	953	72	28	1	42,075

Canada.

	Young People's.	Junior.	Inter-mediate.	Mothers'.	Parent.	Total.
Alberta	11	2				13
Assinibola . . .	49	9				58
British Columbia	49	8	1			58
Manitoba	122	25				147
New Brunswick	228	34	3			265
Newfoundland	6					6
Nova Scotia	407	72	1			480
Ontario	1,786	303	15	1		2,105
Prince Edward Island . .	72	5				77
Quebec	198	72	1		?	273
Saskatchewan	5					5
	2,933	530	21	1	?	3,487

Foreign.

	Young People's.	Junior.	Inter-mediate.	Mothers'.	Senior.	Total.
Africa	115	9			12	136
Australia	2,004	278			4	2,286
Austria	2					2
Belgium	1	1				2
Bermuda	7					7
Brazil	3	1				4
British Guiana	11					11
Bulgaria	1					1
Burmah	15					15
Chili	5	1				6
China	130	18				148
Columbia	3					3
Cuba	4					4
Denmark	2					2
Egypt	3	1				4
Ellice Islands	6					6
England	4,255	785	5	6	?	5,053
France	68	1				69
Germany	96	3			?	101
Gilbert Islands	2					2
Guatemala . . .	3					3
Hawaiian Islands . .	12	5				17
Holland	3					3
Hungary	2					2
India	382	70		1	1	454
Ireland	218	25				243
Italy	3					3
Japan	66	5				71
Labrador	1					1
Laos	28	1				29
Madagascar	93					93
Marshall Islands	13					13
Mexico	76	32				108
Norway	4					4
Philippine Islands	2					2
Persia	3	1				4
Russia	3					3

Foreign.
(*Continued.*)

	Young People's.	Junior.	Inter-mediate.	Mothers'.	Senior.	Total.
Samoa	13					13
Scotland	536	60				596
Siam	1	1				2
Spain	16	15		5		36
Sweden	35					35
Switzerland . . .	8					8
Syria	6	1				7
Tokelan Islands . .	2					2
Turkey	38	17				55
Upper Hebrides . . .	1					1
Wales	339	8				347
West Indies	93	18				111
	8,733	1,357	5	12	21	10,128

Recapitulation.

	Young People's.	Junior.	Inter-mediate.	Mothers'.	Senior.	Parent.	Total.
United States . . .	28,228	12,793	953	72	28	1	42,075
Canada	2,933	530	21	1		2	3,487
Foreign	8,733	1,357	5	12	21		10,128
Floating Societies . .							123
	39,894	14,680	979	85	49	3	55,813

COMPLETE INDEX OF THE REPORT.

Topics of Services. — Themes of Addresses, Sermons, Etc. — Conferences, Rallies,
Studies, and Special Meetings. — Illustrative Anecdotes. — Greetings,
Resolutions, Presentations, Etc. — Some Convention Incidents.
— Illustrations. — Reports and Statistics. — Open
Parliaments. — Special Music. — Personnel.

www.ingramcontent.com/pod-product-compliance
Lightning Source LLC
Chambersburg PA
CBHW051820040426
42447CB00006B/294